A HISTORY OF GL

Anglicanism can be seen as irredeemably English. In this book Kevin Ward questions that assumption. He explores the character of the African, Asian, Oceanic, Caribbean and Latin American churches which are now a majority in the worldwide communion, and shows how they are decisively shaping what it means to be Anglican. While emphasising the importance of colonialism and neo-colonialism for explaining the globalisation of Anglicanism, Ward does not focus predominantly on the churches of Britain and North America; nor does he privilege the idea of Anglicanism as an 'expansion of English Christianity'. At a time when Anglicanism faces the danger of dissolution Ward explores the historically deep roots of non-western forms of Anglicanism, and the importance of the diversity and flexibility which has so far enabled Anglicanism to develop cohesive yet multiform identities around the world.

KEVIN WARD is Senior Lecturer in African Studies in the Department of Theology and Religious Studies, University of Leeds. He is a trustee of the Church Mission Society and a member of the General Synod of the Church of England.

A HISTORY OF GLOBAL ANGLICANISM

KEVIN WARD
University of Leeds

CAMBRIDGE UNIVERSITY PRESS
Cambridge, New York, Melbourne, Madrid, Cape Town, Singapore, São Paulo

Cambridge University Press
The Edinburgh Building, Cambridge CB2 2RU, UK

Published in the United States of America by Cambridge University Press, New York

www.cambridge.org
Information on this title: www.cambridge.org/9780521008662

First published 2006

Printed in the United Kingdom at the University Press, Cambridge

A catalogue record for this publication is available from the British Library.

Library of Congress Cataloguing in Publication Data

Ward, Kevin, 1947–
A History of global Anglicanism / Kevin Ward.
p. cm.
Includes bibliographical references and index.

ISBN-13 978-0-521-80395-3 (hardback)
ISBN-10 0-521-80395-0 (hardback)

ISBN-13 978-0-521-00866-2 (paperback)
ISBN-10 0-521-00866-2 (paperback)

1. Anglican Communion – History. I. Title.
BX5005.W37 2006
283.09–dc22
2006025236

Contents

Maps

Preface

A book of this global nature and scope depends more than most on the good-will of others, and so there are many debts. Firstly I wish to thank my colleagues in the Department of Theology and Religious Studies at the University of Leeds for their support and encouragement, in particular the successive heads of department: Professor Haddon Willmer, Professor Kim Knott, Dr Hugh Pyper and Dr Al McFadyen. I owe a particular debt of gratitude to Bishop Stephen Charleston, the President of the Episcopal Divinity School, and to the faculty there, for the award of a Proctor Fellowship. This enabled me to spend an exciting semester in Cambridge, Massachusetts in 2002, with access to the magnificent libraries of Harvard. Professors Ian Douglas, Christopher Daraysingh and Frederika Thompsett stimulated my thinking about the nature of Anglicanism as a world communion.

I wish to thank the library and academic staff of a number of institutions, most especially the Selly Oak Campus of the University of Birmingham, the Centre for the Study of Christianity in the Non-Western World at the University of Edinburgh, Scotland, the Oxford Centre for Mission Studies, the Henry Martyn Library at Westminster College, Cambridge and the library of the Uganda Christian University, Mukono, Uganda.

Kevin Taylor and Kate Brett at Cambridge University Press have been very patient and supportive. Special thanks to Dr Alistair Mason for his careful reading of the typescript, his perceptive advice on how to improve it, and his keen eye for detail.

Finally, thanks to Amos and Sonia Kasibante (Uganda, Guyana and England) Mongezi and Justine Kapia (South Africa and Namibia), Abiaaza and Betty Kibirige (Uganda and South Africa), Godfrey and Deborah Makumbi (Uganda), Anijo and Shilpi Mathew (India and USA), Margaret and Peter Larom (USA and Uganda), Angela and

Andrew Wingate (England and India), Peter Gossip (Scotland, India and South Africa), John Webber (Bangladesh, Wales and England) and Philip and Beatrice Musindi (Uganda and Wales) for friendships which encompass the world Anglican communion and . . . beyond.

Abbreviations

ACC	Anglican Consultative Council
ACK	Anglican Church of Kenya
ACS	American Colonisation Society
AIM	Africa Inland Mission
AME	African Methodist Episcopal (Church)
ANC	African National Congress
BCMS	Bible Churchmen's Missionary Society (Crosslinks)
CAPA	Council of the Anglican Provinces of Africa
CCA	Church of Christ in Africa
CEFACS	Centre for Anglican Communion Studies (Birmingham)
CESA	Church of England in South Africa
CHSKH	Chung Hua Sheng Kung Hui (the Holy Catholic Church of China)
CIM	China Inland Mission
CMJ	Church Mission to the Jews, now known as the Church's Ministry among the Jews
CMS	Church Missionary Society/ Church Mission Society
COI	Church of Ireland
COU	Church of Uganda
CPK	Church of the Province of Kenya (now the Anglican Church of Kenya)
CPSA	Church of the Province of South Africa/Church of the Province of Southern Africa
CPWI	Church in the Province of the West Indies
CSI	Church of South India
DP	Democratic Party (Uganda)
DRC	Dutch Reformed Church
ECS	Episcopal Church of Sudan

ECUSA	Episcopal Church in the United States of America
EDS	Episcopal Divinity School, Cambridge, Massachusetts
ISPCK	Indian Society for Promoting Christian Knowledge
JRA	*Journal of Religion in Africa*
LMS	London Missionary Society
LRA	Lord's Resistance Army
MRI	Mutual Responsibility and Interdependence
NCCK	National Christian Council of Kenya; now known as National Council of Churches of Kenya
NGO	Non-Governmental Organisation
NSKK	Nippon Sei Ko Kai (the Holy Catholic Church of Japan), the Anglican/Episcopal Church of Japan
NSW	New South Wales
NZ	New Zealand
PEC	Philippine Episcopal Church
PIC	Philippine Independent Church
PNG	Papua New Guinea
SAIACS	South Asian Institute of Advanced Christian Studies
SAMS	South American Missionary Society
SPCK	Society for Promoting Christian Knowledge
SPG	Society for the Propagation of the Gospel
SPLA	Sudan People's Liberation Army
SWAPO	South West Africa People's Organisation
TRC	Truth and Reconciliation Commission (South Africa)
TSPM	Three-Self Patriotic Movement (China)
TTS	Tamilnadu Theological Seminary
UDF	United Democratic Front (South Africa)
UDI	Unilateral Declaration of Independence
UMCA	Universities' Mission to Central Africa
UNISA	University of South Africa
UPC	Uganda People's Congress
USPG	United Society for Propagating the Gospel
VOC	Vereenigde Oost-Indische Compagnie (Dutch East India Company)
WCC	World Council of Churches
YMCA	Young Men's Christian Association
YWCA	Young Women's Christian Association.

CHAPTER I

Introduction: 'not English, but Anglican'

The Anglican communion describes itself as a 'fellowship' or 'communion' of autonomous Christian churches, united by a common history, confessing a common faith and (traditionally) a common liturgy. There are thirty-eight distinct and independent Anglican churches or 'provinces', existing in a particular country or spread over a number of countries. Provinces vary in size from the big churches such as the Church of England (26 million baptised members), the Church of Nigeria (17.5 million), the Church of Uganda (8 million) and the Episcopal Church of Sudan (5 million) to the tiny communities of the Southern Cone of America (22,490), Mexico (21,000), the Anglican Church of Korea (14,558) and the Episcopal Church in Jerusalem and the Middle East (10,000).[1]

This book is an attempt to write a history of the Anglican communion from its inception as a worldwide faith, at the time of the Reformation, to the present day. While it does not ignore the contribution of the Church of England or of those of British extraction who have established Anglican churches in other parts of the world, its emphasis is on the activity of the indigenous peoples of Asia and Africa, Oceania and America in creating and shaping the Anglican communion. In the British Isles, attention is paid to Welsh, Irish and Scottish contributions, not least because they played a disproportionate part in the establishment of Anglican churches in other parts of the world, both as colonists and as missionaries.

[1] These figures are taken from the 2004 *Church of England Year Book* (London: Church House Publishing, 2004). The statistics are based on the reporting of numbers by the individual churches and vary from a very precise enumeration in some of the smaller churches to the rough estimates commonly used in calculating the numbers of the bigger churches. Only the entry for the Church of England uses the category 'baptised members' in these statistics. All the others talk simply of 'membership', which may well hide very different rules for inclusion (baptised/confirmed/active membership/adherents).

In areas of the world where the church is largely white, attention will be paid to the role of minority communities: Native Americans, African Americans and Hispanics in the United States, First Nation peoples and Haitians in Canada, Aboriginal people in Australia and Maoris in New Zealand. In Britain itself, the contribution of black 'ethnic-minority' people to the Church of England will be explored. In areas traditionally seen as the 'subject' of missionary work from Britain and America – India, China, Africa – the emphasis will be on the local appropriation of the faith rather than on missionary activity as such. This is not meant to devalue missionary work. In fact, one of the important themes which this approach highlights is the importance of missionary work engaged in by Anglican Christians who were not British, and who worked outside their own homeland. The often remarkable missionary work of Tamils, Chinese, Baganda and Yoruba, to name a few, needs general recognition for making Anglicanism what it is.

Anglicanism is commonly seen as incorrigibly English, a hangover of the British Empire, an anachronism. Its very name seems to proclaim its limitations. Human beings normally don't choose their names. Some are proud; others feel resentful and wish their parents had given the matter more consideration. Christian churches are sometimes named after great theological themes: *Catholic*, *Orthodox*, *Evangelical*, *Pentecostal*, *Aladura*. Some recall important founders: *Luther*, *Kimbangu*, *Wesley*. Some point to important organisational principles: *Reformed*, *Methodist*, *Congregational*. The Anglican communion seems peculiarly unfortunate in being saddled with what appears to be either a specific place or a particular ethnic group. 'Anglican' is, after all, simply another word for 'English'. How can a communion be truly worldwide with such a parochial name? How can it be truly *local* in Ghana or Uganda, Barbados or Brazil?

Some churches have solved this conundrum by abandoning the term 'Anglican' altogether in their title. And so, on the model of the 'Church of England', but without the English connotation, we have the 'Church of the Province of Southern Africa' or the 'Church of Uganda'. (In colonial days, Ugandan Anglicans belonged to the 'Native Anglican Church' – a strange contradiction: 'native' and 'English'.) Some have preferred the term 'episcopal', such as the churches of the United States, Brazil or the Sudan. But this usage may seem just as problematic as 'Anglican', suggesting a hierarchical pattern of organisation rather than the whole people of God. Most provinces have been content to include it in their title. Kenyan Anglicans for a long time called themselves the 'Church of the Province of Kenya'. But they have recently decided officially to be known as the 'Anglican Church of Kenya'. The name is widely recognised and understood by Kenyans generally, in a way that the 'Church of the Province' never was.

People learn to live with their names, to triumph over them. It is generally better to be open about one's origin than to try to hide it. Anglican Christians in Africa, as in other parts of the world, cannot hide the fact that their history is intimately bound up with colonialism. Anglicanism was and remains strong wherever British rule was exercised. It was and remains weak in parts of Africa which were not at some time British. 'Anglicane? Qu'est-ce que c'est? Vous êtes chrétien? C'est une secte, ou quoi?' asks a local in Lubumbashi, in the Congo Democratic Republic, when asked the way to the Anglican church.[2] The surprising thing may be that there is an *église anglicane* in the Congo Democratic Republic or Madagascar, Rwanda or Burundi, Haiti or Quebec.

The British Empire had more Muslim subjects than the Ottoman and Persian empires combined, boasted one Anglican missionary in Cairo in 1909. 'Who would doubt the issue of this glorious conflict?', he concluded, confident that Islam would wither away under the combined onslaught of Christian mission and colonial rule. But he himself lived to see the disadvantages of British colonial rule in Palestine when he became bishop in Jerusalem, with a largely Arab membership. There can be little doubt that belonging to the 'dini ya Queeni' (the religion of Queen Victoria and her successors) had had a powerful prestige in the colonial period itself. Anglicanism easily slotted into an 'establishment' mentality. If Christianity and 'power' (political/educational/cultural) went together, then Anglicanism was a form of Christianity which had its attractions for those whose lives were dominated or circumscribed by the colonial reality. Few missionaries could be sanguine about the future of African Anglicanism in the era of the independence struggle of the 1950s. That Anglicanism has not only survived but flourished in Africa since independence is a fact of great significance whose consequences have yet fully to be realised in understanding what Anglicanism is.

The term 'Anglican' originated in the medieval Latin designation for the Catholic Church in England, *Ecclesia Anglicana*: a geographical location rather than a theological description. At the Reformation, the reformed Church of England asserted its identity and continuity with that medieval church. But the term 'Anglican' only developed its modern

[2] Tim Naish in Andrew Wingate, Kevin Ward, Carrie Pemberton and Wilson Sitshebo (eds.), *Anglicanism: A Global Communion* (London: Mowbray, 1998), pp. 161–5.

use in the nineteenth century, first of all as a theological identity marker rather than a geographical description. The Tractarians used the term to signify participation in the universal church, but as a unique branch distinguished from Roman, eastern and Protestant Christendom. By the 1860s the term 'Anglican communion' was becoming a useful descriptor for churches outside Britain. In appealing for a General Council of Churches, the Provincial Synod of the Canadian Church in 1865 urged the Archbishop of Canterbury to look for ways 'by which the members of our Anglican Communion in all quarters of the world should have a share in the deliberations for her welfare, and be permitted to have a representation in one General Council of her members fathered from every land'.[3] Archbishop Longley, however, avoided using the term when he issued his invitation:

> I request your presence at a meeting of the Bishops in visible communion with the United Church of England and Ireland, purposed (God willing) to be holden at Lambeth, under my presidency . . .[4]

Indeed, the term 'Anglican' only gradually came to be used within the Church of England itself. English people, whether communicants or not, identified themselves as 'Church of England' rather than as part of a wider communion. But, by the late twentieth century, the term 'the Anglican Church' had come popularly to be used (in the press and elsewhere) as a synonym for the established Church of England.

Anglicanism ceased to be the established religion in Ireland in 1867 and in Wales in 1922. It has never been the established church in Scotland. Anglican establishments in Canada and the Caribbean were dismantled in the nineteenth century. In India, although the Anglican Church was officially an establishment until well into the twentieth century, it was always understood to be the established church for English people in India, not for the native population. In this case, both the East India Company and its imperial successor utilised the fact of establishment as a way of inhibiting the extension of Anglicanism among the native Hindu, Sikh and Muslim population. There were no similar religious sensitivities to conciliate in much of sub-Saharan Africa, and missionaries were not discouraged from evangelising. But the British were careful to maintain an official neutrality, both between religions and between different Christian denominations. They were particularly sensitive to aggressive evangelism in predominantly Muslim areas. Perhaps with the Irish

[3] [Davidson,] *The Six Lambeth Conferences 1867–1920* (London: SPCK, 1929), p. 4. [4] Ibid., p. 5.

experience in mind, they were also anxious not to offend Catholic missions. Nevertheless, the Anglican church was perceived to be the church of the government in much of British Africa. In 1914 Yoswa Kate of Uganda denounced the cathedral at Namirembe in Kampala as a *ssabo* (shrine) of the English traditional religion. The cathedrals of Nairobi in Kenya and Salisbury in Southern Rhodesia were even more closely identified with the colonial administrations, in this case largely because they were dominated by the white settler community.

WRITING ABOUT ANGLICANISM

Books which consider 'Anglicanism' as their overall theme have largely been written from theological perspectives, typically with a strong interest in ecclesiology: they attempt to locate Anglicanism as a distinctive part of classical Christianity, examining its 'Catholic', 'Reformed', 'Evangelical' and 'Liberal' characteristics, and how these characteristics relate to, and are in tension with, each other. In encapsulating what is special about Anglicanism, writers often emphasis its privileging of common prayer over doctrinal uniformity; its preference for a familial rather than a centralised and bureaucratic structure; its role in reconciling Catholic and Reformed understandings of the faith. The Indian priest Emani Sambayya expressed this sense of Anglicanism well in an essay entitled 'The Genius of the Anglican Communion', written in 1948. After his conversion as a young man and employment by the Student Christian Movement in India, he finally decided to seek ordination in the Anglican church. His preference for Anglicanism arose from the sense of common worship, rather than the individualism of other Protestant bodies, enshrined in the Book of Common Prayer, which he saw as 'a precious heirloom for posterity' and one which 'lends itself to adaptation by various peoples, according to their peculiar temperaments and needs'. Alive to the colonial and class bias of Anglicanism, he nevertheless found it 'possible to envisage the emergence of the catholicism of the African people, or of the Chinese, or of the Indian nation within the confines of Anglicanism'. Sambayya rejoiced in the 'double heritage' of Anglicanism – Catholic and Reformed. He was thankful for its freedom from excessive emotion, but critical of its failure to commit itself in the nationalist struggle from which India was just emerging in 1948.[5] This theme of the

[5] E. Sambayya, 'The Genius of the Anglican Communion' , in E. R. Morgan and Roger Lloyd (eds.), *The Mission of the Anglican Communion* (London: SPCK and SPG, 1948), pp. 18–29.

'genius' of Anglicanism is perhaps more redolent of an Anglo-Catholic than an Evangelical temperament. Anglo-Catholics have felt greater need than Evangelicals to give a justification for the distinctive location of Anglicanism in the Christian world. Evangelicals traditionally have had more pragmatic, utilitarian reasons for being Anglican.

In recent decades, Stephen Sykes in England and John Booty in the USA have been active in developing a rigorous theological understanding of Anglicanism and its ecclesiology. They describe their 1988 collection of essays *A Study of Anglicanism*[6] as an 'introduction to the history and ethos of the Churches which constitute the Anglican Communion'. They recognise that the days of 'classical Anglicanism' may be numbered with the global shift of Christianity to the south. One of the chapters, by the Ghanaian theologian John Pobee, speaks of the 'Anglo-Saxon captivity of the church'. But he is the only representative of the 'South' in this collection. This, and similar books whose theme is the nature and ethos of the Anglican tradition, are largely still bound within those 'classical' patterns of thinking. *The Anglican Tradition*,[7] 'a handbook of sources', is organised on a chronological schema. The majority of extracts relate to England, though there is a good attempt to include material from other parts of the world in the final chapters. *Love's Redeeming Work: The Anglican Quest for Holiness*[8] also adopts a chronological pattern. Only in Part 3 (1830–2001) is there much attention to material from outside Britain. The writings of South Asian Christians (mainly Indian) are represented by 10 entries, out of the 136 in this section.[9] The only other 'non-white' included is Ini Kopuria, the founder of the Melanesian Brotherhood. Surprisingly, perhaps, there are no extracts at all from African Anglicans, partly because of the editorial decision to include only extracts from those who had died, partly perhaps because of the lack of opportunities for Africans to publish internationally and in English. Bishop John V. Taylor died just in time to be included, with a generous selection of his meditations and poems – but none draw directly from the African experience which shaped his life.

6 Stephen Sykes and John Booty (eds.), *The Study of Anglicanism* (London: SPCK, 1988).

7 G. R. Evans and J. Robert Wright (eds.), *The Anglican Tradition: A Handbook of Sources* (London: SPCK, 1991).

8 Geoffrey Rowell, Kenneth Stevenson and Rowan Williams, *Love's Redeeming Work: The Anglican Quest for Holiness* (Oxford: Oxford University Press, 2001).

9 Krishna Mohan Banerjea, Nilakantha Nehemiah Goreh SSJE, Krishnan Pillai, Appasamy Pillai, Pandita Ramabai Sarasvati, Sundar Singh, Aiyadurai Jesudasen Appasamy, Lakdasa Jacob de Mel, Emani Sambayya, Lakshman Wickremesinghe.

Bishop Stephen Neill (1900–84) was a theologian and historian who exemplified the expanding horizons of Anglicanism, with his experience as a missionary (1924–45) and bishop (1939–45) in South India and his work with the World Council of Churches in Geneva and as Professor of Mission in Hamburg (1962–7). After retirement he was appointed as Professor of Religious Studies in the University of Nairobi (1969–73) in Kenya. In 1964, he wrote what is still the standard textbook on the history of Christian missions, published as the final volume of the *Pelican History of the Church*. His rather earlier historical work for Penguin, *Anglicanism* of 1958, was predominantly about the Church of England.[10] The work turns to events outside Britain only on p. 278, in a text of some 400 pages, with a chapter entitled 'Expansion in the English-Speaking World'.

Lamin Sanneh has noted that both Kenneth Latourette and Stephen Neill, in their great works on mission, witnessed to the fact that this was the age when Christianity was freeing itself from the dominance of Europe:

> Yet it remains an astonishing fact that, given their gifts of intellect and sympathy, both Neill and Latourette should proceed to tell the story of Christianity as essentially a phase of Europe's worldwide ascendancy after they had noted the cultural shifts that in their view were constitutive of the religion itself.[11]

The thrust of Sanneh's critique is directed not so much against these writers as against the post-colonial generation of Christian thinkers:

> [I]t is a curious thing that western academic theologians (alas!) have scarcely shown any sustained interest in the subject, having decided to turn their backs on world Christianity as the offspring of mission's outdated theology of territorial expansionism.[12]

Sanneh's strictures serve to put in context the difficulties with which theological and historical articulations of global Anglicanism have laboured since the 1960s. Only in 1993 was there a history which seriously attempted to view Anglicanism systematically in a global context. This was the work of the American Episcopalian, William Sachs: *The Transformation of Anglicanism: From State Church to Global Communion*.[13] Like Neill, Sachs adopts a chronological framework, but now about half of the

[10] Stephen C. Neill, *Anglicanism* (Harmondsworth: Penguin, 1958).

[11] Lamin Sanneh, 'World Christianity and the New Historiography: History and Global Interconnections', in Wilbert R. Shenk (ed.), *Enlarging the Story: Perspectives on Writing World Christian History* (Maryknoll: Orbis, 2002), pp. 94–114.

[12] Ibid.

[13] William L. Sachs, *The Transformation of Anglicanism* (Cambridge: Cambridge University Press, 1993).

text is concerned with the global perspective, beginning with Chapter 5, 'The Church and Empire'. The trajectory of the story is that of 'expansion' (to utilise Neill's term) – from colonial to national, from English to multi-cultural, from state church to a family of independent churches. Sachs also wants to address theological questions about the nature of Anglicanism: 'It is the story of a search for a clear idea of the Church's nature under the impact of modern social and intellectual life.'[14] He hopes thereby that the book will be a contribution to the question of 'Anglican identity' which has become problematic precisely because of its global expansion:

> By the late twentieth century the integrity of Anglicanism had become the Church's central concern. Why did this challenge arise? How did Anglicans succeed in expanding globally yet ultimately doubt their resolve?[15]

Paul Avis has commended Sachs as providing a fascinating history of global Anglicanism, but is unconvinced by its theological conclusions in the final chapter, which concerns the Anglican response to modernity, the search for 'the authentic Church' and 'the loss of coherence'. Avis' *Anglicanism and the Christian Church* is a theological analysis of 'classical' Anglicanism, as defined by Sykes and Booty.[16]

Bill Jacob's *The Making of the Anglican Church Worldwide* (1997) eschews theology and aims to present a more straightforward historical account.[17] After an initial chapter on the Reformation in the British Isles, the subsequent chapter is entitled 'The Church of England Overseas 1670–1780'. Every chapter thereafter addresses the global character of Anglicanism. As Jacob acknowledges, it is primarily a history of the institutional expression of the communion. The story ends in 1960 when these structures were still heavily English in ethos, and when the episcopates of almost all provinces were still very predominantly English, or white, or both. The institutional perspective does not easily lend itself to extensive discussions of local culture and agency.

THE ORIGINS AND STRUCTURE OF THIS WORK

This present work aims to take into account the strictures of Sanneh about writing history in a world context. The particular project emerged

[14] Ibid., p. 3. [15] Ibid.

[16] Paul Avis, *Anglicanism and the Christian Church* (Edinburgh: T. & T. Clark, 2002), pp. 326–8 (1st edn 1989).

[17] W. M. Jacob, *The Making of the Anglican Church Worldwide* (London: SPCK, 1997), p. vii.

from my collaboration in an earlier project pioneered by the Centre for Anglican Communion Studies (CEFACS) in Birmingham. CEFACS was the creation of the two Anglican mission colleges of the Selly Oak Federation of mission colleges, the United College of the Ascension (USPG) and Crowther Hall (CMS). The Principal of Ascension, Andrew Wingate, inspired the creation of a collection of short essays entitled *Anglicanism: A Global Communion*, with over seventy contributions from a wide range of scholars and church workers from all parts of the worldwide Anglican communion. The book reflected the rich variety of what was going on in the communion. Its publication coincided with the 1998 Lambeth Conference, in which it was widely anticipated that the churches of 'the South' would make a full and distinctive contribution in a new way.

The kaleidoscopic nature of *Anglicanism: A Global Communion* seemed to highlight the need for a wide-ranging historical account of the communion which would serve to highlight the role of Christians from the South in establishing and developing the worldwide Anglican communion. I had recently been appointed as Lecturer in African Religious Studies at the University of Leeds, a post created on the retirement of Professor Adrian Hastings, the great historian of African Christianity. My own background was also as a historian of Christianity in Africa. I had first gone to Kenya as a schoolteacher in 1969 and did doctoral studies on Kenyan Protestantism. I had then taught in the Bishop Tucker Theological College at Mukono, Uganda, from 1976 to 1990. I was ordained in 1978 by Archbishop Silvanus Wani, who had succeeded Janani Luwum as leader of the Church of Uganda, after Luwum's murder at the hands of the Amin regime.

Taking the strictures of Lamin Sanneh to heart, I have attempted, in this book, to construct an account of Anglicanism which is primarily concerned with the 'commitment, engagement and action' of Anglicans from Asia and Oceania, Africa, the Caribbean and Latin America, rather than focusing on the Church of England or on people of British origin in other parts of the world. It aims to take seriously the experience of local people and societies in their decisions to accept or reject the Anglican forms of Christianity which were on offer. The focus is thus not on the British missionaries who 'planted' their form of Christianity, but on the local response and appropriation, the creation and recreation of the Christian message within a particular context. The relative lack of concern with missionary societies and missionaries does not thereby undervalue mission. Indeed, it intends to prioritise the essential missionary nature of Christianity, by highlighting the work of local Christians, both in creating their Christian world and in being missionaries to their neighbours. Thus the narrative gives prominence to the crucial role played by Chinese Anglicans in establishing the church in the Asian Pacific beyond China, to the activities of African evangelists far from their home area and to the pioneering role of African Caribbean Anglicans in establishing the church in Latin America, as well as to the presence of a Japanese Anglicanism in Brazil.

The prioritising of local agency does not mean that I am blind to the unequal power relationships between the representatives of the British (or North American) missionary movement and the colonial 'subjects'. For good or ill, metropolitan influences shaped and channelled the development of local Christianities.[18] Africans and Indians, Chinese and Pacific Islanders, were rarely free simply to espouse (or reject) a Christianity disconnected from its British origins. But this should not be allowed to over-determine the conversion process, unduly to narrow the creative appropriation, to shut down the possibility that, even in the replication of English liturgy or practice, something new and distinctive has emerged. If at times Anglicanism seems peculiarly ill adapted to the local culture, a fish out of water, it has also, often, become so thoroughly incorporated in the local environment that its superficial resemblance to the Church of England may, on further investigation, be highly misleading.

It was clear to me that the chronological approach adopted by previous histories of Anglicanism would have to be abandoned. Such an approach almost inevitably prioritises England in terms of space and time. The work is planned, rather, on a regional basis. But, since the passage of time is essential to historical appreciation, each regional section has its own chronological framework. This principle of organisation prevents Britain from dominating the story. It does allow more space than would otherwise be given to areas of comparative weakness for Anglicanism: for example the Middle East and Latin America. These were particularly exciting sections to write precisely because they normally tend to be neglected in considerations of Anglicanism as a whole. A precedent for this approach is found in Adrian Hastings' *A World History of Christianity*, an edited collection. Hastings notes the drawbacks of the

[18] This theme is discussed in Andrew Porter, *Religion versus Empire? British Protestant Missionaries and Overseas Expansion, 1700–1914* (Manchester: Manchester University Press, 2004), pp. 4–6.

regional approach, particularly that it may underplay the international dimensions of Christianity. But, he says,

> [a]t least it emphasizes a primary truth: that the writing of Christian history needs to escape imprisonment within a Europe-centred story in order not only to serve the needs of the many hundreds of millions of Christians who live elsewhere but also to provide an objectively balanced account of a straightforwardly historical kind of something which has for long been seen in too Eurocentric a way.[19]

'Non Angli, sed angeli' ('Not Angles, but angels'), Gregory is supposed to have punned.[20] His encounter with the slave boys in the Roman market sowed the seeds of a plan which bore fruit, once he had become Pope in 590, in the mission to England led by Augustine, the first Archbishop of Canterbury.[21] 'Not English, but Anglican' is the theme of this present book: a concern for the non-English majority which makes up the modern world Anglican communion. However, it would be strange and rather perverse to exclude the Church of England from the story altogether. The second chapter examines the Anglican churches of the Atlantic Isles (to use Diarmaid MacCulloch's description[22]). The shape of Anglicanism worldwide was decisively moulded by the contestations of religion which the Reformation engendered in these islands. But the chapter also draws attention to the non-English dimension in that history: the relationship between the Church in Wales and the Church of England, and the separate importance of Irish and Scottish Episcopal churches in the wider British context. It was in Scotland and in Ireland that Anglicans first learnt to adjust to minority and non-established status – this would eventually be the normal experience of Anglicans in the world Anglican communion. The Irish and the Scots also provided a disproportionate number of overseas colonists and clergy, with important implications for the development of the colonial Anglican church.[23] The Irish and the Scots worked in surprising numbers as missionaries for Anglican societies.

Chapters 3–6 are concerned with the New World, with chapters on the United States and Canada, on the Caribbean and Latin America. In the

19 Adrian Hastings (ed.), *A World History of Christianity* (London: Cassell, 1999), p. 5.

20 F. L. Cross and E. A. Livingstone, *The Oxford Dictionary of the Christian Church*, 3rd edn (Oxford: Oxford University Press, 1997), entry for St Gregory I, pp. 706–7.

21 Bertram Colgrave and R. A. B. Mynors, *Bede's Ecclesiastical History of the English People* (Oxford: Clarendon, 1969), pp. 132–5.

22 Diarmaid MacCulloch, *Reformation* (London: Allen Lane, 2003), p. xxvi.

23 Thomas Devine, *Scotland's Empire* (London: Penguin, 2003).

nineteenth century, America also began a significant missionary role to other parts of the world, particularly to China and Japan and other parts of the Pacific, as well as to Africa and Latin America. The North American Anglican missionary enterprise diverged in significant ways from the British model, tending to focus on areas outside the sway of the British Empire. Within North America itself, the contribution of First Nation/Native American, African American, African Caribbean and Hispanic peoples to the overall development of the Episcopal and Anglican churches is investigated. Latin America is the area of the world where Anglicanism is weakest in numerical terms. Yet it is one of the most complex and diverse areas in terms of its expressions of Anglicanism, with considerable variation of origin, tradition and ethos.

The experience of black slaves and ex-slaves in America and the Caribbean provides the link with the next chapters on Africa (Chapters 7–9). The continent of Africa itself provides wide contrasts in the development of Anglicanism. Often these arise more from the diversity of cultures and historical experience within Africa than from the diversity of Catholic or Evangelical Anglican traditions which are represented on the continent. Chapter 10 deals with Anglican expressions in the Middle East. Anglican communities here are numerically small and comparatively insignificant, but they have a fascinating role in the development both of Christian–Muslim relations and in relating to the ancient Christian traditions of the area. This chapter includes a discussion of the large and growing Episcopal Church of the Sudan, which links the Anglicanism of East Africa with that of the Middle East.

Chapters 11 and 12 deal with Anglicans in the complex religious pluralism of the Indian/South Asian and Chinese civilisations. Chapter 13 examines the rest of the Asian Pacific, profoundly influenced by China, both in its general cultural development and in the strategic importance of Chinese Christian missionary work, but also with very distinctive forms of Anglicanism in Japan and Korea. Chapter 14 is concerned with Oceania, a region noted for its diverse native and aboriginal cultures, for the impact of white settlement and for the interaction between these cultures in shaping its characteristic Anglicanism. Finally, Chapter 15 looks at the phenomenon of the Anglican communion as a whole, tracing the historical development of communion-wide institutions and the role of those institutions in the developing shape of Anglicanism on a world arena.

Although this book is about the world Anglican communion, it aims to be more than a denominational history. It is alert to the location of the church within the wider culture, civil society and the state. It seemed not only right but my bounden duty to write about the (united) Churches of the Indian subcontinent and the Three-Self Patriotic Movement in China (the non-denominational form of Protestant Christianity in which Anglicans have participated in decisive ways). Moreover, it would be against the spirit of these ecumenical ventures to look only for 'Anglican' survivals in these new forms of church. Issues of a lingering Anglican imperialism within united structures is a problem which needs to be addressed.

I have not been concerned to define the nature of Anglicanism too precisely, to extract the 'genius of Anglicanism'. I have operated with the self-definitions which characterise the different parts of the Anglican communion. Quite a number of provinces of the communion would see themselves as 'Protestant' – in the United States the 'Protestant Episcopal Church' is still an official designation, while in Ireland, it was, in the eighteenth century, the name which distinguished the Church of Ireland from all other Christians, Roman, Presbyterian and dissenting. In Uganda 'Protestant' is still generally used to mean 'Anglican', distinguishing the Church of Uganda from the Catholic church and from the 'born-again' churches which in other contexts and other societies would be seen as pre-eminently 'Protestant'. Sydney diocese has a much more explicitly confessional understanding of what it means to be Anglican than many Anglicans would feel comfortable with, defined in terms of the Reformation theology of the Book of Common Prayer and the Articles. Even in areas of the world where the Anglican tradition would be reluctant to call itself Protestant – the UMCA areas of Central Africa or Melanesia and Papua New Guinea, for example – the sociological reality may often be that these churches operate, as far as governments and local perceptions are concerned, as other Protestant churches do. But their own self-understanding is in marked contrast to that of Sydney.

SOURCES FOR A HISTORY OF WORLD ANGLICANISM

A work of this nature is dependent on an enormous range of research and writing, by scholars approaching Anglican history from academic perspectives and by committed members of the church writing as 'insiders'. The quality and extent of writing about particular Anglican churches varies greatly. Though small in proportion to the overall population, the importance of Christianity in India and China means that there is a large and sophisticated discussion of its role in the creation of modern society.

Anglicans are central to defining that role in India, but perhaps less so in China, where the Episcopal Church was a small part of a much larger Protestant contribution. In Africa, generally, modern historiography recognises the key role of missionary Christianity in colonial times, and of indigenous forms of Christianity for the development of post-colonial Africa. Anglicans have had a high profile in those developments, well recognised by historians. In contrast, small Anglican communities like those of Korea, Egypt or Latin America may escape the radar of general historical scholarship, and also be weak in the generation of in-house historical work concerned with the specifics of denominational history.

My research has encompassed both works of historical scholarship dealing with the more general issues of Christianity in society and denominational history making. This kind of literature is often locally published and may not find its way into western libraries. For example, both India and many parts of Africa have important secular and church publishing houses which encourage local studies, of a scholarly as well as a more devotional kind. It is often a matter of chance whether such works find their way to western libraries. In this regard, the sabbatical which I spent in the fall of 2002 at Cambridge, Massachusetts at the Episcopal Divinity School was invaluable. In addition to the EDS-Weston Jesuit library, the stunning resources of Harvard provided essential material without which this work could not have been undertaken.[24] Mission libraries in Britain have also been utilised, particularly the library of Partnership House (USPG and CMS) in London. Special university collections have been invaluable –particularly the collection in the Orchard Resource Centre at the Selly Oak campus of the University of Birmingham, the library of the Centre for the Study of Christianity in the Non-Western World in New College, in the University of Edinburgh, and the Henry Martyn collection at Westminster College in Cambridge.

The unpublished dissertations of recent scholars from Asia, Africa and the Caribbean who have studied in Britain are particularly useful in providing information about Anglican churches, securely based in the regional context. The library of the Uganda Christian University (Bishop Tucker Theological College) has been an important source for my own research into the Church of Uganda, as have other theological institutions in Kenya and Tanzania for Anglicans in East Africa. Undoubtedly there would be a wealth of similarly vital local information in other parts of the

[24] Particularly useful at Harvard were the Widener Library, the Divinity School library and the Yenching Library, with its collection of East Asian materials.

world. It would require an enormous research budget, unlimited time and inexhaustible stamina adequately to tap into these local resources. It is my hope that in every region I have been able to utilise some extant contemporary scholarship as it bears on issues of Anglicanism. Overwhelmingly, the material which I consulted was in English (part of the colonial and post-colonial legacy of Anglicanism). But much of the regional scholarship of others which I consulted has its origins in field work and oral interviews and diocesan and parish archives in vernaculars.

THE CRISIS IN WORLD ANGLICANISM

Arguments over homosexuality surfaced as a communion-wide issue at the Lambeth Conference of 1998 just as I was beginning to plan this book. Since that time, and particularly since the ordination of Gene Robinson as a bishop in the Episcopal Church of the USA in November 2003, homosexuality has increasingly preoccupied the debates within the communion, appearing to threaten the very survival of Anglicanism as a global communion. The prominence of bishops from Africa in particular in the condemnation of ECUSA has thrown into high relief the issue of the southward shift in Anglicanism, not least the fact that debates about Christian doctrine and ethics can no longer be conducted as if the Christians of the South were merely passive observers.

> Like it or not, Anglicanism is at a crossroads that could make or break the fragile family of churches that is the Anglican Communion. On the surface it appears as if the current debates in Anglicanism are about conflicting positions on human sexuality, or differing biblical hermeneutics, or contradictory understandings of truth and/or doctrines of the church. As important as these concerns are, what really is at stake in Anglicanism today are ecclesiological conflicts over identity and authority. What exactly is our common vocation as Anglican Christians globally? Who has the power to say who is or is not an Anglican?[25]

I will explore some of these issues in the last chapter of the book. It may be that the communion will hold together. A tighter discipline or a looser federation may emerge. Anglicanism may fragment in bitter recrimination. Whatever the outcome, this account attempts to articulate the ways in which individuals, local fellowships and churches worldwide have already contributed to the creation, shaping and continuing witness of

[25] Ian Douglas, 'Anglicans Gathering for God's Mission: A Missiological Ecclesiology for the Anglican Communion', *Journal of Anglican Studies* 2.9 (2004), pp. 9–40.

the Anglican communion, in the hope and expectation that Anglican communion continues to have a distinctive role in Christian mission.

A SUMMARY OF THE THESIS OF THE BOOK

The main purpose of this book is to give an account of worldwide Anglican Christianity outside what previously has been regarded as its heartlands in Britain, as well as in North America and Australasia, where Anglicans are largely of British or European descent. As far as these churches are concerned, the book pays particular attention to the indigenous and non-European ethnic groups who constitute significant minorities. But, the major focus of the book as a whole is on those parts of the world often characterised as 'the global South' – Africa, Asia, Latin America, the Caribbean and Oceania. In these places, the 'English' or 'British' heritage, however constitutive of what it means to be Anglican, is only one element in a distinctively local appropriation and expression of Anglicanism.

Clearly, it would be unwise to dismiss the colonial heritage as a trivial, accidental or irrelevant legacy. It has often stifled local initiative and autonomy, and it has too often demeaned or undermined native creativity and cultural expression. In liturgy and architecture, in styles of theology and discipleship, and not least in its relation to secular power, Anglicanism worldwide has often reflected, all too closely, its cultural origins. But the thesis of this work is that the English/British cultural hegemony, however powerful, does not preclude or negate the agency of local Christian communities; nor can it be allowed to shape the writing of Anglican history in a worldwide context. Moreover, the religious/cultural assertiveness of former subjects of empire is not a phenomenon simply of the collapse of empire. It does not begin, ex nihilo, with the establishment of a post-colonial world. In fact, local agency and creativity operate from the very beginning, with the first responses to the Gospel.

It is implicit in Scripture translation, one of the first and over-riding priorities of missionary activity, not least Anglican. Translation is premised on the active participation of indigenous people, and even when the resulting Scriptures followed all too faithfully the syntax and tone of the English Authorised Version (as first translations tended to do), the result was, nevertheless, a genuine 'incarnation' of the Gospel in the local culture. Even the adoption of foreign forms (for example church organisation, architecture, or, more importantly, a style of life or pattern of doing theology) takes on new meanings in different contexts. There is a disjunction between what was preached and what was heard, but this does not simply mean that people 'misheard'; rather it means that the Christian message must always be heard in context. This book is, therefore, primarily about the Anglican church which local people constructed and the meanings which they gave to the Christianity which they received through Anglicanism.

The history of Anglicanism as a global 'communion' is not unique. Parallel histories of world Roman Catholic, Lutheran, Methodist and Reformed Christianity can be written. Pentecostalism is equally global, but its history can hardly be written in denominational terms. If the Anglican communion as it has developed worldwide has a particular cohesion, this is derived partly from the political unity of the English nation as expressed through its national church, partly from the extension and persistence of British empire. It is also derived from the importance of a uniform ecclesial structure based on Catholic forms, order and liturgy, and on Reformation principles, but in which a great diversity of faith and practice can flourish. Roman Catholicism, as the pre-eminent form of world Christianity, is more concerned about policing faith and morals. It is also much more clearly multi-national; it cannot be identified with any specific European origin. Churches of the Reformed tradition are more diverse in their national origins. Historically they have been much less insistent on ecclesiastical uniformity. Methodism shares with Anglicanism a specific English origin. But non-British Methodism has played a much more decisive part in its worldwide extension, and as an ecclesial community it is less cohesive. Lutheranism shares many similarities with Anglicanism in the dominance of a single culture in its formation – in this case the German. But in relation to the Lutherans as a global communion, German colonialism was less pervasive and more transient. It was also more traumatic. As a result, Lutheran churches in the global South have been forced to confront more critically the significance of their national origins. Moreover, Scandinavian and (English) American forms of Lutheranism have influenced world Lutherans, alongside German forms. Nevertheless, within world Lutheranism there is a high degree of awareness of a Lutheran spiritual tradition embodied in worship and hymnody, in biblical hermeneutics, doctrine and confession of faith, which transcends its Northern European origin, yet makes the Evangelical Lutheran communion distinctive.

The challenge for the world Anglican communion is similarly to develop a self-understanding which enables the communion to appreciate its common heritage of faith and order, its worship and discipleship, in ways which both acknowledge and transcend Anglicanism's ethnic, national and colonial origins. It needs, further, to develop a common Christian identity and confession which does not privilege 'Englishness', but which honours the distinctively local forms in which the Gospel has been appropriated and rooted, and which must constantly be interpreted anew. It is the purpose of this book to provide historical tools to help foster that appreciation and critical evaluation.

CHAPTER 2

The Atlantic isles and world Anglicanism

The general burden of this book is that the diverse forms of Anglicanism which have developed in Asia and Africa, in Oceania and the Americas, are not simply clones of the English church. They have a dynamic and an integrity which derive from the special circumstances of their own history and geography and the engagement of the Gospel with the local cultures. But one important issue for all these churches, for some the dominant issue, is the historical legacy of British Christianity. This chapter will explore some of the major characteristics of the Anglican churches in Britain and Ireland since the Reformation and the effects of this history on the shape and self-understanding of the communion worldwide.

Since so much discussion of Anglicanism is Anglocentric, it is important to stress, at the outset, that the Church of England is neither the sole established church in Britain nor the sole representative of Anglicanism. The Church in Wales and the Church of Ireland are both Anglican, but they are no longer the 'established' churches of their respective lands. The Episcopal Church in Scotland is Anglican, but is not, nor (arguably) has it ever been, the established church in Scotland. That role is occupied by the (Presbyterian) Church of Scotland.

If there had been no Reformation, there would, doubtless, have been a distinctive English Catholicism which impacted worldwide. The Spanish and Portuguese Empires created their own special, idiosyncratic, forms of Roman Catholicism, closely allied to Iberian political power. French missionary enterprise equally strove to establish a Catholicism which embodied French values – after the French Revolution often at loggerheads with state republican secular values, but imbued with a strong nationalistic and patriotic spirit nevertheless. The English Reformation coincided with the beginnings of empire and the spread of English and (after the Union of 1707) British influence beyond these islands. The creation of informal and formal empires, the migration of British people throughout the world and the British missionary movement, were all bound up, in one way or another, with the diffusion of the established Church of England and its particular ethos.

Notoriously, Henry VIII's break with Rome in 1534 was motivated by dynastic considerations – the need to produce a son and heir. In the 1970s President Amin of Uganda, wishing to discredit the Church of Uganda for opposing his tyranny, mocked the 'sexual insatiability' of Henry and portrayed the Anglican church as a trumped-up religion concocted by a tyrant.[1] In fact, Henry felt that he had strong biblical reasons to justify the annulment of his marriage, and was angered that the Pope refused to recognise this. The break with the Papacy was not meant by Henry to be a break with the Catholic tradition of the church. The king had no sympathy for the new Evangelical movement which was setting the rest of Europe ablaze. Once the break was effected, however, Henry found himself reliant for the implementation of his church policy on ecclesiastical leaders who were increasingly influenced by the reforms initiated by Luther and by the Swiss. In 1536 Henry had a hand in the execution of William Tyndale, the great English Bible translator, who had fled to Antwerp. But he also allowed his Archbishop, Thomas Cranmer, to provide an English bible (largely based on Tyndale's work) in every parish in the land. With the accession of Henry's six-year-old son, Edward VI, in 1547, Cranmer was able to take the initiative in a thorough Evangelical Reformation of the Church.[2] The Book of Common Prayer of 1549, and its more radical revision of 1552, created a pattern of worship in the vernacular which breathed Evangelical values while remaining respectful of traditional forms. The Articles of Religion provided a moderate but clear statement of Reformation theology. This was done within the context of a continuity with the ancient church of the land, with its three orders of bishop, priest and deacon, its diocesan and parochial structure. The restoration of Roman Catholicism by Mary (1553–8) put an end to the Evangelical experiment. It was only in the long reign of Elizabeth (1558–1603) that a reformed Church of England was able to flourish.

The circumstances of the English Reformation created an ambiguity about the place of the Church of England in the spectrum of Reformation churches. Many within the church looked for further reforms of the church so that it would conform with Evangelical truth. In opposition to

[1] Kevin Ward, 'Archbishop Janani Luwum: The Dilemmas of Loyalty, Opposition and Witness in Amin's Uganda', in David Maxwell (ed.) with Ingrid Lawrie, *Christianity and the African Imagination* (Leiden: Brill, 2002), pp. 199–224.

[2] 'Evangelical' is the word used by Diarmaid MacCulloch to describe the general movement of Reformation ideas, *Thomas Cranmer* (New Haven: Yale University Press, 1996), p. 2.

this 'Puritan movement', there developed an apologia for the Church of England as it had emerged in 1559. The person who came to be regarded as the quintessential spokesman of the Church of England, as it actually existed rather than as it ought to be, was Richard Hooker (1554–1600), whose great work *The Laws of Ecclesiastical Polity* set out a theological justification for Anglicanism. In debate with those who demanded that the church conform precisely to what they considered clear scriptural models, Hooker defended its constitution and episcopal government by appealing to the principle of 'adiaphora' (things indifferent). Put simply, the argument is this: there are many ways of ordering church life, as of personal Christian life. God does not prescribe a single pattern. Churches are at liberty to order their external life as they deem fit, always assuming that such ordering does not contradict the Gospel. Hooker exalted prayer over preaching. He emphasised that the church was coterminous with society as a whole, rather than a gathering of the saved:

> There is not any man of the Church of England but the same man is also a member of the commonwealth; nor any man a member of the commonwealth which is not also of the Church of England.[3]

The Puritans might develop aspects of Calvin's system in ways unacceptable to the establishment, but Anglican leaders continued to speak respectfully of Calvin's theological insights. Their understanding of the Eucharist was recognisably 'Reformed' rather than Lutheran or Catholic. In political terms, there was a strong identification with the fate of Protestant communities generally in Europe, and particularly of Reformed groups in the Netherlands and the French Huguenots. The St Bartholomew massacre of French Protestants in 1572 was felt as an assault on English Protestants too, and a century later Huguenot refugees received a warm welcome in England. Many were absorbed into the established church (in Ireland and New York as well as England). English representatives (including the Bishop of Llandaff) attended the Synod of Dort in 1618–19, a consultation which provided the doctrinal and ecclesiastical framework for the Reformed church in the Netherlands.

In subsequent conflicts the Church of England distanced itself from 'Calvinism' as a set of beliefs and attitudes which were blamed for the civil war, and the consequent abolition of the monarchy and of episcopacy in the 1640s. But there has always been a strain of Calvinism (in the narrow sense of an identification with doctrines of grace and

[3] Paul Avis, *Anglicanism and the Christian Church* (Edinburgh: T. & T. Clark, 2002), p. 49.

predestination) within sections of the Church of England. In the eighteenth century those Evangelicals who remained within the Church of England and who did not join the Methodist exodus were characterised by a 'Calvinist' understanding of predestination, over against John Wesley's 'Arminianism', or emphasis on human freedom and responsibility to respond to the Gospel. In the need to emphasise its distinctiveness over against Roman Catholicism, the Church of Ireland has often demonstrated a much greater sympathy for Reformed theology. In the twentieth century, the diocese of Sydney in Australia would claim to confess the full Reformation heritage of Anglicanism, in ways which most other Anglican churches would now regard as decidedly un-Anglican.

Much of religious value disappeared as a result of the Reformation upheaval – the historian Eamon Duffy stresses the vitality of pre-Reformation English Catholicism.[4] He has shown that much of the lay participation in parish life in the Devon parish of Morebath centred on its gilds and fraternities. At the Reformation this was replaced, at least at first, by a less participatory church life, less popular forms of worship and spirituality.[5] But by the end of Elizabeth's long reign the Reformation had begun to create a new form of popular devotion based on hearing and reading the Bible in English, participating in an English liturgy which retained a sense of awe and mystery, and promoting a sense of English national solidarity under God. As the Elizabethan settlement achieved stability, it became clear that the old faith could not be entirely eradicated. But it was marginalised. There might be a residual nostalgia for the old faith among all ranks of society, but it was generally only high-status families who were able to maintain an overt adhesion to Catholicism. Until the nineteenth century, there was a strong suspicion that Catholics were political subversive. They were accused of supporting England's rivals: Catholic Spain remained the main threat in the sixteenth and early seventeenth centuries. France, especially after the Revocation of the Edict of Nantes and the repression of the Huguenots in 1685, became the enemy. A Protestant identity helped powerfully to define what it meant to be English. England's growing interest as a world power, especially in the New World, was undertaken in opposition to the empire of Catholic Spain. In England itself, the sense of being an 'elect nation' was popularised, and sustained, over generations, by the *Acts and Monuments* of John Foxe, which recounted the heroic stories of the English Protestant martyrs.

[4] Eamon Duffy, *The Stripping of the Altars* (New Haven: Yale University Press, 1992).
[5] Eamon Duffy, *The Voices of Morebath* (New Haven: Yale University Press, 2001).

The Reformation also aroused the hopes of a common Protestant identity for all the kingdoms of the British Isles. The union of the English and Scottish crowns in 1603 seemed to augur well for this project, but it was to prove elusive. Scotland valued its particularly Reformed identity too strongly to fall in line with the different trajectory of English Protestantism. The Church of Scotland was unenthusiastic about the creeping episcopacy which the Stuart kings tried to impose upon it, and openly rebelled when Charles I in 1637 attempted to impose a liturgical uniformity with England. The civil war which ensued in all three kingdoms resulted in the collapse of an attempt to produce a uniform Protestant church for the three kingdoms (of England, Ireland and Scotland) based on the episcopal model of the Church of England. In the late 1640s the Westminster Assembly attempted to provide an alternative based on a robust Calvinist statement of faith and a Presbyterian church order. But this did not survive even the Commonwealth period: Cromwell and the army preferred a church which was altogether less coercive and centralised, and one with a wider toleration (as long as it did not subvert the new republic). It is difficult to imagine precisely what would have eventually emerged if the Commonwealth had survived – possibly a form of Protestant Christianity rather like that which obtained in the Netherlands with a 'public' church in which Calvinism would have provided the dominant theological orthodoxy but in which more liberal tendencies would have had a voice, and in which minorities were more respected and tolerated.[6] 'Anglicanism' itself would have had a very different identity.

With the Restoration of the monarchy in 1660, episcopacy was revived. The renewed attempt to impose an episcopal church order in all three kingdoms met with resistance in Scotland, though there was no attempt to impose a Book of Common Prayer there. Eventually, in 1690, after the flight of the Roman Catholic king James II and VII, Parliament for the first time established the principle that the sovereign must be a Protestant and that he or she be required to swear an oath 'to maintain the Protestant Reformed Religion established by law'. The new rulers, William and Mary, abandoned the elusive search for a uniform Protestant (and, therefore, Anglican) identity by the restoration of Presbyterianism in Scotland. This was enshrined in the Act of Union between Scotland and England in 1707. The new British identity was consequently based on a general Protestantism rather than a specifically Anglican one. In England itself, although the government ceased actively to repress dissent, the

[6] Jonathan Israel, *The Dutch Republic* (Oxford: Clarendon, 1995).

concept of an Anglican confessional state, in which full citizenship was dependent on membership of the Church of England, remained strong. The debate within the established church was between those who wanted sharply to define the boundaries of the Church of England over against dissent, emphasising 'high'-church doctrines of apostolic succession and the sacraments (the Tories) and those who wished the church to be as inclusive as possible by emphasising common Protestant elements and to grant increasing civil liberties to those who conscientiously refused to be included (the Whig understanding). An acceptance of a legal establishment of religion remained a bedrock of Church of England identity for both groups, until the whole idea of a confessional state, supporting a church establishment, came under severe pressure in the early years of the nineteenth century.

Before examining the implications of the church–state connection, embodied in establishment, for the development of a worldwide Anglicanism, it is useful to explore how Anglican identity was constructed and conceived outside England.

WALES

Wales was most closely bound up with England, politically and in its ecclesiastical structure. The Reformation served to strengthen these ties institutionally. The Welsh dioceses were an integral part of the Province of Canterbury, though generally poorer than English dioceses. One of the signs of the success of reformation in Wales was the realisation that it must be conveyed through the medium of Welsh, which remained until the nineteenth century the language of a large majority of the inhabitants. William Morgan's 1588 translation of the Bible was of enormous significance for Welsh culture and the long-term viability of Welsh as a language. The Book of Common Prayer appeared in Welsh even earlier, in 1567. The Reformation thus proved, for the Welsh, an important element in the preservation of Welsh language and culture in the face of creeping Anglicisation.[7] The Anglican church was as important in that process as it was to be among the Yoruba or Baganda in nineteenth-century Africa. In the eighteenth century, the newly established Society for the Propagation of Christian Knowledge played a vital role in promoting Welsh-language books on theological themes and spiritual issues. The leaders of the Welsh Great Awakening, William Williams of

[7] Glanmor Williams, *The Welsh and their Religion* (Cardiff: University of Wales Press, 1991).

Pantycelyn, Daniel Rowland and Howell Davis, were all Anglicans. Their achievement, apart from their profound impact on the way people understand religious commitment, was to eschew the largely 'imitative and derivative' forms of literary Welsh and to utilise, in their sermons and hymns, a form of Welsh which 'grew organically' from the spoken language.[8] However, the eighteenth-century Welsh episcopate, in marked contrast to that of Elizabeth, was largely non-Welsh and non-Welsh-speaking. The tragedy of the Great Awakening for Welsh Anglicanism was that it could not be contained within the established church, and resulted in a serious haemorrhage of church support. By the 1851 census, three-quarters of people in Wales belonged to Nonconformist churches. The late nineteenth century saw some recovery – with a vigorous church planting in the industrial areas, and (with the growth of Anglo-Catholicism) a renewed sense of the distinctive nature of a Welsh Anglican identity. In the 1905 census it was still the largest denomination in Wales. But by this time it had long been on the defensive against a self-confident and socially radical Welsh Nonconformism.

The Welsh church was the last of the non-English Anglican churches to be disestablished, in 1922. The church retained, by and large, its property. Unlike the Irish church it could still claim, in some sense, to embody Welsh national identity. It was decided, however, partly in deference to Nonconformist sensibilities, to name the new body 'the Church in Wales', rather than 'the Church of Wales', though even this terminology could be interpreted as implying an unwillingness to accord full ecclesial status to dissenting bodies.[9] Through its parochial system, it continues to understand itself as having a mission to all people living in Wales. Consequently, the Church in Wales probably provides a significant model of how the Church of England might be constituted if it were ever disestablished.

IRELAND

If the Reformation in Wales demonstrates how Anglicanism could transcend Englishness with considerable success, the Reformation in Ireland illustrates how difficult was the task. By the end of the sixteenth century the Reformation had made little impact on Ireland. Both native

[8] Derec Llwyd Morgan, *The Great Awakening in Wales* (London: Epworth, 1988), p. 133.

[9] C. C. Harris and Richard Startup, *The Church in Wales: The Sociology of a Traditional Institution* (Cardiff: University of Wales Press, 1999).

Gaelic-speaking Irish and the old Anglo-Irish aristocracy resisted the new church. The schemes to 'plant' English and Scottish settlers in Ireland and to dispossess Irish peasants added a racial dimension to the Reformation. The establishment of Trinity College Dublin, in 1591, was an attempt to provide a supply of ministers born and bred in Ireland, and to give the Reformed church a stronger local base. There were efforts to translate the Bible and Prayer Book into the Irish (Gaelic) language, but the process was slower, more fitful and less enthusiastic than in Wales. Only in 1602 was an Irish New Testament completed, and it never achieved wide distribution. Gradually Protestants in Ireland, dismayed at their failure to win over the bulk of the population, tended to blame their difficulties on the 'backwardness' of Irish culture. The best way of advancing the Protestant faith was to promote 'civility' and the use of English. Enthusiasm for utilising the Irish language for evangelistic purposes tended to lie with individuals rather than the Church of Ireland as a whole. Aware that it existed in a strongly Catholic environment, the Church of Ireland in the seventeenth century tended to emphasise its Reformed, Calvinist heritage, where differences between 'elect' and 'reprobate' came to have a racial as well as a theological signification.

To the vast majority of the Irish, Protestantism came to be regarded as the religion of the English. This was reinforced by the considerable plantation of Protestants from England and Scotland and the eventual alienation of land from Catholics. The Irish can be seen as the original victims of English/British colonialism, a process which preceded the Reformation but which was given added dimension by religious conflict.[10]

Protestants saw themselves as a beleaguered and separate people. The 1641 massacres of Protestants, particularly intense in Ulster, came to symbolise the dangers of Catholic aggression and the need to keep the Catholic majority under control. Long into the eighteenth century the Church of Ireland annually commemorated the 1641 killings.[11] With the triumph of William of Orange (King Billy) over the Catholic king, James II, at the battle of the Boyne in 1690, Catholicism seemed decisively defeated as a political force. During the 'Protestant Ascendancy' of the eighteenth century, Catholic gentry were dispossessed of their land and denied access to the professions. Some Catholic families felt constrained

[10] Stephen Howe critically examines this idea in *Ireland and Empire* (Oxford: Oxford University Press, 2000).

[11] Toby Barnard, *Irish Protestant Ascents and Descents 1641–1770* (Dublin: Four Courts Press, 2004), Chapter 4.

to conform to the Church of Ireland, or encouraged certain members so to do, in order to maintain their position – the political philosopher Edmund Burke came from such a family.[12] Presbyterians also were discriminated against: in eighteenth-century Ireland, even the word 'Protestant' was often used to refer exclusively to the established Church of Ireland; other non-Catholic churches belonged to 'dissent'. For long the bishops of the Church of Ireland had been appointed by the government in London. After the Act of Union of 1801, the Church of Ireland legally became part of a 'United Church of England and Ireland' (though its bishops did not sit in the House of Lords).

The Church of Ireland entered the nineteenth century in both hopeful and fearful mood. The impact of the Evangelical movement brought a new enthusiasm and optimism about the possibilities of claiming Ireland as a whole for the Protestant religion. Church leaders saw signs of a 'second reformation'. Societies for the education and uplift of Irish people proliferated. There was renewed activity in producing literature in the Irish language. Foreign missions were embraced – the CMS came to occupy a much more central role in Church of Ireland life than it ever did in the Church of England.[13] These hopes were to be shattered by the political crisis of the early nineteenth century over the place of establishment, by the revival of the Catholic Church, and by the rise of Irish Nationalism. The established church, under criticism in England for denying civil rights to dissenting minorities, found its position even more problematic in Ireland. The decision by the Whig government of the 1830s to suppress a number of uneconomic and unsustainable Irish dioceses precipitated a major crisis for Anglican establishment. The Tractarian movement attacked the 'Erastian' nature of the Church of England and Ireland, its being treated as an arm of the state. In 1867 the Church of Ireland was disestablished and substantially disendowed (though it still kept its pre-Reformation buildings). This did, at last, enable the church to be realistic about its position. Dublin and Northern Ireland remained growth areas. But the church was already seriously in decline in the rural areas, especially in the West, a process precipitated by the Famine and by emigration.

Contrary to the popular image, taken overall, almost as many Irish Protestants as Catholics emigrated to America or Australia. Protestants

[12] Conor Cruise O'Brien, *The Great Melody* (London: Sinclair-Stevenson, 1992).
[13] Alan Acheson, *A History of the Church of Ireland, 1691–2001* (Dublin: Columba Press, 2002), pp. 124–7.

carried with them their own strong anti-Catholic prejudices, which had an important impact, particularly on Canadian and Australian religious as well as secular politics. Meanwhile in Ireland itself, the renewed vigour of the Church of Ireland attracted Catholic suspicion of aggressive proselytism – especially if it appeared that welfare schemes were taking advantage of misery and hunger to secure conversions.

In the twentieth century, sectarian division assumed new force with the creation of an independent Ireland, and the partition of Ireland. The creation of Northern Ireland in 1922 – 'a Protestant state for a Protestant people' – established what many saw as a sectarian state. The Orange Order had been established in 1795 to commemorate and consolidate the events of a century earlier which had secured the Protestant cause. By the middle of the twentieth century, it had become a major vehicle of working-class Protestant religious identity in Northern Ireland. Associated often with a bitter and narrow doctrinal expression and anti-Catholicism, it is not, however, the exclusive expression of fringe or extremist Protestants. Many of its members were and are members of the Church of Ireland. In the 1990s, the Orange march at Portadown (incidentally an epicentre of the 1641 massacres) became a flashpoint between Catholic and Protestant, with Drumcree Church of Ireland the site of an Orange service.[14]

Meanwhile, in the Republic of Ireland, the Church of Ireland had long learnt to live peacefully as a minority, protected more by its residual status as the church of a privileged group than by specific legal safeguards. The church continues, as an institution, to embody the unity of Ireland as a whole, despite the political division between North and South. The church emphasises its Irishness, continuing to argue a historical continuity with the early and medieval church, and the legacy of Celtic Christianity. In Northern Ireland that Irish identity is supplemented by an emotionally even stronger identity as British and Unionist. At the leadership level, the Church of Ireland in the North has strongly emphasised its peace-building role, through work like that of the Corrymeela community, an ecumenical venture in which Church of Ireland members have participated strongly.[15] When, in the early years of the twenty-first century, members of the Anglican communion were seeking for ways to live together, despite the crisis over homosexuality, it is not

[14] Dominic Bryan, *The Politics of Ritual, Tradition and Control* (London: Pluto Press, 2000).

[15] See Trevor Williams, 'Corrymeela: Healing the Division', in Andrew Wingate, Kevin Ward, Carrie Pemberton and Wilson Sitshebo (eds.), *Anglicanism: A Global Communion* (London: Mowbray, 1998), pp. 286–93.

surprising that they should look to the Archbishop of Armagh to chair the commission.

Irish migration has been of great significance for the development of worldwide Anglicanism. The development of the Anglican Church in Ontario (Canada) was highly influenced by Protestant and Catholic antagonisms between Irish settlers. The distinctiveness of the diocese of Sydney in Australia, with its unusual degree of Protestant theological definition, is due partly to Irish Protestant migration, as well as to the social tensions resulting from the high percentage of Catholic Irish among the early convicts transported for political reasons. Irish Anglican clergy provided a high proportion of colonial clergy, while Irish missionaries have been prominent. Among important Hibernian CMS missionaries were James Long, the great missionary to Bengal, Philip O'Flaherty, an Irish-speaking convert who pioneered work in Uganda, Archdeacon Owen of Kenya, a persistent critic of British colonial rule in East Africa, and the redoubtable Mabel Ensor of Uganda.[16]

SCOTLAND

In 1690 King Billy's victory at the Boyne had ensured the ascendancy of the Anglican Church of Ireland. In the same year he brought an end to the elusive attempt to conform the Church of Scotland to an Anglican pattern. Presbyterian order was finally established, enshrined and strengthened by the terms of the Treaty of Union of 1707. Some Episcopalian ministers hung on for a number of years as incumbents in the parishes of the established church, a dwindling band. Since the Reformation, Aberdeen and the North-East had identified with an Episcopalian tradition and spirituality, and it was here that the beginnings of a dissenting church emerged, equipped with bishops. Their sympathies were with the Anglican Non-Jurors who had left the Church of England because of their continuing loyalty to the Stuart dynasty. The strong connection between Scottish Episcopalianism and Jacobitism meant that between 1715 and 1792 it was subject to penal laws, and for a time the Book of Common Prayer (always likely to arouse Scottish sensibilities at the best of times) was proscribed.

Religious coercion was fitful, and a small network of 'qualified chapels' began to emerge in the lowland urban areas. Their ministers agreed to take an oath of allegiance to the Hanoverians in return for legal

[16] Jack Hodgins, *Sister Island: A History of CMS in Ireland* (Dunmurray: CMS Ireland, 1994).

protection. But this put them at loggerheads with the Jacobite sympathies of the Aberdeen Episcopalians. Whereas the lowland chapels used the Book of Common Prayer of the Church of England, the North-Eastern group experimented with a distinctive Scottish liturgy, incorporating indigenous high-church traditions, the spirituality of the Non-Jurors, and Eastern Orthodox influences. Thus, whereas the Church of Ireland tended to emphasise its Protestant roots in the face of a Catholic majority, the fragmented Episcopal communion in Scotland emphasised its high-church heritage in contrast to the established Church of Scotland. For much of the eighteenth century a coherent Episcopal Church did not exist. It was only with the dropping of Jacobitism as a lost cause at the end of the century that the way was open for a full union of the disparate groups into the Episcopal Church in Scotland, agreed at Laurencekirk in 1804. For long Episcopalians maintained the fiction that they were the legitimate Church of Scotland, inheritor both of the medieval Catholic tradition and of the Reformation church before 1690. The harsh reality was that they were a small 'sect', though one which had status and influence: many of the Scottish lairds (the land-owning class) chose to identify with the Episcopal Church, and to finance its building programme – even though this same group continued to have responsibilities for the established church. In popular perception the Episcopalians became the church of the lairds, while the established church was the church of the urban, business and professional classes, and (before the 1843 Disruption) of by far the greater part of the population as a whole. This animus against the Episcopal Church persisted well into the twentieth century. As Agnes Muir Mackenzie put it in 1943, Presbyterians think 'that the Episcopal Church is an English exotic brought in by the laird with his background of an English public school, or by the laird's English wife, and supported mainly by people who hope the laird will ask them to dinner'.[17]

In fact, Scottish Episcopalianism was distinctively Scottish. But, as it came out of the ghetto, it had difficulty in avoiding being seen as a satellite of the English church. The dominance of the Oxford Movement in shaping the ritual and theology of the nineteenth-century Scottish church, the reliance on a large number of English priests, and the increasing tendency to appoint English bishops gave some credence to this. In this the Scottish church resembled the colonial Anglican church,

[17] *Scottish Guardian*, 15 January 1943, quoted in Gavin White, *The Scottish Episcopal Church: A New History* (Edinburgh: General Synod of the Scottish Episcopal Church, 1998), p. 121.

where a preference for the appointment of English clergy as bishops persisted until the second half of the twentieth century. In addition, the growth of the Scottish Episcopal Church in the nineteenth century was, to a large extent, sustained by the influx of English and Irish Anglicans to work in the central industrial lowlands. In contrast, the Episcopal Church found it hard to maintain pastoral support in those Gaelic-speaking areas of western Scotland where it had a presence, and by the end of the nineteenth century had few native Gaelic-speaking priests.[18]

Not only did the Scots provide a significant proportion of the British emigrants to the colonies, and a high proportion of the British Empire's administrators and soldiers, but there was also a disproportionate number of Scots clergy serving overseas as Anglican clergy. The first clergy sent to America by the SPG were Scots Episcopalians. John Strachan from Aberdeen, regarded as the chief architect of the Anglican church in Ontario, had been a member of the Church of Scotland before he decided to take Anglican orders in Canada. The Episcopal Church in Scotland did not itself manifest the same missionary zeal which characterised the Church of Ireland, nor could it compete with the vigour of the three main Scottish Presbyterian traditions. But a large number of SPG, CMS and UMCA missionaries were Scots, not all of them Episcopalian. One of the greatest CMS missionaries was Alexander Mackay of Uganda, the son of an Aberdeenshire minister of the Free Church of Scotland. The Scottish Episcopal Church has special ties with the diocese of St John's in South Africa and of Nagpur in India.

The Scottish Episcopal Church has become linked historically with the establishment of the episcopate in the American church, when three Scottish bishops consecrated Samuel Seabury on 14 November 1784 in Aberdeen, shortly after the end of the American War of Independence. It was a connection full of ironies. Seabury, like the majority of Anglicans in America, was a loyalist. He had reluctantly made his peace with the new republic, but was still regarded with some suspicion by more patriotic Americans. The Scottish bishops had not yet formally decided to abandon their objection to swearing an oath of loyalty to the Hanoverians. In the nineteenth century, the Scottish Episcopal Church accepted the reality that it existed as a small denomination within a strongly Protestant (and non-Anglican) country. In this sense it confronted similar challenges

[18] One Gaelic speaker was Arthur John Maclean (1858–1943), though he was not a native speaker. He became the leader of the Archbishop of Canterbury's mission to the Assyrians, Bishop of Moray and eventually Primus of the Scottish Episcopal Church.

to those facing the Episcopal Church in America, which had the task of reinventing itself in the aftermath of revolution. Both accepted that they could not be the 'established' church in their land. Both needed to differentiate themselves from the Evangelical ethos of the dominant form of religion in their land. Both found congenial the spiritual renewal associated with the Oxford Movement and the reaffirmation of the 'catholic' nature of the church.

A number of contradictory currents seemed to operate within nineteenth century Scottish Episcopalianism: a desire to emphasise the distinctiveness of the Scottish tradition over against English innovation struggled against a need to emphasise links with the established Church of England. The Scottish rite struggled to maintain its place against those who argued that only the 1662 (English) prayer book should have legal authority. These tensions were only resolved in the twentieth century with the production of a new Scottish prayer book in 1929, in which liturgies from both English and Scottish traditions were authorised.[19] The Scottish Episcopal Church has been in a number of conversations with the Church of Scotland, most predicated on the introduction or re-introduction of episcopacy within a Presbyterian framework. In the 1950s and 1960s, these attempts revived in the popular imagination (aroused by the press and by sections of the kirk) residual fears of 'prelacy' and of Anglican/English imperialism. As all churches have begun to confront the problems of rapid secularisation in Scotland since the 1960s, the appetite for institutional reunion schemes has diminished, in favour of a courtesy, a recognition of a common mission to a secular society. A less pretentious and stuffy, more critical and innovative, Episcopal Church emerged at the end of the twentieth century, symbolised by the popular radicalism of the Bishop of Edinburgh, Richard Holloway.

ANGLICANISM BEYOND BRITAIN: THE DEVELOPMENT OF A MISSION CONSCIOUSNESS

After the Restoration of the monarchy after the Commonwealth period, episcopacy was restored within the Church of England, and in 1662 a new Book of Common Prayer was produced. It remains the authorised prayer book of the Church of England and became the basis for the prayer books for practically all the other members of the communion, either in English

[19] Rowan Strong, *Episcopalianism in Nineteenth-Century Scotland* (Oxford: Oxford University Press, 2002).

or in translation. One of the few substantial amendments to Cranmer's 1552 book was the introduction of a baptism liturgy for 'those of riper years'. The disruption of the previous twenty years, 'the growth of Anabaptism' and 'the licentiousness of the late times crept in amongst us' necessitated such a service. As an afterthought, the preface to the 1662 Book of Common Prayer also noted that the service 'may be always useful for the baptizing of Natives in our Plantations, and others converted to the Faith'. It was to be another forty years before the implications of the expansion of the church overseas began to be addressed in any coherent way. In 1695 the Revd Thomas Bray was appointed by the Bishop of London to help in the organisation of an Anglican parochial system in Maryland in America, over which the bishop had oversight. Bray's recognition of the needs of the church overseas led to the establishment of two societies which were profoundly to affect the development of Anglicanism. The Society for Promoting Christian Knowledge (SPCK) was founded in 1698. Its aim was to foster education, the supply of Christian literature and help in the theological formation of ministers. The Society had a significant role in Christian education and diffusion of literature within Britain, but it always had overseas interests. The SPCK's great overseas work lay in the printing of vernacular prayer books and other Christian literature in India. It continues to provide theological literature for Anglican theological colleges throughout the world. In the eighteenth century, the SPCK also sponsored the missionary work of the Danish Lutherans in South India. Bray's other organisation, the Society for the Propagation of the Gospel in foreign parts (SPG), was established in 1701, with a more specifically missionary brief: to work among British settler communities and to evangelise non-Christian peoples 'subject to the Crown'.

The SPG understood its role as a handmaid of the church. It upheld a high-church tradition going back to Hooker, but not in any partisan spirit. Dan O'Connor, the modern historian of the Society, puts it well:

> It included a high view of the Church, of church order and apostolic succession, liturgy and sacraments, exemplified in an early decision that 'no Bibles be sent by the Society into the Plantations without Common Prayer Books bound up with them'. An important consequence … was the understanding that a missionary was answerable to the Church and the bishop to which he was sent, and only secondarily to the Society. Accompanying this high ecclesiology was a political theology which saw church and state intimately associated, two aspects of a single national community.[20]

[20] Daniel O'Connor, *Three Centuries of Mission: The United Society for the Propagation of the Gospel 1701–2000* (London: Continuum, 2000), p. 8.

It was, as O'Connor usefully puts it, an *ancien régime* concept of the relationship of church and state. The church was an integral part of an ordered, hierarchical 'commonwealth', a corporate society in which religion was part and parcel of the way of life, and in which aristocracy and rank were sanctioned. By the late eighteenth century, this vision of a Christian society was increasingly at odds with the revolutionary values of the time.

While by no means radical in its political vision, the Church Missionary Society, founded in 1799, more clearly articulated these changes. The CMS was a fruit of the Evangelical revival in England. Associated, from the 1730s, with John and Charles Wesley and George Whitefield, all Anglican priests, the Methodist movement began as a voluntary movement within the church. It aimed to spread 'biblical holiness' throughout the land. The Wesleys were for a time SPG missionaries, sent in the 1730s to Georgia. Their attempts to impose a godly discipline in frontier parishes was not a success. It was their bitter experience in America, as well as contact with the continental Pietist movement and the Moravians, which provoked the conversion experiences of the Wesley brothers in 1739 once they had returned to England. Released from the burden of good works, John Wesley preached a message of justification by faith, appropriated through a specific and sudden conversion experience. The bishops were alarmed by the 'enthusiasm' provoked by John Wesley, and his unwillingness to comply with parish boundaries. Reluctantly, but decisively, the Methodists established their own organisation, which could not fit into the Church of England structure. The rapid expansion of Methodism in America during the revolutionary period came at a time when the Anglican church in America was disorientated and confused, and from which it did not fully recover: Methodism soon far outstripped the Episcopal Church in numbers.[21]

Though the church and Methodism parted company, the Evangelical revival made a profound impact. The Evangelical party within the Church of England preferred to work through the parochial system, rather than ignore it, as John Wesley had done. They wished to revive what they saw as the flagging spiritual life of the established church from within. The Evangelical founders of the Church Missionary Society also

[21] For 1970, Barrett puts the United Methodist Church (the main but by no means the only branch of Methodism) at 14 million compared with the 3 million of the Episcopal Church. David Barrett, George Kurian and Todd M. Johnson, *World Christian Encyclopedia* (2 vols., Oxford: Oxford University Press, 2001), Volume 1, pp. 782–9.

brought a new kind of missionary consciousness. Conservative in many aspects of social life, and strongly against the 'godless' doctrines of the French Revolution, Evangelicals were strongly in a favour of the abolition of the slave trade and of slavery itself. It was not the CMS's intention to conflict with the SPG. It also supported the established church – but, as John Venn said, it was founded on 'the church principle', not the 'high-church principle'. If the SPG had tended to blur the boundaries between voluntary society and church, and between church and state, the CMS defined those boundaries much more clearly. The CMS was willing to co-operate with the British government where it was useful to evangelism. But it did not see its work as dependent on British authority overseas. In parts of India, in Yorubaland, in Uganda, among the Maori, the CMS operated long before the onset of colonial power – in some cases it contributed to the factors which led to British imperial expansion, but neither was this its aim nor in many cases did it initially welcome such expansion. In similar ways, the CMS wanted to keep the church authorities at arm's length. Missionary work was distinct from planting ecclesiastical institutions. It aimed to produce an indigenous church, but it was for that native church to decide how best to organise itself ecclesiastically. Henry Venn, between 1841 and 1872 the guiding force behind the CMS, expressed this in his famous dicta of the 'euthanasia of the mission' and the 'three-self principle': self-government, self-propagation and self-finance. Venn expected the local church to be constituted on recognisably Anglican lines. But he was quite willing to contemplate separate national churches which were definitely not 'Church of England'. And yet Venn, like all the early CMS strategists, welcomed the establishment principle. They urged the duty of British imperial officials to support the church financially and materially and to promote its Christian values in society as a whole. What they found less easy to accept was the authority of a colonial bishop in the native church, if that bishop was not himself Evangelical.

The CMS was anxious, in a way that the SPG was not, to emphasise the autonomy of missionaries from episcopal direction. In the nineteenth century, the CMS was incomparably the greatest Anglican force in spreading Christianity worldwide. But it was relatively unconcerned with the ecclesiastical form which Christianity should take, and was often suspicious of high-church emphases. Venn's understanding of independent native churches can be seen as bearing fruit in the way in which the united churches of India have transcended their Anglican and other western denominational heritages, and also in the Three-Self Church in

China. It has also been influential in the recognition of the three cultural traditions of the New Zealand church. But Venn's theory, in so far as it is intended as a blue-print for the development of an Anglican communion, has been a minority one. By the end of the nineteenth century it gave way, even in CMS circles, to the acceptance of a more organic, unitary and cohesive sense of Anglicanism as a distinctive ecclesial body.[22]

THE RISE OF CHURCH PARTIES WITHIN THE CHURCH OF ENGLAND AND ITS EFFECT ON MISSION

The SPG always set great store on a high doctrine of the church. 'High church' signified an attachment to the church's corporate identity, its three-fold ministry, its ministry of word and sacrament. But 'high church' has come to have another series of meanings within Anglicanism – that representing a particular group or party within the church. It was only in the nineteenth century that this more partisan and factional view came to dominate the self-understanding of the church. This arose as disputes between Evangelicals and Anglo-Catholics intensified.

The Tractarians (later to be known as the Oxford Movement and then, more generally, Anglo-Catholicism) had first arisen in the 1830s at a time of crisis about the status and being of the church in British society. With the growth of civil and political liberties for those Dissenters and Catholics who conscientiously refused to conform to the established church, governments began to question the privileged status of the church, with its exclusive claims. The Whig government of the 1830s wanted to reduce its powers, even perhaps to disestablish it. John Henry Newman and the members of the Oxford Movement saw this, not as a useful reform of an anachronistic institution, but as an attack on the claim of the established church to be the church, divinely instituted by God, which the government should recognise and support but not attempt to run as a department of state. The Tractarians believed that they were speaking out for the church as such, not defending a partisan opinion. But increasingly they seemed to denigrate or attack the Protestant heritage, blaming it for the liberal secularism which threatened the place of Christianity in society. Unlike other confessional revivals on the continent, the Anglo-Catholic movement emphasised Anglican distance from the Reformation. The alliances between Lutheran, Reformed and

[22] Peter Williams, *The Ideal of the Self-Governing Church: A Study of Victorian Missionary Strategy* (Leiden: Brill, 1990).

Moravian in the eighteenth century, which had been so important for the SPG in providing personnel for their work in America and their collaboration in India, were now deemed to compromise Anglican self-identity – most famously in the dispute over the Anglo-German project to establish a Protestant bishopric in Jerusalem in the 1840s. The SPG was revitalised by the Oxford Movement, but it now distanced itself from alliance with continental Protestants. The CMS continued to rely heavily on continental missionaries. But, after the 1860s, the growing importance of European nationalism made co-operation across nations more difficult. As Paul Jenkins says, 'the heightened confessional consciousness in both Anglican and Lutheran communions made cooperation more problematic and the awareness of a common Protestant identity less easy to take for granted'.[23]

The development of the church overseas was hampered by the legal establishment and exacerbated by the fissure in the mission movement between Catholic and Evangelical. One thing which both societies could agree upon was that the mechanisms for creating an episcopate overseas were unwieldy and highly unsatisfactory. Before 1840 some ten overseas bishoprics had been created by the government, in Canada (the 1790s), the Caribbean (the 1820s) and India (from 1814). Such creations were costly, both of parliamentary time and of money. Moreover, with the crisis of the 1830s, it became clear that a government which was suppressing bishoprics in Ireland would not easily create new ones in other parts of the world, where Anglicans were inevitably a minority and where there might be political sensitivities just as great as in Ireland. The creation of the Colonial Bishoprics Fund in 1841 enabled the church itself to take the initiative in the creation of dioceses – still, in areas of British control, with letters patent from the crown, but without requiring the government funding which would have made their creation impossible. Bishop Samuel Wilberforce, who pioneered this development, was impressed by the action of the Episcopal Church in the United States in commissioning 'missionary bishops'. Wilberforce advocated that the Church of England might similarly appoint bishops beyond British territory. The clearest example of this came with the consecration of Bishop Charles Mackenzie in 1859 to be bishop in Central Africa, followed in 1862 by the consecration, on the urging of Henry Venn, of Samuel

[23] Paul Jenkins, 'The CMS and the Basel Mission', in K. Ward and B. Stanley (eds.), *The Church Mission Society and World Christianity 1799–1999* (Richmond: Curzon and Grand Rapids: Eerdmans, 2000), p. 65. See also N. Railton, *No North Sea: The Anglo-German Evangelical Network in the Middle of the Nineteenth Century* (Leiden: Brill, 2000).

Crowther as 'Bishop on the Niger', although the appointment went against Venn's view that the bishop was the 'crown' of the church – the mark of an already existing self-supporting, self-governing and self-propagating church. That there were inconsistencies can be expected as the missionary expansion of the church created unprecedented situations.

Both the weakening of state–church links in the 1830s and the experience of 'planting' the church overseas affected the way in which the Church of England itself was run, leading eventually to the 1919 Enabling Act, which created a Church Assembly and the beginnings of synodical government – things which had been enjoyed in many other parts of the Anglican communion for decades. But the degree of self-government within the Church of England remained inhibited by the state connection: Hastings has noted the paucity of the lay element in the assembly, dominated by Tory MPs and 'the Cecil family and their relatives'.[24]

The Church of England has been affected by the worldwide communion in numerous ways, though ones which are often unacknowledged. Notoriously, Owen Chadwick's great work *The Victorian Church* failed completely to mention the role of mission, strange for an author who wrote such a sensitive biography of Bishop Mackenzie and his work in Central Africa. The CMS, through its 'auxiliaries', established a solid base of support, and created a network of parishes which took an active interest in the mission world. Missionary service was a contributory force to social mobility. Women, in particular, found outlets in missionary work which were denied them in Britain.

The conflicts of the early nineteenth century gave the impression that the church's two societies were serving particular constituencies within the church, rather than the church as a whole. The proliferation of missionary societies in the latter half of the nineteenth century tended to reinforce that understanding. The Universities' Mission to Central Africa, the Cambridge and Oxford Missions to India and the Melanesian Mission all represented various shades of 'high'-church tradition; the South American Missionary Society, the Evangelical tradition. In 1922 the unease of conservative Evangelicals led to a further splintering of mission work with schism within the CMS and the establishment of the Bible Churchmen's Missionary Society. Significantly, this was a time when, in America, whole denominations were splitting over similar issues.

[24] Adrian Hastings, *A History of English Christianity 1920–1985* (London: Collins, 1986), p. 242. Ken Farrimond, 'The Policy of the Church Missionary Society concerning the Development of Self-Governing Indigenous Churches 1900–1942', Ph.D. dissertation, University of Leeds, 2003.

One of the consequences of the Church of England's unwillingness or inability to co-ordinate its missionary work (unlike the Presbyterian and Methodist churches) was the creation of much more compact and cohesive versions of Anglicanism in many parts of the world. Even in parts of the world, like China, Japan or India, where a diversity of societies operated, local districts (which often became dioceses) tended to express a particular and distinctive form of Anglicanism. The spectrum of church traditions embodied in the Church of England translated in only a minority of cases to the worldwide Anglican communion.

THE DISTINCTIVE MARKS OF AN ANGLICAN PIETY

The publication of the Authorised Version of the Bible in 1611 produced an English translation which remained standard for Anglicans, and Protestants generally, in England and among British settlers until the second half of the twentieth century. Bible translation was an essential task for Anglican missionaries. Some early translations into vernaculars tended to echo the grammatical forms and turns of phrase of the English Bible – a covert form of the 'colonisation of the mind', perhaps, seeming to allow the Bible to speak in a familiar tongue, yet the bearer of a foreign mentality. Vernacular translations have been revised as knowledge of the local culture has deepened. But in many cases the power of the first translation – one can think of the 1897 Luganda translation by Pilkington and Duta – has created a sacred language in the new language as powerful as the English of the Authorised Version. Just as pervasive have been the local translations of the 1662 Book of Common Prayer, powerfully shaping the liturgical expression of Anglicanism throughout the world. Until the latter part of the twentieth century this uniformity was often regarded as a strength of worldwide Anglicanism. Now it is more likely to be seen, at least by native English speakers, as a somewhat bizarre and exotic survival.

For a long time the Church of England did not use hymns in its formal services, relying on metrical psalms. In the eighteenth century, hymn singing became a vital component of the Evangelical Revival. The Church of England was rather late in incorporating hymns into the normal structure of its worship, and when it did so in the mid nineteenth century, it tended to be the Anglo-Catholic, rather than the Evangelical hymns of the previous century, which provided the distinctive ethos of Anglican hymn books. Charles Wesley's hymns certainly appeared – though they did not have the central place which they had in Methodist collections. But hymnody is rarely as precise about denominational boundaries as other aspects of church practice. The eighteenth-century dissenting tradition (of Isaac Watts and others) eventually found a place. The Church of England resisted the popular revivalist hymns of Moody and Sankey. These were much more likely to be incorporated into vernacular missionary collections. They were overwhelmingly translations from hymns belonging to the European or American tradition, with the significant exception of the Tamil Church of South India, where there was a long tradition of local composition. The extensive diffusion of sol-fa notation in the early twentieth century was intended to impose a musical orthodoxy. But hymn singing is rarely entirely amenable to precise direction of this nature.

Hymns began to take on a resonance, in word and music, which may well be very different from that originally intended. Take the example of 'Daily, daily sing the praises', introduced into Buganda in the late nineteenth century. A hymn from *The English Hymnal*, it was probably first sung at the coast in UMCA missions, but made a successful transition to Evangelical missions in Buganda, translated as 'Bulijjo tutendereza'. It achieved an enormous popularity as the hymn sung by the martyrs executed for their faith in 1885–6. It was sung with enormous poignancy and heartfelt yearning almost a hundred years later when Archbishop Janani Luwum was murdered in 1977. Movements of revival, and times of pressure and persecution, are also important for developing more indigenous creativity.

Apart from the Bible, the Book of Common Prayer and the Thirty-Nine Articles, a number of devotional works can be seen to represent a distinctively British Anglican heritage: the prayers and sermons of Lancelot Andrewes, Jeremy Taylor's *Holy Living* and *Holy Dying*, the poems of Herbert and Vaughan and William Law's *A Serious Call to a Devout and Holy Life*. These works would all be seen as nourishing a distinctively 'high' Anglican tradition. For Evangelical Anglicans, in addition to the hymns of William Cowper and John Newton, William Wilberforce's *Practical View* was an outstanding guide. For a long time Foxe's *Book of Martyrs* was normative for understanding England's Protestantism. None of these works, however, was exportable (apart from their use among British settlers).

The one book which did have universal resonance was not written by an Anglican at all, and that was John Bunyan's *The Pilgrim's Progress*. Written by a man imprisoned for his dissent from the Church of England, it was hardly the book which could be seen as enshrining Anglican values. But it became the most translated text of British Christianity. The story was adaptable and flexible. The early engravings which accompanied the book could be altered to show Pilgrim as an African dressed in traditional clothing, or a schoolboy in shorts. Translations were made by Scots Presbyterians and English Methodists, by Baptists and Congregationalists, but Anglicans were eager to produce Bunyan for their adherents too: David Hinderer produced a Yoruba version in 1866, Bishop Colenso, a Zulu version in 1868. There was a Luganda version in 1896 and a Luo version in the 1920s. Apart from Colenso's version, these had a CMS origin. But in 1888 the UMCA produced a Swahili Bunyan: Anglo-Catholics, too, saw the usefulness of Bunyan.[25]

THE SOUTH COMES NORTH: THE IMPACT OF AFRICA AND ASIA ON THE CHURCH OF ENGLAND

Until the end of the twentieth century, most British Anglicans saw their church as a national church of 'English' people, incorporating a Celtic minority tradition which could either be marginalised, as in the Anglicising trajectory of modernisation; or cultivated, as in the discovery of 'Celtic' forms of spirituality. The implications for the worldwide extension of the church have rarely been tackled directly within the Church of England. The Reformation had attacked foreign domination of the church (especially by clergy), but had also cultivated a Protestant internationalism which remained important into the nineteenth century and beyond. The first substantial religious refugees were French Huguenots. Although at first they tried to sustain their identity as part of an international Reformed community, gradually most were absorbed into the Anglican system. In Ireland they played a particularly important role, but they were also significant in America, particularly in colonial New York.

Although black people have been part and parcel of English society since the sixteenth century, their presence has only been considered significant for the nature and well being of the Church of England from the late twentieth century.[26] Equiano Olaudah, the great abolitionist of the eighteenth century, an Igbo from West Africa enslaved in the Caribbean, was perhaps historically the most famous of black Britons who contributed to the life of the Church of England. The black presence in

[25] Isabel Hofmeyr, *The Portable Bunyan* (Princeton: Princeton University Press, 2004).
[26] Peter Fryer, *Staying Power: The History of Black People in Britain* (London: Pluto Press, 1984).

London, a distinct and growing community from the late eighteenth century, was represented in baptisms, marriages and burials and, for some, regular attendance at the parish church. In the nineteenth century, the CMS's training institute at Islington provided education to a succession of Maori, Canadian First Nation, Indian and African students. This student tradition, now in higher education, was important in twentieth-century Britain. Many students were active Christians, but their contribution was often more to the political life of their home countries, and the growth of an anti-colonial movement within Britain, than a contribution which impacted directly on the life of the Church of England.

The very idea that the church could or should be transformed by its black presence remained alien to most thinking about the meaning of the church. After the Second World War, Caribbeans provided the first large settlement of people of non-European descent. Many of those who came to Britain from the Caribbean in the 1950s and 1960s had an Anglican background. The rejection and hostility from white church people was both shocking and unexpected. African Caribbeans responded by joining Pentecostal and Holiness groups, where it was easier to retain a sense of solidarity and active participation. But, remarkably in view of the disdain they received, there was also a 'staying power' of black people within the Anglican church. A seminal report of 1980 by the black priest David Moore, *Invisible People: Black People in the Church of England*,[27] was an important milestone. Black Anglicans began to organise, to demand visibility, to be treated seriously as a distinctive expression of what it means to be Anglican. The *Faith in the City* report of 1985 recommended a more concerted attention to promoting the black (including Asian) presence.[28] Wilfred Wood, born in Barbados (that most 'English' of Caribbean islands), was consecrated Bishop of Croydon (a suffragan of the Bishop of Southwark) in 1985. Glynne Gordon-Carter became Secretary to a newly formed Committee for Black Anglican Concerns in 1987. But there was often a misunderstanding of, or indifference to, the black presence. In 1989 a recommendation to ensure larger black representation in the General Synod of the Church was defeated. This was seen as a painful rejection by black Anglicans. In the frustration of defeat,

[27] John L. Wilkinson, *Church in Black and White* (Edinburgh: St Andrew's Press, 1993).

[28] In much of the discussion about ethic minorities in the church, Asian Anglicans have seen it as important to be identified as 'black', as a statement of the joint struggle of African, African Caribbean and Asian peoples for full inclusion.

Bishop Wood referred to some Synod members being trapped in 'their Christian slave owners thinking . . . they wanted black people to be happy, but under conditions they provided, and without requiring any adjustment to their comfortable state'.[29] The failure to ensure adequate representation of ethnic-minority communities in the structures of the church continues to be a hard-fought battle. The legislation of 1989 had envisaged a minimum of twenty-four black members. Even a decade later, the 2000 Synod could still only muster fifteen members, including Bishop Michael Nazir-Ali, the Bishop of Rochester, who had been born in Pakistan.[30]

By the 1990s a major new development in the black presence within the Church of England was taking place, the consequence of a new migration from Africa itself. Nigeria and Uganda both have large Anglican churches, and Anglicans were strongly represented among the Nigerians and Ugandans who settled in Britain. The sense of alienation was nothing like as severe as that of the 1950s. It was now rarer to find the overtly racist attitudes of the earlier generation. African Christians have become a significant constituency in a number of parishes, particularly in London. But Africans have, like the Huguenots before them, also felt the need to maintain their distinctive cultural identity, including its Anglican expression, in their new home, particularly to worship in congenial styles and in ways which support their life in diaspora. A full-time Anglican chaplain to the Nigerian community operates in London, offering a service both to permanent members of the British Nigerian community and to those here for shorter periods. Nigerians have managed to form networks which are inclusive of all Nigerians. This has been more problematic for Ugandans, especially as the reasons for migration to the UK are bound up with political tensions with regional and ethnic dimensions. Thriving Acholi- and Luganda-speaking groups, which value their Anglican heritage, meet regularly.

For such fellowships, Anglicanism is particularly important in safeguarding and fostering cultural and ethnic solidarity, to set over against the strong powers of Anglicisation operating in society at large and through the education system. Especially among the second generation of African settlers, a wider 'black' or African/African Caribbean identity is embraced. Pentecostal churches, utilising English (rather than vernacular

[29] Glynne Gordon-Carter, *An Amazing Journey: The Church of England's Response to Institutional Racism* (London: Church Publishing House, 2003).

[30] Ibid., Appendix 14.

languages) and emphasising global identities, are often more attractive than either the Church of England or the ethnic fellowships of their parents. At the beginning of the twenty-first century it has been estimated that more than half those who go to church on a Sunday in London are from immigrant groups. Even if most do not go to the Anglican church, there are enough black people who do to make it a very important constituency for the future of the Church of England. This makes the English church rather different from the established Protestant churches of the Netherlands, Germany or Scandinavia, where African migrants have, by and large, failed to find a home. The presence of African diaspora communities in Europe have given Anglican chaplaincy churches a new lease of life. Formerly the havens of diplomats, the retired and transient tourists, these churches now often minister to a significant group of people from outside Europe, whether students, professional people or working-class immigrants, who wish to worship in English.

The appointment of John Sentamu as Bishop of Stepney meant that, for the first time, an African became a bishop of the Church of England. His membership of the Macpherson Inquiry into institutional racism in the Metropolitan Police after the murder of Stephen Lawrence gave Sentamu a national profile. In 2003 he became Bishop of Birmingham, and in 2005 the Archbishop of York, 'Primate of England'. Two reports, *Seeds of Hope* and *The Passing Winter* (1991 and 1996), commissioned by the Committee on Black Anglican Concerns/the Committee for Minority Ethnic Anglican Concerns, trace and evaluate the changes in the black and Asian contribution to the life of the church.

> [S]lavery and colonisation ... have distorted the encounters between people of differing ethnic groups, and left a legacy where black people have for centuries experienced injustice, discrimination and exploitation in various forms at the hands of white people ... It would be surprising if this seepage from our national life did not find its way into the Church, and its cancerous potential for the whole life of the Church must not be underestimated. Racism is sin.[31]

The way in which the black and Asian voice is esteemed, and its presence incorporated in the life of the Church of England (and the other Anglican churches of the British Isles), remains one of the most important themes for the future of Christianity in a multi-racial, secular society.

[31] Committee on Black Anglican Concerns, *Seeds of Hope: Report of a Survey on Combating Racism in the Dioceses of the Church of England* (London: General Synod of the Church of England, 1991). The second report is: Committee for Minority Ethnic Anglican Concerns, *The Passing Winter: A Sequel to Seeds of Hope* (London: Church House Publishing, 1996).

Not least, it questions the inevitability of secularisation in Britain. But this may not be good news for the British churches. The nostalgic hope that, somehow, the church worldwide may come to the rescue of an otherwise dying Christian society in Britain is likely to be a dangerous and self-defeating delusion.

CHAPTER 3

The United States

The beginnings of English expansion overseas coincided with the consolidation of England as a Protestant nation in the reign of Elizabeth I. English patriotism became particularly associated with the struggle against Spain and the preservation of the Protestant faith. As for the Dutch, whose war of liberation against Spain England strongly supported, the guidance and preservation of the nation and its place in the world became bound up with being Protestant. Sailors often espoused a militant Protestantism (frequently with a sympathy for its more radical, Puritan tendencies). To fight the King of Spain on the high seas was a religious and patriotic duty. This struggle brought the English into contact with the New World. The initial encounter with the native peoples of America was to be one of mutual benefit. The seal of the Massachusetts Bay Company incorporated the figure of an American Indian appealing 'Come over and help us.' This appropriation of a biblical phrase was not only a Puritan conceit. It expressed the ideal of the Anglican settlers on the Chesapeake also.[1]

Despite the English hostility to the Spanish, Iberians did have an experience of Christian mission which could serve as a model for England: making treaties with native people, in which baptism symbolised a process of assimilation by which 'barbarians' adopted 'civilisation'. The cultural and religious forms of civilisation were not differentiated. For the English it meant an English Protestant civilisation. At Roanoke Island, Sir Walter Raleigh attempted the first English plantation in the 1580s. Manteo and Wanchese, 'chieftains' from Roanoke Island (off the coast of modern North Carolina), were kidnapped and transported to England. Queen Elizabeth is reported to have given her approval to an alliance: 'it seeming probably that God hath reserved these Gentiles to be introduced

[1] Nicholas Canny, *The Origins of Empire: British Overseas Enterprise to the Close of the Seventeenth Century* (Oxford: Oxford University Press, 1998), p. 52.

into Christian civility by the English nation'. Wanchese's experiences in England made him hostile to English civilisation and religion. But Manteo was more positive, and on his return to Roanoke Island he was baptised, on 13 August 1587. The Roanoke settlement did not last. There was no plan for sustained evangelisation of the native population. One serious problem for Protestants was that they lacked the religious orders, the chief means of effective missionary work among Catholics.

The same motives characterise the establishment of a permanent English settlement at Jamestown in the Chesapeake Bay. The instruction to the settlers was that 'the true word of God be preached, planted and used not only in the colonies, but also as much as might be, among the savages bordering upon them, and this according to the rites and doctrines of the Church of England'. The clergyman who accompanied the first 104 settlets spoke optimistically: 'they are a very witty and ingenious people, apt both to understand and speake our language. So that I hope God ... will make us authors of his holy will in converting them to our true Christian faith.' The first native convert in Jamestown was the legendary Pocahontas, the daughter of the chief of the area, Powhatan. Pocahontas had interceded for the life of Captain William Smith early on in the encounter with the settlers. A few years later she was held hostage on a ship in the James River. John Rolfe, a widower who was to initiate the tobacco trade on which Virginia's economy was to be based, expressed his desire to marry her: 'for the good of the plantation, the honour of our country, for the glory of God, for mine own salvation and for the converting to the true knowledge of God and Jesus Christ'.[2] She was baptised Rebecca, and married Rolfe on Maundy Thursday, 1 April 1613. Later she visited England, where she died of smallpox. As a contemporary put it with mordant wit: she 'came to Gravesend, to her end and grave'.[3]

Pocohontas' father remained sceptical. By the 1620s there was conflict over land. The idea of an alliance with the settlers seemed increasingly to offer only danger to the Indian communities of the coast, as settler insatiability with regard to land became ever more pressing. From the settler side too ideas of converting natives, as part of a national mission, gave way to hostility and a struggle for survival in which notions of civility had little place.

[2] Ibid., p. 159.

[3] Owanah Anderson, *400 Years: Anglican/Episcopal Mission among American Indians* (Cincinnati: Forward Movement, 1997), p. 7.

THE CHURCH OF ENGLAND IN THE COLONIES OF AMERICA

Virginia and the South

The Church of England became established in Virginia, which in 1622 became a crown colony – that is, it had a governor appointed by the king. (The alternative was a proprietary colony, in which a company or individual had a charter.) But there were many difficulties in transplanting the Church of England structures to America. Clergy were always in short supply. The real power lay with the vestry, appointed from the local community. They had civil as well as ecclesiastical responsibilities, and were in effect the arm of government in the localities. In Virginia the vestry in effect became a self-perpetuating institution in which existing members appointed new members: an oligarchy of the most powerful families. Vestries had the right to choose and appoint their minister. They often maintained a very strict control over him by employing him on a yearly contract. All members of the colony were required to pay a tax for the maintenance of the church. Ministers themselves were paid in tobacco. The church was an arm of civil society, providing for the rites of passage, its moral compass. But, as resentment against Britain mounted in the eighteenth century, so the church came to be seen increasingly as part of the repressive structures of the colony.

In other parts of the South, Virginia provided a template. The Church of England became established in Maryland in the 1690s, though here the governor retained powers to appoint clergy. In South Carolina the established church grew in vigour; it was much weaker in the less developed North Carolina and Georgia. In the 1660s the young John Locke worked out a constitution for a colony of Carolina. The parliament would

> take care for the building of Churches and the publick Maintenance of Divines, to be employed in the exercise of Religion, according to the Church of England, which being the onely true and Orthodox, and the National Religion of all the King's Dominions, is so also of Carolina.

Nevertheless, other churches were to be tolerated, 'that the Civil Peace may be maintained amidst the diversity of Opinions'.[4]

New England

In contrast to Virginia, Anglicans in New England were not only a minority, but hardly tolerated at all. The pioneers of Massachusetts

[4] J. C. D. Clark, *English Society 1660–1832* (Cambridge: Cambridge University Press, 2000), p. 128.

included clergy of the established church in England, but they had left England precisely because they were committed to establishing a Reformed church according to Puritan ideals. A congregational church structure emerged – not unlike that in Virginia in the extent of interpenetration of the civil and the ecclesiastical, but one in which episcopal ordination was not required of its ministers, in whose churches the liturgy of the prayer book was not said and where the idea of a 'godly commonwealth' – the 'city on a hill' – was much more strenuously envisaged and systematically implemented. And yet, as commercial life flourished and diversified, merchants with Anglican sympathies did emerge, critical of the Congregational elite.

In 1686 the new king, James II, a Roman Catholic, imposed crown colony status on Massachusetts. The new governor demanded that one of the Congregational churches in Boston be appropriated for the rites and usages of the Church of England. The South Meeting House was requisitioned and became known as the King's Chapel (i.e. representing the official religion of the crown, despite James' personal Catholicism). The action was bitterly resented. There was therefore much relief when James was overthrown in 1688. The Puritans had been no more in favour of religious toleration than the Anglicans, but, under a new charter which restored many of their liberties, they were now prepared to allow a limited toleration to the Church of England. The King's Chapel chose one of their number, Samuel Myles, to go to England, where he was ordained. Anglicanism in New England was strengthened in the eighteenth century by conversions from the Congregational establishment of the upwardly mobile sons of the old Congregational elite.

The middle colonies

Between Anglican Virginia and Puritan New England were a number of colonies where no religion dominated and where a wide toleration prevailed. Pennsylvania had been founded as a place of toleration by William Penn, the Quaker. However, the Penn family in the eighteenth century had conformed to the Church of England. Anglicans became identified with the ruling elite in Pennsylvania. New Amsterdam was captured from the Dutch in 1664. The Church of England became the established church in the four coastal counties of the state in 1693. But in practice the government had to recognise the existence of a wide variety of churches, including the Dutch Reformed Church. Some of the European immigrants into New York from state churches (Dutch Reformed, Swedish and German Lutherans), as well as Huguenot refugees, conformed to the Church of England. Anglicanism in New York was probably the most prosperous and vigorous in pre-Revolutionary times of all the Anglican communities in America. One reason for this was the wealth of Trinity Church in Lower Manhattan. It was founded as the parish church of New York in 1697; in 1702 Queen Anne granted a tract of land on the west side of Manhattan – an area which included what would become the Wall Street financial centre. Trinity Church endowed King's College (chartered in 1654) as New York's answer to Harvard, Yale and Princeton: what was to become Columbia University. In 1704 Elias Neau, a Huguenot refugee funded by the SPG and working with the rector of Trinity Church, established work among the African American community, against the opposition of the slave owners.[5]

CONCERN FOR THE SPIRITUAL LIFE OF THE COLONIAL CHURCH

In the 1690s Thomas Bray was appointed by the Bishop of London as his 'Commissary', charged with exploring ways of developing a more ordered Anglican church life in the American colonies. His brief experience in America led to the creation of the Society for the Propagation of the Gospel (SPG), whose aim was to promote 'a religious, sober and Polite people'.[6] The Revd Samuel Thomas, the first SPG missionary in South Carolina, reported that the settlers were 'in such a wilderness and so destitute of spiritual guides and all the means of grace' that they 'were making near approach to that heathenism which is to be found among negroes and Indians'. The Wesleys, SPG missionaries in Georgia in the 1730s, were equally concerned to inculcate disciplined religion in their rude and unruly congregations. The immorality of settlers was often compared unfavourably with that of 'savage' Indians and black slaves.

The preoccupation with civility and polite manners was seriously to inhibit the appeal of the Episcopal Church during the colonial years. Anglicans remained very suspicious of the outburst of religious fervour which characterised the Great Awakening in the 1740s. The great revivalist preacher George Whitefield made a considerable impact among Congregationalists

[5] Gerald J. Barry, *Trinity Church: 300 Years of Philanthropy* (New York: The Hundred Year Association, 1997), pp. 10–20.

[6] Daniel O'Connor, *Three Centuries of Mission: The United Society for the Propagation of the Gospel 1701–2000* (London: Continuum, 2000), p. 39, quoting the first historian of the society, David Humphreys (1730).

and Presbyterians. But his unguarded criticisms of the Church of England in America, as well as the decidedly impolite and uncivil emotions which he raised in his hearers, alienated him from members of his own communion. More seriously, in the early years of the new republic, the church was to appear out of touch with the increasingly populist, democratic tenor of the American Republic, representing a more patrician style and ethos.[7]

One of the particular concerns of the SPG was the fact that the colonial church seemed unable to understand its obligations to the 'heathen' whose miserable state it seemed to approach or surpass. One of the chief objects of the SPG was to preach the Gospel to native Americans. Usually it proved impossible to combine commitment to missionary work with care for the settler community. But one area of some potential was work among the Iroquois people (the five nations, of whom the Mohawk were one), who lived on the borders between the British colonies and the French dominions to the north. A delegation of Iroquois *sachems* (leaders) visited London in 1713. They put forward their need for assistance and desire for friendly relations with Britain (and their suspicions of France). Queen Anne received them and presented them with silver communion vessels, which became hallowed treasures of the nation.[8]

Mission among African slaves was also undertaken by the SPG. Two black Americans, known only in the surviving literature as Henry (or Harry) and Andrew, were employed in the Carolinas as evangelists and teachers of their fellow African slaves. The SPG ignored a state law of 1749 that slaves should not be taught to write.[9] Like the Mohawk, a significant number of African American people supported the British cause in the revolutionary war. Their subsequent migration to the Bahamas and to West Africa was to be significant in the extension of Christianity, and the Anglican church, to those parts.

A CHURCH WITHOUT BISHOPS

One of the marks which separated the Church of England from other religious groups in America was its insistence that a church needed to

[7] John Wigger, *Taking Heaven by Storm: Methodism and the Rise of Popular Christianity in America* (Oxford: Oxford University Press, 1998), p. 11.

[8] Owanah Anderson, 'Anglican Mission among the Mohawk', in O'Connor, *Three Centuries*, pp. 235–48.

[9] See Albert J. Raboteau, *Slave Religion: The 'Invisible Institution' in the Antebellum South* (New York: Oxford University Press, 1978); Sylvia R. Frey and Betty Wood, *Come Shouting to Zion: African American Protestantism in the American South and British Caribbean to 1830* (Chapel Hill and London: University of North Carolina Press, 1998).

have bishops and that clergy should be episcopally ordained. In practice the church existed for nearly 200 years without bishops. There were numerous attempts in the eighteenth century to remedy this anomaly. But all of them foundered. A number of English bishops were enthusiastic, but governments were lukewarm, if not actively hostile to the idea. In the early years, such appeals were often seen as having a covert political motivation devised by Tories, Non-Jurors and Jacobites. Later in the century, relations with the colonists were sufficiently delicate for a desire not to add a further grievance. In the colonies there was a general suspicion. Puritans equated bishops with the Laudian prelacy from which they had escaped. Americans generally saw bishops as another form of oppressive royal interference. Even Anglicans (especially in Virginia) feared that the right of vestries to appoint and control their minister would be compromised.

The only significant group who wanted a bishop were New England clergy converts from Congregationalism. The promoters of an American bishop in the 1760s (led by Samuel Johnson of Connecticut and Thomas B. Chandler of New Jersey) talked of a bishop shorn of any prelatical powers – simply one who would ordain and confirm and provide a pastoral discipline for the clergy. But when most Americans thought of bishops they thought of palaces, and grandeur and despotic royal power. A bishop, however simple and apostolic at first, would not remain so for long. 'It would be as unsafe for an American Bishop . . . to come hither, as it is at present for a distributor of Stamps.'[10]

THE CHURCH AND THE WAR OF INDEPENDENCE

Two-thirds of the fifty-five signatories of the 1776 Declaration of Independence were Anglicans, including General George Washington (the first President) and James Madison (the third). Nevertheless, the War of Independence made life difficult for the Church of England in America. Nearly half of the clergy, mindful of their oath of loyalty to the crown, fled or chose to leave the country. There was an exodus of other Anglican loyalists. Boston lost some of its wealthy 'Tory' merchants. The new republic's decision for a separation of church and state affected the Church of England more than any other – it had been established in nine of the thirteen states. In Virginia, where the relationship between church

[10] Charles Martyn to the Bishop of London, 20 October 1765, quoted in Frederick V. Mills Sr, *Bishops by Ballot* (New York: Oxford University Press, 1978), p. 110. The reference to 'a distributor of Stamps' is to the hated Stamp Act.

and state had been particularly close, churches were closed or did not have ministers for many years after the revolution. Was the church identified so closely with the old regime that it would not survive the revolution?

These were the questions which loyal churchmen had to face during the war and in its aftermath. In 1782 William White, the rector of two Philadelphia churches, produced a pamphlet which became the basis for a reconstitution of the Church in America: *The Case of the Protestant Episcopal Churches in the United States Considered.* A patriot (i.e. a supporter of the independence struggle), White proposed to reform the church in line with the new republic, giving it a constitutional framework, with both lay and clerical representation in the governance of the church. Episcopacy should have a part in this system, he argued, but if (as seemed likely) it was difficult to obtain bishops, then 'a temporary departure from episcopacy' might be warranted: Hooker's *Ecclesiastical Polity* and the writings of other churchmen of the Reformation period were cited in support of this.

Eventually many of these proposals were to become embodied in the constitution of the church. But there was immediate alarm from the New England Anglican tradition, particularly the clergy of Connecticut, whose high-church principles were fundamentally challenged by these proposals. They tended, also, to be loyalists, and were coming to terms with the new republic with difficulty. In 1783 a small group of Connecticut clergy gathered and chose one of their number, Samuel Seabury (the son of a convert to Anglicanism), to journey to England to seek consecration as bishop. Seabury spent eighteen frustrating months in England. The Archbishop of Canterbury judged that he was not able to ordain a bishop who would not swear an oath to the king; that legislation would be needed to dispense with this oath; and that Parliament was unlikely to grant such a request. Seabury finally decided to go to Scotland, and there the Primus Robert Kilgour, Bishop of Aberdeen, Arthur Petrie, Bishop of Ross and Moray, and John Skinner, Kilgour's coadjutor, ordained Seabury to the episcopate on 14 November 1784.

In retrospect the event is regarded as a key event in the life of the church in America. But, in the short term, it threatened to produce a schism. White dismissed the Scottish orders as invalid (taking his cue from English suspicion of a Non-Juring church whose orders were not recognised). One American historian has referred to the Scottish bishops as a 'poignant band of Anglican outcasts'.[11] The lack of lay representation

11 Allen C. Guelzo, *For the Union of Evangelical Christendom: The Irony of the Reformed Episcopalians* (Pennsylvania: Pennsylvania State University Press, 1994), p. 28.

envisaged in the New England constitutional plans was also a major stumbling block for White and patriots generally. In 1786 the church conventions of New York, Philadelphia and Virginia (constituted with full lay representation) elected three bishops. The Archbishop of Canterbury now felt able to consecrate them (he was aided by the decision of the Scottish bishops to take the oath of loyalty to the crown). William White of Pennsylvania and Samuel Provoost of New York sailed for England and were consecrated on 4 February 1787 in Lambeth Palace. Eventually the differences between the two American groups were patched up sufficiently to allow all three Americans bishops to participate in the consecration of new bishops for other American states.[12] The creation of an episcopacy which was not connected with the state was to be of great significance for the development of the Anglican communion as a whole.

THE PROTESTANT EPISCOPAL CHURCH

If the Episcopal Church made a surprisingly successful transition from colonial dependency to the era of the new republic, its growth in the new era was nevertheless hampered by a number of limitations. It was not anything like as successful as the Baptists and Methodists in adapting to the era of democratic populism symbolised by Andrew Jackson's presidency in 1830s. Methodism had began to expand dramatically in the revolutionary period. In 1784 Francis Asbury became the first bishop of what became the Methodist Episcopal Church (even before the Episcopal Church had obtained its first bishop).[13] During the next few decades the Methodist movement, with its emphasis on an emotional rather than a rational religion and its use of lay preachers with little formal education, was the fastest-growing denomination in the United States, catching the spirit of the frontier.

Episcopalians had no wish to emulate this. They remained committed to a college-trained clergy, and recruited from a social class markedly different from that from which itinerant preachers were drawn. Samuel Hobart (1775–1830), Bishop of New York from 1811, developed a theology, in the old high-church tradition, which located the Episcopal Church as a divine society, standing out against the secular society embodied in the new republic. Episcopalianism was presented as an attractive alternative both to the Calvinist-derived spirit of the republic and to the newer democratic revivalism. Hobart's motto was 'Evangelical

[12] Mills, *Bishops by Ballot*, Chapters 8–12. [13] Wigger, *Taking Heaven by Storm*, p. 23.

truth and apostolic order'. The church aimed to be an 'ark of refuge' amidst the increasing clamour of conflicting politics, especially in the acrimonious dispute over slavery which increasingly divided America. There continued to be conversions of college-educated, professional and business men. Episcopalianism seemed to offer a superior product attractive to the discerning consumer in the religious emporium. But this was at odds with the claim to speak as the 'conscience of the nation', as the Hobartian tradition envisaged. For much of the nineteenth century it fulfilled this role with a somewhat Olympian detachment.

Episcopalians tended to abstain from the moral crusades which Evangelicals engaged in: the sabbatarianism or abstinence movements, or, more seriously, the campaigns against slavery. This preserved the unity of the church when other denominations were splitting, but it did appear to some to be built on a 'cosmic Toryism', a somewhat anachronistic conception of society.[14] Episcopalians prided themselves on their ability to avoid the social and ethical disputes which split many Protestant churches. On the other hand, there was plenty of acrimony within the church over internal ecclesiastical issues, particularly between Evangelicals and the new Tractarian high-church movement.

If the Episcopal Church was losing its position to other churches on the East Coast, it was having an even more difficult time in the West. A mission strategy which depended so heavily on clerical initiatives needed a more centralised strategy if it was to make an impact on the frontier. In 1835 the General Convention of the Episcopal Church decided to create missionary districts, and to appoint missionary bishops to energise the task. Tacitly the Convention divided mission work into two: missions within the USA, which became the province of the high-church constituency, and foreign missions, which Evangelicals engaged in. Their first choice of missionary bishop was Jackson Kemper from New York, who was appointed to supervise the extension of the church in the Midwest. Kemper's energetic pioneering work had many heroic qualities about it. The patterns of church planting which he established ensured that the church did develop a presence on the frontier, and Episcopalians were represented in every state – not surprisingly often attracting the more prosperous sections of the new society, who looked for a moderate, respectable form of religion. Kemper and his successor bishops were, however, strongly constrained by the chronic lack of clergy. For a church

[14] Robert Bruce Mullin, *Episcopal Vision/American Reality: High Church Theology and Social Thought in Evangelical America* (New Haven: Yale University Press, 1986), p. 80.

which relied so heavily on a priestly ministry, the actual reluctance of clergy to give up lucrative parishes in the East (reminiscent of the English problems of missionary recruitment in the nineteenth century) was a major constraint.

One missionary area for which Bishop Hobart in particular is remembered is his support for mission among Indian groups. He encouraged work among the Oneida and followed Indians as they began to be displaced westwards, into Dakota. At his consecration, Kemper said that 'the needs of the red men are a weight upon my soul'. In 1841 Nashotah House was established in Wisconsin as a semi-monastic college with a concern for mission among Native American people. Bishop Benjamin Whipple (1822–1901), with responsibility for Indian people in Minnesota, ordained Enmagahbowh (an Ottawa Indian) and Paul Mazakuta (a Dakota Sioux) as priests in 1867 and 1869, and in 1881 David Pendleton Oakerhater (Cheyenne) as deacon. The period after the civil war was a time in which Indian peoples were particularly hard pressed by the relentless pursuit of land, the decline of their herds, and increasing government control. The church played a dual role. It sometimes appeared to be little more than a government agency (handling government grants) in a policy which resulted in a devaluing of Indian culture and encouraged assimilation on unequal terms to white American values. On the other hand, the church stood as an advocate of humane treatment and worked for the preservation of some cultural cohesion among Native American peoples. In Dakota the Episcopal Church established a non-geographical jurisdiction of Niobrara for Indian work, and a special committee on Indian affairs. These policies could mitigate some of the injustice done to Native American people in specific cases, but did not change the overall situation.

BLACK EPISCOPALIANS

'If a black man is anything but a Baptist or a Methodist, someone has been tampering with his religion.'[15] This quip, attributed to Booker T. Washington, expresses the common feeling that all the traditions of the Episcopal Church militated against its being a home for Americans of colour. In the eighteenth century, whites tended to be indifferent or opposed to black education. Religion was deemed to militate against obedience and control. In the ante-bellum South, slave owners encouraged their blacks to

[15] Harold T. Lewis, *Yet with a Steady Beat: The African American Struggle for Recognition in the Episcopal Church* (Valley Forge: Trinity Press, 1996), p. 1.

become part of the church community – now seen as encouraging obedience and subservience, the values of a patriarchal society. Blacks were allowed to participate, but consigned to the gallery in the church. Many African Americans naturally saw more scope for self-improvement and assertion and esteem in black-led churches. The civil war saw an even greater desertion of the racially stratified Episcopalian churches of the South.

In the North, Episcopalianism did offer scope for black initiative and pride. St George's Methodist Church in Philadelphia contained white and black members, but after a gallery was completed in the church, the blacks were told to remove themselves from the body of the church and occupy the gallery. Absalom Jones (1746–1818), Richard Allan and the black parishioners walked out in a body. Richard Allan was to go on to establish the African Methodist Episcopal Church, a new denomination in which he became bishop. Jones established the St Thomas' African Episcopal Church in Philadelphia, and sought affiliation with the Episcopal Church. He was ordained by Bishop White as deacon in 1795 and priest in 1804, the first black man to be ordained not only in the Episcopal Church but in any of the mainline denominations of America. St Thomas' became one of the most important congregations of the Episcopal Church in Philadelphia. Similar congregations were established in other northern cities – for example St Philip's in New York. In the period before the civil war, some twenty-five black priests were ordained, mainly working among free black congregations.

Although black people established a footing within the church, with their own congregations, they were hardly welcome to mix freely with white people or to be accorded equality. For long, black congregations were excluded from attendance at diocesan conventions. One of the outstanding African American Episcopalians of the nineteenth century was Alexander Crummell (1819–98). Refused entry to General Theological Seminary in New York on the grounds of his colour, he was eventually ordained as deacon in 1842 (and priest in 1844). He became rector of the Church of the Messiah in New York City and provoked a crisis by challenging the exclusion of black clergy from the diocesan convention. The convention justified continuing such a policy on these grounds:

> We object not to the color of skin, but we question their possession of those qualities which would render their intercourse with the members of a Church Convention useful, or agreeable, even to themselves ... It is impossible, in the nature of things, that such opposites should commingle with any pleasure to either.[16]

[16] Ibid., p. 32.

Since blacks themselves had recognised this by forming separate congregations, the convention delegates argued, speciously, that there seemed no reason for them not to be separate in other areas of church life.[17] Crummell subsequently graduated from Cambridge University in England, and became an outspoken campaigner for the abolition of slavery and the development of people of colour in America, a missionary educator in Liberia and a rector in Washington. An intellectual, he produced work on African identity which influenced W. E. B. Du Bois and a whole tradition of pan-African thinking in West Africa.[18]

In the South, the outbreak of civil war led to an exodus of black people from the Episcopal Church. In the aftermath of defeat, Episcopalians, in parallel with many other northern agencies, poured resources briefly into schemes for the uplift of freed slaves. Educational institutions were founded, such as St Augustine's Normal School (a teacher-training institution) and College at Raleigh, North Carolina. But after the period of reconstruction, segregation in the South meant that black congregations for nearly a century were denied full participation in the life of the church.

In 1883 there was a proposal at the National Convention at Sewanee to establish separate non-geographical dioceses for coloured people. This was defeated by opposition from the North, in particular from black clergy, who feared the institutionalisation within the church of segregation and Jim Crow laws. In 1918 two black suffragan bishops were elected in the South – Edward Demby in Tennessee and Henry Beard Delany in North Carolina. But the move was unpopular – they were dubbed the 'deaf and dumb' bishops and 'Uncle Toms' by black clergy. Southern society remained adamantly opposed to blacks ever being put in positions where they might have authority over white people. According to Montgomery Brown, Bishop of Arkansas, this was a 'God-implanted race prejudice' which should never be tampered with.[19]

EPISCOPAL WOMEN

In work on behalf of both Indians and black people after the civil war, women paid a particularly notable part. They had long constituted the majority of committed members of the church, and had always played a significant role within the home in catechising (children and, in the

[17] Wilson J. Moses, *Alexander Crummell: A Study of Civilization and Discontent* (New York: Oxford University Press, 1989), p. 44.

[18] Paul Gilroy, *The Black Atlantic: Modernity and Double Consciousness* (London: Verso, 1993).

[19] Lewis, *Yet with a Steady Beat*, p. 75.

South, servants and slaves). In the latter half of the nineteenth century they began to play more important public roles. More or less totally excluded from official positions in the liturgy and preaching, they sought outlets in social service. Tractarian interest in establishing women's religious orders was at first (as in England) met with fears and suspicions. Anne Ayres was the first woman to be professed. Her Sisterhood of the Holy Communion (1852) concentrated on ministry to the sick at St Luke's hospital in the parish of the great New York rector William Muhlenberg. The Sisterhood of St John the Baptist, with its house in Brooklyn, worked in the Lower East Side of New York among German immigrants. The deaconess order was given canonical recognition by the Episcopal Church in 1889, 'to assist the minister in the care of the poor and sick, the religious training of the young and others, and the work of moral reformation'.[20] University-educated women were becoming interested in working in 'settlements' in areas of urban deprivation and in establishing women's hostels. By the twentieth century, deaconesses and other parish workers were providing vital professional work in the life of church. Women were more likely to be volunteers. Where they were paid, their salaries were lower than men's. By 1916, 39 per cent of missionaries of the church were single women or widows – not to mention the unacknowledged work which married women did in this field.[21]

Women were also particularly important in financing and organising help for missions, both inner and foreign. In 1871 a Women's Auxiliary to the Foreign Mission was established. In 1889 the United Thank Offering of the Women's Auxiliary was created. It became a major contributor to the funding of mission projects, quite apart from the ordinary giving of the churches, much of it by women. The Women's Auxiliary was the most important way in which women had a voice in the central administrative boards of the Episcopal Church until well into the twentieth century. But it had its definite limitation – it was, after all, only an 'auxiliary', and they were still excluded from discussions of policy and the exercise of power. In 1919 there was an unsuccessful attempt to have women elected to the General Convention of the church – this had to wait till 1970.[22] The Depression had eliminated many from the pay rolls of the church; these picked up again after the war, but pay and conditions for women in the specialised roles in the church continued to be inferior.

20 David Holmes, *A Brief History of the Episcopal Church* (Harrisburg: Trinity Press, 1993), p. 133.

21 Mary Donovan, *A Different Call: Women's Ministries in the Episcopal Church 1850–1920* (Wilton: Morehouse-Barlow, 1986), p. 119.

22 Ibid., pp. 164–5.

FOREIGN MISSION

For much of the nineteenth century, Episcopal mission had been concentrated on Liberia, the African state established by American abolitionists as a home for freed slaves. The morality of repatriation was always fiercely contested, particularly by black free men and women suspicious of white intentions. Sometimes emigration to the Caribbean was seen as an alternative to Africa. A black Episcopalian priest, James Holly, established Episcopal work in Haiti, which, since the revolt against the French led by Toussaint L'Ouverture in the early years of the century, had seemed a beacon of freedom and independence to many black Americans. As Americans began to exert more influence in the world, Episcopalians, in common with other Protestants, began to look for areas of the world where they might exert a Christian influence: Americans had always had a special interest in Latin America, but because of the general diffusion of Catholic Christianity, Episcopalians were reluctant to be involved in proselytism, and for a long time confined their activities to supplying pastoral support to expatriates. The opening up of Japan and the growing economic interest in China meant that this part of the Pacific basin became a focus for Episcopal activity. And then, at the very end of the century, a new interest in direct power arose in the aftermath of the war against Spain of 1896, and the sense of 'Manifest Destiny': Puerto Rico, the Philippines, Panama, Hawaii all became (or were given renewed attention as) fields of mission for the Episcopal Church.

SOCIAL ACTION

Apart from the popular chauvinism which the events of the 1890s generated in Americans, and from which the Episcopalians were no more immune than other Protestant bodies, much of the justification for Episcopal involvement in mission was put in the context of the church's role in the nation: what Ian Douglas has identified as the 'national church ideal'.[23] Leading churchmen such as William Muhlenberg and William Reed Huntington (both of New York) elaborated a sense of the Episcopal Church, with its unique blend of Catholic and Protestant elements, having a mission to the nation as a whole, in terms of providing both a possible ecumenical consensus and a moral vision for society. This was to be a much less elitist vision than that of the Hobart tradition, but one of

[23] Ian T. Douglas, *Fling out the Banner! The National Church Ideal and the Foreign Mission of the Episcopal Church* (New York: Church Hymnal Corporation, 1996), Chapter 2, pp. 73–137.

involvement which incorporated the essence of Anglican establishment and an engagement with social problems sustained by a vision of an ethical society. Intellectually, F. D. Maurice provided an important model. Father James Huntington was inspired by the Sisters of St John the Baptist to found a male community, the Order of the Holy Cross, to live and work in the Lower East Side. He conceived this society as embodying, not a 'British-aristocratic ethos', but an 'American-democratic' one. He also founded the Church Association for the Advancement of the Interests of Labor. The Episcopal Church thus made its own distinctive contribution to the Social Gospel movement, linked to a strong incarnational theology.

Vida Scudder (1861–1954) presents a particularly interesting example of an Episcopal woman deeply involved in understanding, practically as well as intellectually, the nature of church presence in society. She was born into a prominent New England Congregational family. Her father was a missionary of the American Board of Missions in South India. In the twentieth century, a relative, Dr Ida Scudder, became famous as a Congregational missionary and the founder of Vellore Hospital of the Church of South India (in which former Congregationalists and Anglicans participate). Vida Scudder spent her life as a college teacher at Wellesley, both a committed socialist and an Episcopalian, involved in the College Settlements Associations, and in contact with labour leaders. For many years she was a key member of the Society of the Companions of the Holy Cross. She wrote works on spirituality – on Catherine of Sienna and Francis of Assisi – as well as being 'an apologist for international socialism of a Marxist kind' before events in Russia after 1921 made such enthusiasm difficult to sustain.[24] In the 1930s she was a supporter of Roosevelt's New Deal, which attracted substantial interest from Episcopalians. The first American woman Cabinet minister, in the Roosevelt administration, was an Episcopalian, Frances Perkins, Secretary of Labor. Scudder herself is an important voice in the intellectual engagement of an incarnational theology and in feminist thinking.

CIVIL RIGHTS

In the South, the Episcopal Church was anything but prophetic. The segregation which became part and parcel of the postbellum South – 'Jim

[24] Bernard Kent Markwell, *The Anglican Left: Radical Social Reformers in the Church of England and the Protestant Episcopal Church 1846–1954* (Brooklyn: Carlson, 1991), p. 191. See further Chapter 6, 'Vida Dutton Scudder: A Socialist Churchwoman'.

Crow' – was reflected in Episcopal church life. South Carolina was the last diocese to remove racial barriers on black parishes sending delegates to the diocesan convention – in 1954.[25] As late as the 1950s, the institutions of the church remained largely separate, but hardly equal. In Sewanee seminar in Tennessee the Confederate flag hung in the chapel, and the faculty resisted the admission of black students until forced to integrate in the early 1950s. Many white Episcopalians in the South had little sympathy for the desegregation of schools order by the Supreme Court in the landmark decision in *Brown* v. *Board of Education* (1954). African American Episcopalians campaigned against holding the 1955 General Convention in Houston, Texas, since segregation was still rampant in the state. In 1958, at a time when Episcopal congregations generally were growing, Tollie Caution (a black priest who headed the Episcopal Church's Division of Racial Minorities) noted that black communicants had declined by 10,000 over a ten-year period.[26]

A small number of white Episcopalians became prominent in the civil rights campaigns. Sarah and Carl Braden of Louisville, Kentucky, were activists from 1954 and suffered threats and a bomb attack on their home.[27] Some priests began to talk of the 'suburban captivity of the church' (a phrase coined by Gibson Winter) and 'the captive Christianity of Gothic arches and Tudor prose' (Bishop Stephen Bayne). Jonathan Daniels, a seminarian from New Hampshire, was killed by a white gunman while taking part in a voter registration campaign in the South.[28]

In 1964 the church elected John Hines, previously bishop coadjutor of Texas, as Presiding Bishop. During his tenure of office he aligned the Episcopal Church strongly on behalf of radical and progressive social issues.

NATIVE AMERICANS

The civil rights era focused on the issue of black participation in the life of the church. The issue of Native Americans in the life of the Episcopal Church did not have a similar profile. Around the beginning of the century in Oklahoma, David Pendleton Oakerhater, a Cheyenne, served as a deacon for thirty-six years (he retired in 1916 and died in 1931). Although he was never counted ready to be ordained priest, his work

[25] Lewis, *Yet with a Steady Beat*, p. 142. Gardiner H. Shattuck Jr, *Episcopalians and Race: Civil War to Civil Rights* (Lexington: Kentucky University Press, 2000), p. 55.

[26] Shattuck, *Episcopalians and Race*, p. 96. [27] Ibid., p. 73. [28] Ibid., pp. 156–8, 217.

more than any other secured a substantial Indian presence in the Episcopal Church – which according to one estimate comprises 15 per cent of the Episcopal membership in the Oklahoma diocese.[29] In 1984 Bishop McAllister of Oklahoma restored land previously ceded to the diocese to its proper owners, the Indian community.

The Navajo of the South-West constitute the largest single ethnic group of Native Americans, stretching over a number of dioceses. In 1976 the church voted to establish a Navajo episcopal district in the area which could allow an autonomous Navajo Episcopalian cultural identity to flourish. Alaska has also developed a distinctive Native American style of Episcopalianism. Between 1992 and 1996 its bishop was an Oklahoma-born Chocktaw Indian. The Niobrara Convocation of Nebraska, 'the single most distinctive institution of American Indian Episcopalians', was first held in 1870 and has continued to provide an important meeting point, significant for the development of a sense of pan-Indian co-operation. Two-thirds of Native Americans now live in urban areas. 'Once in the strange city the Indians quickly discovered that "The Episcopal Church Welcomes You" sign did not consistently apply' – instead 'a heartless bigotry' pervaded.[30] In a reception which paralleled that accorded to Absalom Jones two centuries earlier, Indians in Minneapolis were told to stand at the wall of the church. They established St Matthew's as a Lakota-speaking congregation in Rapid City, South Dakota. Minneapolis has become a major centre, a pan-Indian city with the Maxzakuta Memorial Church established in 1976 as a multi-ethnic congregation serving Ojibwa, Sioux and Winnebago as well as blacks, whites and Hispanics. Milwaukee, north of Chicago, is an important centre for Oneida Indians, and 10 per cent of Milwaukee's Indians are Episcopalian.[31] In 1954 the Episcopal Church set up an Indian Office to co-ordinate and promote its Indian work. This was directed from 1984 by a Choctaw Indian woman, Owanah Anderson.

THE CHURCH IN THE LATE TWENTIETH CENTURY AND BEYOND

The modern Episcopal Church has become very different from the rather Olympian church of the post-revolutionary birth of the nation. This radicalism has been resented by more conservative sections of the church (both politically and theologically). But there has also been a problem of

[29] Anderson, *400 Years*, p. 164. [30] Ibid., p. 283. [31] Ibid., pp. 283–9.

competing radicalisms. The women's movement has often linked its struggle with the civil rights issues. Unwilling to wait for the church to come to a decision, in 1974, eleven women were ordained priest in the black Church of the Advocate in Philadelphia.[32] By their action the advocates of women's priesthood aligned their struggle with that of black civil rights. A black laywoman, Barbara Harris, acted as crucifer. She was later to become the first woman bishop in the Episcopal Church. But behind this solidarity, real as it was, there were tensions, and differing priorities. White feminists were disturbed by the Black Power movement, with its aggressive masculinity. Black people detected a pervasive racism in much of the rhetoric of the white feminist movement.[33]

The liberal profile of the Episcopal Church has been attractive to individual Christians in other denominations – for example, a number of Catholic women have joined the Episcopal Church because of its attitude to women's priestly ministry. But such an influx of individuals is not likely to reverse the long-term decline in membership, which conservatives blame on the unprecedented level of change within the church. In 1979 a new Book of Common Prayer, to replace the older book, was authorised, after years of debate and revision. This and the controversies over women's ordination have produced a number of schisms. The only substantial schism of the nineteenth century had been that of the Reformed Episcopal Church of 1873. This had been an Evangelical protest against Catholic practices and 'ritualism'. By the 1990s the major contentious issue was the question of homosexuality. Gradually (and far too slowly for an important minority within the church) attitudes to homosexuality have mellowed. But at the same time an outspoken opposition has become more vociferous. There has been an alliance of conservative Evangelicals and Catholics. The debate on homosexuality at the Lambeth Conference of 1998 proved decisive in the polarisation of attitudes. Episcopalian traditionalists realised that they could tap into a level of support in the worldwide communion which they had not previously considered. Supporters of an Episcopalian group called the Anglican Mission in America persuaded Archbishop Moses Tay of Singapore to assist in the consecration of a bishop for the Anglican Mission; then in 2001 four other bishops were consecrated in Denver, Colorado,

[32] G. H. Shattuck Jr, 'A Whole Priesthood: The Philadelphia Ordinations (1974) and the Continuing Dilemmas of Race in the Episcopal Church', EDS Occasional Papers, No. 6 (Cambridge, April 2001).

[33] Shattuck, *Episcopalians and Race*, p. 10, citing Louise Michele Newman, *White Women's Rights: The Racial Origins of Feminism in the United States* (New York: Oxford University Press, 1999).

by Archbishop Kolini of Rwanda.[34] The election and consecration of an openly gay bishop, Gene Robinson, in 2003 further deepened the crisis within the Episcopal Church, as well as threatening the unity of the Anglican communion worldwide. ECUSA avoided schism in the days of slavery. It was largely immune from the bitter disputes over fundamentalism which divided other Protestant churches in the early part of the twentieth century. The issue of sexuality has gravely compromised the internal cohesion of ECUSA, quite apart from its ramifications internationally.

CONCLUSION: ECUSA'S PLACE IN WORLD ANGLICANISM

It has not been possible within the scope of this book to give an adequate account of the internal development of the Episcopal Church. I have concentrated on ECUSA's work among minority groups, and others who have struggled to find a voice within Anglicanism generally. The importance of ECUSA for world Anglicanism lies in the fact that it was the first Anglican church to learn, not only to exist outside state establishment, but positively to embrace its status as a free, Reformed Catholic church. The Episcopal Church, not without great anguish, cast off its royalist and establishmentarian past. It came to defend republican values, but to position itself as a conservative force amidst what it sometimes regarded as the extremes of more democratic, populist forms of Evangelical Protestantism within the new American society. Despite its small size in comparison with other denominations, ECUSA advanced the claim to embody the ideal of a 'national church' – a kind of establishment without establishment. This was a somewhat conservative, patrician vision, but it could also convey a strong and progressive, socially radical critique of existing society. For William Reed Huntington the 'idea of a national church' was one which welcomed unity with other churches on basis of a Catholic and Reformed ecclesiology, the particular gift of Anglicanism to the universal church.

As an autonomous church, ECUSA, in the nineteenth century, continued to be influenced by many aspects of English Anglicanism, not least the Oxford Movement. But it also developed new ways of being Anglican, particularly synodical forms of government which placed a high value on lay representation. It was strongly conscious of having a missionary task within the United States. The pioneering of missionary

[34] *Church Times*, 29 June 2001.

bishops as instruments for the evangelisation of the American frontier was an innovative ecclesiological development of great importance for the worldwide Anglican communion. Through its Domestic and Foreign Missionary Society, ECUSA endeavoured to articulate missionary work as part of the very fabric of its life as a church, a task which could not be devolved to voluntary missionary societies. ECUSA's international work, particularly in China and Japan, was of great important in transmitting an American ideal of a non-established yet national Episcopal Church which could be seen as a way forward in the growth of autonomous churches overseas.

Especially after the Second World War, American Episcopalians were instrumental in fostering and financing an emerging world Anglican communion, which could be seen as more than a vague, somewhat vacuous, ideal. Bishop Stephen Bayne's appointment as the first executive officer of the Anglican communion in 1958 was a landmark. Actual conciliar forms of global Anglicanism were set in place for the first time, not least the Anglican Consultative Council. American Episcopalianism was thus crucial in the building of Anglicanism as a world communion in a post-colonial world. Not that ECUSA could escape its own styles of imperialism in a world in which the United States was a super-power, eventually the only super-power.

In the post-war years ECUSA itself increasingly became internally divided. The revision of the prayer book, the long debates over the ordination of women, the increasing identification, as a church, with liberal and progressive causes – these developments were at first accepted stoically by many brought up in more socially and theologically conservative forms of Episcopalianism. The debate about homosexuality, growing in urgency from the 1970s, and the willingness of the church as an institution to accommodate and affirm same-sex relations have become increasingly difficult for disaffected sections of the church to tolerate.

For a long time, these tensions were acrimoniously disputed within the Episcopal Church itself, with only minimum attention to the implications for the worldwide communion. Lambeth 1998 enabled conservative sections of the Episcopal Church to become conscious, in a new way, of the potential for an alliance with leaders in the worldwide communion. The church in the global South was seen as generally more conservative in matters of faith, and overwhelmingly more conservative on ethical matters in general and on the acceptance of homosexuality in particular. It remains to be seen whether this alliance of conservative forces between

North and South will prove sufficiently powerful and persuasive radically to change the direction of Anglicanism as a whole. A weakness is that northern conservatives may have underestimated the complexity of ethical issues in the South, and may be unable to understand that perspectives on sexuality are changing rapidly within the South itself. It is unlikely that attempts to ostracise a 'liberal' and 'revisionist' ECUSA can, in the end, succeed, precisely because the churches of the South are themselves already engaging with complex ethical issues – not necessarily the same issues, but nevertheless ones which are as unamenable to simple solutions as are issues of homosexuality.

CHAPTER 4

Canada

Henry Cabot reached Newfoundland on 24 June 1497, the feast of St John the Baptist. Cabot (like Columbus) was an Italian, but he was working for Henry VII, King of England, and the event is included in the calendar of the Canadian Anglican Church. In reality, the English had little interest in these northern areas for over two centuries. The SPG sporadically sent missionaries to Nova Scotia in the eighteenth century to minister to British settlers and to work among First Nation (Native American) communities. But Catholic missionaries had a much greater importance. British interest in the area was transformed by the capture of Quebec in 1759. At the Treaty of Paris in 1763 France accepted the conquest. In turn, 'His Britannic Majesty . . . agrees to grant the liberty of the Catholic religion to the inhabitants of Canada.' British government policy was to secure loyalty to the crown on the part of the French settlers through a policy of religious toleration. By contrast, the Church of England got little tangible support and encouragement. The concern to conciliate Canada's Catholic population was something new for Britain. British Catholics as individuals and the Catholic church as a body were still subject to legal restrictions. In Ireland, penal legislation was in force.

The weakness of the established church in British North America began to be addressed in the years after the American Revolution. The British realised the importance of forging stronger ties between the home country and the colonies if they wanted to avoid a repetition of the War of Independence. The Church of England was potentially an important weapon to accomplish this strategy. If a parochial system could be established, it would serve as a force for stability and loyalty in the community. The influx of loyalists into the Maritime Provinces in the wake of the American Revolution gave this strategy some chance of success, and at last convinced the British government that it should establish an episcopate in North America. In 1787 Charles Inglis was appointed by letters patent as Bishop of Nova Scotia, with general episcopal oversight in British North America. Inglis was Irish, an American loyalist, an SPG missionary and a former curate at Trinity Church, New York.

Bishop Inglis presided over the church in the Maritime Provinces of British North America. It was a 'limited Anglican establishment'. The bishop had no civil or temporal powers. Although the loyalists who settled in the Maritimes in the 1780s included many Anglican clergy, most of the refugees were not Anglican at all. Methodism made rapid strides in Nova Scotia. Inglis wanted to mitigate the popular force of Methodism by establishing a well-ordered parochial structure, and by concentrating on educational institutions. He was not willing to adapt Anglican formality and decorum to the new populism – he continued to oppose the inclusion of hymns in services. One Methodist complained of Anglican preaching that such 'discourses were not adapted to awaken the sleepy Sinner'.[1]

Nancy Christie speaks of the church foundering on 'the smug assumption . . . that the traditions and rituals of the Anglican church need not be adapted to colonial circumstances'.[2] Anglicanism in the Maritime Provinces exhibited a quiet conservative character which it has tended to retain.[3]

The government also appointed a Bishop for Quebec, to have a seat on the Governor's Legislative Council. It chose someone from England, Jacob Mountain, who had never visited America before his appointment. One factor in the choice of Mountain was that he was from a Huguenot family, though that did not endear him to the French Protestants whom the governor had earlier appointed as chaplains in Canada, and whose understanding of Anglican practice did not meet with Mountain's approval. Mountain had expected a fully established church. In reality he found a church which hardly existed physically on the ground, and one circumscribed by the virtual establishment of the Roman Catholic Church, which the government, for reasons of state, was not willing to jeopardise. Mountain, nevertheless, acted the part of an English establishment bishop, visiting York (the future Toronto in Upper Canada) in 1812, 'bewigged, gentlemanly, sitting in an armchair in a canoe paddled by eight Indians'.[4] The Anglican church in Quebec was to remain

[1] Judith Fingard, *The Anglican Design in Loyalist Nova Scotia 1783–1816* (London: SPCK, 1972), p. 67.

[2] Quoted in M. E. Reisner, *Strangers and Pilgrims: A History of the Anglican Diocese of Quebec 1793–1993* (Toronto: Anglican Book Centre, 1995), p. 39.

[3] Joan Marshall, *A Solitary Pillar: Montreal's Anglican Church and the Quiet Revolution* (Montreal: McGill University Press, 1995), pp. 58f.

[4] J. L. H. Henderson, *John Strachan 1778–1867* (Toronto: Toronto University Press, 1969), p. 20.

primarily the church of government officials and of the growing English settler community around Montreal and Ottawa.

ANGLICANISM IN ONTARIO

In Ontario (Upper Canada) the Mohawk loyalists were the largest single group of Anglicans. They settled in Brantfort, bringing with them the silver Communion plate which had been a gift from Queen Anne, and continued strongly to identify with the Anglican church under the leadership of Thayendandegea (Captain Joseph Brant), who translated the Bible and the Book of Common Prayer into Mohawk. Other Indian communities in this area were useful strategically to the British, with whom they signed treaties. With the establishment of cordial relations with America after 1814, such Indian alliances ceased to be important. The economy of the 'treaty Indians' was threatened by British settlers, but the government no longer had much incentive to protect them. But Christianity had become important for the treaty Indians, and although Methodism had many attractions, a number of chiefs remained attached to the 'religion of the king'.

Among the immigrant community the Anglican church was weak, just one of a range of competing Christian groups. A key figure in building up the church was John Strachan. Strachan was from Aberdeen, a member of the established Church of Scotland, and ambitious for a career in the church. When he was unsuccessful in his application to become minister of the Presbyterian church in Montreal, the Lieutenant Governor of Upper Canada offered him a living as a Church of England clergyman. He accepted and was ordained by Bishop Mountain in 1803, transferring from one form of established religion to the other. Strachan (a great admirer of Thomas Chalmers, the most prominent Scottish churchman of his day) rapidly became the linchpin of the church in Ontario, and in 1839 was consecrated the first Bishop of Toronto. Strachan strenuously advocated 'restraint, order and establishment',[5] and saw the church as essential for the taming and civilising of the country, a collaborative enterprise of church and state. 'A Christian nation without a religious establishment is a contradiction', he believed.

The state recognised this by paying the stipends of a number of clergy of the established church. In 1791 the state had established what became

[5] William Westfall, *Two Worlds: The Protestant Culture of Nineteenth Century Ontario* (Kingston: Queen's University Press, 1989), p. 24.

known as the Clergy Reserves, by which the government set aside one-seventh of its land allocation for 'the maintenance and support of a Protestant clergy'.[6] For many years (especially since land prices were very cheap) the Reserves did not produce much in the way of tangible support for the clergy. But were the Reserves to be used only to support the Church of England? Scots Presbyterians also demanded their share, as did the dissenting churches. But by the 1840s they were agitating for the complete abolition of the Reserves as part of a radical political agenda, which aimed at undermining the 'Family Compact', the oligarchy widely seen as monopolising office and unduly benefiting from land deals. The Reserves were abolished in 1854. Bishop Strachan had to turn his attention to self-support within the church.

It was his great achievement that, in the face of the collapse of his establishment ideal, he was able to accomplish a radical rethinking of the basis of the church, to pursue policies aimed at self-reliance and congregational giving, and to reconstitute the church as an autonomous body within a 'secular' state. The Disruption of the Church of Scotland in 1843 (in which Strachan's former mentor Chalmers was involved) and the ecclesiology of the Tractarians helped Strachan to rethink the place of the church in colonial society. The state had deserted the church. It was now the task of the church to re-establish itself on other foundations. Strachan helped to give it a strong constitutional identity, with synodical government and procedures for the election of its own bishops, and investment in education.[7] An indication of the relative strength of the different denominations in Ontario is given by the census of 1842. The Methodists led the way with 28.5 per cent of the population, followed by Presbyterians at 22 per cent, Anglicans at 20.4 per cent, and Catholics at 16.9 per cent.[8] The figures show that the Anglican church had always been on weak grounds in claiming to be 'The Church' of the land. But Anglicans did have a strong corporate identity compared with the fragmentation of Methodists and Presbyterians.

The Irish constituted the largest group of immigrants from the British Isles to Canada (between 1825 and 1850 they were more than the combined numbers of English and Scots immigrants). The 1871 census gave the national origin of Canadians as 31.1 per cent French, 24.3 per cent Irish, 20.3 per cent English and 15.8 per cent Scottish.[9] Scots clergy were a

[6] Ibid., p. 95.

[7] John Webster Grant, *A Profusion of Spires: Religion in 19th Century Ontario* (Toronto: Toronto University Press, 1988), p. 150.

[8] Ibid., p. 158. [9] The figure for England would include Welsh immigrants.

strong influence in the Church of England in Canada: some cradle Episcopalians and many, like Strachan himself, converts from Presbyterianism. But there were relatively few people of Scottish extraction in Anglican congregations; overwhelmingly Scots joined one of the three strands of Presbyterianism which existed by mid-century. Both Catholic and Protestant Irish people migrated to Canada, but Protestants outnumbered Catholics by two to one before 1850, and in this period 23 per cent of all Irish people belonged to the Church of Ireland. They were heavily to influence the character of lay Anglicanism in Ontario in particular. A larger proportion of Protestants than Catholics became land owners, and they constituted an important core of support for the church in the rural areas. Orange Lodges encouraged the strong anti-Catholic strain in Ontario politics.[10]

The Anglican clergy, in contrast to many of the laity, were anxious to distance themselves from other Protestants. In the years after Strachan's death in 1867, the 'irresistible force' of a lay Evangelical (largely Irish) leadership in the Synod met the 'immovable object' of a clerical establishment strongly imbued with high-church ideals.[11] The disputes between clergy and Evangelical laity were particularly acute during the episcopate of Strachan's successor, another Presbyterian convert, John Bethune. The Synod became an arena for party politics of a particularly vigorous kind. Trinity College had become identified (at least to its Evangelical opponents) with a high-church ecclesiology. In 1857 a new diocese of Huron had been created, based on London, Ontario. It became much more identified with Evangelicalism, and under its vigorous Irish bishop, Benjamin Cronyn, had established an Evangelical college, Huron College. In 1877 an Evangelical seminary was opened in Toronto diocese: Wycliffe College, an important institution for producing an Evangelical clergy, and in promoting foreign missions.

The years of the late nineteenth century and the early twentieth century were ones in which a rich associational life of all the churches flourished. Most important for the Anglican church was the Women's Auxiliary. In a church which still excluded women from almost all forms of recognised office (membership of synods, not to mention ordination), the Women's Auxiliary (modelled on ECUSA practice) became a formidable space in which women could exercise their own initiative as

[10] Donald H. Akenson, *Small Differences: Irish Catholics and Irish Protestants 1815–1922* (Kingston: Queen's University Press, 1988), pp. 89–90.

[11] Alan L. Hayes (ed.), *By Grace Co-workers: Building the Anglican Diocese of Toronto 1780–1989* (Toronto: Anglican Book Centre, 1989), p. 49.

fund raisers and mobilisers, with its own budgets, ministries and paid workers. The Women's Auxiliary funded domestic (i.e. largely Indian) and foreign mission. Women were particularly active in the Social Gospel movement. An order of deaconesses was established, with women working sacrificially, and invariably for much lower wages than their male counterparts, among working-class migrants from Russia or Macedonia, in jails and reformatories, in girls' rescue work.[12] Sunday schools, youth work and the Girls' Friendly Society became an integral part of much parish life, especially in urban areas. The church was confident that it was making a contribution both practically and morally to the building of a Christian, or more Christian, society.

THE CHURCH AND FIRST NATION PEOPLES

The Mohawk loyalty to Britain and to the Anglican church provided a model for other First Nation people, long after the alliance had ceased to have significance as far as the government was concerned. But state support for the church remained an important factor in convincing chiefs of local Canadian nations to seek an Anglican connection, for example the Ojibwa of Sault Ste Marie on the shores of Lake Superior, whose leader Augustine Shingwauk hoped that the Anglicans would provide a great educational institution, perhaps one day a university.[13] Officials of the Indian Department preferred impartiality. As a policy of assimilation became generally accepted as the way to 'deal with' the Indians, all churches were seen as useful civilising agents. Indians had ceased to be valued as military allies and increasingly were seen as an embarrassing welfare problem, as land pressures and the erosion of Indian culture began to produce alcoholism and destitution. In the North, the area of the Hudson Bay Company, the old alliance between Indians as trappers also came under threat as European entrepreneurs began to take direct control. J. R. Miller, the historian of Indian–white relations, has described this nineteenth-century trajectory succinctly: 'from alliance to irrelevance'.[14]

The SPG continued to play a role in providing financial support for the church in Canada, mainly by supplying ministers for settler

[12] Ibid., Chapter 2.

[13] J. R. Miller, *Shingwauk's Vision: A History of Native Residential Schools* (Toronto: Toronto University Press, 1996), pp. 4–6.

[14] J. R. Miller, *Skyscrapers Hide the Heavens: A History of Indian–White Relations in Canada* (Toronto: Toronto University Press, 1991), Chapter 5, pp. 83–98.

congregations, but it did not see Canada as a priority for missionary work among its Indian people. It was the Church Missionary Society which took up this challenge. At first the Society was reluctant to embark upon a new area of work, but agreed to sponsor John West because his salary was paid by the Hudson Bay Company. In 1820 West went to the Red River settlement, a pioneering colony of Cree people and Métis (people of Indian and European descent) near Lake Winnipeg. West and the other missionaries who worked over the next century in the prairies were convinced that Christianity must be an agent of economic change. He spoke in the typical language of a pioneering missionary when he called the Red River settlement 'a heathen land, which Satan hath led bound'.[15] West established a school which proved successful, not least in training a generation of Cree Christian leaders. Foremost of these was Sakacewescam, who became one of the first converts to be baptised. He took the name of Henry Budd (an English CMS supporter). Budd became an important evangelist in the North, along with another convert James Settee.[16] Budd was ordained in 1850, the first American Indian priest. The church adopted the syllabic alphabet introduced by Methodists, which became an important instrument for vernacular literacy among the Cree.

Budd went on to open a mission at Nipawin, among the plains Indians. In the next decades the sustainability of their way of life was rapidly eroded by the slaughter of the buffalo, and by the treaties negotiated by a hard-hearted federal government. Grant says of the work undertaken at this time: 'one misses both the fervour and the native initiatives conspicuous in other parts of Canada'.[17] Indians tended to become clients of missions rather than the self-propagating communities which had been such a feature of the work further north.

Further west in British Columbia, both the SPG and the CMS were active in work among Indians. In 1859, a substantial endowment from the English philanthropist Angela Burdett Coutts enabled a diocese to be established in Vancouver Island and British Columbia. An SPG clergyman, John Booth Good, was invited to work among the Nitlakapamuk (modern orthography Nlha7kapmx) people on the Thompson River, in the southern part of British Columbia. They had previously had contact

[15] Quoted in Janet Hodgson and Jay Kothare, *Vision Quest: Native Spirituality and the Church in Canada* (Toronto: Anglican Book Centre, 1990), p. 64.

[16] Eugene Stock, *The History of the Church Missionary Society*, Volume 1 (London: CMS, 1899), pp. 363–4.

[17] John Webster Grant, *Moon of Wintertime: Missionaries and the Indians of Canada in Encounter since 1534* (Toronto: Toronto University Press, 1984), p. 166.

with the Roman Catholic Oblate mission, but the relationship had soured. But, in a period of rapid European settlement, access to some form of Christianity seemed essential if the Nitlakapamuk were successfully to negotiate the new world.[18] The CMS tradition was also represented in British Columbia. A few years before Good, a layman, William Duncan, began work among the Tsimshian people of Port Simpson, towards the border with Alaska. Duncan developed a radical mission policy which involved separating his flock both from their traditional society and from the onslaughts of western civilisation.[19] He established a Christian community at Metlakatla, which encouraged local initiative and democratic accountability within an authoritarian, even theocratic, framework, based on deference to Duncan as leader. To establish such a hermetically sealed community was in itself a dubious enterprise. Its problems were magnified by the increasingly eccentric and bizarre behaviour of Duncan. Convinced that his converts would not be able to distinguish the elements of the Eucharist from a fetish, Duncan (a layman) outlawed the sacrament at Metlakatla. He criticised the ritualism of the diocese, and would allow the bishop no jurisdiction. In 1887 Duncan negotiated with the American government for his followers to trek over the border to Alaska, where they could live out Duncan's vision of a Christian society untroubled by church or civil constraints.[20]

In their book on First Nation spirituality, Hodgson and Kothare tell a story of how an eruption of revivalism at Metlakatla, with all-night prayer meetings and manifestations of strong emotion, had been snuffed out by Duncan because he feared that it contained too many 'heathen' elements. In 1893 a missionary at Kincolith (not many miles from Metlakatla) had responded to a similar revival by inviting the Church Army to come to the district. Building on the fruits of the revival, the Church Army was able to establish a strong, tightly knit association. The smart grey uniform, the band music and the strict rules (especially against alcohol) had created a community. At times it, like Metlakatla, had appeared detached from the rest of the church. It was only in the 1970s that the local clergyman, John Hannon, was able to integrate the particular spirituality of the Kincolith Christians into the life of the diocese as a whole.[21]

[18] Brett Christophers, *Positioning the Missionary: John Booth Good and the Confluence of Cultures in Nineteenth-Century British Columbia* (Vancouver: University of British Columbia Press, 1998), pp. 9–18.

[19] Eugene Stock, *The History of the Church Missionary Society*, Volume III (London: CMS, 1899), p. 617.

[20] Grant, *Moon of Wintertime*, pp. 129–31; Stock, *History of CMS*, Volume III, pp. 629–30.

[21] Hodgson and Kothare, *Vision Quest*, pp. 113–16.

As a result of these widespread efforts, largely though not exclusively undertaken by British societies, the Anglican church became a major force in the movement of Canadian Indian peoples towards Christianity. Hodgson and Kothare reckon that approximately a quarter of all Canadian Indians are adherents of the Anglican church; and that 10 per cent of the total membership of the Canadian Anglican Church is First Nation. About 85 per cent of Inuit people (Eskimo) are Anglican. Their evangelisation is largely a twentieth-century phenomenon. In 1956 the first Bishop of the Arctic, Archibald Lang Fleming (yet another Scot), published an account of his life. Entitled *Archibald the Arctic*,[22] it is an unashamedly old-fashioned account of pioneering missionary work among the heathen. One searches in vain for any critical reflection on the encounter between western Christian values and indigenous sensibilities. To Fleming, Eskimo music is 'monotonous', their ways 'dirty and degraded', their beliefs 'crude and false or a combination of myth and error'. But 'who are we to judge their value?'[23] It is rather startling to see these sentiments expressed so starkly and unashamedly as late as 1956 (Fleming had retired as bishop in 1947). They were embarrassingly archaic even then.

THE RESIDENTIAL SCHOOLS ISSUE

By the end of the nineteenth century, hardly any Indian people in Canada was in a position to survive as a self-sustaining autonomous community. Indian affairs were a matter for the federal government, whose Department of Indian Affairs was established in 1880. Indians were encouraged to seek entry into the dominant Canadian society by assimilation and enfranchisement. But one could only do so at the cost of renouncing one's status as an Indian. Only 250 opted to take this path between 1885 and 1920. Meanwhile, the regulation and interference in Indian cultural and political life became pervasive, with well-intentioned restrictions on the sale of alcohol, and less benign restrictions on such important religious and cultural symbols of Indian identity as the *potlatch* rituals of gift exchange among the coastal peoples.[24]

[22] His title competes with 'Lucian Upper Nile' for crazy episcopal titles: Lucian Usher-Wilson was Bishop of the Upper Nile in Uganda at about the same time as 'Archibald the Arctic'.

[23] The quotations are scattered about in Archibald Fleming, *Archibald the Arctic* (New York: Appleton-Century-Crofts, 1956).

[24] Miller, *Skyscrapers*, pp. 192–3, and Chapter 11.

Both government and missionaries concentrated their efforts on the establishment of residential schools, an environment in which young people would be prised away from their traditional society and culture, and re-formed as Christians and Canadians. All Christian bodies were complicit in this policy. Catholics and Anglicans were the most active simply because their work among Indians was the most extensive. J. R. Miller, the historian of the residential schools, catalogues the problems which the residential schools faced. They were under-financed, claiming to offer a vocational style of training, but without the resources which such training required. They conducted a 'campaign of linguistic repression', in which use of the mother tongue was heavily punished.[25] 'They took away our brains, our language, our songs – they whipped our spirits.'[26] The result was the creation of institutions of despair and demoralisation, a culture of disdain. In 1986 the Anglican church issued a formal apology. The question of compensation remains. The church has been willing to pay for its institutional sins. But the amounts threaten to bankrupt the church. There is a feeling that the federal government also should not evade its responsibilities.

CANADIAN ANGLICANISM IN THE TWENTIETH CENTURY

In 1900 about 10 per cent of Canadians were active Anglicans.[27] The church entered the new century with a strong institutional base. It had been effective in adapting to a situation in which it did not rely on a state connection. It was surprisingly cohesive. Despite strong tensions between Evangelical and high-church constituents, the church had learnt to live with internal difference of a ritual or doctrinal nature. But apart from its important Indian work, it was socially much less heterogeneous, largely the church of people from the British Isles. In the early part of the century, some work was done among Yiddish-speaking Jewish or east European Orthodox immigrants, largely out of a social rather than an evangelistic concern.[28] Anglicans were worried by the extent of immigration from non-Anglo-Saxon countries. A report of 1927 warned that

[25] Miller, *Shingwauk's Vision*, p. 181.

[26] Witness of a 49-year-old Peigan woman in Brian Maracle, *Crazywater: Native Voices on Addiction and Recovery* (Toronto: Viking Press, 1993), p. 172.

[27] David Barrett, George T. Kurian and Todd M. Johnson, *World Christian Encyclopedia* (2 vols., Oxford: Oxford University Press, 2001), Volume 1, pp. 169–75.

[28] In the nineteenth century, a Polish Jewish convert to Evangelical Anglicanism had become the second Bishop of Huron: Isaac Hellmuth. See Philip Carrington, *The Anglican Church in Canada: A History* (Toronto: Collins, 1963), p. 110.

'[t]he time is not far distant when peoples of Anglo-Saxon origin will be in a minority'.[29] Such unsavoury language has parallels in other parts of the British Empire, and in Britain itself. In 1921 the General Synod chose the Church of England in Canada as its official title. This was changed only in 1955 to the Anglican Church in Canada.[30] A number of factors help to account for the steep decline in membership of the Anglican church (according to Barrett's 2000 figures) to 2.5 per cent of the Canadian population. One of them is the fact that immigration in the twentieth century has been largely non-British. Until the 1960s, the Anglican church remained profoundly British both emotionally and in its perception of itself as the guardian of monarchy and of Canada's links with Britain.

Anglican numbers continued to rise in absolute terms (in line with population growth) until mid-century. In Toronto diocese 'active' Anglicans numbered 151,000 in 1939, and peaked at 236,000 in 1962. By 1989 this had dropped to about 116,000.[31] Decline was steepest in the coastal provinces of the west. It was least noticeable in the old areas of Anglican establishment, the Maritime Provinces. It was significant in large metropolitan areas: Toronto, Ottawa, Montreal, Quebec. The rapid secularisation of Canada reflects the British experience, rather than that of the United States.[32]

In the French-speaking areas of Canada, a combination of factors made the position of the Anglican church particularly vulnerable. Anglicanism had failed to attract a substantial French-speaking constituency. The two communities existed as 'two solitudes', separated by 'ignorance and isolation, by linguistic hierarchy and English unilingualism'.[33] The English-speaking community had for long felt secure because, though a minority in the Province of Quebec, they were part of a wider English-speaking Canadian majority. English speakers constituted a disproportionate part of the business and professional elite within the province. The rise of Quebec nationalism and the so-called 'Quiet Revolution' – the drive by the francophone community to be 'maître chez nous' – has eroded that confidence. One result has been a large out-migration of English speakers. The Anglican diocese of Montreal has seen a 75 per cent decline in membership in thirty years, a result partly of secularisation, but primarily of emigration. For those who are left, there is a 'heightened sense of

[29] Hayes, *By Grace Co-workers*, p. 85. [30] Reisner, *Strangers and Pilgrims*, p. 41.
[31] R. M. Black, in Hayes, *By Grace Co-workers*, p. 97. [32] Marshall, *A Solitary Pillar*.
[33] Ibid., p. 3. The phrase 'two solitudes' is Hugh Maclennan's.

place', in which the church is the locus for affirmation of identity and community, a sense of embattlement and of fear: one woman (ironically descended from Anglicised French settlers) spoke of her fears of 'dying in French'.[34] This is sometimes expressed in a conservative resistance to change, an impatience with the many changes which are perceived as further eroding the church community from within: opposition to prayer-book reform, women priests, or liberalisation of issues such as divorce or homosexuality. Marshall illustrates this with five case studies of parishes in Montreal. Two of the parishes – a well-heeled suburban church in an English enclave and a working-class church in a down-town area – show a classic conservatism. Two parishes – one in a more mixed suburb where anglophones are used to operating in a bilingual situation, another in a rural area which has in recent years become a weekend and permanent home for upwardly mobile professionals – are seen as responding more positively to change. In both cases the charismatic movement is an important factor in that break with ecclesiastical conservatism.

Despite the very special circumstances of Montreal diocese, these varying responses to change can be paralleled elsewhere, in other places where a trend of secularisation has been at work over a long period of time. Marshall's fifth case study illustrates a very different but important development. This is the establishment of a francophone congregation – not of native Québecois but of Haitian immigrants. The Episcopal Church in Haiti has a history which goes back to the mid nineteenth century. Only in the later part of the twentieth century did Haitian immigrants become numerically significant in Canada. The Episcopalian congregation of La Nativité is a congregation which rents room in the anglophone congregation of Rosemount in Montreal. The congregation uses the French version of the prayer book of ECUSA (of which the Haitian church is a part). French Creole is used for hymns and for certain parts of the liturgy. The service occupies most of Sunday afternoon, and there is an informality in timing and in the atmosphere of the service which contrasts with much Anglican worship. The congregation has a Haitian minister, Father Joseph. This is an important if fragile breakthrough of the Anglican church into the francophone world. Montreal Anglicanism remains problematic for Haitian Episcopalians: 'On y trouve toute la culture anglo-saxonne et toute la vision ecclésiale britannique.'[35] It remains a challenge for the church effectively to provide a home for its

[34] Ibid., p. 126. [35] Ibid., p. 139.

Haitian members. This applies equally to other, anglophone Caribbean immigrants and, more recently, African Anglican migrants – for example Ugandans and Rwandese in Ontario and Japanese and other East Asian Anglicans on Canada's Pacific coast.

The Anglican church has made serious, if belated, attempts to come to terms with bilingualism in Quebec, through language training for its ministers and the publication of literature in French. In 1991 a bilingual bishop of Quebec was appointed. French services take place regularly in the cathedral and in some parishes, and a policy of explaining 'l'église Anglicane' to francophones has been embarked upon. In addition to Haitians, there are an increasing number of refugees and migrants from the Congo Democratic Republic, some with an Anglican background.[36]

In many important ways, since the 1960s the church has radically transformed its self-understanding of its role in society. From being the protector of traditional values and the loyal arm of government, the church has come to see its role as one of criticism of government policy and advocacy of the disadvantaged. In retrospect, the holding of the international Anglican Congress in Toronto in 1963 was a watershed. 'Mutual Responsibility and Interdependence' was a key concept which emerged from this conference. The phrase was meant to indicate the future direction of Anglicanism as a worldwide communion. In many ways the church in Canada took this as a standard by which to evaluate both the quality of its life as a church and its relationships with the church internationally, especially under the primacy of Archbishop Edward Scott (1971–81). 'The pluralism of international Anglicanism reinforces our commitment to openness and hospitality in Canada.'[37]

Like the church in Britain or in the USA, the church in Canada has undergone a process of substantial change, transforming its traditional expression. The admission of women to the priesthood was approved in 1975. In 1985, the Book of Alternative Services (the culmination of a number of years of experimental use) was published. The charismatic movement has been important in enabling a loosening of Anglican rigidities, especially with regard to worship. But it has also become important in providing an increasingly articulate opposition to what is perceived as the liberal establishment of the church, and in reaction to the

[36] Reisner, *Strangers and Pilgrims*, p. 198.

[37] Gordon Light, 'Being Anglican in a Pluralist Society: A Canadian Perspective', in Andrew Wingate, Kevin Ward, Carrie Pemberton and Wilson Sitshebo (eds.), *Anglicanism: A Global Communion* (London: Mowbray, 1998), p. 143.

secularisation of Canadian life generally. Whereas in 1940 Canadians were more likely to go to church than Americans, the opposite had become true by 1990.[38]

The Canadian Anglican Church has not escaped the controversy over gay issues. The decision of the diocese of New Westminster to authorise church blessings for same-sex partnerships has been condemned by many Anglican leaders of the global South. Canadian society, on the other hand, is less bitterly divided than the United States on this issue, and the issue has not raised the same degree of fury in Canada itself.

FIRST NATION SPIRITUALITY

One vital aspect of the increasing social awareness of the church from the 1960s was a radical rethinking of its responsibilities to its Indian members. In 1963 Archbishop Carrington could say of Canon Edward Ahenakew that he 'might have been our first Indian bishop if only more imagination had been shown'.[39] Ahenakew had been a moderate leader of the League of Indians of Canada in the 1920, and had written *The Voice of the Plains Cree*, arguing, among other things, for a wholehearted recognition by the church of Cree spiritual insights. In 1967 the General Synod made a declaration of penitence and asked 'forgiveness regarding Anglican participation and the perpetuation of injustice to Indians'.[40] The Synod commissioned a sociologist, Charles E. Hendry, to write what turned out to be a penetrating report, *Beyond Traplines*, published in 1969.[41] It urged support for Indian peoples at all levels, economic and cultural, and aboriginal rights, as well as religious. The Canadian church did give moral and financial support to help in the setting up of the Native Peoples' Convention, a North American-wide forum for religious and spiritual concerns. This was a movement which could not be confined to one denomination, or indeed be kept within the boundaries of institutional Christianity. *Vision Quest: Native Spirituality and the Church in Canada*, a report written in 1990 by Janet Hodgson (a South African), and Jay Kothare, a priest from India who had been ordained in the Church of Canada, criticised the 'constant chaperoning

[38] Robert Bruce Mullin, in Adrian Hastings (ed.), *A World History of Christianity* (London: Cassell, 1999), p. 455.

[39] Carrington, *The Anglican Church in Canada*, p. 255.

[40] Hodgson and Kothare, *Vision Quest*, p. 131.

[41] Grant, *Moon of Wintertime*, p. 207.

of native peoples by whites' as a major factor in smothering native spirituality.[42]

In contrast, the writers held up the work of Archdeacon Andrew Ahenakew (1904–76) of the Sandy Lake Reserve. He had combined his work as a Christian priest with that of a native healer, and interpreter of First Nation culture in Christian terms.

[42] Hodgson and Kothare, *Vision Quest*, pp. 94, 122–4.

CHAPTER 5

The Caribbean

THE CHURCH OF THE PLANTERS

The English began their long connection with the Caribbean in the reign of Elizabeth I.[1] England was just beginning to assert itself as a Protestant nation. Its exploits in the Caribbean were an extension of the war with Catholic Spain.[2] Sir Walter Raleigh had grand ideas of converting Indian rulers to the Protestant faith and joining an alliance against the Spanish; but these remained no more than idle fancies. Protestant England had no more concern for the souls of the indigenous populations, the Carib and Arawak, than had the Spanish. Indeed, less so: there was no Anglican theologian of the stature of the Dominican Fra Bartolomé de las Casas to defend the native Americans as fully human, though the Elizabethan clergyman Richard Hakluyt, who publicised English exploits across the globe, made use of las Casas in his attack on Spain's treatment of the American Indians.[3] The English presence in the Caribbean was an extension of the European conflict between Protestants and Catholics, not a conflict about comparative missionary methods. In any case, by the time that the English began actually to occupy Caribbean islands, the native populations were well on the way to extinction.

The first permanent English possessions in the Caribbean came in the 1620s, with the capture of islands in the Lesser Antilles – the Windward and Leeward Islands. St Kitts was taken in 1624, and successful immigration was promoted, involving conflict with the remaining Carib in the area. Settlement of the neighbouring islands of Nevis, Antigua and Montserrat followed in the next few years, in competition with the

[1] This chapter will concentrate on Anglicanism in the English- and French-speaking Caribbean. The tiny Anglican presence in the Spanish-speaking Caribbean will be discussed in Chapter 6.

[2] Nicholas Canny, *The Oxford History of the British Empire*, Volume 1 (Oxford: Oxford University Press, 1988).

[3] David Armitage, *The Ideological Origins of the British Empire* (Cambridge: Cambridge University Press, 2000), p. 87.

Catholic French and the Protestant Dutch. In 1627 English settlers landed on Barbados – an uninhabited island which, unlike some of the other islands, remained continuously under English (and then British) control.[4] In 1655, during the Protectorate, Jamaica, 'that Spanish backwater', as Oliver Cromwell called it, was captured. It became the most important of the English sugar islands. The seventeenth century also saw the consolidation of English control of two areas on the mainland: Guiana and Belize, which remain to this day anglophone enclaves in Latin America. Gradually the British took control of other islands: Grenada, Dominica, Saint Vincent and Tobago. Trinidad was captured from the Spanish as late as 1797.[5]

The first settlers in the English possessions were English, Irish and Scottish. A few were land owners; most were indentured servants, whose conditions of life were harsh. But with the reliance on sugar came the importation of large numbers of slaves from Africa. Very quickly black people came to constitute a large majority in all the islands. The islands were, nevertheless, 'English'. English civil and ecclesiastical institutions were replicated. Jamaica, for example, was divided geographically into twelve parishes, with names like St Catherine and Manchester. Englishmen and their dependants (and the Irish and Scots in so far as they conformed to the Church of England) constituted civil society. African slaves were not part of 'civil society'; they were property, not members. A major theological issue was the status of slaves who became Christians. Catholic Spain did not hesitate to baptise slaves. It did not affect their status as slaves, but did save their souls. For some Protestants this made the very notion of baptising the heathen questionable, an example of Catholic superstition and 'Popish supererogation' (doing God's work to gain merit).[6] In the Netherlands, the 1618–19 Synod of Dort (which representatives of the churches of England and Scotland had attended) had given a clear Protestant understanding of the relationship between Christianity and slavery: baptised slaves should be accorded the rights of Christian citizens.[7] The Church of England did not formally pronounce on the matter, but the plantation economy depended on slaves, and English settlers had sufficient anxieties about the legal (not to mention

[4] Jan Rogozinski, *A Brief History of the Caribbean: From the Arawak and Carib to the Present* (New York: Facts on File Inc., 1999).

[5] Ibid., p. 194.

[6] A. C. Dayfoot, *The Shaping of the West Indian Church 1492–1962* (Kingston: University of the West Indies, 1999), pp. 85–90.

[7] Robert C.-H. Shell, *Children of Bondage: A Social History of the Slave Society at the Cape of Good Hope 1652–1838* (Hanover: Wesleyan University Press, 1994).

the ethical) implications of slaves becoming Christians for them to be anxious to prevent this from happening.[8]

Despite the advanced Protestant leanings of many of the early buccaneers, the English Caribbean did not become the refuge for any substantial groups of Puritan settlers. The Church of England became the established form of religion throughout the English West Indies, and remained so even after the union with Scotland created a British imperial power in 1707. It was an episcopal church, but without an actual bishop. The Bishop of London exercised a general oversight, and was important in ordaining and licensing priests to work in the Caribbean. But the governors of the various islands had quasi-episcopal powers, acting as 'Ordinary' in relation to the church. They had powers to appoint and 'collate' (install in their office) parish priests, and exercised many of the functions which in England would have been performed by the diocesan bishop. The island legislatures and the parish vestries had considerable powers, not least because they financed the upkeep of the church fabric and paid the stipend of the minister. Priests were sometimes paid in sugar. They themselves became sugar planters and slave owners. While originating from Britain themselves, they came to reflect the mores and attitudes of the plantocracy.[9]

In England the unsatisfactory nature of this state of affairs was acknowledged by three institutions concerned with the religious welfare of the West Indies: the crown, the Bishop of London and, after its establishment in 1701, the Society for the Propagation of the Gospel (SPG). The revised Book of Common Prayer in 1662 found it convenient to include, for the first time, a service of adult baptism, 'for the baptizing of Natives in our Plantations'. In 1741 Bishop Edmund Gibson appealed 'to the masters and mistresses of families in the English plantations abroad' to take their obligations seriously with these comforting words:

> Christianity and the embracing of the gospel does not make the least alteration in civil property, or in any of the duties which belong to civil relations, but in all these respects, it continues persons just in the same state as it found them. The freedom which Christianity gives is a freedom from the bondage of sin and Satan, and from the domination of men's lust and passions and inordinate desires, but as to their outward conditions, whatever that was before, whether bond or free, their being baptized and becoming Christians makes no manner of change in it . . . so far is Christianity of discharging men from their duties of

[8] Dayfoot, *The Shaping of the West Indian Church*, pp. 85–90.

[9] P. F. Campbell, *The Church in Barbados in the Seventeenth Century* (Bridgetown: Barbados Museum and Historical Society, 1984).

station and condition in which it found them; it lays them under stronger obligation to perform these duties with the greatest diligence and fidelity, not only from the fear of God, but from a servant's duty to God and belief and expectation of a future account.[10]

Such pronouncements did not convince the planters that evangelisation of slaves was acceptable or advisable. The SPG did send missionaries with a specific duty of evangelisation, but they were usually located in the existing parishes of the planters. Not being so directly accountable to the local parishioners, they were occasionally able to take a more critical stance regarding slave society. They were concerned that black people were not allowed to contract marriages recognised by the courts. But the Society found it difficult to avoid absorbing the values of plantation society. In 1704 Sir Christopher Codrington,[11] the governor of the Leeward Islands and from a Barbadian family, made a will bequeathing his estates in Barbados to the SPG:

My desire is to have the plantation continued intire and 300 negroes at least always kept thereon, and a convenient number of Professors and scholars maintained there all of them to be under the vows of poverty and chastity and obedience who shall be obliged to study and practise Phisick and Chirurgery as well as Divinity, that by the apparent usefulness of the former to all mankind they may both endear themselves to the people and have the better opportunitys of doing good to men's souls whilst they are taking care of their bodys, but the particulars of the constitutions I leave to the Society composed of wise and good men.[12]

Codrington's vision that only a Protestant religious order was likely to achieve a seriousness about missionary work was perhaps most nearly realised before the end of the eighteenth century by the work of the Moravians. The SPG record in Codrington College itself was more ambiguous. The medical work did not really get established, and the school was for white children only. Missionary work among the 300 slaves was taken seriously. But by the terms of the will the SPG itself became a slave owner, a situation for which it was increasingly criticised by abolitionists and Evangelicals. As late as 1819, the SPG, defensively, justified the status quo:

a system which while it effectively secures the progressive amelioration in the disposition, understanding and habits of the slaves may afford a model for other proprietors to follow, and most ardently may this event be expected, when it is

[10] Quoted in Dayfoot, *The Shaping of the West Indian Church*, p. 108.
[11] Nina Langley, *Sir Christopher Codrington and his College* (London: SPCK, 1962).
[12] Quoted in Dayfoot, *The Shaping of the West Indian Church*, p. 108.

seen in what harmony Religion and Instruction and Flourishing Agriculture subsist.[13]

This provoked a nice bit of invective from an Evangelical abolitionist in London:

> What a frightful mockery is this! A society instituted for the dissemination of a creed whose central principle is charity towards all humankind, tenaciously claiming its due of sweat and labour from the bones and muscle of enslaved man; a Society holding the Bible in one hand and the cart-whip clotted with blood of the African in the other, with one eye fixed in pious veneration on the Cross, the other on the drooping slave degraded down to the lower animals . . .[14]

If the SPG conspicuously failed to take a lead in the abolition movement in the Caribbean,[15] it was a regular parish priest from St Kitts who proved one of the most effective Caribbean Anglican voices in protest at slavery. James Ramsay, a Scot from Aberdeenshire, became a major influence on William Wilberforce. A naval surgeon, Ramsay was ordained by the Bishop of London in 1762 to serve in St Kitts, where he married the daughter of a planter. He was already an abolitionist, appalled by his experience of treating an epidemic among captured slaves aboard a slaving ship. Ramsay's 'duel with the planters' in the 1780s was conducted with considerable tenacity and courage by Ramsay, and was publicised in Britain in the abolitionist press. He returned to Britain and, as a parish priest in Kent, continued to help the anti-slavery campaign.[16] In the Caribbean itself, Quakers and Moravians, Baptists and Methodists, were more critical of slavery. They were not so bound up in the slave economy of the British Caribbean islands as the Church of England (though the Methodist missionary Thomas Coke, in his concern to reach planters as well as black slaves, was reluctant to make too much of an issue of it).[17]

The ending of the slave trade in 1807 did not end the slave economies. But in 1823 the British government initiated a policy of 'amelioration'. A gradualist approach, it involved a programme of religious instruction for slaves. Slaves could testify in court if they could show that they had

[13] Regulations of 1819, quoted by Leroy Errol Brooks, 'The Church and the Abolition Movement in the British Caribbean', unpublished M.Th. dissertation, Columbia Theological Seminary, 1986, p. 61.

[14] Ibid., p. 62.

[15] Noel Titus, 'SPG and the Barbadian Plantations', in Daniel O'Connor, *Three Centuries of Mission: The United Society for the Propagation of the Gospel 1701–2000* (London: Continuum, 2000), pp. 249–61.

[16] Folarin Shyllon, *James Ramsay: The Unknown Abolitionist* (Edinburgh: Canongate Press, 1977).

[17] Dayfoot, *The Shaping of the West Indian Church*, pp. 131–4.

received some education and knew the nature of an oath. Sunday markets should be abolished.[18] The church had long promoted Sunday as a day of rest, for slaves as well as for planters. In 1834, the abolition of slavery was finally promulgated, but it was only on 1 August 1838 that the transitional period of 'apprenticeship' came to an end and liberation was at last achieved. 'Amelioration' was accompanied in 1824 by the belated establishment of an episcopate in the Caribbean. Two bishops were appointed by the government: William Hart Coleridge for Barbados (with responsibility for the Leeward and Windward Islands, Trinidad and Tobago and Guiana) and Christopher Lipscomb for Jamaica (with responsibility for the Bahamas and Honduras). Both these men served for twenty years, and each had a real but limited success in facilitating a process by which the church could escape from its captivity by the plantocracy.

THE ERA OF LIBERATION – JAMAICA AND BARBADOS: A COMPARISON

Jamaica and Barbados, the seats of the two dioceses created in 1824, were the most important British West Indian islands. Both were sugar islands, with black majorities, and both were ruled by a plantocracy who conceived of church and state as exclusively white Creole.[19] In other respects the established churches of the two islands developed in markedly different ways. Jamaica continued to import slaves from West Africa much later than Barbados, and there was a deeper cross-fertilisation with African world views.[20] Jamaican planters emphasised the diversity of slave origins, hoping thereby to pre-empt the rise of a common black Jamaican identity. Barbados evolved a much more homogenous black population, but planters there hoped that black people would passively accept a society of deference which the church would reinforce.

By the time of emancipation, almost half of Jamaica's slave population was reckoned to have some Christian commitment. This had little to do with the established church. The SPG had not been active in Jamaica, and the planters had been indifferent or hostile to evangelisation among slaves. Moravians and Methodists were active among slaves, but the most

[18] Sehon S. Goodridge, *Facing the Challenge of Emancipation: A Study of the Ministry of William Hart Coleridge, First Bishop of Barbados 1824–42* (Bridgetown: Cedar Press, 1981), p. 5.

[19] 'Creole', in this context, meant white people born on the islands.

[20] Shirley C. Gordon, *God Almighty Make Me Free: Christianity in Preemancipation Jamaica* (Bloomington: Indiana University Press, 1996), p. 2.

powerful impact came from black American Baptists such as George Liele, a former slave from Savannah, Georgia, who settled in the Bahamas during the revolutionary war, and in 1784 began to preach in Kingston, Jamaica. A strong Native Baptist Church emerged. British Baptists tried to channel and control its enthusiasm and to free it from the charge of radical political involvement. But they were never able completely to restrain its radicalism. The plantocracy feared Baptist and Methodist activity, but realised that an entirely negative response was no longer appropriate. In 1815 the Jamaican Assembly resolved to 'investigate the means of diffusing the light of genuine Christianity, divested of the dark and dangerous fanaticism of the Methodists'.[21] Government 'amelioration' policies (with their emphasis on slave education and religious instruction) also demanded a response. Bishop Lipscomb envisaged creating a strong diocesan structure which would free the clergy from their dependence on the planters. He invited the CMS to send missionaries to work among slaves and ex-slaves. They were initially greeted with suspicion, but many planters came to value their creation of a class of Christians less likely to cause trouble. Baptists continued to be seen as political agitators – Sam Sharpe's revolt of 1831 and Paul Bogle's rebellion of 1865 (both were Baptist deacons) reinforced this perception.[22] The CMS withdrew its missionaries in the 1840s, partly because of a financial retrenchment, partly because its vision of a native church was as suspicious of episcopal control as the planters had been.[23] The SPG, having resumed activity in Jamaica in the 1830s, withdrew again in the 1860s, partly in protest at the local church's continued indifference to its mission among black people.[24]

The weakness of the missionary societies in Jamaica made it all the more necessary for the bishops to form some counter-weight to the planters. Increasingly, high-church traditions seemed to offer the best opportunity for creating a church independent of the old plantocracy. In Jamaica the strength of Nonconformity meant that the question of disestablishment was a hot political issue in the legislature. The rector of St Ann's, G.W. Bridges, was notorious both for his despising of black people generally and for his intolerance of other Christian

[21] Dayfoot, *The Shaping of the West Indian Church*, p. 165.

[22] Robert Stewart, *Religion and Society in Post-Emancipation Jamaica* (Knoxville: Tennessee University Press, 1992), pp. 161–70.

[23] Eugene Stock, *The History of the Church Missionary Society*, Volume 1 (London: CMS, 1899), pp. 337–48.

[24] R. A. Minter, *Episcopacy without Episcopate: The Church of England in Jamaica before 1824* (Upton-upon-Severn, Worcs.: Self-Publishing Association Ltd, 1990), p. 225.

denominations. It is not surprising that churches which were both attracting and encouraging black leadership should be prominent in the political agitation to disestablish the church. Baptist missionaries from England might be as concerned as the old planters to discourage politically subversive activity, but they were also adamant that the old establishment was neither fair nor, ultimately, conducive to good order, and they led the way in the debates which resulted, in 1869, in a formal separation of church and state and an end to the government payment of clergy stipends. Enos Nuttall, a priest with a Methodist background who eventually became Bishop of Jamaica in 1880, was quite successful in seizing the opportunity of disestablishment to encourage a voluntary system of self-support. He has been called the 'Moses of the Anglican Church of Jamaica'.[25]

The church in Jamaica was much less successful in appearing with any conviction to foster black leadership. As Stewart puts it:

> The Anglican Church was the white man's church not because only whites belonged – that was not the case. It was the white man's church because the clergy in practice showed that white leadership and membership were its only social legitimization.[26]

The first black priest was Robert Gordon. Born in 1830 the son of black Creole parents (i.e. second-generation Jamaican), he was brought up in the Methodist Church. Aged seventeen, he became a Church of England catechist in Kingston. When he sought ordination, Bishop Aubrey Spencer suggested that he go to Codrington to train as a missionary to Africa. Gordon was suspicious of what was an all-white institution. He also feared that he would not be allowed to exercise his ministry in Jamaica itself. Instead he went to England in 1857 and was employed by the Colonial Church and School Society as a missionary in Canada to a black community of ex-slave refugees, living near London, Ontario. The Bishop of Huron ordained him as a deacon. When he returned to Jamaica in 1861, the new bishop, Reginald Courtenay, again urged him to consider missionary work in Africa, but would not employ him as a clergyman in Jamaica. Back in England the Archbishop of Canterbury did give him a licence. Gordon wrote an angry tract entitled 'The Church in Jamaica – Why it has Failed' (1872). Why did Gordon persist in identifying himself with a church which seemed so unwelcoming? One

[25] Dayfoot, *The Shaping of the West Indian Church*, p. 209. Nuttall became Primate of the West Indies in 1893 (with the title of Archbishop from 1897). See Frank Cundall, *The Life of Enos Nuttall, Archbishop of the West Indies* (London: SPCK, 1922).

[26] Stewart, *Religion and Society*, p. 67.

reason was his perception that the dissenting tradition in Jamaica was incapable, by itself, of overcoming 'the contempt for blackness' in Jamaican society, which would persist 'as long as institutions of undeniable power such as the Anglican church continued to be white in structures of authority and command'.[27]

Barbados, equally reliant on sugar, had abandoned the import of slaves from Africa much earlier than Jamaica, relying on natural increase to provide its labour requirements. Barbados had a black majority, but its culture was more uniform and more shaped by 'Englishness' than that of Jamaica. In Barbados, the seat of the second diocese, Anglicanism achieved an unrivalled authority. Nonconformity did exist, but it was kept in its place much more effectively than in Jamaica. There was no equivalent agitation for the disestablishment of the church. Indeed, at the time of the disestablishment of the church in other parts of the Caribbean, the Barbadian legislature voted to retain establishment. This continued until 1969, some years after independence. But establishment was a mixed blessing. In the late nineteenth century, Bishop John Mitchinson felt that the church would never develop a sense of its own identity as long as it relied so heavily on government financial support. Mitchinson was instrumental in affiliating Codrington with the University of Durham. He berated Barbados for its 'absence of culture, of literature and a taste for art and science', and 'the self-complacency, and narrow prejudice of its ruling society'.[28] Given this disdain for the rulers, one might have expected a greater sympathy for the aspirations of black Africans. But his somewhat haughty elitism prevented him from real engagement with popular religion and politics.

The Barbados church also had problems with the idea of black clergy. Richard Rawle, the Principal of Codrington in the 1850s and 1860s (and later to be Bishop of Trinidad) was enthusiastic about encouraging black people to engage in a West Indian mission to West Africa, particularly the Gambia (Rio Pongas). J. H. A. Duport, a young catechist trained at Codrington, went out as a missionary and in 1856 was ordained in Sierra Leone. But the Mission House did not long survive Rawle's tenure at Codrington.[29] One of its graduates, John Nathaniel Durant, of mixed race, felt a vocation to work in Barbados rather than go to Africa. He was

[27] Ibid., p. 198.

[28] Kortright Davis, *Cross and Crown in Barbados: Caribbean Political Religion in the Late 19th Century* (Frankfurt: Verlag Peter Lang, 1983), p. 19.

[29] G. C. Simmons, 'The History of Codrington College, Barbados 1710–1875', Doctor of Education dissertation, Graduate School of Education, Harvard University, 1962, pp. 158–63.

not ordained, and in 1860 attended the Philadelphia Divinity School, one of the first American Episcopalian seminaries to admit black people. He was ordained deacon in Virginia in 1869. His imminent return to Barbados precipitated a crisis in Barbados, and a special Act had to be passed by the Barbadian legislature to allow him to officiate as a clergyman in his home country. He was ordained priest in Barbados, but sent to Tobago, a less sensitive location with a weaker English elite – but even here, he was deployed as a curate to an incompetent priest from England. He never held a benefice in Barbados, but for many years served as chaplain to the Westbury cemetery in Bridgetown. Kortright Davis writes acerbically, 'The burial of the dead was the only official function to which the Anglican Church assigned Durant until his own death in July 1904.'[30]

One of Durant's problems, as far as the authorities were concerned, was that he was an outspoken and articulate critic of the status quo. The other black Barbadian priest at this period was E. Sandford Thomas. After excelling as a student at Codrington, he went to King's College, London. He was ordained deacon a year before Durant. Less radical than Durant, he was nevertheless kept in subordinate pastoral positions in the diocese until he was made a rector in 1884. It is not surprising that, given the reluctance to trust black people with responsible positions in the church in their homeland, few African Caribbeans felt attracted to the plan to send them as missionaries to Africa.

Barbadian society was defined by class and race consciousness, and this continually permeated the church. In 1831 black freedmen had objected to being obliged to sit in the slave gallery in St Michael's Cathedral, and demanded admittance to the pews. Forty years later, in 1870, Miss Eliza Goddard found herself passed over at the Communion rail because she had made the 'mistake' of coming forward along with the white people. Her formal complaint to the bishop was met with a lecture about keeping the rules. At this time there was debate about the inclusion of people of colour in church choirs – even though by far the greater part of the population was black or of mixed ancestry, and the Anglican church claimed the allegiance of 88.9 per cent of the population.[31] Yet, for black Barbadians a distinctive sense of standing over against white culture was more difficult to develop than in Jamaica. Barbados was 'little England'. This can be interpreted as 'colonisation of the consciousness' among an overwhelming black population with no biological or geographical connection with the British Isles; but also as an identification with a code

[30] Davis, *Cross and Crown*, p. 38. [31] Ibid., pp. 69–70.

of life which gave dignity and self-respect, akin to the 'Englishness' of Sierra Leone. George Lamming's great novel about growing up in Barbados, *In the Castle of my Skin*, expresses this memorably. Lamming recounts an incident in the Anglican church school in the 1930s. One student retells a story he has heard from an old woman in the neighbourhood, about how Queen Victoria had freed the slaves, including her. The schoolchildren are puzzled. They know about being freed from prison, but what was a slave? The teacher explains, but denies that the old woman could have been involved – it was too long ago.

> And moreover it had nothing to do with the people of Barbados. No one there was ever a slave, the teacher said. It was in another part of the world that those things happened. Not in Little England.[32]

Was this collective amnesia? Or was it a refusal to be conditioned by history, an assertion of freedom not simply from slavery but from its insidious legacy?

By the end of the century, black ordinands did not meet quite the same official discouragement as they had done earlier. It was becoming acceptable throughout the Caribbean for black men to become clergymen, even in the Anglican church. But the racial stratification which still obtained there, combined with the privileged position of clergy from England, meant that black people were grossly under-represented, not least in comparison with Methodists and Baptists.

AFRICAN CULTURE AND CARIBBEAN ANGLICANISM

'The Afro Caribbean Jamaican religious tradition has consistently reinterpreted Christianity in African, not European, cultural terms.'[33] Despite the inertia of the Church of England in Jamaica, by the time of Emancipation, in 1838, a good proportion of the population had had some contact with Christianity. Indeed, Christian adhesion and liberty went together. Dissenting chapels proliferated in 'free villages' away from the sway of the plantations. For the Anglicans, though the vestries and councils of the Anglican church continued to be dominated by white clergy and laity, the actual membership of the church became predominantly black. The structures of the church may have provided less scope for black leadership than did the Baptists or Methodists, but the

32 George Lamming, *In the Castle of my Skin* (Ann Arbor, MI: University of Michigan Press, 1991), pp. 57–8 (first published 1953).

33 Neil Parsanlal in *Caribbean Journal of Religious Studies* 17.1 (April 1996), p. 7.

established church was important in education. There was a certain cachet in being Anglican, not least for a growing African and mixed-race middle class. As Stewart puts it: 'The church allegiance of Jamaican blacks tended to be pragmatically flexible and simultaneous: they would shift their attachment for what European religious ministers saw as secular reasons.' People became members of the Anglican church 'while retaining truly affective and cognitive commitment to Afro-Creole religious groups and practices'.[34]

In Jamaica, as in other parts of the Caribbean, many aspects of traditional African culture and religious sensibilities survived in the new world. In the British Caribbean the term *obeah* was used to describe this African world. It particularly impacted on the lives of black folk in relation to the rites of passage: birth, marriage and death. 'To deprive them of their funeral rites seems to negroes a greater punishment than death itself', wrote the rector of St Catherine's, a statement which poignantly shows the incomprehension of the clergyman and the power and the tenacity with which people wrenched from their home country and kin endeavoured to honour the burial customs of their ancestors.[35] Divination was a powerful force in this regard, but an area of African cultural survival which had to be kept secret. *Obeah* was universally condemned by church leaders, Dissenters as well as Anglican. They portrayed it as the dying remnant of a superstitious religious system. Church leaders equally condemned *Myalism*, a synthesis of African and Christian elements. But, while Anglicans disdained African religious sensibilities in general, the Baptists were more responsive, and this was reinforced by the revival which swept Jamaica in 1861. The Anglican church, strongly imbued by this time with Anglo-Catholicism, was suspicious of the exuberant Evangelicalism which came to characterise much Caribbean Christianity. The plantation community, whose anxiety was augmented by the prolonged economic downturn which followed the freedom of the slaves, continued to be intolerant and isolationist.[36]

Nevertheless, in his study of Anglicanism and culture in the Bahamas (part of the diocese of Jamaica until 1861), Kirkley Sands paints a picture of a church which, despite its rigidities, did have strong appeal to Africans. Its educational provision and its rich Anglo-Catholic liturgy, combined with an awareness of the emotional appeal of religion, made

[34] Stewart, *Religion and Society*, p. xviii. [35] Minter, *Episcopacy without Episcopate*, p. 151.

[36] Winston Arthur Lawson, *Religion and Race: African and European Roots in Conflict – A Jamaican Testament* (New York: Peter Lang, 1996), pp. 65–8.

the Anglican church in the Bahamas attractive. By the late nineteenth century, a number of Baptists and other Dissenters had joined the church.[37] Sands also mentions how elements of African culture persisted, for example in the carnival-like celebrations of Junkanoo (Jonkanoo in Jamaica), and in the extra-liturgical celebrations around Christmas and New Year. In these cases the celebrations' cultural origins in West African yam festivals, rather than Myalism, with its political implications, rendered them relatively harmless.

HAITI AND THE EPISCOPAL MISSION

So far the story of Caribbean Anglicanism has been about its transplantation and hesitant adaptation (or non-adaptation) to the British West Indies. For many aspiring West Indian Anglicans, such as Gordon of Jamaica and Dupont in Barbados, the development of political and cultural self-consciousness among black people in the United States presented a contrast to their own situation, even though the position of black people in the USA was hardly ideal. In Haiti an Episcopal church developed which had nothing at all to do with British colonialism (and little to do with the American nationalism which often informed the white American Episcopalian missionary consciousness).[38] The mission to Haiti was pioneered by a remarkable African American. James Theodore Holly was born in 1829, the son of free parents 'of color'. Educated in Brooklyn, he became deeply involved as a young man in the abolition movement, a friend of Frederick Douglass. He had had a Roman Catholic upbringing, but in 1852, while in Detroit, was confirmed as an Episcopalian. Some years before Robert Gordon, he worked among freed slaves who had settled in Canada.

In 1855 Holly was ordained deacon, by the Bishop of Michigan, and priested in 1856. He had become interested in the possibility of Haiti as more congenial for black settlement than the African colonisation programmes devised by white Americans. Haiti had particular resonance for black people in America because of Toussaint L'Ouverture, who had led a slave revolt against the French in 1791 and founded a black republic.

[37] Kirkley Sands, 'The Anglican Church and Bahamian Cultural Identity: The Role of Church-Sponsored Education, Prayer Book Liturgy and Anglo-Catholic Rituals in the Development of Bahamian Culture 1784–1900', unpublished Ph.D. dissertation, University of Edinburgh, 1998.

[38] Ian Douglas, *Fling out the Banner! The National Church Ideal and the Foreign Mission of the Episcopal Church* (New York: Church Hymnal Corporation, 1996).

Denied official recognition for a missionary venture by the Episcopal Church's Board of Missions, Holly embarked on the mission nevertheless, and began a fifty-year association with Haiti. Holly had been initiated into Freemasonry, a badge of honour for an aspiring black American middle-class man at this period. Many of the Haitian elite were also Masons, and, given Catholic opposition, Holly hoped to influence them. The work did not win large numbers of converts. But it was successful in attracting idealistic black Americans to the mission, which betokened black initiative and self-esteem.

The lack of endorsement by ECUSA was frustrating for Holly, as it limited the resources on which he could call. But he had the confidence to go ahead with an enterprise clearly managed by blacks for blacks. He named the church L'Eglise Orthodoxe Apostolique Haitienne. Rather against the odds, in 1874, Holly did persuade ECUSA that the Haitian church needed a bishop and that Holly was the right man for that position. Bishop Holly continued to struggle to build up his little church until his death in 1911. At that stage the church had some 2,000 members, twelve priests and two deacons – the numbers reveal both the difficulty of making much headway in Catholic Haiti and the attractiveness of the enterprise to young educated African American and Caribbean men who constituted the majority of its clergy. After Holly's death the church asked formally to become a mission district of the Episcopal Church, and it had a succession of white bishops until the election of a native Haitian in 1971, Luc Garnier.[39] Despite the strong American economic and strategic interest in Haiti (including military occupation in the early part of the twentieth century), members of the Episcopal Church have remained a small minority, estimated at 1.3 per cent of the total population.[40]

THE CHURCH AND CARIBBEAN SOCIETY IN THE TWENTIETH CENTURY

By the twentieth century, Caribbean Anglicanism remained a powerful force, still linked to British colonialism in its structure and mentality, but with a large black majority, whose 'ownership' of the church was given only grudging public expression. The church now faced new challenges

[39] David M. Dean, *Defender of the Race: James Theodore Holly, Black Nationalist Bishop* (Boston: Lambeth Press, 1979).

[40] David Barrett, George T. Kurian and Todd M. Johnson, *World Christian Encyclopedia* (2 vols., Oxford: Oxford University Press), Volume 1, p. 339.

from political movements which were even more assertive of black values and aspirations. In 1917 Marcus Garvey, a Jamaican, founded in New York the Universal Negro Improvement Association, which soon established branches throughout the British Caribbean as well as in the States. Garveyism has become one of the definitive political movements of twentieth-century Jamaica, as well as having a profound effect on Pan-Africanism in Africa. It is difficult to imagine the Anglican leadership of the 1920s having a good word to say for Garveyism. Nevertheless, there is an interesting Anglican connection, in the person of George Alexander McGuire. McGuire had something of Holly's ambition and persistence, as well as a desire to show the competence of the 'black race'. He was an Antiguan, son of a Moravian mother and an Anglican father, born in 1866. Moving to the States, he was ordained (as deacon in 1896 and as priest in 1897) and had a varied career in the States, including serving as rector of St Thomas' Church, Philadelphia, the church of Absalom Jones and the oldest black Episcopal church in the USA. His father-in-law was Bishop William Montgomery Brown of Arkansas, who had controversially campaigned for a separate 'black' diocese in the American South.

McGuire himself moved back to his native Antigua in 1913, and in 1919 Garvey appointed him as the chaplain-general of his new movement. It was at this point that McGuire decided to abandon his Episcopalian allegiance and establish an independent church for African people, which he named the African Orthodox Church (was he mindful of James Holly's name for the church in Haiti?). McGuire received bishop's orders from Joseph René Vilatte in 1921. He probably hoped that Garvey would recognise the church as the religious arm of the Universal Negro Improvement Association. This Garvey was not prepared to do. McGuire had to accept that the two movements would remain distinct. But he did devise some liturgical compositions for the Association. They show his Anglican roots, often adapting collects of the Book of Common Prayer explicitly to express a non-racial message:

> O God, who has made of one blood all nations of men for to dwell on the face of the whole earth . . . Grant that men everywhere may seek after Thee and find Thee. Bring all nations into one fold and hasten the day of Universal brotherhood.[41]

[41] Randall K. Burkett, *Garveyism as a Religious Movement* (Metuchen, NJ: Scarecrow, 1979), pp. 71–4.

His 'Universal Negro Catechism', while not so derivative of the Book of Common Prayer, has a similar form and spirit:

> Q. Did God make any group or race of men superior to another?
> A. No, He created all races equal, and of one blood, to dwell on the face of the earth.[42]

Both Garveyism and the African Orthodox Church were to have an influence in Africa. In Uganda a young Anglican, Reuben Spartas, obtained copies of the Universal Negro Improvement Association newsletter, *The Negro World*. In 1929, at the end of the Sunday service in Bombo, he announced the formation of a new church for 'all right thinking people', all who wanted to be 'masters in their own house and not house-boys'. A small but vigorous African Orthodox Church continues to exist in Uganda.[43]

THE ANGLICAN CHURCH IN THE POST-COLONIAL CARIBBEAN

Men like Gordon and Durant, Holly and McGuire, show that there were black Anglicans who had a vision for a church in which English race superiority was displaced, and pride in black identity was affirmed. They represented most immediately the educated black middle class, a group most clearly constrained by the racial stereotypes of white Creole society. But they were a tiny minority of the overall population of the West Indies. Their first interest was not in rescuing and restoring African values – to have done so would often have been to detract from their claim to be admitted into 'civilised' society. Meanwhile large groups of ordinary black people – peasants and agricultural labourers, the small urban proletariat and lower-middle-class people – found spiritual sustenance in the Anglican liturgy, enlivened to a limited extent by extra-liturgical services and customs. Membership of the church had a prestige, it was important for educational purposes and it provided a cohesive community ethic, even if it was not as alert to the potential of black leadership as were the Baptists and Methodists. At the top, the church remained remarkably dependent not simply on white leadership but on leadership from Britain. There had been a sprinkling of white Creole bishops since the late nineteenth century, but the first bishop of African ancestry, Percival William Gibson, was only consecrated in 1956.[44]

[42] Ibid., pp. 71–4. [43] Fred Welbourn, *East African Rebels* (London: SCM Press, 1961), Chapter 5.
[44] Dayfoot, *The Shaping of the West Indian Church*, p. 209.

In the 1960s and 1970s, the era of political independence, there was rapid change in the church.

Dioceses typically now had local bishops rather than English imports; the majority of the clergy were black. In the 1970s, as the Black Power movement provided much of the intellectual energy for those discontented with the status quo in society or government, there grew up an articulate clergy ready to question the traditions of a conservative church. The Anglican church still seemed too tied to English values and personnel.[45] In the 1970s Knolly Clarke, a parish priest from Trinidad, expressed the problem of Anglican worship by quoting a character from Austin Clarke's novel *Easter Carol*:

> I was the only one in my village who belonged to the Church of England. My mother, who was brought up in this Church, had recently started to attend the Church of the Nazarene because she felt its services were more like a part of her life, more emotional, more exciting, more tragic and more happy . . . There she could clap her hands and stamp her feet till the floor boards creaked with emotion, and jump up in the air and praise God and for all that feel God was listening. But in the Church of England she was regimented to sit-and-stand exercise of dull, religious drilling.[46]

Although the Community of the Resurrection, which had been invited to run Codrington College in 1955, assisted in an imaginative revising of the Communion service for the Church of the Province of the West Indies, it is unlikely that their efforts did much to address the issues raised in *Easter Carol*.[47] That had to wait for a more general questioning of the place of the Anglican church in an independent West Indies.

The Antiguan Anglican theologian Kortright Davis, in his *Emancipation Still Comin'*, describes four phases in the Caribbean church's relation to the people. It began as 'The Church and the People', in which the 'people' were seen as a threat. In post-Emancipation times it became 'The Church for the People', providing educational and social welfare. The post-colonial church now emphasises that it is 'The Church of the People', in which clergy attempt to incorporate African spirituality into the worship of the church. But there is, says Davis, a fourth stage, 'The

[45] Claude Berkley, 'Partnership is a Leaky Ship: An Evaluation of the Relationship between the Church in the Province of the West Indies (CPWI) and the United Society for the Propagation of the Gospel since the Time of Independence', unpublished M.Phil. dissertation, University of Birmingham, September 2000.

[46] Knolly Clarke, 'Liturgy and Culture in the Caribbean: What is to be Done?', in Idris Hamid (ed.), *Troubling of the Waters* (San Fernando, Trinidad: St Andrew's Theological College, 1973), p. 141.

[47] The presence of the Community of the Resurrection from Mirfield in the North of England can be seen as a belated fulfilment of Codrington's will.

Table 5.1. *Anglicans as a percentage of the total population*

	1900 (%)	2000 (%)
Barbados	75.0	28.6
Antigua and Barbuda	47.0	33.3
Bahamas	46.0	08.9
Jamaica	39.0	04.0
St Kitts and Nevis	28.4	25.1
Haiti	0.1	1.3

Source: Barrett, Kurian and Johnson, *World Christian Encyclopedia*, Volume 1, pp. 70, 93, 101, 339, 409, 635.

People's Church', in which the clericalism of the church is replaced by an acknowledgement that it is the people as a community who constitute a church. 'It is taking a long time to move to this.'[48] For Davis this new emancipation will not be given from above, but must be grasped by the people themselves. For centuries they have, in a way, done this surreptitiously, through covert strategems.

> The black Anglican archbishop in solemn procession in his cathedral has much more in common with the Spiritual Baptist archbishop in his mourning ceremony and the orisha priest at his palais ritual, than he may realize.[49]

The Anglican church is now a small minority even in those Caribbean societies where it formerly had a formal establishment status, as shown in Table 5.1.

Other denominations are now more likely to be seen as allies than as rivals in the attempt to make the church a people's church. Pentecostalism is more of a problem, not least because of its dynamism, and its lack of concern for traditional denominational boundaries. Charismatic forms penetrate the liturgy and life of the parishes, especially among the young, whose allegiance to the Anglican church cannot be taken for granted. Pentecostalism is critical of the political theology espoused by many young Anglican priests at the time of independence. It may appear to be yet another manifestation of American values. In earlier times, the United States offered an attractive alternative to the hide-bound colonialism of Caribbean society. Now its pervasive cultural and religious influence

[48] Kortright Davis, *Emancipation Still Comin': Explorations in Caribbean Emancipatory Theology* (Maryknoll: Orbis, 1990), p. 72.
[49] Ibid., p. 63.

on the Caribbean seems more ambiguous, blamed for the sexual permissiveness which erodes society's cohesion, and yet offering a new ethical conservatism. This often appears unsympathetic to age-old Caribbean family realities, which have never conformed to Christian ideals,[50] and hostile to gay rights. Archbishop Drexel Gomez (of the Bahamas) has taken a particularly hard line in the crisis over homosexuality.

There is still in Caribbean Anglicanism a reluctance to give a voice to women. Davis says:

> Women are by far the dominant sector, numerically, in the life of the church in the Caribbean, just as they are in other areas of the Christian world. The lifeblood of the church would be seriously malnourished if women were to withdraw their full participation and support. Yet church leaders in the Caribbean continue to be ambivalent and hesitant about the significance of such participation and about the value of women in the leadership structures of the Christian movement.[51]

These remain pressing moral issues for Caribbean Anglicanism, but can only be addressed satisfactorily in an ecumenical context.

[50] J. L. Springer, 'West Indian Value Systems and the Church's Validating Role', in Hamid, *Troubling of the Waters*, pp. 125–38.

[51] Davis, *Emancipation Still Comin'*, pp. 90–1.

CHAPTER 6

Latin America

Latin America is different from almost all other regions in that neither British colonialism nor the widespread diffusion of the English language has been a major factor in the development of the Anglican church. Anglicanism in Ireland and Australia has been confronted by a strong and cohesive Catholic culture, but in both cases the Anglican church has traditionally been part of the 'establishment'. Trinidad and Quebec are areas with Catholic majorities which pre-date British rule, but the Anglican church gained prestige once the British took over. Anglicanism in Latin America is numerically weak, even insignificant. According to Anglican statistics, the Igreja Episcopal Anglicana do Brasil has 103,021 members (out of a population of about 150 million). The Province of the Southern Cone (Argentina, Chile, Bolivia, Paraguay, Uruguay and Peru) has 22,490 members. Episcopal membership in Central America (from Mexico to Ecuador) amounts to perhaps 40,000.[1] Protestants in an overwhelmingly Catholic culture have traditionally faced problems of state hostility. For some Anglicans, particularly from the Anglo-Catholic tradition, there has also been a reluctance to proselytise in a Catholic country. The 1910 Edinburgh conference on world mission excluded Protestant work in Latin America on these grounds, though it was recognised by the International Missionary Council of Jerusalem in 1928.

Anglican work began primarily as a pastoral initiative for British (and later American) expatriates. But it was not confined to expatriates. The South American Missionary Society combined concern for English-speaking people with a missionary zeal to reach the Native American (Indian) peoples. The missionary work of ECUSA, in contrast, especially in Brazil, was from the beginning focused on the Hispanic population. A fourth, important strand of work has been ministry to migrant workers

[1] *The Church of England Year Book 2000* (London: Church House Publishing, 2000), pp. 336, 341, 360.

from the English-speaking Caribbean islands, who from the late nineteenth century worked on plantations and railway and canal building in Central America and who settled permanently.

With the collapse of Spanish and Portuguese power in Latin America in the early and mid nineteenth century, there was a large fund of goodwill for Britain among newly independent states. British naval superiority could prevent attempts to reimpose the old order. Brazil became the first state to allow the British to establish a chaplaincy. The royal family of Brazil had been in exile in Britain during the Napoleonic Wars and had warm feelings towards their protector. The Catholic church generally was opposed to allowing Protestants to gain a foothold, but the Bishop of Rio spoke in favour of allowing the English to establish a chapel:

> The English really have no religion at all, but they are a proud and obstinate race. If we oppose their wish in this matter, they will not only persist in it more and more, but will make it a matter of infinite importance. But if, on the other hand, we give way to them, they will build their chapels, and no one will ever go there.[2]

The former Spanish territories were even more suspicious. Permission to build a chapel in Valparaiso, Chile, was granted 'only if the building was behind a high board fence and without a steeple or bell'.[3] But chapels were allowed in Rio (1819), Buenos Aires (1825), Valparaiso (1841), Montevideo (1845) and Lima (1849). British commercial interests in South America were strong throughout the nineteenth century, ensuring a continuous number of expatriates, especially in Argentina.

THE WORK OF THE SOUTH AMERICAN MISSIONARY SOCIETY

Direct evangelistic work among the nominally Catholic populations of South America was thus prohibited by governments and discouraged by British officials concerned with good relations. An opportunity for mission did, however, present itself among Native American societies which appeared remote from Hispanic culture and religion. In 1844 Captain Allen Gardiner established his Patagonian Missionary Society. After his death it was renamed the South American Missionary Society (SAMS).[4]

[2] Quoted in Douglas Milmine, *The History of Anglicanism in Latin America* (London: South American Missionary Society, 1994). This is Milmine's translation of his book *La Comunión Anglican en America Latina* (Santiago, Chile: La Verdad os Hará Libres, 1993).

[3] Quoted by John Sinclair, 'Historical Protestantism', in Paul E. Sigmund (ed.), *Religious Freedom and Evangelization in Latin America: The Challenge of Religious Pluralism* (Maryknoll: Orbis, 1999).

[4] Phyllis Thompson, *An Unquenchable Flame: The Story of Captain Allen Gardiner, Founder of the South American Missionary Society* (London: Hodder & Stoughton, 1983).

Gardiner had had a colourful career, ranging from South Africa to Bolivia.[5] Finally he settled on the island of Tierra del Fuego (Patagonia) as the theatre for his sustained missionary endeavour. He saw the people as 'degraded', with 'no name for God', but mercifully spared contact with Spanish Catholicism. His attempts to reach the Yahgan Indians eventually led to his death. All four members of his missionary expedition died of hunger and exposure in 1851, an event which served to awaken interest in the enterprise. Charles Darwin was one of the most unlikely, but nevertheless enthusiastic, supporters of SAMS. On the *Beagle* in 1831, he had travelled back to England with some Patagonians. He was disturbed by the wretched state of the people he encountered in Tierra del Fuego, and saw mission as the most likely way to redeem them. In fact, by the end of the nineteenth century, the Yahgan people were well on the way to extinction.

Although SAMS became important for providing pastoral ministry in a number of expatriate churches, the heart of its work has been among two groups of South American Indians: the Araucanian Indians in Chile and the Chaco Indians of Paraguay and northern Argentina. Allen Gardiner Jr, like his father, attempted to establish work among the Mapuche people of Araucania, still in the 1860s outside Chile's jurisdiction. Eventually in the 1880s the Mapuche agreed to become part of Chile in return for a certain amount of autonomy. Their ability to maintain some decision making with regard to land was important for the survival of the Mapuche as a people. In the 1890s SAMS finally established a permanent mission at Cholchol, work associated with Charles Sadleir, who began translation work into the local (Mapudungu) language. Some of the success of the early twentieth century is attributed to the educational provision of the Society. In 1925 Chile made basic education compulsory. The government valued the Anglican contribution and provided grants to Anglican schools, but insisted on Spanish as the medium for instruction. SAMS was going through a particularly lean financial patch at this period and, perhaps against its better judgement, was willing to accept state aid. The basic evangelistic work was given a boost in the 1930s by two dedicated Mapuche evangelists, Segundo Cayul and Juan Antinao, who did much to spread the Gospel beyond the mission station. They were to become the first indigenous clergy.[6]

[5] Milmine, *History*, p. 7.

[6] Wendy Mann, *An Unquenched Flame: A Short History of the South American Missionary Society* (London: SAMS, 1968), pp. 30–8. Milmine, *History*, p. 22.

The work in Paraguay is associated with the pioneering evangelism of W. Barbrooke Grubb, a Scot whose intense commitment to the local people earned him the epithet 'the Livingstone of South America'. He first established work among the Lengua Indians of the Paraguayan Chacos in 1888, extending this to work among the Mataco and Toba people in northern Argentina. His other epithet, 'The Pacifier of the Indians', illustrates the dilemma of the missionary among the ethnic minorities of South America: how far should missionaries collaborate with the extension of state control and the incorporation of Indians into the dominant culture? Grubb aimed to uplift and enhance the peoples as he encountered them, and, to that end, he established a Chaco Indian Association, with strong developmental work. This has continued to be a strong feature of Anglican work in the Chacos regions of both Paraguay and Argentina. The Anglican church has served to protect and advance Indian rights and to help to establish viable economic enterprise. Bishop Maurice Sinclair talks of the contribution to 'the gradual resuscitation of a dying, aboriginal race'.[7] But the problem for the church in sustaining such a task was highlighted by the decline of the diocese of northern Argentina's project work in the aftermath of the 1984 Falklands War, and the departure of foreign personnel which ensued. These areas have remained generally economically backward and marginal. More recently the Anglican church has extended its mission to the Criollo (Spanish-speaking) inhabitants of the Chacos. There are many areas of conflict between the needs of Indians, disadvantaged by their lack of legal title to their tribal lands, and Criollo cattle keepers.[8]

BRAZIL

Although Lusophone Brazil was in many ways more open and hospitable than Spanish America to British evangelistic endeavour, British missionaries were slow to exploit the opportunities. American Episcopalians have largely built up what has become numerically the most important Anglican work on the continent. Episcopalian missionaries had first made attempts to establish a mission in northern Brazil (around Bahia) in the 1850s, but the work had languished. The disestablishment of the Catholic church in 1889 and a law guaranteeing freedom of religion presented new

[7] Milmine, *History*, p. 18

[8] Calvin Miller and Ian Wallace, 'A Review of Iniciativa Cristiana of the Diocese of Northern Argentina and Tear Fund' [n.d., early 1990s]. In the SAMS Library Collection, Crowther Hall, Selly Oak, Birmingham.

opportunities, and in that year Evangelical Episcopalians established permanent work in the far South, at Porte Alegre in Rio Grande do Sul Province. One of this group of missionaries, Lucien Lee Kinsolving, became bishop in 1899, and in 1907 the work came directly under the authority of ECUSA. Kinsolving remained in office until 1928. The mission found a response, particularly among professional people and city dwellers, attracted to the liturgical order and intellectual freedom of Anglicanism. It was also able to recruit a local clergy – by 1928 there were thirty Brazilian priests; by 1950, fifty. The first Brazilian bishop was Dr Athalicio Pithan, who became suffragan bishop in 1940 and died in 1966.

From the beginning of the twentieth century there was a substantial immigration of Japanese to work as tea, coffee and cotton planters in the areas around Rio and São Paulo in central Brazil. A Japanese sailor, Yasogi Ito, pioneered Japanese contacts with the Episcopal Church. Having survived a shipwreck, Ito began a religious quest, which led him to conversion to Christianity, through the Episcopal Church in Brazil. In 1923 he was encouraged by the Anglican Bishop of Tokyo to study for the priesthood. He returned to Brazil and held the first Anglican Japanese service for the growing community of Japanese migrants in Brazil. By the 1960s a third of the membership of the diocese of central Brazil were of Japanese origin, and in 1977 Dr Sumio Takatsu was elected as Bishop of São Paulo.

In the 1970s Edmund K. Sherrill became Bishop of North Brazil. He was the son of a former presiding bishop of ECUSA, Henry Knox Sherrill, who had been active in promoting Episcopal missions. A lively evangelistic work was initiated there with Paulo Garcia.[9] In 1965 Brazil was the first of the Latin American Anglican churches to become autonomous – 'emancipation', as it was called in Brazil itself. The Brazilian church felt ready to assume responsibility for its life and mission. But it did feel uneasy about the way in which ECUSA cut off funding. Bishop Soares felt that this had been a mistake, assuming that the middle-class backbone of the church in Brazil was able to assume the whole burden of church finance, but without taking into account the severe pressures on professional salaries which inflation was having at this time. The professional background of many Brazilian bishops (there is a strong representation of lawyers) and the intellectual sophistication which it has developed contrasts strongly with the native Indian congregations of

[9] Mardi Mauney, *Episcopal Windows on Brazil* (New York: Episcopal Church Centre, 1998). Milmine, *History*, pp. 46–8.

Argentina, Paraguay and Chile. Younger Brazilian Episcopal clergy have been more willing to utilise the language of liberation theology than in other parts of the Anglican church in Latin America, and to articulate political concerns during the authoritarian regimes of the 1960s to the 1990s. The Episcopal Church in Brazil was the first Anglican church in Latin America to admit women to the priesthood, and has been notably more willing to conduct an open debate on homosexuality (though this has itself produced internal tensions).

CENTRAL AMERICA

Anglicanism in Central America[10] has both British and American roots, and is characterised by the strong presence in many countries of English-speaking black Caribbean workers. But the proximity of the United States has meant that American culture cannot be ignored, and this is as true of the Episcopal Church as of other aspects of life. In the 1950s most of the Anglican and Episcopal work in the area was grouped under Province IX of ECUSA. More recently many national churches in Central America have become autonomous provinces.

As a result of the growth of liberalism in Mexico, there occurred, in 1857, a secession from the Catholic church, led by Padre Manuel Aguas. He called his church the Church of Jesus (Iglesia di Jesus). In 1859 he invited the Episcopal Church to collaborate with them, but ECUSA was insufficiently prepared fully to seize the opportunity. It did send a missionary, Henry Chauncey Riley, and he eventually became bishop in Mexico in 1879. But previously he had divided his time between assisting the Reformed Episcopal churches in Spain and Portugal and the work in Mexico. The Mexican Episcopal Church catered as much for expatriate Americans as for the discontented Mexican Catholics who had first initiated the work. By 1910 there were twenty-one English-speaking congregations with fourteen clergy, compared with thirty-five Hispanic congregations with only ten clergy. The strong anti-clericalism unleashed by the 1910 revolution brought further hard times. But in more recent years the church has developed ministries with a wide cross-section of the Mexican population: professional people, peasants, Indians, and English speakers.

[10] See three articles in *Anglican and Episcopal History* 57 (1988): John Kater, Jr, 'At Home in Latin America: Anglicanism in a New Context', pp. 4–37; John Kater, Jr, 'The Beginnings of the Episcopal Church in Panama, 1852–1904', pp. 147–58; and Robert Renouf, 'Anglicanism in Nicaragua, 1745–1985', pp. 382–96.

American influence is predominant throughout Central America. But in many parts there was an earlier British or British Caribbean presence. The British occupied Belize (British Honduras) from the late eighteenth century until 1974. There was at first a joint Anglican–Presbyterian establishment, with a succession of Evangelical chaplains, divided in their loyalties between black woodcutters who had escaped slavery in the islands and white adventurers who would have liked nothing better than to re-enslave the black population. The SPG eventually began a ministry specifically to Jamaican contract labourers, but in 1947 the main responsibility for the church passed to ECUSA. In 1900 some 21 per cent of the population nominally belonged to the Anglican church. Even in 1970 it was 13 per cent. But by 2000 this percentage had dropped to 4.2 per cent.[11]

Jamaican, Trinidadian and Barbadian economic migration to Central America increased markedly in the latter part of the nineteenth century. Black Caribbeans looked for work on the banana, tea and coffee plantations, in the mines, and as navvies on the railways and in the construction of the Panama Canal. Black Anglicans became the nucleus of Episcopal work in Costa Rica, Guatemala, Honduras, Nicaragua and Panama. In Panama, particularly, the relatively large presence of American workers in the Canal Zone meant that certain segregationist features of the southern states were replicated.[12] Unlike the Americans, blacks have settled permanently in these countries. Anglican work has thus become progressively more Hispanic as the next generation have adopted Spanish, in addition to or instead of English. Many of the first generation of local bishops have tended to be Spanish speakers of British Caribbean origin, such as Bishop Lemuel Shirley, a Panamanian citizen who became bishop in 1971.[13]

An Anglican presence in the Spanish-speaking islands of the Caribbean largely originates from American Episcopalian influence. In the Dominican Republic, the work was conducted under the auspices of the Haiti Episcopal Church. During the Trujillo dictatorship from 1930 to 1961, an American missionary, Charles Barnes, was executed for publicising details of the massacres of Dominican citizens. Work in Cuba

[11] Wallace R. Johnson, *A History of Christianity in Belize, 1776–1838* (Washington: University Press of America, 1985). The statistics are from David Barrett, George T. Kurian and Todd M. Johnson, *World Christian Encyclopedia* (2 vols., (Oxford: Oxford University Press, 2001), Volume 1, pp. 107–9.

[12] Ian T. Douglas, *Fling out the Banner! The National Church Ideal and the Foreign Mission of the Episcopal Church* (New York: Church Hymnal Corporation, 1996), pp. 111–12.

[13] Milmine, *History*, pp. 58–75.

began in earnest in the aftermath of the independence war of 1895, and the subsequent war between America and Spain. One of its chief American architects in the early twentieth century was Bishop Hiram Richard Hulse, a Christian socialist. He in turn deeply influenced Bishop Romualdo Gonzales, who was bishop in the early years of the Castro regime, 1961–6. During the Castro years, the Episcopal Church, like all other Christian bodies, has been under pressure. In view of its American connections, the Episcopal Church has had to stress its autonomy (it is not part of Province IX of ECUSA!).[14] In 2000 the Cuban Anglican community numbered 3,000, which is tiny compared with the 74,000 in 1960. The factors which led to the expansion of Cuban Episcopalianism in the early part of the twentieth century – the espousal of liberal democratic values and the opportunity for entrepreneurial and professional advance – were strongly associated with the USA, and became a liability once the unyielding hostility of America to the Castro regime became entrenched. Moreover, Cuban Episcopalians were precisely that section of the community whose social standing made emigration to the USA attractive.

THE FUTURE OF ANGLICANISM IN LATIN AMERICA

Bishop David Leane has talked of Anglicanism in Latin America as 'an empty bus desperately needing to be filled'.[15] There has always been a strong optimism among people involved in mission in South America that there is an Anglican-shaped gap in Latin American spirituality just waiting to be filled. Anglicans have consistently noted that Latin America is 'not as Roman Catholic' as would seem at first glance, with perhaps only 20 per cent of the total population having more than a superficial encounter with Catholicism (figures vary, but all are more or less based on subjective criteria). The general Catholic shaping of culture is acknowledged. Anglicanism seems perfectly designed to appeal to those dissatisfied with the Catholic church, but for whom colour and liturgy and a sacramental approach to life are more appealing than Protestant alternatives. Unfortunately for this optimistic view, the evidence seems to point to a great increase in Protestantism, particularly in its Pentecostal

[14] Douglas, *Fling out the Banner*, p. 103.

[15] Patrick Butler, 'The Growth of the Evangelical Church in South America and the Place of the Anglican Church within that Movement', unpublished dissertation, All Nations College, 1994, p. 11. In the SAMS Library Collection, Crowther Hall, Selly Oak, Birmingham.

forms, rather than to the modified forms of Catholic worship and the cerebral literary (biblical) focus which many see as typical of Evangelical Anglicanism. The 'Anglican' nomenclature, so advantageous in the nineteenth century, had become a liability as a result of the Falklands War. In 1984 the tiny Peruvian church decided to drop the term altogether, and call itself the Iglesia Cristiano Episcopal del Peru (rather than Anglicano Episcopal). Bishop Stirling's diocese of the Falkland Islands had once been the largest diocese in the world. In 1977 the Falkland Islands (Malvinas) were reluctant to become part of the new Anglican Province of South America, and eventually came under the direct jurisdiction of the Archbishop of Canterbury.[16]

Although the SAMS work among Indian communities of Chile, Argentina and Paraguay has been outstanding in its faithfulness and attention to development issues, it has to be said that, with a few exceptions, the work remains marginal to these communities. The economic and cultural precariousness of the native Indian communities has, according to Bishop Milmine, inhibited the development of a self-confident Christian community willing to take charge of its own affairs or to assert its presence in the nation. In contrast, the Brazilian church has always had a strong sense of the possibility of engagement in national affairs. These distinctions are clearly factors in the differing responses of the Anglican churches to the homosexual debate. A visitor to the Araucanian churches of Chile in 1990 presented a picture of extreme discomfort at changes in the wider Anglican community, in particular on the questions of women's ordination and homosexuality.[17] In contrast, the Brazilian church has been more open to debating the issue, and moves for gay rights within the church have received some episcopal support. It is significant that social attitudes to sexuality in Brazil tend to be both more varied and generally more tolerant. In advocating a more indigenous theology, the Brazilian priest Jaci Maraschin encourages the Brazilian church to develop and deepen its involvement in the social issues of Brazilian society, to encourage a contextual reading of Scripture, to devise its own liturgy expressive of our 'bodily culture . . . in gestures, dances and songs', and to cultivate a pastoral style of theological

[16] Peter J. Millam, 'A Brief History of the Diocese of the Falkland Islands', 1996. In the SAMS Library Collection, Crowther Hall, Selly Oak, Birmingham.

[17] Ian Prior, 'A Study of the Iglesia Anglicana de Chile'. Unpublished report of a visit, September 1990. In the SAMS Library Collection, Crowther Hall, Selly Oak, Birmingham.

thinking.[18] Despite its relative insignificance, the theologian Samuel Escobar commends the Anglican church in Latin America for the diversity of its work. It is, he says, 'the only non-Roman Church that is effectively evangelizing all levels of society'.[19] But the image of the empty bus evoked by Bishop Leane remains a poignant one.

[18] Jaci Maraschin, in Andrew Wingate, Kevin Ward, Carrie Pemberton and Wilson Sitshebo (eds.), *Anglicanism: A Global Communion* (London: Mowbray, 1998), p. 150.

[19] Butler, 'The Growth of the Evangelical Church', p. 11.

CHAPTER 7

West Africa

QUAQUE: THE FIRST AFRICAN ANGLICAN PRIEST

Anglican engagement with Africa coincided with British involvement in the Atlantic slave trade. The Society for the Propagation of the Gospel (SPG) responded to requests for a chaplain for the British traders on the Gold Coast of West Africa (present-day Ghana), appointing Thomas Thompson to serve as chaplain to the Castle, the British fort at Cape Coast. Thompson stayed from 1751 to 1756, when ill health (the constant hazard for Europeans before effective treatment for malaria became available in the late nineteenth century) caused him to return home. His main task was to provide pastoral service to the transient European traders and the mixed-race community at the Castle. The slave trade being the sole reason for the existence of the fort, missionary work was difficult to undertake. Long after he left Africa, in 1772, Thompson wrote a pamphlet defending the slave trade – the very year of the Mansfield judgement, which undermined the legal basis for slavery in England itself. But one of Thompson's actions did have missionary consequences. In 1754, he had arranged with a local chief, Caboceer Cudjoe [Kodwo], to send three youths to England to be educated. Two of the boys died, but the third, Quaque (Kwaku), who was thirteen, survived and was baptised Philip. In 1765 he was appointed by the SPG to minister at the Castle. Before leaving England, he was ordained deacon and priest and thus became the first African (and, indeed, non-white) priest of the Anglican communion. As well as chaplain, he was to be 'missionary, school master and catechist to the Negroes on the Gold Coast'. Quaque remained in this position for over fifty years. His first wife, the Englishwoman Catherine Blunt, died soon after their arrival. He had to confront prejudice and obstacles in accomplishing both parts of his job, not made easy by what has been described as the 'scandalous neglect' of his Society.[1]

[1] Daniel O'Connor, *Three Centuries of Mission: The United Society for the Propagation of the Gospel 1701–2000* (London: Continuum, 2000), p. 27.

As a young missionary, Quaque sought advice from one of the most distinguished New England Episcopal clergymen, Samuel Johnson, a supporter of the SPG's work. Two letters have survived from what seems to have been a larger correspondence. They poignantly express his hopes and frustrations. Quaque is pleased to hear of the 'flourishing condition of the body of Christ in your parts ... Notwithstanding the efforts of the Presbyterians and our Dissenters'. In Africa, he says, our problems are of an altogether different order:

> the stir of religion and its everlasting recompense is not so much in vogue as the vicious practice of purchasing flesh and blood like oxen in market places.[2]

Quaque's perspective on the slave trade differed substantially from Thompson's. In the letter, Quaque alludes to the breakdown of stable relationships engendered by the slave trade. He speaks of the disdain with which he is often regarded by the traders, the hostility of the 'mulatto' men to their women attending his classes, and his general pessimism about the success of his mission.

Quaque did live to welcome the British legislation which ended the slave trade. He died, in 1816, on the brink of a new era in missionary work in West Africa. After his death a school was established in his honour by a 'Bible band' at the Castle, and it was this group which in 1822 invited Methodists to come to Ghana. Methodists and Presbyterians, rather than Anglicans, were decisively to influence this part of West Africa for Christianity.

EQUIANO OLAUDAH: AFRICAN ABOLITIONIST

Quaque's life has a somewhat elegiac character,[3] very different from that of his contemporary Equiano Olaudah. *The Interesting Narrative of the Life of Olaudah Equiano* was first published in 1789. It is one of the great abolitionist writings, and a profound spiritual autobiography.[4] Olaudah

[2] Herbert and Carol Schneider (eds.), *Samuel Johnson, President of King's College: His Career and Writings: Volume I* (New York: Columbia University Press, 1929), p. 425. Letters from Quaque, 26 November 1767 and 5 April 1769.

[3] Something of this elegiac quality is admirably conveyed in a novel by Arthur Japin, *The Two Hearts of Kwasi Boachi*, translated from the Dutch by Ina Rilke (New York: Knopf, 2000). The novel, based on historical events, describes the experiences of two cousins, Akan boys, sent to the Netherlands in the early nineteenth century.

[4] There are many modern versions of *Equiano's Travels*, including a Penguin Classic edited and introduced by Vincent Carretta (1995) and a scholarly facsimile of the first edition, *The Life of Olaudah Equiano, or Gustavus Vassa, the African, 1789*, with a new introduction by Paul Edwards (2 vols., London: Dawsons of Pall Mall, 1969).

was born in the Igbo region of what is now Nigeria in the 1740s. He was about eleven years old when he was enslaved and taken to Barbados, and then to Virginia. He had a variety of owners and was given various names. Olaudah spent many years at sea, and visited England, where he was baptised in 1759. He obtained his freedom in 1766, but remained at sea; in 1774 he had an Evangelical conversion experience while in Cadiz harbour. In 1779 he approached the Bishop of London about being ordained as a missionary to Africa, but no action was taken. By now Olaudah was a recognised leader of the growing black population of London. He became an active abolitionist when, in 1783, he contacted Granville Sharp about the case of thirty slaves who had been thrown into the sea, so that the insurance could be claimed. Olaudah's autobiography went through eight editions during his lifetime, giving him a sizeable income and considerable fame. Like Quaque, Equiano married an English woman, Susannah Cullen, and they had two daughters, Maria and Joanna. Olaudah died in 1797 and is buried at St Andrew's Church, Chesterton, in Cambridge. For Olaudah, as for many freed slaves, Evangelical religion was a religion of freedom, associated not only with emancipation from physical freedom, but liberation of soul and spirit.

THE PROVINCE OF FREEDOM

One of Equiano's roles within the London black community in the 1780s was to encourage a movement for resettling Africans on the continent. That part of the West African coast named Sierra Leone was chosen. It was the abolitionists' hope and intention that this would be a 'province of freedom'.[5] There was some scepticism in the black community itself – was this simply a plan to rid England of a 'black problem'? The settlers themselves faced tremendous difficulties in their first years. The colony received new energy in the early 1790s from an influx of freed slaves from Canada and the Caribbean, British loyalists during the American War of Independence. Many of this group had adopted forms of Evangelical religion through Methodist and Baptist preachers in America. To these settlers the established Church of England represented the religion of the slave owners. The CMS work which began in the early years of the new century was more concerned with evangelising indigenous peoples (Susu and Temne) and in establishing a mission along the Rio Pongas

[5] John Peterson, *Province of Freedom: A History of Sierra Leone 1787–1870* (Evanston: Northwestern University Press, 1969).

(present-day Gambia) than in ministering to settlers.[6] The future of the colony itself was in serious doubt in the early years. What saved Sierra Leone, and gave the CMS a major role, was the British abolition of the slave trade in 1807 and the establishment of a blockade to try to prevent other countries from continuing the trade. The little colony became the place of emancipation of 'recaptives': slaves rescued by the British Squadron. One of the colony's early governors, Sir Charles Macartney, though a Catholic himself, incorporated the CMS into his plans to create an English-style local government. Thirteen parishes were established in the environs of Freetown, with such patriotic names as Wilberforce, Leicester, Wellington, Waterloo, Regent and Hastings. The church was the centre of the parish, with the missionaries (many of whom were German Lutherans) having some civil, as well as educational and ecclesiastical, responsibilities.

Over the next thirty or forty years, Sierra Leone played an important role in the reception and rehabilitation of the displaced people, who came from a wide variety of ethnic groups. The dominant group consisted of the Yoruba, from a region in modern Nigeria where traditional power structures had rapidly disintegrated at the end of the eighteenth century, leaving an outlet for slave traders. The Yoruba were nicknamed 'Aku' by their fellow recaptives. Governor Macarthy and the CMS hoped that agriculture would become the mainstay of the economy. But very quickly it emerged that there were more opportunities in trade, and Freetown prospered as a commercial emporium for trade with the hinterland and overseas. Education became the other great desideratum for the recaptive community. Although a significant minority of recaptives became Muslim, the majority enthusiastically adopted the Christian religion, the effective cause of their liberation. Christian services were conducted in English, and for Anglicans the Book of Common Prayer and its rituals became part and parcel of religious identity. The formality of the prayer book with its discipline and austerity (as interpreted by Evangelicals) was supplemented by class meetings of a more heart-warming, revivalist kind – something of the strong Methodist presence in Sierra Leone was adopted by the Anglicans. In turn, Sierra Leone Methodists came to demand Anglican formality for their Sunday services. A rivalry between 'church' and 'chapel' became a strong feature of Creole society in the nineteenth century. 'Creole' was the term used for the second generation of recaptives.

[6] Eugene Stock, *The History of the Church Missionary Society*, Volume 1 (London: CMS, 1899), Chapter 13.

The CMS, which at first tended to interpret its work as that of primary evangelism only, gradually accepted the importance of providing the whole range of educational possibilities. Fourah Bay Institute, for vocational training (especially of teachers), was established in 1827. In the 1840s secondary education for boys was initiated by the opening of the CMS Grammar School in Freetown; and in the 1870s a parallel school for girls was established. This process culminated in the affiliation of Fourah Bay College to Durham University in 1876 (around the same time as the affiliation of Codrington in Barbados). The enormous importance attached to education by Creoles is indicated by the fact that in 1850 a larger proportion of children attended school in Sierra Leone than in England.

SAMUEL AJAYI CROWTHER

The dynamism of the Sierra Leone church stimulated Henry Venn's influential theories on mission. Venn became Honorary Clerical Secretary of the CMS in 1841 and provided an approach which has always been particularly appreciated throughout West Africa for its faith in the African capacity for leadership. Venn believed that mission was at the heart of any serious Christianity. But missions to particular places ought to be temporary – there ought to be a 'euthanasia of the mission', as he put it, as evangelism gives birth to a 'self-governing, self-supporting and self propagating native church'.[7] The final mark of a fully autonomous church would be the establishment of a native episcopate, the 'crown of the church'. Venn's vision was radically different from the ideas of missionary bishops being propagated in America by Bishop Hobart and in England by Samuel Wilberforce, in which a bishop pioneered mission, and around whom a native church grew.

For Venn, Creole Anglicanism in West Africa was a clear exemplar of the possibilities of the rapid euthanasia of a mission. Much of his hope focused on a remarkable freed slave, Samuel Ajayi Crowther, who was in London studying for ordination just at the time when Venn became CMS Secretary. Ajayi was born in Osogun, in the Yoruba state of Oyo, around 1806.[8] He was enslaved in 1821, and his boat was captured by the British Squadron. He soon took advantage of the educational

[7] See T. E. Yates, *Venn and Victorian Bishops Abroad* (London: SPCK, 1978) and Wilbert R. Shenk, *Henry Venn: Missionary Statesman* (Maryknoll: Orbis, 1983).

[8] Jesse Page, *The Black Bishop* (London: Hodder & Stoughton, 1909). J. F. Ade Ajayi, *A Patriot to the Core* (Ibadan: Anglican Diocese, 1992). Professor Ajayi is working on a new full-length biography.

opportunities offered by Freetown and accepted the new religion. He was baptised in 1825, made his first visit to England in 1826 and became one of the pioneer students at the new Fourah Bay College, training as a teacher. He married a fellow teacher, Susan Thompson, also a recaptive. Crowther volunteered for the ill-fated Niger Expedition of 1841. In 1842 he was back in London, studying at the CMS Islington institute, and was ordained in 1843. He joined the recently established Yoruba mission in Abeokuta and in 1846 was reunited with his mother. Crowther was largely responsible for the translation of the Yoruba Bible. He saw the necessity of allowing for a gradual convergence of local norms and Christian values, always affirming the liberative power of the Gospel for individuals and societies. He always had his critics, both among what Sanneh calls 'cultural prescriptivists' who demanded a more thoroughgoing transformation of society and among 'evangelical pietists' who devalued all human culture.[9] But even his critics recognised his exceptional gifts. In 1864 Venn, with some difficulty, persuaded Crowther to take on the arduous task of being bishop 'on the Niger'. He was consecrated bishop in Canterbury Cathedral as Bishop in West Africa 'beyond the Queen's dominions'. Sierra Leone and Lagos were thus excluded from his jurisdiction, and (in deference to the missionary-in-charge at Abeokuta, Henry Townsend) he did not have authority in the Yoruba mission either, though that was also not part of the Queen's dominions. The specification was fraught with practical problems; it was also a strange outworking of Venn's theory of mission.

THE SIERRA LEONE PASTORATE CONTROVERSY

Sierra Leone had got its first missionary bishop in 1852, and went through a succession of European bishops over the next twenty years, many of whom succumbed to the climate. By 1861, eighteen Africans had been ordained priest,[10] and in that year the running of the Sierra Leone church was transferred from the CMS to the native pastorate: an implementation of Venn's 'euthanasia of the mission'. There were practical problems: missionaries on the spot were never as convinced as Venn of the practicality of the policy. Venn had a strong belief in the equal capacity of all races transformed by Christ. Missionaries increasingly made sharp

[9] Lamin Sanneh, *Abolitionists Abroad: American Blacks and the Making of Modern West Africa* (Cambridge, MA: Harvard University Press, 1999), p. 163.
[10] Bishop T. S. Johnson, *The Story of a Mission* (London: SPCK, 1953), p. 144.

distinctions between races, and argued that native peoples needed a long period of tutelage before they could be given responsibility. Their strongest weapon was the fact that the church in Sierra Leone was nowhere near being financially self-supporting. The disparity between the aspiring optimism of the local church in its capacity to conduct its own affairs and the pragmatic 'realism' of many missionaries came to a head in a lively controversy over the pastorate which occurred between 1871 and 1874.[11] The controversy was sparked off by the activities of Edward Blyden, a Caribbean by birth and Liberian by adoption. He was the most formidable West African intellect of his age and was briefly professor of Arabic at Fourah Bay. Blyden exerted a strong influence on the Creole intelligentsia, not least a young priest called James Johnson, ordained in 1863. Blyden and Johnson conducted a vigorous newspaper campaign in Blyden's paper *The Negro*, demanding complete autonomy for the Sierra Leone church. They articulated a strong sense of African racial solidarity – and had been disappointed by the failure to appoint Crowther as bishop in Sierra Leone in 1870. In 1874, Johnson left Sierra Leone to become the pastor of the Breadfruit Church in Lagos, where he was to continue to have a crucial role in the development of West African Anglicanism.[12]

Despite the vigour of the Creole church, Sierra Leone Anglicanism has been heavily criticised for two salient characteristics. The first is its uncritical acceptance of the trappings of Victorian religion. This accusation began early. A mid-nineteenth-century visitor complained of church weddings where 'the most extravagant and costly dress, the richest articles of food and luxury, intoxicating drinks, and a company of attendants' were seen as essential. A consequence of this was that many delayed marriage for years until they could afford it, and suffered from years of debt afterwards. 'Yet few can be found to go against this ridiculous, slavish custom.'[13] The problems highlighted here were, and are, by no means peculiar to the Creole Anglicanism of Sierra Leone. The second charge is an indifference to mission among the local people. Stephen Neill, the historian of mission, puts this point of view abrasively:

> Sierra Leone suffered from one of those premature and ill-considered attempts to create an independent Church ... The theory ... was that the Christians of the

[11] Hollis Lynch, 'The Native Pastorate Controversy and Cultural Ethnocentrism in Sierra Leone 1871–4', in O.A. Kalu (ed.), *History of Christianity in West Africa* (London: Longman, 1980), pp. 270–92.

[12] E.A. Ayandele, *Holy Johnson: Pioneer of African Nationalism 1836–1917* (New York: Humanities Press, 1970).

[13] Gilbert W. Olson, *Church Growth in Sierra Leone* (Grand Rapids: Eerdmans, 1969), p. 83.

colony area would gradually spread out into the interior and bring the Gospel to their African brethren. What happened, as ought to have been foreseen, was exactly the opposite.[14]

This is rather unfair, both to the missionary zeal actually shown by Creoles and to their delicate position as descendants of men and women settled in a strange land. The very setting up of Sierra Leone created intractable problems between Creole and indigenous peoples. It should be noted that the present boundaries of Sierra Leone only came into being at the end of the nineteenth century, when large areas were incorporated which had already become heavily influenced by Islam, which remains the predominant religion of the country as a whole.

LIBERIA: A DIFFERENT FREEDOM

American plans for resettling free black people in Africa date from the late eighteenth century, and were promoted particularly by the American Colonisation Society (ACS), an alliance of northern white abolitionists, southern slave owners (who saw no place for free blacks in America) and a small number of idealistic free people of colour. From the first it was a private venture – a major difference from Sierra Leone, where British government involvement and finance were so important in establishing a viable colony.

Lamin Sanneh makes this contrast:

In the founding of the Sierra Leone colony, antislavery as the culmination of evangelical social activism became a public cause in the sense of commitment to establishing a new society based on public morality, freedom, human dignity, integrity, the rule of law, and justice. In Liberia by contrast, antislavery was compromised by being privatized and prescribed as an individual inducement for southern emancipation. Weighed down as such with the bells and whistles of antebellum America, antislavery languished in Liberia.[15]

The fact was that Liberia was a beleaguered huddle of unwanted blacks who left America, where their race conflicted with their freedom, to find refuge in Africa, where their freedom conflicted with their security.[16]

The Liberia experiment began in 1820, with the first small group of settlers arriving at Shebro, under white leadership. The second group in 1821 included two white Episcopalian priests. In the 1830s the Episcopal

[14] Stephen Neill, *The Unfinished Task* (London: Edinburgh House Press, 1957), p. 166. See also Stephen Neill, *A History of Christian Missions*, revised edn (London: Penguin, 1986), p. 259.

[15] Sanneh, *Abolitionists Abroad*, p. 238. [16] Ibid., p. 210.

Church began to train black leaders for church work in Liberia, including Edward Jones, who subsequently transferred to Sierra Leone, where he had a distinguished career as Principal of Fourah Bay College.[17] He married the daughter of one of the German CMS missionaries. A particularly important early black missionary of the Episcopal Church in Liberia was Elizabeth Mars Johnson. Her husband died just two weeks after arriving in Liberia. She remarried James Thomson, already working in Monrovia as a lay reader. Elizabeth opened a school for children of the indigenous population. In 1835 the Thomsons went to Cape Palmas to pioneer missionary work among the Grebo people of eastern Liberia.[18]

Many of the pioneer American settlers in Liberia were Baptist. Their leader, Lott Carey, was a Virginia slave who had bought his freedom. Episcopalian leadership, by contrast, was largely white. In 1836 there began a long connection between Virginia Theological Seminary and Liberia. John Payne, one of the first of the Virginian missionaries, became the first Bishop of Cape Palmas. The focus of mission work was among the indigenous Grebo community. Relationship between settler Episcopalians and the missionaries tended to be fraught. Eli Stokes, a black priest from Baltimore, tried unsuccessfully to interest the Scottish Episcopal Church in a Liberia mission to act as a counter-weight. In Alexander Crummell (1819–98), Bishop Payne had an even more articulate African American to contend with.[19] Crummell combined an Evangelical faith with a belief in the responsibility of black Americans for the uplift and civilisation of their brothers and sisters in Africa, and their common identity as 'the Negro race'. Like the Creoles of Sierra Leone, he equated Christian faith and English civilised values and culture.

> At the core of Crummell's vision is a single guiding concept: race. Crummell's 'Africa' is the motherland of the Negro race, and his right to act in it, to speak for it, to plot its future, derived – in his conception – from the fact that he too was a Negro . . . Crummell was one of the first people to speak *as* a Negro in Africa, and his writings effectively inaugurated the discourse of Pan-Africanism.[20]

Crummell arrived in Liberia in 1850 with grandiose plans for the establishment of a 'national' (African) church in the country. But his rhetoric often exceeded his powers of implementation, and Sanneh notes

[17] Eugene Stock, *The History of the Church Missionary Society*, Volume II (London: CMS, 1899), p. 102.

[18] D. Elwood Dunn, *A History of the Episcopal Church in Liberia 1821–1980* (Metuchen: Scarecrow Press, 1992), p. 40.

[19] For Crummell's career, see Chapter 3.

[20] Kwame Anthony Appiah, *In My Father's House* (Oxford: Oxford University Press, 1992), p. 5.

that 'he reflected without transcending the shortcomings of Liberian colonization'.[21] Crummell's Pan-Africanist ideas were developed in new and brilliant ways by the greatest genius of nineteenth-century West African thinkers, Edward Blyden, whose contribution in Sierra Leone has already been noted. Blyden was convinced of the power of Christianity, but critical of the forms in which it was being conveyed by missionary Christianity. By contrast, Blyden contended, Islam had adapted more naturally to the indigenous culture. Islam was a positive force in the development of Africa and might prepare the way for Christianity, but only if Christianity did not forfeit its inheritance. Both Blyden and Crummell had faith in the possibilities of Liberia and Sierra Leone as crucibles for this great Christian experiment for the betterment of Africa. At a time when white missionaries were magnifying their own essential role in Africa and belittling that of Creoles or African Americans, Crummell and Blyden saw the missionaries themselves as a major impediment to the attainment of an authentic African Christian civilisation. Blyden was not himself an Episcopalian (he was a minister of the Presbyterian Church), but he influenced a generation of Christian Africans not least in Sierra Leone, the place where he eventually settled. Thousands, Christians and Muslims, attended his funeral in Freetown in 1916.

In 1885, for the first time, a Liberian became bishop, Samuel David Ferguson, the first black bishop in the Episcopal Church of the United States (of which the Liberian diocese was a part). Ferguson's wholehearted identification with the Liberian government's policy of 'Americanisation', with its concomitant policy of assimilation of indigenous people, exacerbated the tensions between native and settler.[22] This can be seen in the career of one of the great Grebo Christians, perhaps the most successful evangelist Africa has produced, Prophet William Wade Harris. Born around 1860, Harris came from a Christian family and was baptised in the Methodist Church. He learnt English at an early age and was to use English, the lingua franca of the West African coast, throughout his evangelistic campaigns. In 1888 Harris was confirmed by Bishop Ferguson, having recently married his wife, Rose, in an Episcopal church. For nearly twenty years, Harris was a teacher and lay reader in the Episcopal Church. He became active in local politics, protesting against Monrovia's

[21] Sanneh, *Abolitionists Abroad*, pp. 222–30.

[22] David Shank, *Prophet Harris, The 'Black Elijah' of West Africa* (Leiden: Brill, 1994). Shank says, rather unkindly, of Bishop Ferguson, 'He was a light-skinned black who tried to prove his unlimited loyalty to white American values.'

denial of Grebo rights, and in 1910, during a series of disturbances, he even raised the British flag on Grebo land as a gesture of defiance. During his subsequent imprisonment he had a vision in which the Angel Gabriel ordered him to break with the 'fetishism' of western Christianity. He embarked on his remarkable campaign to establish a more indigenised, less elitist, Christianity 'without fetishes', whether of African or European origin. His break with the Episcopal Church was final – when asked about his former religious allegiance, he always stressed his Methodist upbringing rather than his Episcopal employment.[23] Harris' evangelistic journeys took him far beyond the boundaries of Liberia, and led to the establishment of L'Eglise Harriste in the Ivory Coast. Anglicanism was never so successful in appealing to francophone parts of West Africa.

THE YORUBA MISSION

Black American Liberians had an emotional and ideological commitment to Africa, but no actual home there. For the Yoruba of Sierra Leone, home was an attainable reality. From the 1830s they began to return as traders, just at the time when the city state of Abeokuta was founded as a new home for Egba Yoruba people disrupted by the wars. The *Alafin*, the ruler of the new state, while not himself becoming a Christian, encouraged Christians to settle in his state. They were given certain privileges and were nicknamed 'Saro', perhaps because of their strange 'English' greeting (Hello). In 1842 (a month after the Methodists) the CMS established a mission in Abeokuta, under the direction of a young missionary, Henry Townsend. Work among Yoruba people spread to Lagos, which became a British colony in 1861. Some of the older Yoruba cities invited missionaries. The German CMS missionary David Hinderer and his wife Anna worked for many years in Ibadan, a great Yoruba cultural centre. Christians, both Saro and missionaries, were valued as brokers between the Yoruba and the British, whose power was growing steadily. At other times the association of Saros with the missionaries was a liability. In the 1860s missionaries were expelled from Abeokuta and other Yoruba towns, during the period known as the *ifole*, the time of troubles, as fears of British political power grew.

The major missionary role was undertaken by the Sierra Leone Yoruba, and by converts such as David Olubi, first employed by the Hinderers in Abeokuta. He accompanied them to Ibadan, and eventually became the

[23] Ibid., p. 106. See also G. M. Haliburton, *The Prophet Harris* (London: Longman, 1971).

first 'home-grown' Yoruba Anglican priest. Yoruba (either Creole or native) mission agents far outnumbered the European missionaries. They wrote regular reports back to the CMS in London, describing their confrontations with the *orisa*, the divinities of the traditional religious system, criticising many aspects of Yoruba society and telling of their struggle to attain a hearing for the Christian Gospel. Peel has this to say of the reports of one Creole mission agent, James White:

> White addresses the quality of his converts' faith in rather different terms from, say, Townsend, and in a way which expresses a distinctively African perspective. He is less concerned about whether their inward state corresponds to the outward forms of their religion than with the manifest overall consistency of their lives. What really matters to him is that the exercise of Christian faith should be integrated with the quotidian or 'secular' business of life.[24]

While as enthusiastic as their English and German colleagues about overcoming the *orisa*, the Yoruba CMS agents had an insider knowledge of the society denied the Europeans. This was combined with an intense Yoruba nationalism – a pride in their ancient culture, powerfully expressed in the great work of a Yoruba priest, Samuel Johnson: *The History of the Yorubas*.[25] Written towards the end of his life in the 1890s, just as Britain was consolidating its rule over the whole of what was to become Nigeria, Johnson's book is the story of the Yoruba nation, a great people, once united. He deprecates 'the spirit of tribal feelings and petty jealousies now rife among us'. It is not a work of Christian propaganda as such, but underlying the narrative is an optimism that Christianity (preeminently in the Anglican form in which it has been received) will play an important part in the regeneration and transformation of the Yoruba people.

Nevertheless, Johnson is critical of certain aspects of the Christian legacy, not least the loss of the old patterns of naming children. This might seem rich from a man calling himself Samuel Johnson, but he was reflecting a common concern among Creoles of the time that Yoruba culture should not be forgotten. The completed manuscript of *The History of the Yorubas* had a turbulent history. In 1897 it was sent to the CMS in London with a view to publication.[26] But this proved something of an embarrassment – Dr R. N. Cust described the 647-page manuscript

[24] J. D. Y. Peel, *Religious Encounter and the Making of the Yoruba* (Bloomington: Indiana University Press, 2000), p. 256.

[25] Samuel Johnson, *The History of the Yorubas* (London: Routledge & Kegan Paul, 1921). The book was reprinted in 1966.

[26] Ibid., p. ix.

as prolix and 'the subject matter so very unimportant both from a secular and a religious point of view that I have not what to recommend' (an unusually crass remark for Cust).[27] The CMS then 'lost' the manuscript. In 1901 Samuel Johnson died, and his brother, Dr Obadiah Johnson, resolved to reconstruct the lost text from notes and drafts. Completed in 1914, the manuscript was again sent to Britain. Alas, the boat in which the manuscript was placed was captured by the Germans. Only in 1921 was it finally published (by which time Obadiah had also died).

The History is a remarkable piece of historical scholarship, the data gathered from hundreds of oral informants and decades of keen observation. Far from being unimportant it is a vital document, not only about the Christian appropriation of a Yoruba identity, but about the creation of a common Yoruba identity out of diverse and competing polities and religious affiliations.[28]

CROWTHER AND THE NIGER MISSION

Crowther's greatness lies in the breadth of his involvement in the story of West African Christianity, and in the depth of his understanding of the nature of Gospel and culture. Apart from his work among the Yoruba, Crowther had a long association with the Niger. He had been part of the disastrous Niger Expedition of 1841. Conceived as a bold plan to strike at the slave trade at its source and to establish new patterns of productive trade for the benefit of African societies and European capitalism, and as a means of commending Christianity, the mission had ended in failure and the death of many of the European missionaries. It set back the cause of overseas missions in popular British estimation for a generation (until Livingstone's expeditions gave it a renewed popularity). Crowther returned to the Niger in 1854 and began serious missionary work among the Igbo people, the people of the Niger Delta, and made contacts with Muslim rulers further north. But when he became bishop in 1864, the work was still in its infancy. There were only a few permanent catechists, nearly all from Sierra Leone, and even fewer priests. Crowther was inadequately supported financially by the CMS, lived far from his diocese, in Lagos, and was reliant on a trading boat whose timetable was geared to trade rather than pastoral needs.

[27] Peel, *Religious Encounter*, p. 308. For a discussion of Cust's relatively enlightened views in other matters, including the Niger crisis, see Peter Williams, *The Ideal of the Self-Governing Church: A Study in Victorian Missionary Strategy* (Leiden: Brill, 1990).

[28] Peel, *Religious Encounter*, p. 278.

The Creole community was critical of the limitations imposed on Crowther. Why had he not been appointed Bishop of Sierra Leone? Why did he have no authority in Abeokuta (the centre of Yoruba Christianity) or Lagos (where he lived)? The fact is that the episcopate of Crowther was resented by missionaries convinced that the Creoles were a liability to missionary work. When CMS missionaries did become directly involved in the Niger mission, in 1878, they were hostile and critical of the work of the Sierra Leonians, though they proved equally incompetent and venal. Then, in 1887, there arrived a group of young, enthusiastic missionaries influenced by the Keswick movement. Their most charismatic member was a 25-year-old layman, Graham Wilmot Brooke, a freelance missionary of no particular profession, but possessing a tremendous confidence. These 'young, impetuous, uncharitable and opinionated' men mocked the catechists for their European clothes and pretensions to education, their lack of missionary zeal, and the poor quality of their converts. One insulted Creoles as ex-slaves, the rejects of their own society and the 'dregs of humanity'.

The CMS Keswick missionaries, on the other hand, were determined to adopt Muslim attire for the work which the Creoles had so conspicuously failed to engage in. Disregarding the church structures and duly constituted authority (including the bishop himself), they instituted a purge of congregations, prohibiting 'sinners' (those who were living in polygamous relationships or cohabiting; those suspected of consorting with traditional religious practices) from Holy Communion. They pitied Crowther, and were convinced that his easy tolerance was responsible for the state of affairs. They urged that when the bishop died, it was vital that an African should not succeed him.

It is easy to caricature the exploits of these naïve and destructive firebrands, and they have received a universally bad press. Tasie has argued that moral indignation must not disguise the fact that there were serious problems between the Creole agents who dominated church life and the local populations on the Niger.[29] What is more difficult to explain or justify is the attitude of the CMS in the post-Venn years in failing so signally to believe in the native agency which had been responsible for the vigour of West African Anglicanism.[30]

[29] G. O. M. Tasie, *Christian Missionary Enterprise in the Niger Delta 1864–1918* (Leiden: Brill, 1978).

[30] Peter Williams, *The Ideal of the Self-Governing Church*, is an important examination of the abandonment of Venn's ideals.

WEST AFRICAN ANGLICANISM IN THE COLONIAL PERIOD

The Niger crisis came at the beginning of a traumatic decade in West Africa. By 1900 Britain was well on the way to taking over the whole of the area and creating the populous and complex colonial state of Nigeria. Some Yoruba Christians decided that the CMS (and therefore the Anglican church) had behaved so badly in its treatment of Crowther, and its failure to replace him by an African, that they formed their own independent churches: part of the growing 'Ethiopian' movement. Such churches often kept the liturgy and rituals of Anglicanism. There was hope that James Johnson, the pastor of the strategic Breadfruit Church in Lagos since 1874, might become leader of such an independent church. If he had done so, this would have had very grave consequences for the future of Anglicanism. But, despite his outspoken criticism of the CMS, he refused to leave the church. Yet he decisively refused to be a 'half-bishop' when offered the office of assistant to the white bishop. He only accepted this position in 1900, on what turned out to be an elusive promise that his episcopal area in the Niger Delta would become a separate diocese once funds permitted. The Niger Delta had just been reconciled to the CMS in 1897, after the CMS had apologised for its behaviour in the crisis of 1889–91.[31]

The CMS did not suffer as much as it might from these controversies because it entered into a period of rapid expansion which further side-lined the Creole community. In the early colonial period, the CMS consolidated a complex network of local schools. These became feeders for high schools. Educational work both promoted vernacular languages at the primary level and gave young people an aspiration to learn English. Bishop Shanahan, the Irish missionary of the Holy Ghost Fathers (the Spiritans) realised that Catholic success depended on following this path, and soon the resources of the Catholic church outstripped those of the Anglicans in Igboland, creating a Catholic majority in that area. But Anglicanism also consolidated its position. Chinua Achebe (whose father was an Igbo Anglican catechist) writes powerfully about the destructive consequences of Christian penetration in his area in his early novel *Things Fall Apart*.[32] The tragic hero, Okonkwo, laments the loss of the old world and struggles against the new. In the process his own personality falls apart and the story ends in his suicide. Okonkwo's fate represents the trauma of a whole society in the face of colonialism. For many, however,

[31] Ayandele, *Holy Johnson*, pp. 259ff.

[32] Chinua Achebe, *Things Fall Apart* (London and Lagos: Heinemann, 1959), Chapter 22.

an identification with Christianity became essential for survival and progress in the colonial period. Another great Nigerian writer, Wole Soyinka, winner of the Nobel prize for literature, is a great-grandson of the first indigenous (Egba) Yoruba priest, David Olubi. Soyinka describes growing up in Ake, near Abeokuta, a place dominated by the Anglican church, by the home where Bishop Crowther had once lived, by the CMS school. Canon J. J. Ransome-Kuti, musician and preacher, also seemed to overshadow the community.[33]

In colonial West Africa, the leadership of the Anglican church everywhere (with the exception of Liberia, where African Americans were able to keep some control) passed into the hands of missionaries. It was only in the 1950s that an African diocesan bishop was again appointed. But the missionary work continued largely to be in the hands of local pastors and evangelists. In 1951 A. B. Akinyele became Bishop of Ibadan, the first African diocesan bishop since Crowther. Akinyele had been an assistant bishop since the 1930s.[34] His brother Isaac Akinyele was a powerful political figure in Ibadan, eventually becoming the Olubadan (king). He was also a supporter of the Christ Apostolic Church, one of the many Aladura (independent) churches which had arisen in Yorubaland since the 1920s.[35]

In nineteenth-century Lagos, the Christian elite distinguished itself from the rest of the population by its adhesion to Christian marriage customs. Abigail Oluwole, the wife of Bishop Isaac Oluwole (one of the despised 'half-bishops' appointed after Crowther's death) advocated the adoption of Christian marriage in a pamphlet she wrote for the Mothers' Union, an organisation which she helped to pioneer in Lagos. But it proved difficult to enforce rigidly Christian norms with regard to sex and monogamous marriage. Many baptised men secretly took additional wives, according to Yoruba custom. They were deliberately imprecise about the exact nature of these relations, to evade church discipline or prosecution under the Marriage Ordinance code. Women from the elite were more likely to identify strongly with the strict Christian marriage which the church promoted: for them it offered security and status. Women were much more vulnerable than men if they failed to conform. Adel Coker, a daughter of an Anglican priest, having twice become pregnant as an unmarried girl, reluctantly felt obliged to accept the offer

[33] Wole Soyinka, *Ake: The Years of Childhood* (New York: Random House, 1981).

[34] T. B. Adebiyi, *The Beloved Bishop: The Life of Bishop A. B. Akinyele* (Ibadan: Daystar Press, 1969).

[35] Adrian Hastings, *The Church in Africa 1450–1950* (Oxford: Clarendon, 1994), p. 518.

of marriage to Dr Ogontola Sapora according to Yoruba traditions, but insisted that she have the privileges of 'head of table' accorded to a wife married in church. Things did not work out, and Dr Sapora informed Adel that he was going to marry another woman in church. Adel persuaded Herbert Macaulay (a grandson of Samuel Crowther and one of the founders of the Nigerian Nationalist movement) to file a legal objection to this marriage, something he was glad to do as part of a political campaign against Sapora's brother.[36] African and European marriage customs were difficult to combine successfully, however much Yoruba Christians certainly wanted to affirm both.

The CMS encouraged women's education. Some of the elite children went to England for part of their education. Education was important for 'marrying well', and to enable women to achieve an independent role. On the other hand, some of the traditional spheres in which West African women operated successfully, as traders and 'market women', were frowned upon by a Christianity which overly emphasised domesticity and family values. Bishop Crowther's wife, Susan, was criticised for engaging in trade. She passed on her aptitude to her daughter Abigail, who became the wife of the Revd Thomas Babington Macaulay, and who needed to supplement her husband's clerical income to support their eleven children.[37] Gradually women's education opened up new possibilities for Christian women. Funmilayo Ransome-Kuti (1900–78) was one of the first girls to go to Abeokuta Grammar School. She finished off her formal education in England in the 1920s. She married I. O. Ransome-Kuti, son of the Anglican canon and musician. Funmilayo's husband himself became a priest and a teacher, one of the founders of the Nigerian Union of Teachers. Funmilayo became a political activist, a role which took her outside the traditional church women's organisations. In the late 1940s she organised protests by trading women against unjust taxation. A pan-Africanist, with radical left-wing sympathies, she deplored the ethnic particularism of independent Nigeria. Her son, Fela Kuti, inherited his grandfather's musical gifts in the very different idiom of African popular music, becoming internationally famous for his music and for his unorthodox life style (he was a multiple polygamist). But he also adopted the radical political stance of his mother. Funmilayo was no conventional pastor's wife: she was concerned with social justice rather than the affairs

[36] Kristin Mann, *Marrying Well: Marriage, Status and Social Change among the Educated Elite in Colonial Lagos* (Cambridge: Cambridge University Press, 1985), pp. 80–1.
[37] Ibid., pp. 78–9.

of the church; her faith was inclusive and non-dogmatic. She was buried in Abeokuta next to her husband, who had died twenty years before.[38]

THE INDIGENISATION OF ANGLICANISM?

The story of the Ransome-Kuti family is the story of the transformation of an elite, its reintegration into central aspects of African life. The Anglican Church in Nigeria became a popular, 'folk' church, with an appeal to substantial sections of the peasantry and urban working class, whose perceptions of Anglicanism were only superficially shaped by the dominant elite. The Ijebu are a Yoruba people, inhabiting the hinterland of Lagos, who had consistently and successfully resisted the Christianity emanating from Lagos and Abeokuta. But in the twenty years after the British takeover in 1896, conversion both to Islam and to Anglican Christianity was phenomenal. It was encouraged by the substantial number of recaptive Christians of Ijebu parentage who lived in Lagos (Bishop James Johnson was one of them). But a movement of this unprecedented magnitude inevitably changed the character of the church, making it more responsive to the needs of a predominantly rural constituency, and one which had not been through the same acculturation process.

Similar movements were already going on in the Niger Delta. There a strong influx into the church was combined with discontent with a church which was still largely controlled by the Sierra Leonians and by Igbo speakers. In 1916 a popular movement occurred under the guidance of Prophet Garrick Braide, a native of the delta. Braide was baptised in 1910 and confirmed by Bishop Johnson in 1912. Shortly afterwards he had a vision during Communion and embarked on a life of evangelism and healing, which profoundly affected Bonny and the whole Delta region. He became known as Prophet Elijah II. Bishop Johnson, who might well have sympathised with Braide's evangelistic zeal, was alienated by its increasingly militant expression. Braide was arrested by the British authorities in 1916. He was released and died in 1918, having established the Christ Army Church.[39]

[38] Cheryl Johnson-Odim and Nina Emma Mba, *For Women and the Nation: Funmilayo Ransome-Kuti of Nigeria* (Chicago: Illinois University Press, 1997).

[39] G. O. M. Tasie, 'The Prophetic Calling: Garrick Sokari Braide of Bakana', in Elizabeth Isichei (ed.), *Varieties of Christian Experience in Nigeria* (London: Macmillan, 1982), pp. 99–115. See also Tasie, 'Christian Awakening in West Africa 1914–18', in Kalu, *History of Christianity*, pp. 293–308.

Braide's meteoric career resembled that of Harris in Liberia: a dream, a commission, a startlingly successful campaign. Both campaigns were cries for a more indigenised form of Christianity than Anglicanism was at that time ready to accept. In the 1920s a series of independent churches emerged which became known as Aladura (praying) churches. The garb and rituals, the emphasis on prayer and healing, the engagement with Yoruba understandings of spiritual forces, all marked these churches off from the formalised, prayer book-based services of the Anglican church. Some of the founding prophets, such as Josiah Oshitelu and Moses Orimolade, founder of the Christ Apostolic Church, had an Anglican background. Isaac Akinyele, Orimolade's financial backer, was raised in a devout Anglican family and his brother became a bishop.[40] Although Nigerian Anglicans long ignored and dismissed the Aladura movement, there has been a gradual, if somewhat reluctant, recognition of the authenticity of its religion.[41] But in practice the Nigerian Anglican church has remained remarkably conservative in its adhesion to the prayer book forms which it inherited. It is ironic that, just as Nigerian Anglican theologians were urging the church to be more sympathetic to the Aladura tradition, the rise of a vigorous charismatic renewal movement in Nigeria's schools and universities in the 1960s has tended to increase the gulf. This new Evangelicalism, which by the 1980s had become heavily influenced by Pentecostal understandings of the spirit world, has exacerbated or revived the negative assessment of the traditional religious environment which Aladura is seen to inhabit.

CHRISTIANITY AND ISLAM IN NIGERIA

From the beginning, Christianity in Nigeria has existed alongside an equally vibrant and expansive faith, that of Islam. Islam was already established among the Yoruba when Christianity made its appearance, and remains the faith of a substantial minority. The Yoruba are used to negotiating religious difference, not least in the context of kinship and family. Moreover, Bishop Crowther set a good example of patient dialogue with Islam in his missionary work at Lokoja on the Niger.[42] What has become increasingly contentious in the modern Nigerian state is

[40] Hastings, *The Church in Africa*, pp. 516–18.
[41] Afe Adogame and Akin Omoyajowo, 'Anglicanism and the Aladura Churches in Nigeria', in Andrew Wingate, Kevin Ward, Carrie Pemberton and Wilson Sitshebo (eds.), *Anglicanism: A Global Communion* (London: Mowbray, 1998), pp. 90–7.
[42] See John Loiello, 'Bishop in Two Worlds', in Isichei, *Varieties*, pp. 34–55.

relations between the two faiths at the national and political level. The British had ruled the two parts of Nigeria (a predominantly Muslim North and an increasingly Christian South) in very different ways. They had established a concordat with the Muslim rulers of the North which limited and circumscribed Christian missionary activity. Under Dr Walter Miller, the CMS had established good relations with the ruler of Zaria and had, uniquely, been allowed to establish his mission in the town itself.[43] His contacts with a group of (heterodox) Muslims who had a special regard for the prophet Isa, the Isawa, helped to establish a small Hausa-speaking Anglican church in Zaria (from which group President Yakubu Gowon, the son of an Anglican catechist, was descended).[44] But the Christian presence in northern Nigeria consisted largely of southerners who lived in separate quarters of cities.

With the coming of independence, the new government relaxed the restrictions on evangelism, since Nigeria was to be a secular, unitary state with freedom of religion enshrined in its constitution. This provided new opportunities for evangelistic work, especially in the Middle Belt, which had been under the political domination of Muslim emirates but whose life had hitherto been shaped only partially by Islamic practice. In post-independence Nigeria, political and religious identity has been one of the most hotly contested areas of national life. The North feared domination from southern politicians, whose Christianity was of a secular kind. They have been particularly critical of the overt political character of the Christian Association of Nigeria (CAN). Many northern Nigerian states have tried to entrench their Islamic way of life by constitutional means, including the re-introduction of Sharia law.

There have been clashes with Christian minorities, both southerners and northern minority groups. After the Kaduna riots of 1987, Bishop Gbonigi, Anglican Bishop of Kaduna, sent a strong message to the government that Christians (many of whom worked in government offices) could not go back to work until they received more protection from the federal government. He urged Christians to gather in their churches every day to pray for peace.[45]

The Christian Association of Nigeria has acted as a political pressure group, urging successive Nigerian governments to deal robustly with

[43] Walter Miller, *An Autobiography* (privately printed in Zaria, Nigeria, n.d.) (Miller died in 1952 and the book was published posthumously).

[44] E. P. T. Crampton, *Christianity in Northern Nigeria* (London: Cassell, 1975), pp. 129–36.

[45] Toyin Falola, *Violence in Nigeria: The Crisis of Religious Politics and Secular Ideologies* (Rochester: Rochester University Press, 1995), p. 186.

political Islam. It has also urged Christians to bring faith into politics, because faith ought to have political consequences and implications – something which Islam has always argued.[46] The growth of Pentecostalism, with its impact on and within the older churches, has equally tended to harden the lines of the religious debate. The Anglican church, as one of the largest and most influential churches in the country, advocates a robust defence of Christian political interests in a country finely divided demographically between Christian and Muslim, and a robust debate between the two communities as people of faith. It has been particularly concerned for evangelism in the North, and the rapid growth of missionary dioceses is a mark of that evangelistic commitment.

This chapter has concentrated on the history of Nigerian Anglicanism because Nigeria is overwhelmingly the most important part of the Anglican communion in West Africa, and indeed is rapidly overtaking England as the most populous Anglican country. It has a vibrant, confident style, typified by its Primate, Archbishop Peter Akinola, Bishop of Abuja. The church is strongly evangelistic and robust in its assertion of Anglican identity, and has a long tradition of financial self-support. It is conservative in its attitude to issues such as liturgical revision – the 1662 Book of Common Prayer, both in English and in its many vernacular translations, is still seen as providing the staple nourishment of Nigerian Anglicans, though both the Aladura and the Pentecostal movements have had an informal impact on many aspects of worship, in fellowship meetings and extra-liturgical settings. The massive strength of Nigerian Anglicanism was one of the factors which led to the collapse of the church unity discussions between Protestant churches in the 1960s. Anglican strength and confidence was seen as breeding insensitivity to the apprehensions of other churches, particularly the Methodists.[47] To cater for evangelism and expansion, the church has been divided into eight provinces, with 'missionary' dioceses in the North supported by the rest of the church. In 2004 there were seventy-eight dioceses in total.

Despite the Aladura movement, despite the Pentecostal challenge, the church in Nigeria remains a giant in both African and Anglican terms. Reckoned to number in 1900 some 35,000 adherents or 0.2 per cent of the total population, by 2000, according to Barrett's calculations, the church numbered 20 million, or 18 per cent of the population,

[46] Iheanyi M. Enwerem, *A Dangerous Awakening: The Politicization of Religion in Nigeria* (Ibadan: Institut Français de Recherche en Afrique, 1995).
[47] Ogbu Kalu, *Divided People of God* (Lagos: NOK Publishers, 1978), p. 72.

considerably more than other Protestant churches (12.6 per cent) or the Catholic church (12 per cent).[48] The Nigerian Anglican church has shown no enthusiasm for ordaining women.

ANGLICANISM IN THE REST OF WEST AFRICA

Compared to the church in Nigeria, other West African Anglican churches are tiny.

If Nigerian conservatism is a factor of its strength, the conservatism of the Ghanaian Anglican church is a factor of its weakness. The SPG only re-established a significant presence there in 1904, when it helped to sponsor the first Anglican bishop. In 1900 the Anglican population was reckoned to be 2,000, or 0.1 per cent of the population. By 2000 that number had grown to 50,000 Anglicans in seven dioceses. But this was still only 1.2 per cent of Ghanaians.[49] In the nineteenth century a strong Methodist and Presbyterian presence had established itself in Ghana, and these groups have provided the cutting edge of Protestant Christian work in the way that the Anglicans have done in Nigeria. The Anglican church has consolidated its high-church traditions and rituals, and has remained a distinctive minority church, in colonial times utilising its connections with the British colonial authorities – a limited and depreciating asset. The Sisters of the Holy Paraclete, a British Anglican order, has worked in Ghana, and encourages vocations from within Ghana. But the church as a whole has not been enthusiastic about women's ordained ministry. One Ghanaian priest blames the church for concentrating on 'obsolete and unrelated rituals', for failing to support initiatives such as the Anglican Student Youth Movement in college and university campuses, for not encouraging the ministry of the laity and being too hesitant about evangelism.[50] Attention to all these issues is important. But the church may need to accept its position as a small minority church, and look strategically at promising areas for growth. It is not in a strong position to

[48] David Barrett, George T. Kurian and Todd M. Johnson, *World Christian Encyclopedia* (2 vols., Oxford: Oxford University Press, 2001), Volume 1, p. 549. Compare with the slightly more modest figures of the *Church of England Year Book 2004* (London: Church House Publishing, 2004): 17.5 million members. Barrett's figure for members of independent churches is 23,075,000, or 21.5 per cent of the total population of Nigeria. This seems to include both membership of Aladura-type churches and the more recent Pentecostal churches – groups which in many cases would not recognise a common identity.

[49] Barrett et al., *World Christian Encylopedia*, Volume 1, pp. 307–11.

[50] H. F. Orland-Mensah, 'The Ministry of the Laity as Agents for the Growth of the Anglican Church of Ghana', D. Min. dissertation, Episcopal Divinity School, Cambridge, MA, 1993.

compete with Methodists, Presbyterians and Catholics in terms of corporate strength, or to compete with the charismatic movement in its appeal to young people.

The churches of Liberia and Sierra Leone have found it difficult to overcome the limitations of their origins in the abolition movement of the nineteenth century. According to Barrett, Sierra Leone had 20,000 Anglicans (2 per cent of the population) in 1900, and 25,000 in 2000 (0.5 per cent); Liberia had 2,200 Episcopalians (0.7 per cent) in 1900, and 34,5000 (1.1 per cent) in 2000.[51] Both states have been racked by violence, and by the resurgence of apparently regressive and inhuman forms of religion (traditional witchcraft and Masonic anti-democratic secret societies, as well as anti-social and anti-democratic Christian tendencies).[52] The Anglican churches, while hardly directly responsible for the collapse of the Sierra Leonian and Liberian states in the 1990s, were part of a structure of dominance which has now come to an end. It remains to be seen what form their churches will take when a new political order does eventually establish itself. Paul Gifford records a Sunday visit in 1989 (during Doe's regime and before the descent into chaos) to the impressive Episcopal cathedral in Monrovia (with an organ donated by the Firestone Company which more or less ran Liberia in the early part of the twentieth century). A total of 274 people attended its three services. Next door, in a rented school, the Transcontinental Evangelistic Association Church hosted 1,600 people at its morning service. As elsewhere in Africa, the Episcopal Church is finding it difficult to compete with the vitality of the newer Pentecostalism.[53]

When the Province of West Africa was created it was hoped that the diocese of Liberia would become a member, but Liberia was reluctant to forgo its connection with ECUSA and the financial support which this entailed. In 1982 the Liberian bishop George Browne was elected as Archbishop of the Province of West Africa, and Liberia did become part of the province. Under his leadership, the Liberian church has adopted a number of progressive policies on social issues. Browne was particularly concerned about issues of Freemasonry and its effects on both the church and the political life of the country. He has ordained a number of women. Since 1986 the church has honoured William Wade Harris as 'a

[51] Barrett et al., *World Christian Encylopedia*, Volume 1, pp. 307, 452.

[52] See Stephen Ellis, *The Mask of Anarchy: The Destruction of Liberia and the Religious Dimension of an African Civil War* (London: Hurst, 1999).

[53] Paul Gifford, *Christianity and Politics in Doe's Liberia* (Cambridge: Cambridge University Press, 1993), p. 190.

hero of the Church'. ECUSA and the diocese negotiated an 'endowment' to enable the Liberian church to be self-financing. The onset of the civil war in the 1990s put all such arrangements in jeopardy, but the theological college at Cuttington does continue to have a precarious existence.[54]

Although small, the churches in the Province of West Africa have made significant contributions to African theology, particularly through Canon Harry Sawyerr, who worked for many years at Fourah Bay University, John Pobee, a Ghanaian theologian who worked for many years in Geneva with the WCC, and Canon Burgess Carr, Secretary General of the All African Conference of Churches in the 1970s. In a small way, Anglicans have begun to establish themselves in francophone areas. In the Cameroons, the Anglican church began as an expatriate community for Nigerians. More recently it appointed a bishop from Rwanda, to provide direction for the growing work among the francophone part of the country.

[54] George D. Browne, *The Episcopal Church of Liberia under Indigenous Leadership* (Lithonia: Third World Literature Publishing House, 1994). Wade Harris Day is 6 May (p. 32). Browne, not himself a Mason, has a long section on Freemasonry in the church, and reckons that about 50 per cent of priests are Masons (p. 119).

CHAPTER 8

Southern Africa

BEGINNINGS

The origins of the Anglican Church in South Africa could hardly have been more different from that of West Africa. In West Africa, Anglicans came to a 'province of freedom' to participate in the building up of a new liberated humanity. In South Africa, the Anglican church was first established to minister to soldiers whose task was to protect a society dependent on slavery for its existence. Throughout the nineteenth century, military expansion brought more and more independent African societies under colonial rule. On the walls of Grahamstown Cathedral are commemorative plaques to British soldiers who died in the 'Kaffir wars' against the Xhosa people. 'Kaffir' occurs with such embarrassing frequency on the inscriptions that in liberated South Africa statues have been turned to face the wall, and offensive words on plaques have been deleted.[1]

Cape Town was established in 1652 by the Dutch East India Company (VOC[2]) as a staging post for its operations in Batavia (modern Indonesia). In 1806, the British permanently took over the colony. They guaranteed the status of the established Dutch Reformed Church (DRC). The Dutch community, which also contained people of French Huguenot and German origin, strongly differentiated themselves from Khoi pastoralists and San hunters (the 'Hottentots', as they were disdainfully called). In 1806 slaves were still being imported from Malaya, Bengal, Madagascar and Mozambique. They slightly outnumbered white people. To the north and east lived Bantu speakers, with complex societies based on agricultural and pastoral economies. Baptism defined the boundary between Christian and heathen, civilised and savage. Consequently,

[1] 'Kaffir' (in various spellings), originally an Arabic word denoting 'pagan', was applied specifically to Xhosa people by Europeans at the Cape, and, by extension, to all Bantu-speaking Africans.

[2] Vereenigde Oost-Indische Compagnie.

baptism of slaves was discouraged and missionary work among the native population frowned upon.[3] The missionary endeavours of the Moravians in the early eighteenth century had come to grief when Martin Schmidt attempted to baptise his converts. Revived in the nineteenth century, the Moravian settlement at Gnadendal became a model for an alternative economy and society and was admired for its discipline by Bishop Gray.

The British occupation brought revolutionary changes at the Cape. Slave trade throughout British territories was ended in 1807. The 1834 proclamation ending slavery came into effect in South Africa in 1838. In the early years of the British occupation, the missionary movement, led by the largely Congregational London Missionary Society (LMS), had become involved in a series of high-profile controversies with the Boer community over the status and economic plight of the Khoi and ex-slaves, led by the indefatigable campaigners Johannes Theodore van der Kemp, a Dutch aristocrat, and later John Philip, a Scot from Aberdeen.

When, in 1848, Robert Gray was appointed as the first Bishop of Cape Town, the Anglican church had only a tenuous existence, ambiguous as to its established status, and with little prestige in comparison with the Reformed church. Anglicans had no mission work to speak of. The Anglican church could not even claim a majority of the English settlers who had arrived in the eastern Cape in 1820. Methodists, whose ministers had accompanied the settlers, had a much stronger presence. When Gray arrived, his diocese consisted of some 10 churches, 16 priests and perhaps 10,000 adherents. Gray's major achievement was one of organisation – he created not simply an efficient diocese but, by the time of his death in 1872, a whole province, with five dioceses, a synodical structure and a strong corporate identity (the Church of the Province of South Africa: CPSA).[4] In a period when some other denominations were organising separate churches for different racial groups, Gray firmly established the principle of a church inclusive of all races. In practice, Anglicans failed substantially to embody that catholicity, in a society saturated by racial division. But Gray's work did provide a basis for the prophetic stand of later opponents of apartheid.

3 Robert Shell, *Children of Bondage: A Social History of the Slave Society at the Cape of Good Hope 1652–1838* (Hanover: Wesleyan University Press, 1994); J. N. Gerstner, *The Thousand Generation Covenant* (Leiden: Brill, 1991).

4 Charles Gray, *The Life of Robert Gray* (2 vols., London: Rivington, 1876); Peter Hinchliff, *The Anglican Church in South Africa* (London: DLT, 1963); J. Suggit and M. Goedhals, *Change and Challenge* (Cape Town: CPSA, 1998).

Gray's own theology was strongly influenced by the Oxford Movement. He was a friend of Bishop Samuel Wilberforce. His wife, Sophy, had architectural skills, and she designed a number of churches, built in the 'correct' Gothic style favoured by the high-church movement.[5] It served to distinguish 'English' Christianity from the meeting houses of the Nonconformists or of the Dutch church, at least before Gothic became the dominant ecclesiastical style. While stressing the high-church principle of independence of state control in spiritual matters, Gray was also a patriotic Briton who did not demur when the governor, Sir Harry Smith, magnified his office to some Xhosa chiefs, emphasising Gray's status as bishop of the 'religion of the Queen'. 'Now I trust the way is paved for future missions', noted Gray.[6] Belonging to the 'religion of the Queen' did have a certain cachet. But it was no substitute for the solid work which other missions had already embarked upon. To try to make up for lost time, Bishop Gray and the next governor (Sir George Grey) embarked on a joint scheme for a school for 'native chiefs', situated at Zonnebloem in Cape Town. In its early days it recruited some notable figures: children of Moshoeshoe (King of the Basutho) and Moroka (leader of the Rolong Tswana). At the first baptisms in the school in 1860, a number of the sons of chiefs were baptised, including three who chose the name George, a suitably British patriotic name. But the educational experiment was not an unmitigated success, as Janet Hodgson, the historian of the college, makes clear:

> Educated as black English ladies and gentlemen, they found on their return home that they were alienated from their countrymen, yet were not accepted by white frontier society and on occasion became pawns in the political arena.[7]

Edmund Sandile and his sister Emma, children of the Xhosa chief Sandile, were unable easily to adjust to their ambiguous position as mediators between British colonialism and Xhosa nationalism once they had left the school.[8] Later, Zonnebloem changed direction and took on the less socially ambitious but more practical task of training catechists, including Bernard Mizeki, the martyr of Mashonaland.

[5] Robert Ross, *Status and Respectability in the Cape Colony 1750–1870* (Cambridge: Cambridge University Press, 1999), p. 109.

[6] Mandy Goedhals, 'Ungumpriste: A Study of the Life of Peter Masiza, First Black Priest in the CPSA', *Journal of Theology for Southern Africa* 68 (September 1989), p. 19.

[7] Janet Hodgson, 'Mission and Empire: A Case Study of Convergent Ideologies in 19th Century Southern Africa', *Journal of Theology for Southern Africa* 38 (March 1982), p. 34.

[8] Ibid., pp. 46–8.

BISHOP COLENSO

In 1852 Gray had managed to raise money (with the help of the SPG) to establish the two new dioceses of Grahamstown and Natal, each with a strong emphasis on mission work, among the Xhosa and Zulu respectively. John Colenso, a mathematics don whose school book 'Colenso's Arithmetic' served for generations as the standard text, was appointed to the diocese of Natal, a new British colony. The theologian F. D. Maurice was a family friend of Colenso's wife, Frances, and a great influence on Colenso, teaching him to look for signs of God's revelation in other religious systems. While always conscious of his duties to the English settlers, Colenso rapidly threw his energies into mission to the Zulu people. Zululand itself was an independent state north of Natal. But many Zulu lived within the colony, either as independent farmers or as labourers for European farmers. Colenso spent long hours immersing himself in the language and in translation work. He was assisted by a number of native speakers, the most important being William Ngidi (a Christian convert, from the American Congregational mission).

Unlike Zonnebloem, far away from the home environment of its students, Colenso wanted his school at Ekukhanyeni to use the medium of Zulu and to be steeped in the local culture. His critics made fun of the seriousness with which Colenso allowed Ngidi's questionings to shape his own thinking. It is this aspect of Colenso's work which appeals to modern sensibilities. His literalistic approach to the numerical data in the Pentateuch seems a blind alley in comparison. Colenso's reshaping of the doctrines of sin and justification in his commentary on Romans seemed at the time to go beyond acceptable limits. His theories about Zulu religion now seem naïve.[9] His appreciation of the social function of marriage in African communities led him to suggest that polygamy should not be a barrier to baptism: this too remains an area which African theologians and ordinary Christians alike continue vigorously to debate. Colenso was adamant that Christians, once baptised, should not become polygamists, and he remonstrated with his friend Ngidi when he decided to take another wife. Ngidi eventually moved away from Ekukhanyeni, and distanced himself from Christian commitment altogether.

Bishop Gray was so alarmed by Colenso's departure from the traditional teaching of the church that he made the decision to try Colenso as a heretic, using the new synodical structure which he had created. The

[9] David Chidester, *Savage Systems* (Charlotteville: Virginia University Press, 1996), Chapter 4.

result was that in 1863 the Church in South Africa declared him a heretic. Colenso appealed to the British courts, on the grounds that he had been appointed by the queen and that Gray had no jurisdiction over him. Colenso won the court battle and remained Bishop of Natal for the rest of his life. The Church in South Africa proceeded to appoint an alternative bishop, to be known as the Bishop of Maritzburg. Both groups claimed the same cathedral. Farcical scenes followed as the bishop claimed the right to enter his cathedral 'to discharge the duties committed to me by the Queen', and the dean pronounced anathemas from the high altar.[10] Two constitutional views of the Church of England and its relation to the wider Anglican communion were starkly outlined by the controversy and led to the first Lambeth Conference in 1867.[11]

Colenso won his battle in the English courts, but his Erastian view of the Church in South Africa had little future, if only because the British government had no intention of financially underwriting the churches overseas. Colenso found it almost impossible to keep the remnant of his church afloat in Natal, not to mention any thought of posting missionaries to Zululand.

Ironically, considering his views of the constitutional links between church and state, some of Colenso's greatest battles and his greatest achievements were to come from his fearless criticism of the British government in Natal. It led him to an irreversible breach with his erstwhile friend Sir Theophilus Shepstone, for many years the Commissioner for Native Affairs in Natal. The trouble began in 1874, when Colenso chose to defend Langalibalele, chief of the Hlubi people, from charges of rebellion. Colenso believed that the protest had actually been fomented by British agents. Then in 1878 Colenso vigorously defended the Zulu nation, protesting against the British invasion after the Zulu victory at Isandhlwana. In what must be one of the very great Anglican sermons, Colenso spoke on the text 'What does the Lord require of thee, but to do justly and to love mercy?'

> Wherein in our invasion of Zululand, have we shown that we are men who love mercy? Did we not lay upon the people heavily, from the very moment we crossed their border, the terrible scourge of war? Have we not killed already, it is said, 5000 human beings, and plundered 10000 heads of cattle? It is true that, in that dreadful disaster . . . we have ourselves lost many precious lives . . . But are there no griefs – no relatives that mourn their dead – in Zululand?[12]

[10] Peter Hinchliff, *John William Colenso* (London: Nelson, 1964), pp. 172, 181.
[11] A. M. G. Stephenson, *The First Lambeth Conference* (London: SPCK, 1967).
[12] Jeff Guy, *The Heretic* (Pietermaritzburg: Natal University Press, 1984), pp. 275–80.

Colenso died in 1883, anguished and worn out by the destruction of the Zulu kingdom. He was buried before the altar in the cathedral, with the simple inscription 'Sobantu' ('Father of the people') on the tombstone. His work was brilliantly continued by his daughter Harriette, *Udlwedlwe*, the guide and support of her father. She mastered the parliamentary Blue Books which her father had also utilised. She became counsellor and advocate to the Zulu royal family (the exiled King Cetshwayo and his son Dinizulu). Over the years she was involved in endless correspondence and writing, representation of the royal house at the treason trial in Eshowe (the capital of British Zululand), and visits to England to lobby Parliament and to St Helena, where Dinizulu was exiled for a time. Eventually she had the satisfaction of seeing the restoration of the royal family to an important role in Zulu affairs.[13]

Many of the royal family and their counsellors became Anglican, and the CPSA diocese of Zululand flourished in the aftermath of the British occupation. But the Church of the Province, as guardian of Anglican orthodoxy, continued for many years to regard Colenso simply as 'the heretic'. One legacy of the quarrel was the establishment of a rival form of Anglicanism, the Church of England in South Africa, critical of Gray's constitution and determined to emphasise a more Protestant, and eventually more Evangelical, biblically conservative, Anglicanism. Primarily a church for English people, it did not develop the missionary impetus which had motivated Colenso himself. In a democratic, non-racial South Africa, there has been a reassessment of Colenso's legacy in KwaZulu-Natal. In 2002 a resolution of the Durban diocesan council asked that Colenso's case be reopened, with a view to rescinding his excommunication. The resolution noted that Colenso had 'sought to rethink Christian theology and the interpretation of Scripture in the light of his understanding of the Zulu people and their culture' and that he and his family had dedicated their lives 'to fighting for the preservation of Zulu culture and autonomy, and for justice for the Zulu people'. 'His theology, though radical for his day, may not have transcended the bounds of what today would be considered acceptable theological diversity.'[14]

[13] Jeff Guy, *The View across the River: Harriette Colenso and the Zulu Struggle against Imperialism* (Cape Town: David Philip, 2001).

[14] Email: CPSA.chat. Resolution of the Bishops of Natal and Zululand to the Anglican Triennial Synod September 2002. I am grateful to John and Judy Gay of Cambridge, MA, for drawing my attention to this important resolution.

OTHER WORK AMONG THE ZULU AND XHOSA

Another important missionary to the Zulu was Henry Callaway, who had joined Colenso in 1854. Also influenced by Maurice, Callaway developed a sensitive appreciation of Zulu religion, which he published in *The Religious System of the Amazulu* in 1870. He utilised the testimony of a large number of informants in this work, particularly the insights of his assistant, Mbande, later to be ordained. Mbande was in fact the co-author of the work – some of the chapters are largely translations of Mbande's testimony.[15] Unsurprisingly, Callaway did not support Colenso in the dispute with Gray. In 1873 he was elected as first Bishop of Kaffraria (later to be known as St John's, in the heart of Xhosa country), where he built up Umtata, the capital of the Transkei, as an important church centre.

Much of the early Anglican work among the Zulu was with those living in Natal. Work in the independent Zulu kingdom to the north of the Tugela River was halting. The king, Cetshwayo, held that allegiance to Christianity was incompatible with the obligations of young men to the state, particularly entry into the age-grade regiments, which was required of all Zulu males. The first martyr, a member of the Lutheran mission, Maqhamusela Khamyile, was killed in 1877, just as tensions between the Zulu and the British were mounting. He is commemorated in the CPSA calendar.[16] The struggle between Gray and Colenso further impeded serious mission work. The first CPSA bishop was appointed by Gray in 1870, soon after the collapse of the independent Zulu kingdom.

Both Zululand and the Transkei became important centres of Anglican influence. Anglicans were never the dominating Christian influence – the Presbyterians (with their great centre of Lovedale) and the Methodists provided much of the dynamic of late-nineteenth-century Protestant Christianity among the Xhosa. Among the Zulu, Scandinavian and German Lutherans, American Congregationalists and British Wesleyans ensured that there was a rich mix. In 1882 the Trappist monastery of Mariannhill was established in Natal, and this became a centre of Catholic mission work among the Zulu. Anglicans were always just one church among others. They were even weaker in Lesotho, where the Paris Evangelical Mission and the Catholics had established a dominance which did not give much scope for Anglicans. In Bechuanaland, the LMS had become in some respects the 'established' church by the end of the nineteenth century. In the 1920s Batswana migrant workers returned

[15] Chidester, *Savage Systems*, pp. 152–66. [16] See the Book of Common Prayer of CPSA, 1988.

from the Rand, having been baptised as Anglicans. They wished to establish an Anglican church in their home area, but faced harassment and official discouragement.[17] The Anglican church continues to be a very small group, less than 1 per cent of the population. Anglicans in Swaziland (4 per cent) and Lesotho (4.7 per cent) are also fewer than the South African figure of 6.6 per cent.[18]

Anglican educational influence could not match the power of Lovedale, the Presbyterian institute near Alice in the Ciskei. Something of the vitality and self-confidence of late-nineteenth-century Xhosa Christian culture is missing from the Anglican work. Mandy Goedhals' portrait of the first black priest ordained after the formation of the CPSA in 1872, the Revd Peter Masiza, shows a man of limited abilities and imagination. 'He accepted paternalism both in church and state, and provided living proof of Christianity as an instrument of oppression, by the effacement of his own personality and interests in search of an identity acceptable to Europeans.'[19]

As the Anglican church came to minister more successfully to British immigrants, so there often emerged a tension between the establishment of white congregations and the mission of the church to Africans. The dioceses of the Orange Free State and Pretoria tended to stress the priority of pastoral work among British members. Indeed, the first Bishop of Pretoria, H. B. Bousfield, put it bluntly: 'I never can consent to putting the black before the white population.'[20] Bishop Colenso could never have made such a statement!

THE ANGLICAN CHURCH AND APARTHEID

Long before the victory of the National Party in 1948 and the formal institution of the policy of apartheid (separate development), the Anglican church was part and parcel of a racially saturated society – one in which British cultural values and English speakers lorded it over Boer farmer as much as 'native'. Naturally, Anglicans supported the British side in the South African war of 1899–1902, the 'Boer War'. The church was in no position to resist the rapid industrialisation of South Africa after the discovery of diamonds and gold. This further tipped the scales in

[17] Information from Maggie Tema of Francistown (MA student, Leeds University, 1997).

[18] David Barrett, George T. Kurian and Todd M. Johnson, *World Christian Encyclopedia* (2 vols., Oxford: Oxford University Press, 2001), Volume 1.

[19] Mandy Goedhals, 'Ungumpriste: A Study of the Life of Peter Masiza', p. 28.

[20] O. M. Suberg, *The Anglican Tradition in South Africa* (Pretoria: UNISA, 1999), p. 58.

favour of 'English' values over those of the Afrikaners. But, in the aftermath of the Boer War, the creation of the Union of South Africa in 1910 was widely welcomed as a way of overcoming the conflict between the two white communities. The fact that it completely denied voting rights to non-whites in Natal, the Orange Free State and the Transvaal, and curtailed those rights in the Cape, was not generally seen as an issue. Nor did the Anglican church have much to say about the Land Act of 1913, with its fatal consequences for African land rights.[21]

The unexpected victory of the National Party under Dr D. F. Malan in 1948 was a blow to English South Africa, not least to its churches. Even before 1948, policies of racial segregation and job reservation had become common in South Africa, supported, indeed demanded, by English capitalists and industrial workers alike. After 1948 these trends were formalised and radicalised by the implementation of the policy of apartheid: 'to maintain and protect the purity of the white race by means of territorial segregation, by regarding the presence of the urban black as temporary, by labour control, by the suppression of trade unions, by separation of political representation'.[22] Something of the anxiety about segregation had already been articulated in Alan Paton's novel *Cry, the Beloved Country*, written in the years before the National victory and published in 1948. The story tells of Stephen Kumalo, a Zulu Anglican priest, and his journey into the maelstrom of Johannesburg in search of his son Absalom.[23] For the next four decades Paton stood as a representative of that small white English South African minority whose opposition to apartheid was persistent and principled and informed by a deep Christian spirituality, in Paton's case nourished by his Anglican commitment. But he also came to represent the limitations of the 'white liberals' against whom another Anglican, Steve Biko, protested.[24]

The 1950s saw a growing rift between the Anglican church and the National government. Education became a particular flash point. The 1953 Bantu Education Act was designed to restrict the opportunities of African people through insisting on vernacular language training (even for Africans in urban areas). It was also an attack on the mission schools, which had been the major players in black education for a century. The

[21] James Cochrane, *Servants of Power: The Role of English-Speaking Churches in South Africa 1903–1930* (Johannesburg: Ravan, 1987).

[22] The Sauer Report, quoted in R. Elphick and R. Davenport (eds.), *Christianity in South Africa* (Cape Town: David Philip, 1997), p. 203.

[23] Alan Paton, *Cry, the Beloved Country: A Story of Comfort in Desolation* (New York: Scribner, 1948).

[24] Peter Alexander, *Alan Paton* (Oxford: Oxford University Press, 1994), p. 380.

churches protested, but, threatened with the withdrawal of the government grants on which they depended, most felt compelled to work within the system. The Catholic church put up a vigorous fight. Among the Anglicans, only Bishop Ambrose Reeves of Johannesburg refused, preferring to close the schools rather than allow them to become agents of the apartheid ideology. His fellow bishops felt uncomfortable with his stubbornness. Reeves became increasingly active politically. He established a close collaboration with John Collins, canon of St Paul's in London, whose Defence and Aid Fund helped activists who were standing trial (including Mandela's defence at the Rivonia trial).

Trevor Huddleston, a member of the Community of the Resurrection, denounced the destruction of Sophiatown, one of the few areas of Johannesburg where black people owned property. Sophiatown was cleared to make way for a white housing estate – the blatantly named Triomf.[25] Huddleston, who joined the ANC and associated with Communists, became such a troublesome and outspoken critic that he was forced to leave South Africa.[26] His account of the destruction of Sophiatown in *Naught for your Comfort* (1956) served further to alert an international audience to the evils of apartheid.[27] Archbishop Clayton of Cape Town was distressed by what he considered the intemperate political campaigning of Reeves and Huddleston, but even he decided that he must face up to the regime when it introduced legislation which would restrict the freedom of churches to hold worship services involving different racial groups. Clayton drafted a letter to Prime Minister Verwoerd, on behalf of the bishops, in which he gave notice that:

> The Church cannot recognise the right of an official of a secular government to determine whether or where a member of the Church of any race ... shall discharge his religious duty of participation in public worship ... We recognise the great gravity of disobedience to the law of the land. We believe that obedience to secular authority, even in matters about which we differ in opinion, is a command laid upon us by God. But we are commanded to render unto Caesar the things which be Caesar's, and to God the things that are God's. There are therefore some matters which are God's and not Caesar's.[28]

[25] The subject of a bitter satirical novel of post-apartheid days by Marlene van Niekerk, *Triomf* (London: Little, Brown, 1999).

[26] Robin Denniston, *Trevor Huddleston: A Life* (New York: St Martin's Press, 1999), pp. 45–51.

[27] Trevor Huddleston, *Naught for your Comfort* (London, 1956).

[28] Alan Paton, *Apartheid and the Archbishop: The Life and Times of Geoffrey Clayton* (New York: Scribner, 1973), pp. 278–80.

On 7 March 1957, the day after signing this letter, the 73-year-old Archbishop died. Eventually the government amended its bill. Clayton's successor, Joost de Blank, like all his predecessors, was from Britain. He shared Reeves' impatience with the National government and made it plain, despite his Dutch origin, that he had no sympathy for the stance of the Dutch Reformed Churches.

In 1960, in the African township of Sharpeville, a Pan-Africanist Congress demonstration was called to protest against the extension to women of the pass laws, by which the daily lives of Africans were subject to continual control and harassment. Soldiers fired on the crowd, and sixty-nine people were killed. Sharpeville was a suburb of Vereeniging, in Bishop Reeves' diocese. Reeves immediately started a campaign to publish the facts and to denounce the government.[29] Fearing that he was to be arrested, he fled to neighbouring Basutoland (a British protectorate) and thence to England. Reeves was much criticised for his flight and eventually returned, but was immediately deported. It was hoped that he would find preferment in England, but neither Archbishop Fisher nor Prime Minister Macmillan was keen to exacerbate relations with South Africa at a time when the question of its leaving the Commonwealth was on the agenda.

Gonville Ffrench-Betagh, Dean of Johannesburg, was another cleric who was deported for his outspoken opposition to apartheid. Helen Joseph, a member of the cathedral congregation and a South African, served a number of banning orders for her activities. Hannah Stanton, an English woman working at the Tumeleng Anglican mission in the Lady Selborne township of Pretoria, was deported.[30] Archbishop Joost de Blank resigned at the end of 1963 and returned to England.[31] South Africa had left the Commonwealth by this time. Clayton had been the last English Archbishop of Cape Town who carried sufficient prestige within South Africa to influence events through the inherited status of the Anglican church. De Blank's more polemical confrontational style had alienated the regime, but did not have the power to force change. The post-Sharpeville church, like the African nationalist movement itself, was ruthlessly silenced. The CPSA became acutely aware of its limitations, of the boundaries between criticism of apartheid on Christian grounds and

[29] Ambrose Reeves, *Shooting at Sharpeville* (London, 1960); John Peart-Binns, *Ambrose Reeves* (London: Gollancz, 1973).

[30] Hannah Stanton, *Go Well, Stay Well* (London: Hodder & Stoughton, 1961).

[31] J. Peart-Binns, *Archbishop Joost de Blank: Scourge of Apartheid* (London: Muller, Blond & White, 1987).

anything which could be remotely construed as political involvement and subversion. After Sharpeville the World Council of Churches convened a consultation of all the member churches in South Africa at Cottesloe in Johannesburg, in which a common statement of concern at the direction in which the government was going was drafted. But in the end, political pressure on the Afrikaner churches led to their disowning their delegates. In 1964, Beyers Naudé was dismissed from his church for his activities with the multi-racial Christian Institute.[32] For long he remained almost alone in his brave stand as an Afrikaner Christian against apartheid. His voice was important for Anglicans in South Africa not least because it tempered their instinctive distaste for the 'Calvinist' theology of the Reformed churches. At a later stage of the struggle, Archbishop Tutu was to work closely with Allan Boesak, a member of the coloured branch of the DRC.

With the failure of the Cottesloe agreement, the English-speaking churches worked alone to produce what they hoped would be a significant critique of the apartheid regime within the circumscribed possibilities of the time. In 1968 the South African Council of Churches issued its Message to the People of South Africa, in many ways modelled on the famous Barmen Declaration of 1934, which had opposed the Nazi perversion of church teaching. The Message challenged a doctrine of racial separation as 'a false faith, a novel Gospel. It inevitably is in conflict with the Gospel of Jesus Christ, which offers salvation, both individual and social, through faith in Christ alone.'[33]

Part of the importance of this statement was that it spoke to a government keenly aware of its Protestant Christian identity in a language which came out of the Reformation as well as the German church struggle. It was important that Anglicans, with their sense of a distinctive Catholic identity, committed themselves to this ecumenical statement. The constant complaint of the government was that the Anglican church leadership represented discredited imperial British values. It was a criticism which the CPSA could not easily counter as long as its clergy, and particularly its leaders, were so overwhelmingly of British origin. In 1974 Bill Burnett became the first South African-born Archbishop of

[32] Johann Kinghorn, 'Modernization and Apartheid: The Afrikaner Churches', in Elphick and Davenport, *Christianity in South Africa*, pp. 135–54; Peter Walshe, *Church versus State in South Africa: The Case of the Christian Institute* (London: Hurst, 1983).

[33] Quoted in Zolile Mbali, *The Churches and Racism: A Black South African Perspective* (London, SCM, 1987), pp. 45–6; John de Gruchy, *The Church Struggle in South Africa* (Cape Town: David Philip, 1979).

Cape Town, but this could not by itself overcome what Adrian Hastings has called the failure in 'imaginative response' to the crisis. 'Its discriminating clerical salary scales remained unchanged, and having chosen not to keep its African schools but to keep its white bishops ... its appeal to the black majority was inevitably a diminishing one.'[34] In order to explore the emergence of the black Anglican voice in the CPSA we need to look back at developments earlier in the century.

THE EMERGENCE OF A BLACK SOUTH AFRICAN ANGLICANISM

The Order of Ethiopia

Africans had long been aware of the weak foundations of Anglicanism within South Africa's racial society. James Calata, a priest from Cradock in Grahamstown diocese, was one of the few Anglicans to take a prominent role in the early years of the African National Congress. Some time in the 1930s or 1940s he wrote a memorandum, along with Maishite Maimane, a priest from Pretoria, in which the two priests expressed their frustration at their experience as black people within the Anglican church.[35]

They proposed that African work in each diocese should come directly under an African assistant bishop, or should be amalgamated with the Order of Ethiopia, so that an 'African Branch of the Catholic Church' could be established 'in order to enhance, and use to the full, the African spiritual gifts and powers'. The Order of Ethiopia had grown out of the 'Ethiopian' movement of the late nineteenth century, a protest by educated African Christians, particularly Xhosa, against the practice of discrimination and segregation within the mission-founded churches. A variety of independent churches was established, including one which affiliated with the African Methodist Episcopal Church, a black American church.[36] James Dwane was appointed 'vicar-bishop', but he became disillusioned with the unfulfilled promises made by the AME Church and began negotiations with the CPSA, which resulted, in 1900, in the signing of a compact. Dwane's group was received into the Church of the Province of South Africa as a separate religious Order, with Dwane as

[34] Adrian Hastings, *A History of African Christianity 1950–1975* (Oxford: Clarendon, 1994), p. 228.

[35] Quoted in Richard Shorten, *The Legion of Christ's Witnesses* (Cape Town: Centre for African Studies, University of Cape Town, 1987).

[36] T. D. Verryn, *A History of the Order of Ethiopia* (Cleveland, Transvaal: Central Mission Press, 1972); Hinchliff, *The Anglican Church*, pp. 200–5; Suberg, *The Anglican Tradition*, pp. 68–70.

'Provincial'. The group hoped that its bishop would retain his status, but Anglicans had no intention of going that far: Dwane was simply ordained a deacon. The compact has been described as 'a model of missionary restrictiveness'.[37] Tensions mounted. At one time Dwane was suspended, and it was only in 1910 that he was priested. He died in 1916 without ever having been made the bishop of the Order. Only in 1982 did the Order of Ethiopia finally get its own bishop with the consecration of Sigqibo Dwane (grandson of James Dwane). At present the Order (which prefers its Xhosa name Umze wa Tiyopia) is negotiating to be recognised as an autonomous ecclesial grouping, separate from the Anglican church, but in full communion with it.[38]

Iviyo

Kwazulu provides a contrasting African initiative. In 1948, two Zulu priests, Alpheus Zulu and Philip Mbatha, formed the Iviyo lofakazi bakaKristu, the Legion of Christ's Witnesses, as a fellowship of committed Anglicans. Both were influenced by the discipleship modelled by the Community of the Resurrection.[39] The greeting 'Ukristu uyiNkosi' ('Christ is Lord') became common among members, to which the reply was 'Uyabusa' ('He reigns'), a practice which is reminiscent of the Balokole revivalists of East Africa. In its concern for purity, its close-knit structures of support and its evangelistic zeal Iviyo also resembles the Balokole. But it is unashamedly Anglo-Catholic in its piety and discipline, with a Eucharistic focus and devotion to the Virgin Mary. Nevertheless, at first other Anglicans accused Iviyo of being 'Zionist'. Zionist independent churches were particularly active in Zululand at this time, and were seen as a particular threat to the established churches.[40] The Legion was critical of both Zionist and Catholic churches for the prominence they gave to the ancestors – like Callaway and Mbande in the nineteenth century, they were convinced that a cult of ancestors was not a proper base for Christian devotion. Iviyo got early support from the bishops in Natal and Zululand, and eventually its own members were to become bishops: Alphaeus Zulu became the first diocesan bishop when he

37 James Campbell, *Songs of Zion* (Oxford: Oxford University Press, 1995), p. 220.
38 Mandy Goedhals, 'The Order of Ethiopia', in Daniel O'Connor, *Three Centuries of Mission: The United Society for the Propagation of the Gospel 1701–2000*, (London: Continuum, 2000), pp. 382–94.
39 Shorten, *The Legion of Christ's Witnesses*, p. 30.
40 Bengt Sundkler, *Bantu Prophets in South Africa* (London: Lutterworth, 1948).

was consecrated Bishop of Zululand in 1966. Jacob Dlamini, who became Bishop of St John's in the Transkei, was also an active supporter. Iviyo's membership has been predominantly women: Mrs Meriet Ngubane and Mrs Judith Sitole established the movement among schoolgirls, and encouraged the formation of a religious order with links to Iviyo: the Community of the Holy Name, with Veronica Mkhonza as Superior. The predominance of women is also connected to the prevalence among males of migrant work in the mines. Iviyo is firmly a rural movement, and has not spread strongly into urban industrial areas, or outside Zulu circles. In this connection it has been accused of being uninterested in politics and more sympathetic to the Inkatha movement than to the African National Congress.[41]

BLACK ANGLICANS AND THE FREEDOM STRUGGLE

In other parts of Africa the 1960s were years of optimism. African theology became established as a legitimate development in the search for an authentic Christianity. Anglican churches achieved autonomy and an overwhelmingly black leadership. In South Africa, by contrast, black people were systematically excluded from power and, even in the church, had little sense of ownership. Then, in 1976, there was the explosion of the youth of Soweto, the large black township to the south-west of Johannesburg. Militancy spread to other urban centres. One of the leaders who gave the new movement direction was Steve Biko, a young medical student from King William's Town in the Ciskei. An Anglican, he was critical of all the mission churches for their failure to take black concerns seriously. Black people had for too long been bamboozled into accepting the white assessment of their culture and faith. They now needed to assert their own identity. Biko inaugurated a movement which became known as Black Consciousness. It valued African culture as distinct and different from European and equally valid. Biko's organising skills and oratory made him a marked man. He suffered several banning orders and in 1977 was arrested. He was tortured and died in his cell a few days later, in a case which was to achieve international notoriety. Biko's friend, a priest of the Community of the Resurrection, Aelred Stubbs, published his writings posthumously in a book called *I Write What I Like*,[42] an important inspiration for a school of Black Consciousness

[41] Stephen Hayes, *Black Charismatic Anglicans* (Pretoria: UNISA, 1990), Chapter 7.
[42] Steve Biko, *I Write What I Like* (London: Penguin, 1988).

protest theology, represented by the Methodist Itumeleng Mosala and the Anglican Barney Pityana. Mamphela Ramphela, a sociologist and community activist, worked with Biko in King William's Town in the 1970s. In the Northern Transvaal she continued to value visits from another member of the Community of the Resurrection, who came to celebrate the Eucharist with her.[43]

Suggestions have been made that Biko should be commemorated in the calendar of the CPSA. But his secular life style, far from 'saintly' in a conventional sense, has led to caution. Biko was important for providing a black Anglican radical voice within the country at a time of bleak oppression. Otherwise, the struggle had to be waged from outside. Trevor Huddleston was for many the voice of Anglican protest through his leadership of the anti-apartheid movement in London. The Anglican layman Oliver Tambo had once approached Bishop Reeves about ordination, but decided on a political career. He became leader of the ANC in exile in Zambia, the friend and colleague of Mandela, who by this time was serving a life sentence in Robben Island.[44]

In 1986 Desmond Tutu became the first black Archbishop of Cape Town. Of Xhosa origin, Tutu was born in Klerksdorp in the Transvaal, and studied for the priesthood at Rosettenville. Briefly he was Dean of Johannesburg before becoming Bishop of Lesotho. He then became the General Secretary of the South African Council of Churches in 1978 and was a crucial voice in the church struggle within South Africa. The young people of the townships, for whom Biko had spoken, were particularly angry and militant (this was the time of the Comrades and necklace killings). At a time when all moderate political activity inside the country was proscribed, the United Democratic Front (UDF) was formed in 1983 by a black leadership worried by the seeming anarchy of the township youth violence.[45] Church leaders rose to prominence in the UDF – Frank Chikane, a Pentecostal and successor of Tutu at the Council of Churches, Allan Boesak and Tutu himself, whose election as Archbishop gave him a strategic position. His creative response and engaging personality gave him a popularity second only to that of Mandela as a leader during the final struggle against apartheid.[46]

43 Frank England and Torquil Paterson (eds.), *Bounty in Bondage: The Anglican Church in Southern Africa* (Johannesburg: Ravan Press, 1989).
44 See the Reeves Papers in Lambeth Palace Library.
45 Jeremy Seekings, *UDF: A History of the United Democratic Front* (Cape Town: David Philip, 2000); Tristan Anne Borer, *Challenging the State* (Notre Dame: Notre Dame University Press, 1998).
46 Shirley du Boulay, *Tutu:Voice of the Voiceless* (London: Hodder & Stoughton, 1988). For a theological analysis see Hendrick Pieterse (ed.), *Desmond Tutu's Message* (Leiden: Brill, 2001).

In 1985, an ecumenical body, the Institute of Contextual Theology, had produced a major new statement on the South African crisis: the Kairos Document. It called for a new 'prophetic' theology to replace the 'church' and the 'state' theology which had hitherto dominated the South African churches. Influenced by black and liberation theologies, it spoke powerfully to 'the situation of death in our country'.[47] Tutu came to embody the strengths of that prophetic, politically committed voice, outspoken, yet eirenic.

The crisis in the South African state was resolved with the sudden ending of the structures of apartheid, the release of Nelson Mandela from his twenty-seven years in jail, and the democratic elections of 1994 – Archbishop Tutu danced joyfully at the polling booth and announced 'At last we are human.' He continued to be a guiding light in the new South Africa, particularly through the establishment of the Truth and Reconciliation Commission. Tutu helped to set its agenda and goals, encouraging the strong religious tone which emerged, not least in its emphasis on forgiveness as a basis for building new democratic structures. This emphasis has not gone without its critics, both from more secular political activists who feel that the churches tend to hijack the discussions and introduce inappropriately theological concerns into what must be a *political* process and, on the other hand, from theologians who stress that a reconciliation which does not also prioritise justice for the victims cannot properly be called Christian. Awareness of the shortcomings in the implementation of the Truth and Reconciliation Commission has not deterred Bishop Tutu from seeing it as one of the signs of hope for the future of a multi-racial, democratic South Africa.[48]

Both Tutu and his successor as Archbishop, Winston Njongonkulu Ndungane, have linked the political freedom struggle in which they were involved as Christians with the continuing struggle for equity among all groups within the church. They have supported the movement for women's ministry, which bore fruit in the decision in 1992 to ordain women to the priesthood. The 1990s have seen the emergence of a vigorous women's movement within the CPSA, with two Anglicans, Brigalia Bam and Denise Ackermann, in prominent positions.[49] Gerald

47 *The Kairos Document: A Theological Comment on the Political Crisis in South Africa*, 2nd edn (London: CIIR/BCC, 1986).

48 Kenneth Christie, *The South African Truth Commission* (Basingstoke: Macmillan, 2000).

49 Denise Ackermann et al. (eds.), *Women Hold up Half the Sky* (Pietermaritzburg: Cluster, 1991); Denise Ackermann, *Claiming our Footprints: South African Women Reflect on Context, Identity and Spirituality* (Matieland: Institute for Theological and Interdisciplinary Research, 2000).

West has explored ways for the churches to develop contextual methods of reading Scripture, not least ones which encourage both women's voices and those of churchgoers in general.[50] Both Tutu and Ndungane have been supportive of gay people in the church. Tutu wrote:

> I come from a section of society that has been deprived, discriminated against, oppressed and marginalised, What I found most attractive about Jesus Christ was just how he identified with those who belonged to such a group of persons ... What Jesus did was to say they belonged, they were insiders too, not strangers, not aliens.[51]

The Anglican Church in South Africa can be said to have emerged from the struggle against apartheid with some integrity. Nevertheless, it is still a church with big tensions, not least among whites who feel alienated by the 'political' character of the church. The emergence of a strong charismatic strand within white congregations has been ambivalent: it has allowed whites for the first time to get alongside black congregations and to appreciate African styles of worship; it has at times seemed to retreat from the messiness of political involvement. The Church of England in South Africa continues to offer an alternative Anglican identity for white people, a refuge for some who feel uneasy at the black leadership of the CPSA. Others are joining the large Pentecostal mega-churches, which, while often multi-racial in their appeal, are self-consciously 'non-political' in a way that the CPSA cannot be. Despite everything, Anglicanism in South Africa still struggles to convince Africans that it is really 'for them'. The older African Instituted Churches (AICs) and the newer Pentecostal churches continue to attract. Sometimes they seem to offer a stronger supportive community, a warmer fellowship, than the Anglican church.

NAMIBIA

In front of the parliament building in Windhoek is an impressive statue of a priest: the Revd Theophilus Hamutumpangela. He stands alongside other heroes of the independence struggle.[52] Hamutumpangela was an Anglican priest from Ovamboland, in the north of Namibia. At Mass in his parish of Christ the King mission in 1954 he preached against the intimidation, violence and daylight robbery perpetrated by the South

[50] Gerald O. West, *The Academy of the Poor: Towards a Dialogical Reading of the Bible* (Sheffield: Sheffield Academic Press, 1999).

[51] Paul Germond and Steve de Gruchy, *Aliens in the Household of God: Homosexuality and Christian Faith in South Africa* (Cape Town: David Philip, 1997).

[52] John J. Grotpeter, *Historical Dictionary of Namibia* (Metuchen: Scarecrow Press, 1994), p. 191.

African security forces on Ovambo workers returning home from the mines. Fr Hamutumpangela invited his parishioners to stay after the service to speak about their experiences and voice their complaints. He then smuggled a letter through Angola, addressed to the United Nations, making a formal complaint. The UN took up the case, and other letters followed in which the exploitative migrant labour contract was exposed. The authorities were infuriated, and took steps to remove the priest from Ovambo. He was exiled to Windhoek. Here he collaborated with Sam Nujoma in the formation of the South West Africa People's Organisation (SWAPO), which was to mount an armed struggle against South Africa's occupation of Namibia.[53]

Hamutumpangela's ability to internationalise the issue was facilitated because of the earlier campaigning of another Anglican priest, Michael Scott, an Englishman whose political activities in Johannesburg in the 1940s had led him to gaol and eventually to expulsion from South Africa. Scott had taken up the cause of the Herero people of South West Africa, who had suffered genocide during German rule at the beginning of the century, and, under the leadership of Chief Hosea Kutako, were resisting South African attempts to incorporate the country into the Union of South Africa. Scott tirelessly lobbied the United Nations, the successor to the League of Nations, which had originally granted the mandate to South Africa after the German defeat.[54]

Lutheranism is the dominant Christian tradition in South West Africa. The Herero had been evangelised by German Lutheran missionaries. Further north, in Ovamboland, Finnish Lutherans were active. Anglicanism only arrived in the 1920s. There were congregations of white and coloured people in Windhoek and other towns in the southern part of the country, but the major Anglican missionary work was undertaken among the Ovambo people, on the borders with Angola. St Mary's School, Odibo, became the centre of Anglican educational work. A pioneer nationalist, Herman Toivo ya Toivo, was educated there, and the school played an important role in creating an English-speaking educated class of Ovambo people in a country where Afrikaans was the dominant medium of communication. Fr Hamutumpangela's facility in English was also important for his political campaign. Otto Kapia, a prominent member of the Ovambo community, told me how his own time as a student at

[53] Colin Winter, *Namibia* (Grand Rapids: Eerdmans, 1977), pp. 89–93.

[54] Michael Worsnip, *Between the Two Fires: The Anglican Church and Apartheid* (Pietermaritzburg: Natal University Press, 1991), Chapter 4. Michael Scott, *A Time to Speak* (New York: Doubleday, 1958).

St Mary's between 1945 and 1950 and his knowledge of English enabled him to avoid the normal contract labour in the mines. Kapia was able to find clerical jobs – first in the American geological research centre at Tsumeb, and then in the Transvaal and the Western Cape. It was here that he was confirmed, and married a Xhosa Anglican whose family came from the Kimberley area of the Northern Cape. In the 1950s Kapia had a conversion experience and joined the Baptist Church, eventually returning to Namibia as a pastor. He later became a businessman and a local politician, a mayor of his town.[55] His story illustrates the fluidity of denominational identity in Southern Africa, and the prestige of the Anglican church in Namibia beyond its actual membership.

In the late 1960s and the 1970s, the Anglican church in Namibia became a serious thorn in the flesh of the South African government. At a time when the bishops in South Africa itself were particularly quiescent and cautious, three bishops were deported from Namibia between 1968 and 1975: the American Robert Mize, his successor Colin Winter, and Winter's assistant, Richard Wood. Their political engagement, the continued protests against the treatment of contract workers, their support for the general strike in 1971 and their protests against the increasing militarisation of Ovamboland were a continuation of an Anglican tradition which had been more or less silenced in South Africa itself. Anglicans were only one small Christian voice of protest; Lutherans also played an important part.[56] But the very weakness of the Anglican church in the white farming community (dominated by Germans and Afrikaners), and the fact that its mission work was almost exclusively among Ovambo people (nearly 90 per cent of its membership), enabled Anglican church leaders to identify themselves more clearly and decisively with the freedom struggle. In independent Namibia, the Anglican church plays a full role in the Christian Council of Namibia, with Nangula Kathindi, the first Anglican woman priest in Namibia, as director. Returning from studies abroad in 1986, she became youth director of the church, at a time when young people were the particular target of the South African Defence Forces in their increasingly desperate campaign against SWAPO.[57]

[55] Interview with Mr Otto Kapia, Ondangwa, Namibia, 22 December 2001.

[56] Peter Katjavivi et al. (eds.), *Church and Liberation in Namibia* (London: Pluto, 1989).

[57] N. Kathindi, 'Women's Struggle in the Church: A Namibian Voice', in Ackermann, *Women Hold up Half the Sky*, pp. 254–66.

ZIMBABWE

If the lack of a strong European constituency in Namibia helped the Anglican church to distance itself from white rule, the opposite problem occurred throughout much of the history of the Anglican Church in Southern Rhodesia (Zimbabwe). Bishop Knight-Bruce arrived in 1891, in the wake of Cecil Rhodes' Pioneers column, which marked the beginning of British colonial rule in Central Africa. The bishop had a special place in the hierarchy of the colonial regime. As in South Africa and Kenya, an extensive network of white parishes was established, and white people tended to dominate the synodical councils of the church. Missionary work among the Shona people relied heavily in the early years on a small number of black South African evangelists, pre-eminently Bernard Mizeki. Mizeki's origins were in Portuguese Mozambique among the Bagwambe people of the Inhambane region. Born around 1861, he came to Cape Town by boat in the early 1870s in search of work. He attended a school run by the Cowley Fathers and was baptised by them in 1886. His linguistic skills and work as an evangelist in the slums of Cape Town led to his training as a catechist at Zonnebloem. He volunteered to accompany Bishop Knight-Bruce as a pioneer missionary in Rhodesia. In the Marandellas district of Mashonaland, he established a good rapport with the local chief, Mangwende. Mizeki gathered together a community of young people as the nucleus of a Christian church. He decided not to look for a wife back in Cape Town but to marry Mutwa, a young relative of the chief: Mizeki emphasised the kinship ties between his own people in Mozambique and the Shona. But in 1896 he was suddenly speared to death during the Shona uprising, which protested against foreign rule. Despite his exemplary missionary style, he was identified with the white colonising power by a group of relatives of the chief anxious to take power themselves. But the place of his martyrdom became a shrine, a focus of devotion and pride among the growing black Christian community.[58]

Rhodesia became a self-governing colony in 1922. Africans were excluded from any political power as Rhodesia developed along the lines of South Africa. Successive white bishops in Rhodesia, notably Edward Paget, Bishop of Mashonaland from 1925 to 1957, endeavoured to give equal attention to their white congregations and the African work.[59]

[58] Jean Farrant, *Mashonaland Martyr: Bernard Mizeki and the Pioneer Church* (Cape Town: Oxford University Press, 1966).

[59] Geoffrey Gibbon, *Paget of Rhodesia* (Cape Town: Africana Book Society, 1973).

He supported the St Augustine's mission at Penhalonga, for many years run by the Community of the Resurrection as a centre for education and theological training. In Matabeleland, the Cyrene school developed a particular concern for African visual art and culture. The most remarkable critique of settler society came from a lone priest, Arthur Shearly Cripps, who (alongside his close friend John White, a Methodist missionary) mounted a sustained protest at the increasingly repressive political and land measures of the Rhodesian government. For twenty-six years an SPG missionary, Cripps left to become freelance, building up a strong Christian community at Maronda Mashanu (Five Wounds). A poet and creative theologian, Cripps often dwelt on the 'Black Christ', who 'walked abroad in Mashonaland', participating in the sufferings and daily trials of his people in a land alienated from its rightful owners.[60]

At Rusape, near where Mizeki had died, an inter-racial farm was established at St Faith's. It became an important centre for the nascent nationalist movement in Rhodesia in the late 1950s and remained a focus of opposition to the Rhodesia Front regime, which unilaterally declared independence from Britain in 1965. Guy and Molly Clutton-Brock, lay Anglican workers at the symbolically renamed 'Cold Comfort Farm', remained a thorn in the side of the regime. For African clergy and laypeople in the Anglicanism of Southern Rhodesia, it was more difficult, in church structures dominated by white members and clergy, to make an outstanding contribution. Although the church leaders were very critical of Ian Smith's UDI, they were reluctant to support the *Chimurenga*, the freedom struggle. In 1976 Bishop Paul Burroughs of Mashonaland attacked the 'Marxist power groups' who had taken over in the former Portuguese colonies, and was fearful that a similar fate would overtake Southern Rhodesia. This provoked his suffragan, Patrick Murindagomo, into open disagreement: he spoke strongly against a constitution 'designed to perpetuate the oppression of 6 million Africans'. Bishop Kenneth Skelton of Matabeleland was also more vigorously opposed to the Rhodesia Front regime.[61] But the Roman Catholics were much more outspoken and consistent in their opposition, and they have continued to offer a strong prophetic voice in independent Zimbabwe, criticising the activities of the 5th brigade in Matabeleland. Catholic Archbishop Pius Ncube of Bulawayo has been at the forefront of criticism of the Mugabe

[60] Murray Steele in O'Connor, *Three Centuries of Mission*, p. 378; Douglas Steere, *God's Irregular, Arthur Shearly Cripps* (London: SPCK, 1973).

[61] John Weller, 'Anglican Integration', in Carl Hallencreutz and Ambrose Moyo, *Church and State in Zimbabwe* (Gweru: Mambo Press, 1988), p. 335.

regime. Anglican voices have been more muted, and indeed embarrassed by the blatant support for the regime afforded by the Bishop of Harare, Nolbert Kunonga.

One of the features of the *Chimurenga* was the holding of night meetings (*pungwe*) in which the guerrillas attempted to give political education to local people.[62] After the end of the war, Christians began to incorporate the *pungwe* into their own practices, as an opportunity for spiritual enrichment. Traditionally the night is a time of danger, when malicious spirits walk abroad and witchcraft is practised. The Christian vigils are a means of 'reclaiming' the night. The churches were initially suspicious of a movement which arose spontaneously, which could not be controlled, and which tended to ignore denominational boundaries. But Anglicans, like Methodists and the African Instituted Churches, have become involved in the vigil movement. Preaching, testimony and song are strong characteristics of the vigils, and there may be a Eucharist at dawn. It has proved a way in which the vitality of African traditions of spirituality can be incorporated into an Anglican system for too long dominated by its foreign origins. Bishop Wilson Sitshebo, Bishop of Matabeleland, has argued that the traditional church practices surrounding burial need to incorporate more fully elements of traditional practice (both Shona and Ndebele) while expressing Christian understandings of death and the hope of resurrection. He has been critical of both the church's clergy and its formal liturgical boards, and groups such as the Mothers' Union and the Fisherfolk, the men's fellowship, for being too cautious on these issues.[63]

UMCA WORK IN MALAWI AND MOZAMBIQUE, AND ZAMBIA

The Universities' Mission to Central Africa was formed as a result of David Livingstone's Cambridge Senate Hall speech of 1857, in which he appealed for missionaries to tackle the ills of Central Africa, especially the disruptions of the slave trade. The mission was the first Anglican overseas mission to be shaped decisively by the Anglo-Catholic movement. It provided an opportunity to send a missionary bishop from the beginning to inaugurate the church. Charles Mackenzie (who had been working in Zululand) was consecrated by Bishop Gray in Cape Town for this task,

[62] Titus Presler, *Transfigured Night: Mission and Culture in Zimbabwe's Vigil Movement* (Pretoria, UNISA, 1999) .

[63] Wilson Sitshebo, Ph.D. dissertation, University of Birmingham, 2000.

and he and the other recruits accompanied Livingstone up the Zambesi River to the Shire highlands, in what is now Malawi. The mission quickly experienced the reality of the disruption which Livingstone had preached about. It became involved in warfare with slave traders, and suffered a critical blow when Mackenzie died from malaria.[64] Bishop William Tozer, his successor, decided that the conditions did not allow for the establishment of a mission in the interior. He withdrew to Zanzibar island. This provoked Livingstone's sarcastic remark about St Augustine attempting the conversion of England from the security of the Isle of Wight. The UMCA had a more positive view of islands than Livingstone did. They much admired the work of Iona and Lindisfarne, and took that as a model for mission. Twenty years later they did return to Central Africa, and they established their base on Likoma Island in Lake Nyasa. Unfortunately this, too, was not an altogether happy choice – Bishop Chauncy Maples was drowned there soon after his consecration in 1895. Moreover, Lake Nyasa had become an international boundary between British and Portuguese territories. The Anglican presence on Likoma meant that it became British, but the UMCA was no longer in a strategic position for the evangelisation of British Nyasaland.

The retreat to Zanzibar had enabled the UMCA to concentrate on theological training, and a number of ex-slaves from Central Africa were ordained, including some Yao. The Yao had been involved as slave traders, and were to turn to Islam in large numbers at the end of the century. One Yao priest was Yohanna Abdallah, who pioneered Anglican work at Unangu in Portuguese East Africa (Mozambique), and towards the end of his life wrote a great history of Yao culture and society, *Chiikala cha Wayao*.[65]

In Nyasaland itself, the UMCA based its operations around Nkhotakota in the central region. But it also established work in the South, at Likwenu. Neither of these areas proved to be dynamic areas economically in a Nyasaland which one colonial official called an 'imperial slum'. Anglican work was and remained overwhelmingly rural. This contrasts with the Scots Presbyterian missions around Blantyre in the South and Livingstonia in the North, which developed a strong modernising and entrepreneurial spirit in their converts. The UMCA missionaries, upper-class, Oxbridge, financially self-sufficient, 'were often ignorant of or

[64] Owen Chadwick, *Mackenzie's Grave* (London: Hodder & Stoughton, 1959).

[65] Yohanna B. Abdallah, *The Yaos/Chiikala cha Wayao*, arranged, edited and translated by Meredith Sanderson (London: Frank Cass, 1973), p. xi (Introduction by Edward Alpers).

repelled by the dynamic, self-assured world of Victorian industry. They thus sought in Africa, not to transform societies, but to insert Christianity into them with as little disturbance as possible.'[66] What they did emphasise was a commitment to theological education and ministerial training, and a willingness to trust African priests and catechists, for example in handling the relationship between the young church and the hostile Nyau secret societies, particularly strong in the Nkhotakota area.

In the 1950s, Anglicans were as critical as other African institutions of the white-dominated Federation with Rhodesia, into which Nyasaland was drawn. But it was the Presbyterian Church which provided the main opposition to colonial rule, and which subsequently became most closely identified with the Banda regime and the ruling Congress Party after independence. Anglicans have been able to participate more profoundly, on an ecumenical basis, in the concerted protests and pressure by which the Christian churches secured the end of President Banda's rule and the calling of democratic elections in 1994.[67]

Zambia

In 1907 the UMCA decided that there ought to be a missionary presence in Northern Rhodesia and commissioned Bishop John Hine to pioneer the work. He exchanged his diocese at Likoma for a new missionary diocese, to encompass the whole of Northern Rhodesia. But the Anglicans were latecomers in the field and found it difficult to achieve this aim without conflicting with other missions. Hine wore himself out in establishing and then attempting to supervise three widely separate stations at Mapanza, in the South-West among the Tonga, at Msoro, near Chipata among Chewa in the East, and at Chipili in Bemba country in the North. Another station was added at Fiwila in the centre of the country in 1918. Leonard Kamungu, a priest born to the east of Lake Nyasa in Portuguese territory, became the first African missionary to Msoro. He recruited large numbers of catechumens, conducting the first baptisms in 1912, and supervised the building of a permanent church, constructed with his own hands. His energetic ministry was cut short by his sudden death in 1913; poison was suspected. A convert of Kamungu's,

[66] John McCracken, *Politics and Christianity in Malawi 1875–1940*, 2nd edn (Blantyre: Kashere, 2000), p. 219; Ian Linden, with Jane Linden, *Catholics, Peasants, and Chewa Resistance in Nyasaland 1889–1939* (London: Heinemann, 1974).

[67] Matthew Schoffeleers, *In Search of Truth and Justice: Confrontations between Church and State in Malawi 1960–1994* (Blantyre: Kachere, 1999), p. 256.

Harun Nchewere, continued evangelistic work to the north of Msoro, but he died of pneumonia in 1931, while training for the ordained ministry at St Mark's College, Fiwila. It was another of Kamungu's converts, Patrick Muyawala, and two other men from Msoro, who eventually were priested in 1933.[68] In 1964 the first Zambian Anglican priest was consecrated: Filemon Mataka, also a man from Msoro. Anglican work also expanded into the urban areas of the Copper Belt and into Lusaka.

In 1955 the Province of Central Africa was inaugurated, bringing together the UMCA work. By 2000 the province comprised five dioceses in Zambia, four in Zimbabwe, three in Malawi and one diocese in Botswana. They all share a common Catholic Anglican tradition. None had ordained a woman by 2002. In each of these countries they are a minority Christian tradition, in comparison with much larger Roman Catholic and Protestant churches. The two Anglican dioceses of Mozambique are part of the Province of Southern Africa – many of its membership having strong ties with South Africa, not least through historic patterns of migrant labour in the mines. Bishop Dinis Sengulane of Lebombo has established throughout the Anglican communion a high reputation as an evangelist; within Mozambique he initiated a campaign to transform weapons into hoes. Yao Anglicans continue to be the most important component of the northern diocese of Niassa, going back to the evangelistic endeavours of Canon Yohanna Abdallah over a hundred years earlier. More recently Anglican work has begun in Angola – Ovambo Anglicans were cut off from Namibia during the war with South Africa in the 1970s and 1980s, but returning migrant workers from the mines of Johannesburg have created a desire for Anglican ministrations in other parts of Angola. They are temporarily under the care of the Portuguese-speaking diocese of Lemombo.

[68] John Weller, *Mainstream Christianity to 1980 in Malawi, Zambia and Zimbabwe* (Gweru: Mambo Press, 1984), pp. 167–81; Reinhard Henkel, *Christian Missions in Africa: A Social Geographical Study of the Impact of their Activities in Zambia* (Berlin: Dietrich Reimer Verlag, 1989).

CHAPTER 9

East Africa

INTRODUCTION

East Africa was the last region of Africa in which Anglicans took an interest. But it has become one of the most distinctive regions of the worldwide Anglican communion. The statistics in Table 9.1 show something of the strength of Anglican churches in East Africa at the end of the twentieth century. Though such figures have to be viewed with caution, they do give an overall sense of the importance fof Anglicanism in the region. Noteworthy is the strength of Anglicanism in areas colonised by Belgium. One of the features of this region is the strength of local languages – Swahili and Luganda, in particular, have played the key role which English or Creole English assumed in the extension of Anglicanism in South and West Africa. From an early date, East African Anglicanism developed a vigorous 'vernacular' identity.

Anglicans were not the first missionaries in East Africa. At the end of the fifteenth century, the Portuguese had established alliances with Muslim rulers and established staging posts along the coast, strategically important for securing the sea route to Goa. Fort Jesus on Mombasa Island became a symbol of their military power. Some rulers were converted to Catholicism, but Portuguese interference caused resentment, and as Portugal's power faded, Christianity languished.[1] In 1844, Ludwig Krapf and his pregnant wife, Rosina, landed at Mombasa to renew Christian evangelisation for the Church Missionary Society. One of Krapf's first acts was to dig the graves of his wife and child. Krapf had been expelled from Ethiopia, where he had attempted to win over the Ethiopian Orthodox Church to a more biblical Christianity. Unfortunately, the presence of Protestant missionaries rekindled the suspicions of western Christianity in Ethiopia which had led to the expulsion of Jesuit

[1] G. S. P. Freeman-Grenville, *The Mombasa Rising against the Portuguese, 1631* (Oxford: Oxford University Press, 1980), p. 163.

Table 9.1. *Anglican membership: East Africa*

Country	Anglican membership	Percentage of total population
Uganda	8,650,000	39.4
Kenya	3,000,000	10.0
Tanzania	2,650,000	7.9
Francophone countries		
Rwanda	600,000	7.8
Burundi	443,000	7.2
Congo Democratic Republic	440,000	0.9
Indian Ocean francophone countries		
Madagascar	320,000	2.0
Seychelles	5,200	6.7
Mauritius	5,000	0.4

Source: David Barrett, George T. Kurian and Todd M. Johnson, *World Christian Encyclopedia* (2 vols., Oxford: Oxford University Press, 2001), Volume 1. The figures sometimes differ considerably from those given in the *Church of England Year Book 2000* (London: Church House, 2000), where Anglican membership is assessed more rigorously.

missionaries in the seventeenth century.[2] Brought up in the intense Pietism of Württemberg Lutheranism, Krapf was clear that the Christian cause would not be advanced by appeal to local rulers or to foreign powers:

> Expect nothing, or very little, from political changes in Eastern Africa. As soon as you begin to anticipate much good missionary labour from politics you will be in danger of mixing yourself with them . . . On the contrast, banish the thought that Europe must spread her protecting wings over Eastern Africa, if my work is to prosper in that land of outer darkness.[3]

Nevertheless, his vision was broad – a chain of missions stretching from Mombasa to Cairo, and from the east to the west coast. This would only happen in God's good time. In the mean time, Krapf was content to live simply, preferably at some distance from the Islamic culture of the coast. He established a mission at Rabai Mpya, among the Mijikenda people. From there he and his colleague and compatriot Johannes Rebmann conducted a series of exploratory expeditions to test the feasibility of Krapf's vision. They reported on the snows of Mounts Kilimanjaro and Kenya to a disbelieving audience in Europe. Krapf nearly lost his life on

[2] Donald Crummey, *Priests and Politicians: Protestant and Catholic Missions in Orthodox Ethiopia 1830–1868* (Oxford: Clarendon Press, 1972).

[3] J. Ludwig Krapf, *Travels, Researches and Missionary Labours* (London: Frank Cass, 1968), p. 512 (1st edn 1860).

an expedition to Ukambani and realised that the fears generated by increasing slave trading made the times unpropitious. Forced to retire through ill health, he returned briefly to establish a Methodist mission.[4] Rebmann, who remained at Rabai until the 1870s, lacked Krapf's temperamental serenity, and became increasingly pessimistic.

In 1862 a second Anglican mission was established in East Africa, when Bishop Tozer relocated the headquarters of the Universities' Mission to Central Africa to Zanzibar. Called into being by Livingstone's advocacy, the UMCA was more activist than Krapf in the struggle against the slave trade. It was the first Anglican mission fully to embody the ethos of the Oxford Movement. In a world devastated by slave trading and insecurity, both Krapf and the UMCA hoped to establish alternative communities which modelled Christian values. From the 1870s the UMCA began to establish missions on the mainland, with important work in Usambara at Magila, and at Masasi, on the Ruvuma River to the south-west.[5]

A watershed occurred in 1873, when Sir Bartle Frere, the British negotiator, made an agreement with the Sultan of Zanzibar to prohibit the slave trade between the mainland and Zanzibar. This provided new opportunities for both the UMCA and the CMS. Frere undertook an inspection of CMS work. He was respectful but critical of the German missionaries, and advised the CMS to become more active in the anti-slavery movement by establishing a freed-slave settlement. 'Frere Town' was established north of Mombasa. Already some African freed slaves, educated at CMS stations in Bombay and Sharanpur, near Nasik, had volunteered to return to East Africa. They included David and Priscilla George, William and Jemimah Jones, and Ismael and Grace Semler. Many of the men were Yao (from modern Malawi or Mozambique). A number of their wives were of Ethiopian origin. Like the freed slaves of West Africa, they adopted European names. They had practical skills as blacksmiths and carpenters. Like the West Africans, they were proud of their English Christian culture. But they were also fluent in Swahili, the lingua franca of the coast. Their role in laying the foundations of Anglican Christianity in East Africa was immense.

They were soon augmented by native East Africans such as Isaac Nyondo, the son of Abraham Abe Gunja, a Giriama convert from Rabai; and James Deimler, an ex-slave who grew up in Frere Town. They possessed practical

4 W. B. Anderson, *The Church in East Africa 1840–1974* (Dodoma: CT Press, 1977).

5 Jerome Moriyama, 'Building a Home Grown Church', in Daniel O'Connor, *Three Centuries of Mission: The United Society for the Propagation of the Gospel 1701–2000* (London: Continuum, 2000) pp. 330–42.

and administrative skills and had the energy and enthusiasm to initiate Christian communities away from the coast, such as Jilore, a sanctuary for runaway slaves established in the 1870s by another Giriama convert of Abe Gunja, David Koi. These sanctuaries were intensely disliked by plantation owners, and in 1883 Jilore was raided by the local Swahili chief, M'baruk. Koi was beheaded. He thus became the first Anglican East African Christian martyr, two years before the killings started in Buganda.[6]

Increasingly, however, Bombay Africans and those trained at Frere Town came to resent the insensitive discipline and growing racism of the European missionaries. By the 1890s there was an exodus of residents in search of new opportunities provided in Zanzibar and Mombasa by the onset of British colonial rule. The group of evangelists, like Jones and Deimler, who did continue to work for the mission became discontented by the pay differentials and the lack of esteem for their work. Jones and Semler were made deacons by Bishop Hannington in 1885, but it was to be ten years before they were priested (by Bishop Tucker). Deimler, at one time seen as a potential Bishop Crowther of East Africa, was made deacon in 1896. But he was never priested: he had become too outspoken in his criticisms. One flashpoint became the attempt by missionaries to prevent converts from adopting European dress and to discourage the use of English. Such missionary paternalism was rightly interpreted as an attempt to diminish Africans and to justify discrimination in pay.[7]

Bishop James Hannington was appointed as the first bishop of Eastern Equatorial Africa in 1882. He was the first bishop of the CMS areas, but not the first Anglican bishop – from the beginning, the UMCA had been led by bishops. In 1879 Bishop Steere had ordained the very first East African Anglican deacon, John Swedi. Then in 1886 Bishop Smythies ordained Cecil Majaliwa as deacon; and in 1890 he became the first priest. Like Jones and Semler, Majaliwa was a Yao freed slave; unlike them, he had been specifically prepared for ordination, and had spent some years at St Augustine's College in Canterbury. For the UMCA, a well-educated, classically trained African clergy was a priority, but one which few could aspire to. Bishop Tucker also emphasised the importance of an African clergy, based on locally trained men, with long experience as catechists

[6] Colin Reed, *Pastors, Partners and Paternalists: African Church Leaders and Western Missionaries in the Anglican Church in Kenya, 1850–1900* (Leiden: Brill, 1997). In accordance with Bantu linguistic usage, Buganda signifies the place; Baganda, the people; Muganda, a single person; and Luganda, the language.

[7] Robert Strayer, *The Making of Mission Communities in East Africa: Anglicans and Africans in Colonial Kenya, 1875–1935* (London: Heinemann, 1978).

and evangelists – very different from the UMCA practice, but one which produced much larger numbers of 'peasant clergy'.

UGANDA

In 1886, the newly deaconed William Jones accompanied Bishop Hannington on his ill-fated journey to Buganda. Buganda was the powerful kingdom on the shore of the great lake, ruled by a king (Kabaka), outward-looking and receptive to new ideas, including Islam. But Kabaka Muteesa had become aware of the political dangers of Islam (especially from Egyptian imperialism), and in 1876 executed some of the courtiers who embraced the new religion. He took advantage of the visit of Henry Morton Stanley to appeal for Christian missionaries as a counter-weight. The CMS, aided by an anonymous donation, was able to respond rapidly to this appeal. The first party arrived on 30 June 1877. Although never the leader, the most remarkable personality among the early missionaries was Alexander Mackay, a Scots engineer trained in Berlin. He was a layman, and not an Anglican – his father was a minister of the Free Church of Scotland. He was admired both for his practical skills and for the enthusiasm with which he preached the Gospel. Archbishop Lavigerie's missionary order, the White Fathers, arrived in Buganda in June 1879, much to the disgust of the Protestants. The young Alsatian priest Simeon Lourdel proved a match for Mackay in his debating skills. The stage was set for a competition, often condemned for its unecumenical zeal, but hugely enjoyed by the young pages at court. Three competing religious factions (Muslim, Protestant and Catholic) were now vying for support in Buganda, and won an increasing number of converts. The Kabaka began to clamp down on all expressions of foreign religion. But he was unable to stop the enthusiasm of the converts, for whom a new world was opening up, symbolised by the power of literacy (*okusoma*) on which the religions of the Book put such store. Converts became known as *basomi*, a name which signified not only that they were 'readers' but that they were worshippers of God almighty, Katonda, the creator.

Muteesa died in 1884, leaving his eighteen-year-old successor Mwanga with a series of internal and external problems. The threat from Egypt had by this time abated, only to be replaced by the advent of European imperialism with the sudden eruption of German activity on the East African coast.[8] The same fear which had led to the persecution of

[8] M. S. M. Kiwanuka, *A History of Buganda: From the Foundation of the Kingdom to 1900* (London: Longmans, 1971).

Baganda Muslims in 1876 now worked against the Christian communities. Early in 1885 the first three Anglicans were killed – three adolescents, Nuwa Seruwanga, Marko Kakumba and Yusufu Lugalama. Only a few months later, Bishop Hannington arrived on the east bank of the Nile, without permission and by a new and strategically sensitive route. He and his entourage were deemed to be an invading force. Hannington paid for these indiscretions with his life; 150 of his porters also perished. They included Christians from Frere Town and Muslims from the coast. The next year, Mwanga initiated a persecution of Baganda Christians, mainly young pages, but also some older men. His overall motivation was the need to act decisively to maintain his authority at a time of international crisis. The issue of the refusal by a young page to submit to Mwanga's homosexual demands was one of the triggers, but by no means the most important. Some hundreds of Catholics and Protestants died for their faith, about sixty at the execution site of Namugongo.[9]

For the Christian survivors this established an urgent need to resort to arms to prevent their faith being crushed. A militarisation of the religious groups followed which resulted in the overthrowing of the Kabaka, his subsequent restoration as a puppet ruler, and the beginnings of British colonial rule. This revolution began as a combination of all the new religious groups, but soon developed into a civil war between Muslim and Christian, resulting in a Muslim defeat. A conflict then ensued between Catholics and Protestants, which was only resolved when the British threw in their weight behind the Protestants. The religious geography of Uganda was thus established in the 1890s and was to survive until independence and beyond, with the Anglicans exercising a quasi-established position in the state and the Catholics, politically quiescent, outpacing the Protestants in numbers. The Muslims, having lost out, had to be content with a secure but lowly status in the colonial state.

This state of affairs was rapidly replicated in other parts of what became the Uganda Protectorate, especially in the kingdoms to the west of Buganda – Bunyoro, Tooro and Ankole. Ugandan Anglicanism tended to spread top down. The chiefs in Buganda became agents of conversion among their people. They sponsored and controlled the activities of Baganda catechists and pastors. The first ordinations occurred when Bishop Tucker arrived in 1891. Sir Apolo Kaggwa and Ham Mukasa, high-status converts who had survived the persecution, became great

9 J. F. Faupel, *African Holocaust* (London: Geoffrey Chapman, 1962). Louise Pirouet, *Strong in the Faith* (Kampala: Church Press, 1969).

Protestant chiefs, leaders in church and state. They fashioned a new vernacular literature shaped by Christian ideals, but looking back with pride on the traditions of the Buganda kingdom. By 1897, the missionary George Pilkington and the Muganda convert Henry Wright Duta had translated the whole Bible into Luganda, a remarkable achievement. The vernacular Bible was grafted into Kiganda culture, providing the traditional institutions with a new dynamic and legitimacy. This remarkable convergence of culture and religion in Buganda was transmitted to other parts of Uganda. The Baganda evangelists were to be criticised as 'sub-imperialists', transmitters of a potent cocktail of Kiganda culture, western education, and Christianity. This attempt to use Christianity to extend Buganda's cultural hegemony was resisted. Buganda's example was, nevertheless, imitated, as other societies made their own attempts to incorporate the new values of Christianity into the traditional institutions. But in the north of Uganda, among the Acholi, Langi and Teso, this attempt to spread Christianity through hierarchical institutions was more problematic. It fitted less neatly into the very different social and cultural environment.[10]

Overall, the Anglican Church in Uganda produced a form of Christianity which was strongly 'owned' by its African converts. This is not to deny that many aspects of missionary Christianity were foreign and failed to speak to the religious sensibilities and aspirations of Ugandans. But Christianity was something which had been freely embraced rather than externally imposed. It has often been said that the Catholic church appealed to the peasants in Uganda, and the Anglican church to the elites. By and large, the Anglicans did capture the established elites of Uganda's diverse societies, and its educational system was geared towards producing the new elites (bureaucrats and teachers) of colonial society. But the Anglican church also penetrated deeply into the fabric of society. Its system of bush schools was extremely effective in inculcating the basic elements of the faith in children from peasant backgrounds. Its Ugandan catechists and pastors (largely from humble backgrounds themselves) provided a ministry for the church which was responsive to local needs, if rather conservative and subservient to authority.[11] Bishop Tucker's lasting institutional legacy was the creation of a constitution for the 'Native Anglican Church' of Uganda. The constitution was not what Tucker had wanted – he failed to persuade missionaries to forgo a corporate identity

[10] Louise Pirouet, *Black Evangelists* (London: Rex Collings, 1978).
[11] J. V. Taylor, *The Growth of the Church in Buganda* (London: SCM, 1958).

and simply become part of the church structure. But despite these limitations, the Church of Uganda developed a very strong sense of its own integrity and autonomy, unequalled in Africa.[12]

KENYA

The vigour of the Church of Uganda can be seen in the planting of the church in Kavirondo in western Kenya. Here both Bantu-speaking Luhya people and Nilotic Luo responded strongly to the Gospel message as preached by Baganda evangelists. The school at Maseno (later to become famous under its headmaster Carey Francis) acted as a powerful base for disseminating Anglicanism in the area. But unlike the situation in Uganda, Anglicans here competed with a host of other Protestant missions, many of American origin. Initially part of the Uganda Protectorate, Kavirondo had been transferred to Kenya Colony in 1902, but remained part of the diocese of Uganda until congregations were transferred to the diocese of Mombasa in 1922. Moving from a diocese which had such a strong corporate identity to one divided down the middle by racial divisions was not easy. As part of the development of Kenya as a 'white man's country', congregations sprang up in the 'White Highlands'. A second cathedral for the diocese was built in Nairobi; with its solid Norman architecture, it became the site for the practice of 'English traditional religion'. Despite the growing numerical preponderance of African congregations, representation in the synod of the diocese of Mombasa was divided equally between mission and settler. The church in western Kenya retained a pride in its origins. Under the guidance of its greatest Irish missionary, Archdeacon W. E. Owen, Kavirondo Anglicans were at the forefront in the emergence of a Kenyan African politics of protest, opposing settler political aspirations and labour demands. As in Buganda, the Christians of Kavirondo became enthusiastic missionaries. Luo Anglicans were responsible for planting the Anglican church over the border in the Mara region of Tanganyika in the 1930s.[13]

The other key area for the development of Kenyan Anglicanism was among the Kikuyu people of Central Province. Anglicanism has often been seen as particularly attractive to a hierarchical state like Buganda.

[12] H. B. Hansen, *Mission, Church and State in a Colonial Setting: Uganda 1890–1925* (London: Heinemann, 1984).

[13] [CPK Provincial Unit of Research] *Rabai to Mumias: A Short History of the Church of the Province of Kenya 1844–1994* (Nairobi: Uzima, 1994); K. Ward, 'The Development of Protestant Christianity in Kenya 1910–1940', Ph.D. dissertation, University of Cambridge, 1976.

But acephalous, less centralised, societies, like the Kikuyu, also strongly embraced Anglicanism. At the beginning of the colonial occupation of Kenya, the Kikuyu were subject to a veritable missionary scramble as a host of mission societies moved inland. A 'spheres' system was negotiated in the attempt to control the turf war among missionaries. The CMS, the Church of Scotland Mission, the Africa Inland Mission, the Gospel Missionary Society and the Methodists each agreed to work within designated areas. The Catholic missions were also allocated specific areas by government, though they refused to be bound by the spheres system of the Protestants. A complex patchwork of mission jurisdictions resulted. After a slow start, all missions in Kikuyuland experienced considerable growth, especially after the First World War. The war produced a body of mission converts whose horizons had been widened by their experience in the Mission Volunteer Force, which had taken part in the campaign against the Germans in East Africa.

In contrast to the large, sophisticated Church of Scotland mission stations, the Anglicans developed a range of one-man mission stations in Kikuyu which proved responsive to the aspirations and demands of the young *athomi* converts (*athomi* has precisely the same meaning of 'reader' as *basomi* conveyed in Buganda). The first *athomi* took advantage of new opportunities provided by the missions in the same way that young Kikuyu *ahoi* (people without land of their own) had always done. Kikuyu society had always been highly mobile and enterprising. By the late 1920s, Kikuyu Christianity, conspicuously its Anglican version, provided a potent critique of colonialism, and particularly the land expropriation of settler society.[14]

THE KIKUYU CONFLICT

For English Anglicans in the early twentieth century, Kikuyu was more to do with a particularly heated ecclesiastical crisis than an African people. In 1913 Protestant missionaries met together at the largest Church of Scotland mission centre in the colony, Kikuyu. (Ironically the Kikuyu themselves called the place 'Thogoto', which is the Kikuyu version of 'Scotland'!) The conference included representatives of a wide variety of British and American Evangelical societies, and included the Bishops of Uganda and Mombasa, whose two dioceses covered the colony.

[14] John Karanja, *Founding an African Faith: Kikuyu Anglican Christianity 1900–1945* (Nairobi: Uzima, 1999).

A decision was made to establish a federation of missionary societies which would work towards the creation of a 'united native church'.

The Church of Scotland leader, the Revd Dr John Arthur, celebrated a final Communion service at which the bishops participated. News of the conference alarmed the UMCA Bishop of Zanzibar, Frank Weston. He was disturbed that his fellow bishops were prepared to contemplate dissolving Anglican identity in order to create a church which did not appear to be concerned about Catholic order, sacraments and doctrine. He protested to Randall Davidson, the Archbishop of Canterbury, indicting them for heresy. The storm abated with the onset of war. But in 1916, Archbishop Davidson formally condemned agreements which ignored or devalued Anglican doctrine and practice, but recognised the special circumstances of East Africa. After the war, a further Kikuyu conference was convened. Bishop Weston was invited and attended. The main Kenyan Protestant bodies agreed to establish an alliance (as opposed to a federation) of missionary societies. Hope was expressed that joint ordinations and a common discipline might emerge, a less ambitious plan than a united church. Weston was still not best pleased, but happy that the abandonment of Catholic order was averted.[15] One result of the conference was the establishment of the Alliance High School at the Church of Scotland Kikuyu mission.

Neither Kikuyu nor any other African Christians had been invited to either of the Kikuyu conferences. That they were therefore not party to the agreements was to become a serious handicap. All Protestant missions placed high ethical demands on their adherents. Nevertheless, the CMS was less willing than other missions to lay down precise rules about such matters as drinking as a condition for baptism. In the 1920s, Kikuyu Anglicanism developed a cultural sensitivity to the aspirations of its young converts which marks it off from the other Protestant missions. At the Kahuhia station, the young CMS missionary Handley Hooper and his wife Cecily were particularly noted for their encouragement of local initiative, including political awareness. It was at Kahuhia that the Kikuyu Central Association first flourished, soon to be involved in the bitter dispute about female genital mutilation – 'female circumcision', as it was called at the time.[16]

As among many East African peoples, adolescent initiation was an important rite of passage, marking the transition to adulthood and the

[15] Gavin White, 'Kikuyu 1913: An Ecumenical Controversy', Ph.D. dissertation, London University, 1970.

[16] Jocelyn Murray, 'The Kikuyu Female Circumcision Controversy', Ph.D. dissertation, University of California, 1974.

readiness to assume family responsibilities. The first Kikuyu Christians had overwhelmingly been male. The Church of Scotland mission stations first became aware of female circumcision as a problem. Their boarding schools were more cut off from the local community. Girls began to leave at the time for their circumcision, and many did not return. At first the Scots doctors had agreed to perform infibulation in the hospital – but soon became convinced that there was no medical or ethical justification for this. In 1929 Dr Arthur began publicly to urge the government to ban female circumcision completely. He insisted that all candidates for baptism and all pastors, teachers and mission employees should make a public pledge (*kirore*) to prevent their daughters from being circumcised. The imposition of this pledge caused a mass desertion and infuriated Kikuyu political leaders, especially of the Anglican-founded Kikuyu Central Association. Other missions which fell into line with Dr Arthur soon found that they could not retain their membership.

Anglicans, always unwilling to make membership conditional on particular rules, were reluctant to comply. One missionary in Embu, however, did make the decision to insist on abandonment of female circumcision, almost two years after the initial crisis, with a predictable large falling away of membership. But most other CMS stations refused to make it a condition of baptism and church membership. Consequently Anglicans lost relatively few members at a time when other missions had to cope with the rise of independent churches in their district. The Alliance missions felt let down by Anglican compromise. But among Kikuyu Christians, respect for Anglicans was boosted. The crisis brought a virtual end to any hopes of a united church. Kikuyu Anglicans increasingly refused to submit to the spheres system.

Neither Kikuyu Anglicans nor the dissidents from other Protestant churches were necessarily arguing for the retention of female circumcision. Rather they looked for a slow process of education and enlightenment. But they were convinced that Dr Arthur's attacks were an onslaught on Kikuyu Christian identity. A protest song expressed it this way: 'There were only ten commandments till they reached Dr Arthur's house, then they spread like a gourd.'[17] As the Kikuyu Central Association put it:

> Missionaries have tried on many occasions to interfere with the tribal customs and the question is asked whether, circumcision being the custom of the Kikuyu Christian, he is to be a heathen simply because he is a Kikuyu.[18]

[17] Ward, 'Protestant Christianity in Kenya', p. 197. [18] Ibid., p. 165.

Only the new African unity produced by the East African Revival some two decades later really healed some of the divisions between the Protestant churches which the conflict of 1929 had engendered.

TANGANYIKA

The UMCA also moved inland in the last part of the nineteenth century, at the beginning of the colonial era. For the UMCA it was a move into German East Africa, the colonial power from 1884 until the end of the First World War. Germany's support for German missions and greater reliance on local Islam to provide the lower ranks of administrators and clerks meant that the UMCA in German East Africa developed a much greater distinction between church and colonial power. The UMCA's most formidable missionary was Frank Weston, who first arrived in Zanzibar in 1898, and became bishop in 1908. He was as willing to campaign against colonial injustice as against ecclesiastical fudges, most famously protesting against forced labour in British East African possessions in *The Serfs of East Africa* – policies which affected his own diocese as well as Kenya, since German East Africa had just come under British administration. Not since the days of Bishop Colenso had an Anglican bishop from Africa had such an influence on the shape of the Anglican communion. Weston would not have been pleased with the comparison. But they had this in common: they had a deep and unstinting commitment to Africa and its evangelisation, and were both willing to launch into controversial political and ecclesiastical disputes. Weston was by the early 1920s a leading figure in mapping out a confident role for Anglo-Catholicism within the Anglican communion worldwide, and his death in 1924, at the age of 53, was felt keenly.[19]

The most remarkable mission in Tanganyika was the German Lutheran work among the Chagga of the Mount Kilimanjaro area. Bruno Guttmann developed a mission praxis, based on the concept of a *Volkskirche*, in which the traditional structures and ethos of a people were quite deliberately incorporated into the organic development of the church. The UMCA too aspired to a church which incorporated African communal values, though it put a much greater stress on priestly mobilisation of this vision. The emphasis of both Lutherans and Anglicans accorded well with the commitment to 'Indirect Rule' promulgated by the new British rulers who took over German East Africa

[19] H. Maynard Smith, *Frank, Bishop of Zanzibar* (London: SPCK, 1926).

(now named Tanganyika) as a mandate of the League of Nations. Indirect Rule claimed to utilise traditional authority figures and institutions in government. Tanganyika was not the focus of the same conflict between African culture and the missions. In contrast to the situation among the Kikuyu, the UMCA missionary in Masasi, Vincent Lucas (elected as first Bishop of Masasi in 1926), had for long attempted to 'Christianise' initiation rites, by introducing a Christian *jando* (circumcision guild) as an alternative to the traditional adolescent rite of passage for males. Masasi, in the far south of the country, on the borders with Portuguese Mozambique, was seen as a potential Christian state. One of the rulers, Matola, became a Christian convert in the 1890s. He was described as a 'Clovis or Ethelbert' – UMCA missionaries were inclined to look to early medieval European models. Lucas hoped to convert 'elements connected with paganism to the ends of Christianity' and saw the circumcision guilds as a good candidate for such conversion. The African clergy proved enthusiastic about the Christian *jando*. At a time, during the high noon of colonialism, when missionary paternalism tended to depreciate African skills and enterprise, it gave them considerable influence and prestige which the missionaries could not aspire to. The Christian *jando* was a protracted affair over many weeks. It was suffused with a Christian imagery invented by Lucas and his African clergy.[20]

They were less successful in integrating the rather more secretive and sexually explicit female initiation. But female circumcision as such was not involved, and so the issues did not seem quite so acute. The UMCA was not unique in its stress on what at the time was often called an 'adaptation' strategy, motivated by concerns to avoid 'detribalisation' and limit the corrosive effects of modernity. Such experiments have sometimes been seen as regressive, overly protective and paternalistic and as having little active support from African Christians, especially from young people more concerned with adapting to modern opportunities and stresses than with upholding traditional custom. The Masasi experiment did have an integrity which commands respect. Nevertheless, by the 1960s it had become somewhat fossilised, ceasing to respond very effectively to a society in rapid transition.

The general emphasis on the sacramental gave UMCA liturgy a very different feel from that typical in CMS missions. The UMCA did not

[20] Terence Ranger, 'Missionary Adaptation of African Religious Institutions: The Masasi Case', in T. O. Ranger and I. N. Kimambo, *The Historical Study of African Religion* (London: Heinemann, 1972), p. 239.

simply translate the Book of Common Prayer into Swahili and other vernaculars. Its mission task provided it with an opportunity to overcome the theological inadequacies of Cranmer's liturgical work. The diocese of Zanzibar (under Weston's direction) devised a new prayer book which incorporated African cultural practices, on the suggestion of the African priests. It also facilitated the incorporation of more explicitly Catholic elements which were not allowed at home.[21]

Such liturgical exuberance was bound to put the UMCA at loggerheads with the other Anglicans of the CMS tradition in Tanganyika and elsewhere. The CMS had originally established stations in the 1870s at Mpapwe, Dodoma and Mwanza as part of their supply route from the coast to Uganda. With the establishment of British colonial rule in Kenya this route no longer had strategic value, and the stations seemed devalued and stunted in their growth. The CMS tried to off-load them onto another Protestant mission, but never contemplated handing them to the UMCA! Eventually they did remain Anglican. The Australian CMS assumed responsibility in 1929. Ironically, the most Catholic mission in the Anglican communion was thus joined by the most Protestant.[22] The story goes that the UMCA advised their adherents to attend the Catholic church if they moved to a CMS area, and the CMS advised joining the Moravians or Lutherans if their members found themselves in UMCA territory. It is probably apocryphal (and one can hardly imagine Weston being so cavalier with church order), but nicely illustrates the sense that the two missions occupied different universes.

THE EAST AFRICAN REVIVAL

The East African Revival originated in Uganda and Ruanda in the early 1930s.[23] It has had a profound impact on the character of East African Anglicanism as a whole, and indeed far beyond the Anglican church. The movement is commonly known as Balokole – Luganda for 'Saved People'. The Revival has its roots in classical Evangelical revivalism and the Keswick movement of the late nineteenth century. But from the

[21] Smith, *Frank*, pp. 289–91.

[22] T. O. Beidelman, *Colonial Evangelism* (Bloomington: Indiana University Press, 1982); Raphael Mwita Akiri, 'The Growth of Christianity in Ugogo and Ukaguru', Ph.D. dissertation, University of Edinburgh, 1999.

[23] There is a large literature on the Revival. See Jocelyn Murray, 'A Bibliography of the East African Revival Movement', *Journal of Religion in Africa* 8.2 (1976), pp. 144–7; K. Ward, 'Tukutendereza Yesu', in Z. Nthamburi, *From Mission to Church* (Nairobi: Uzima, 1991), pp. 113–44; P. St John, *Breath of Life* (London: Norfolk Press, 1971).

beginning it was an African initiative. In its early days it was often called the 'Ruanda movement' because of its close connections with the Ruanda Mission of the CMS. In 1922, the CMS had suffered a major schism, after a decade of conflict over questions of biblical authority. The creation of the Bible Churchmen's Missionary Society (BCMS) resulted. Around this time, two medical doctors, Leonard Sharp and Algie Stanley Smith, were pioneering missionary work in the newly created Belgian mandate of Ruanda-Urundi. They were joined by Dr Joe Church and his wife Decie. Sympathising with the dissidents who had created the BCMS, they nevertheless wanted to remain within the CMS fellowship. The result was a special 'Ruanda Mission', which guaranteed that only those who held conservative Evangelical views on the Bible would be sent as missionaries. In addition to Ruanda-Urundi, the mission also worked in the Kigezi region of Uganda. It developed substantial hospital work at Gahini in Ruanda and Kisiizi in Uganda. Ecclesiastically the Ruanda Mission came under the jurisdiction of the Bishop of Uganda. The Ruanda missionaries endeavoured to be loyal Anglicans, but they were Evangelicals first. They were very critical of developments within the Church of Uganda: its compromises with African customs incompatible with true Christianity, the clericalism (*bukulu*) of its institutional life, its stifling 'orthodoxy'.

In this they found allies among the Baganda themselves, in particular Simeoni Nsibambi, a member of one of the elite families. Joe Church struck up a lasting friendship with Nsibambi, and utilised his network of contacts to recruit keen Ugandan Christians as hospital workers at Gahini in Ruanda. It was there that, in 1935, the first outbreak of revival occurred. Nsibambi's brother, Blasio Kigozi, a deacon working at Gahini, brought back the message of revival to the 1936 synod of the Church of Uganda. His fervent plea *Zukuka* (Awake!) made a considerable impression. His prophetic role seemed enhanced by his sudden death shortly afterwards. Revival fellowships began to emerge throughout Buganda and southern Uganda. Members of the fellowship called themselves *ab'oluganda* (brothers and sisters), and saw themselves as belonging to a new clan, a new expression of African communal values and solidarity. They denounced paganism and unchristian compromises (particularly with regard to sexual practice) and espoused a strict monogamy, a puritanical life style and a fierce honesty. The public confession of sin within the fellowship resulted in the singing of the great Revival hymn of absolution, 'Tukutendereza Yesu', which became the characteristic song of the Revival. Their attacks on the clergy did not endear them to either missionaries or African clergy. The Bishop of Uganda, C. E. Stuart, encouraged young Balokole to train for the ministry of the church, and was bitterly disappointed when in 1941 their uncompromising and aggressive behaviour led to the expulsion of twenty-six of them from the theological college at Mukono.[24] Although some of these were ordained later, many, including their leader, William Nagenda, decided to remain as lay evangelists. The surprising thing was that they did not, as they could well have done, leave the church. The Balokole movement as a whole has stubbornly refused to become schismatic. It prefers a stance of critical solidarity with the church.

Preaching a radical message of equality, including the equality of white and black, the Revival movement played a significant part in freeing the Gospel from its association with colonialism. This was to be particularly important as the Revival spread to Kenya, with its increasing political racial tensions in the post-Second World War period. In Kenya the Revival had an impact beyond its Anglican base, making profound inroads into the other Alliance missions, especially those of the Methodists and Presbyterians. It served to bring together Christians who had been bruised and divided by the circumcision conflict. Of all the Protestant missions, the Africa Inland Mission was most resistant to the Revival, despite its own origins in American revivalism. For all missionaries the exuberance and extremism of revivalists presented a danger. AIM missionaries were more anxious than most to impose discipline and order in their congregations. As a result, in the Nandi area of western Kenya, some of those who were influenced by the Revival broke away from the AIM and established a rival Anglican church, a continuing source of religious and political disagreement in the area.[25] In the Mau Mau conflict of the 1950s, Balokole were notable for their refusal to compromise their faith. They were reluctant to join the Home Guard militia formed by the colonial authority. But they absolutely refused to take the oaths required by the Mau Mau: these often involved goat sacrifice, and the revivalists were adamant that only the blood of Jesus could save them.[26]

The Revival became a significant movement in Tanganyika. It made a big impact in a number of missions which had at one time been Anglican but which had been handed on to other missions, such as the Lutherans

[24] K. Ward, 'Obedient Rebels: The Mukono Crisis of 1941', *Journal of Religion in Africa* 19.3 (1989), pp. 194–227.

[25] Christopher Rutto, 'Nandi Identity and Christian Denominationalism', Ph.D. dissertation, University of Birmingham, 2003.

[26] E. M. Wiseman, *Kikuyu Martyrs* (London: Highway Press, 1958).

of Bukoba. The most distinguished theologian of the Revival, Bishop Josiah Kibira, came from this church.[27] The Revival also made an impact in Dodoma, among those CMS stations which had felt neglected for so long. A group of Ugandan laypeople spent a number of years as schoolteachers in Dodoma, including Festo Kivengere, eventually to become Bishop of Kigezi.

The Revival movement put great emphasis on lay witness, and on the ability of women, as well as men, to testify and preach. Eventually revivalists overcame the fears engendered by the Mukono crisis and did encourage men and women to train for ordination. At the time of independence and during the rapid expansion of the church in the years after independence, many Brethren became bishops throughout East Africa. The church as a whole was deeply influenced by the values and ethical standards of the Revival, though the extent to which it became intertwined with the church varied from place to place: very great indeed in Rwanda, Burundi and south-west Uganda; less so in Buganda, which had a proud pre-Revival tradition to defend. The Revival produced a schism from the Anglican church among the Luo of Kenya. A group of moderate revivalists became distressed by the way in which the main Revival seemed to have taken over the church with an uncompromising message of denunciation of ordinary members of the church. Feeling that their message could not be heard, in 1957 Matthew Ajuoga and this group established their own church, the Church of Christ in Africa (CCA). They called themselves Johera – the People of Love – in contrast to Jorema – the People of the Blood, a reference to the revivalist emphasis on the blood of Christ. The CCA established an episcopal structure and remained faithful to the Book of Common Prayer, with the main focus of its work among Kenyan Luo and the neighbouring Luo in the Mara district of Tanganyika.[28]

The Revival has not been without its own inner conflicts. One group became the dominant form of revival in northern Uganda. In the early 1950s, at a time when the mainstream Balokole movement was becoming acceptable to the church at large, a group of revivalists known as the Trumpeters proclaimed a much more combative message. They would stand outside the church with megaphones providing a critical running commentary on the sermon, denouncing the pastor and members of the congregation. Yet for all their abrasiveness they too wished to be counted

[27] Josiah Kibira, *Church, Clan and the World* (Uppsala: Gleerup, 1974).
[28] F. B. Welbourn and B. A. Ogot, *A Place to Feel at Home* (Nairobi: Oxford University Press, 1966).

as Anglicans. In Buganda, in the late 1960s, a conflict developed around a group critical of the growing 'worldliness' of saved people. Calling themselves the Reawakened (Bazukufu), they criticised the Brethren for 'going to sleep', for accepting the standards of the world, for becoming slaves of fashion, braiding their hair, and accepting loans. They particularly denounced a new canon on baptism in the Church of Uganda, which allowed the baptism of children whose parents who had not married in church. Church services were disrupted as Bazukufu walked out on such occasions, or refused to take Communion from a 'worldly' pastor. They created a rival network of weekly and monthly meetings for fellowship. Some of the extremism of the first period of the Bazukufu became modified in the 1980s, but the hyper-rigorous ethic has continued to be attractive to a small but highly cohesive group. For example, in view of AIDS, its emphasis on absolute chastity has an appeal.[29]

For most young people, the old-fashioned moralism of all the Balokole groups makes it more difficult for them to relate to the old Revival. The young have become influenced by the very different style and ethos of modern Pentecostal preaching. This is equally revivalist in its way; it is no accident that in society at large Pentecostal groups are generally called 'Balokole churches'. The Balokole movement remains a vital core of Anglican spirituality throughout East Africa, but since the 1960s it has had to compete, especially in schools, with a vibrant Charismatic youth movement whose strict moral discipline is combined not with the sober personal styles of the 1950s but with modern fashion, and with worship utilising sound systems and modern technology.

THE CHURCH AND INDEPENDENCE

In all three British East African territories the Anglican church suffered from an identity crisis in the late colonial era. The church was producing many of the educated elite who struggled for political independence, but it was also tied to the colonial regime. The 'established' role of the Native Anglican Church in Uganda was both the guarantee of its immense prestige in Ugandan society as a whole and a major problem. As early as 1913 a new protest religion, the Bamalaki, had broken from the Native Anglican Church, protesting against its subservience to an elite led by Sir Apolo Kaggwa, the Katikkiro (Prime Minister) of Buganda, and

[29] Catherine Robbins, 'Tukutendereza: A Study of Social Change and Sectarian Withdrawal in the Balokole Revival', Ph.D. dissertation, Columbia University, 1975.

criticising both Namirembe Cathedral and the government hospital of Mulago as new forms of English paganism just as alien to the Gospel as the traditional religion. Rejecting both the 'scientific' medicine brought by the missionaries and traditional healing practice, they relied on prayer alone. An off-shoot of this group in eastern Uganda, led by Semei Kakungulu, eventually rejected Christianity altogether, in favour of a form of Judaism based on Old Testament law. They became known as the Jayudaya ('Jews'). Persecuted almost out of existence during the Amin years, they have now re-established themselves. Another Anglican schism was the movement initiated in the 1920s by Reuben Mukasa Spartas, whose protest against paternalism led him to establish links with the African Orthodox Church.[30]

Meanwhile, despite the self-governance provided in Tucker's constitution, the church was slow to entrust Ugandan clergy with leadership roles. It was only in the 1950s that Africans became bishops anywhere in East Africa, just a few years before political independence. Only in the years after independence did an African become primate in any of the three ecclesiastical provinces which had emerged. The question of a province had itself been the subject of dispute as early as the 1920s. East African Anglicans consistently opposed the creation of a single province for East Africa because they saw such a move as a parallel to settler attempts to create an East African Federation in which African political progress was sacrificed to the desire for self-rule for settlers.

The question of a federation provoked the events which led to the deportation of the Kabaka in 1953.[31] The crisis shook the Anglican church to its core, and threatened to marginalise it. But it also created the conditions for a new and dangerous involvement in the politics of the independence era in which the old Catholic–Protestant rivalries in Uganda resurfaced in new and greater antagonisms. The Mau Mau struggle meant that the 1950s were even more traumatic for the churches in Kenya. Many missionaries portrayed Mau Mau as a reversion to barbarism, a collective psychosis of the Kikuyu people in the face of modern conditions. This interpretation of Mau Mau led the government to employ psychological warfare to 'cleanse' those who had taken traditional oaths of loyalty to the guerrilla struggle. As part of the de-oathing policy, Howard Church (the brother of Joe Church) and some

[30] F. B. Welbourn, *East African Rebels* (London: SCM, 1961), p. 84.

[31] K. Ward, 'The Church of Uganda and the Exile of Kabaka Muteesa', *Journal of Religion in Africa* 28.4 (1998), pp. 411–49.

CMS colleagues set up a de-oathing camp at Athi River, based on the principles of the Moral Rearmament Movement, in which inmates would be encouraged to confess their involvement and receive cleansing. In some ways this could be seen as an attempt to implement revivalist principles of confession in a more 'secular' setting. But free confession is very different from that forced by political authority. The experiment was not a happy one.[32]

By the mid 1950s many CMS missionaries, in East Africa and in Britain, were beginning to look beyond counter-insurgency and attempts to repress the nationalist fervour in East Africa. CMS General Secretaries Max Warren and John Taylor (himself a missionary in Uganda during the Kabaka crisis) took a very active interest in political developments, acutely aware of the 'winds of change' blowing through Africa.[33]

TANGANYIKA/TANZANIA IN THE INDEPENDENCE ERA

In Tanganyika, the move towards independence was much smoother. Since the days of German rule, Anglicans had not felt such a close identification with colonial governments as in the British possessions to the north. Both the Australian CMS and UMCA, in their very different ways, continued to operate with a highly structured and somewhat authoritarian style. The absence of turmoil in the preparation for independence did not necessitate profound soul-searching. It was the shape of a common Anglican church for the newly independent country, rather than the struggle for independence itself, which gave most heartache. The UMCA had the deeper commitment to establishing an autonomous Anglican church. It was the natural culmination of its ecclesiology. But it inevitably had concerns for the distinctive Anglo-Catholic tradition of the UMCA dioceses in a future province where Evangelicals of a very Protestant kind would play a major role.[34]

In 1961, Tanganyika was the first of the East African countries to become independent. In 1963 Zanzibar also achieved independence, and shortly afterwards entered into a union with Tanganyika. In contrast, Tanzanian Anglicans lagged behind the other East African countries in ecclesiastical self-government. Yohana Omari, from the CMS area, had been the first assistant bishop, consecrated in 1955. He died in 1963. In

[32] Philip Boobbyer, 'Moral Re-Armament in Africa in the Era of Decolonization', in Brian Stanley (ed.), *Missions, Nationalism, and the End of Empire* (Grand Rapids: Eerdmans, 2003), pp. 212–36.
[33] J. V. Taylor, *Christianity and Politics in Africa* (London: Penguin, 1957).
[34] Andrew Porter, 'The Universities' Mission to Central Africa', in Stanley, *Missions*, pp. 79–110.

that year two men from the UMCA area were made assistant bishops: Douglas Soseleye for Masasi, and John Sepeku for Zanzibar. Sepeku became the first African diocesan bishop, for Dar es Salaam, in 1965 and the first Archbishop of the newly inaugurated Province of Tanzania in 1970.[35] Just before independence, in 1960, a new Bishop of Masasi was appointed: Trevor Huddleston. It was an appointment greeted with considerable enthusiasm by the new African politicians as they prepared to assume power.[36] During his eight years as bishop, Huddleston had occasion to criticise the new government, and was particularly exercised about the handing over of church schools to the state. But, on the whole, church–state relations in Tanzania since independence have been much smoother than in the other East African countries. The moral integrity and strong Catholic faith of President Nyerere, together with the strong cohesion of the governing party, Chama Cha Mapinduzi, created an atmosphere which facilitated co-operation between church and state, as well as between Muslims and Christians.[37] The Anglican church was broadly supportive of the socialist vision of the Arusha Declaration of 1967 and the subsequent creation of Ujamaa villages, which required scattered peasants to concentrate into settlements which aimed to provide basic amenities. One consequence of this was that the effectiveness of church provision was enhanced.

At independence there were four dioceses: three from the UMCA area and only one from the CMS. By 2000 the balance had shifted in favour of the Evangelical areas, with eleven of the seventeen dioceses having an Evangelical ethos.[38] If Evangelicals have been rather more aggressively evangelistic, one of the greatest evangelists was from an old UMCA area. Edmund John was from a devout Anglican family from Tanga (north of Dar). His older brother, John Sepeku, became the first Tanzanian Archbishop. Edmund himself was a layman, working as a civil servant. Depressed by the loss of one of his children, in 1967 he experienced a calling to Christian service in a dream. He resigned from his job, sold his car and began a ministry of healing and itinerant evangelism. He cast out spirits in Jesus' name and urged those whom he healed to adopt a strict rule of life. He was never formally connected with Balokole groups, with

[35] Frieder Ludwig, *Church and State in Tanzania: Aspects of a Changing Relationship 1961–1994* (Leiden: Brill, 1999), p. 44.

[36] Deborah Duncan Honoré (ed.), *Trevor Huddleston: Essays on his Life and Work* (Oxford: Oxford University Press, 1988), p. 11.

[37] Lissi Rasmussen, *Christian–Muslim Relations in Africa* (London: British Academic Press, 1993).

[38] Ludwig, *Church and State*, p. 175.

which he had fellowship in the CMS areas, but his stress on repentance and his simple life style resembled that of the Revival Brethren. But he also greatly valued the disciplined Catholic spirituality of his own Catholic tradition. His ministry was short – he died on 9 June 1975. His brother preached at the funeral, and there was a requiem Mass for him in the Cathedral of St Nicholas and the African Martyrs at Dar es Salaam. Edmund John embodied in his life and work the coming together of the two Anglican traditions of Tanzania.[39] It has not been so easy to achieve this harmony institutionally. There have been a number of attempts to unite the two theological colleges of St Mark's in Dar es Salaam and St Philip's at Kongwa, but the obstacles have always seemed insurmountable.

KENYA SINCE INDEPENDENCE

Like Tanzania, Kenya has enjoyed a fair degree of political stability compared with many African independent countries. But relations between the Anglican church and the state have not been anything like as smooth. The Anglican church was regarded as an arm of establishment during colonial times in Kenya in a way that it had never been in Tanganyika. But it was not in fact the dominant church, even among Protestants. The National Christian Council of Kenya (NCCK), the successor of the old Alliance, has often been the forum for criticising government. The NCCK newspapers *Target* and *Lengo* have been conspicuous for their hard-hitting journalism. A courageous editor of both those newspapers was Henry Okullu, later to be Bishop of Maseno. Okullu, a Luo from that western Kenyan stronghold of the Anglican church, worked on the East African Railways in Kampala in the 1950s. He lived with a Balokole family in Kampala (there was at that time a large Kenyan Luo community in the Ugandan capital). Okullu himself was saved and trained for ordination in Uganda. He then worked among migrant labourers in the sugar plantations of Uganda's second city, Jinja. About his time as editor in Nairobi, Okullu wrote:

> By then, I was certain that there was no going back on my firm conviction, formed after a lot of Bible reading, that the Church is not here merely to convert souls. The Church must also be the chief mouthpiece for those who cannot speak for themselves on political, economic and other social issues.[40]

[39] Joseph Namata, *Edmund John, a Man of God: A Healing Ministry* (Canberra: Acorn Press, 1986).
[40] Henry Okullu, *Quest for Justice: An Autobiography* (Kisumu: Shalom, 1997), p. 49.

In 1974 he became Bishop of Maseno South, his home area, where he continued to be outspoken politically. He spoke out against a perceived attempt to subvert the secret ballot by the 'queueing' system advocated by President Arap Moi. He defended the refugees from Uganda who began to flee the brutalities of the Amin regime. Okullu preached at the funeral of a young Kenyan bishop, Gideon Muge of Eldoret, who (like Luwum) died in a suspicious 'car accident' after his vigorous criticism of the regime.[41]

Okullu saw his involvement in social justice issues as springing from his revivalist piety – a remarkable testimony to the way in which the apolitical stance of the early years of the Revival had been transformed by some of its second-generation leaders. Another revivalist who made a similar journey of faith was David Gitari, Bishop of Mount Kenya East from 1975, and then Archbishop of Kenya from 1996 to 2002. Like Okullu, he was deeply committed to a Christianity which engages with the social and political realities of modern Kenya, and security officials were said to attend church to note any seditious content. An important theme for Gitari has been the relationship between righteousness and justice in a nation and God's holiness, often with a strong eschatological dimension.[42] The Anglican Church in Kenya is noteworthy for its interest in liturgical experimentation. The Kenyan Anglican Communion service both incorporates Revival motifs and attempts to articulate features appropriate to the cultural heritage of Kenya's peoples.

UGANDA'S TRAGEDY

At Uganda's independence on 9 October 1963, the Anglican church had achieved an influence on society much greater than that in Kenya or Tanzania. Of the seven Presidents of the republic since independence, six have been Anglican (the exception was Idi Amin, a Muslim). Uganda has had a much more violent history than the other East African states, and relations between church and state have been similarly complex. One of the problems of the deep cultural penetration of the Anglican church into the fabric of Uganda's life has been that it has tended to reflect all the tensions within society as a whole. At independence, the Church of

[41] David Throup, 'The Politics of Church–State Conflict in Kenya 1978–1990', in H. B. Hansen and M. Twaddle (eds.), *Religion and Politics in East Africa* (London: James Currey, 1995), pp. 143–76.

[42] G. P. Benson, 'Kenya's Protestant Churches and the *Nyayo* State', in Hansen and Twaddle, *Religion and Politics*, pp. 177–99.

Uganda was confident that it could exert a strong influence on a government which consisted largely of Anglicans. The Catholics were much less sanguine. The ruling party, the Uganda People's Congress, was nicknamed 'The United Protestants of Canterbury' in contrast to the Democratic Party (DP), which had the sobriquet 'Dini ya Papa' ('the religion of the Pope'). But as divisions opened up within the government itself, tensions surfaced in the church too, especially over the crisis in Buganda, which led to the flight of the Kabaka and the declaration of a republic by Milton Obote. These events traumatised and divided the Anglicans. At the time of Obote's overthrow in 1971, the two Buganda dioceses were threatening to withdraw from the church and set up their own province.[43] The new leader, Idi Amin, was at first welcomed for his ability to knock heads together and broker a deal which might prevent schism. But very quickly the killings began, with Acholi soldiers (Amin's main rivals within the army) being murdered and 'disappearing'.[44] The first African Archbishop, Erica Sabiti, was from a leading family in Ankole and a leader in the Revival. He was used to speaking firmly and without prevarication, but he struggled to understand the devious world of military violence and political machinations. Janani Luwum, his successor, was also a prominent member of the Revival. But he was able to establish a more effective working relationship with Amin. As Amin's rule got bleaker, the disunity of the church was replaced by a common sense of repression. This reached a climax in the preparations for the Anglican centenary in 1977, with the government paranoid that the church was collecting money to supply to exiles preparing for an invasion. Luwum himself was accused of being implicated in a plot to overthrow the President. On 16 February 1977 he was arrested and murdered, along with fellow Luo politicians. A number of other bishops were forced to flee for their lives, including Festo Kivengere, Bishop of Kigezi and renowned evangelist.[45]

During this time the martyr tradition of the church assumed a great importance in making sense of persecution. Luwum's successor was Silvanus Wani, from Amin's home town of Koboko in West Nile Province, a former chaplain in the army. It was hoped that he, like no one

[43] K. Ward, 'The Church of Uganda amidst Conflict', in Hansen & Twaddle, *Religion and Politics*, pp. 72–105.

[44] Louise Pirouet, 'Religion in Uganda under Amin', *Journal of Religion in Africa* 11.1 (1980), p. 38.

[45] K. Ward, 'Archbishop Janani Luwum: The Dilemmas of Loyalty, Opposition and Witness in Amin's Uganda', in David Maxwell (ed.), with Ingrid Lawrie, *Christianity and the African Imagination* (Leiden: Brill, 2002), pp. 199–224.

else, would be able to speak as a kinsman and elder to Amin and restrain his excesses. Wani, like his two predecessors, came from the Revival tradition. Like them, he evinced an honest and straight-forward integrity in the face of evil in the two years before Amin's downfall and in the chaotic years which followed.[46]

The fragile unity of the Church of Uganda was again shattered by the second Obote regime (1981–5), by the revival of sectarian politics, the civil war and the erosion of human rights. It was a time of renewed Catholic–Protestant antagonism, with Catholics resentful of the political domination of the Protestant Uganda People's Congress (UPC) party. Yoweri Museveni began, in 1986, a revaluation of the political culture of Uganda, stressing the need for an end to religious sectarianism and for a new era of public and military accountability.[47] Religious tensions eased in the Museveni era, both between the churches and within the Anglican church itself. But Museveni signally failed to deal with the war in the north of the country associated with the group known as the Lord's Resistance Army (LRA). Far from being the 'fundamentalist' Christian organisation that it is sometimes portrayed as, the LRA has manifested deep hostility to the Christian churches. The Christian leaders of northern Uganda – the Anglican bishops Mac Ocholla, Benjamin Ojwang and Nelson Onono Onwang, and the Catholic Archbishop John Baptist Odama – have been untiring in their defence of their community in the face of rebel barbarism and the cruelties of the government's 'protected village' policy.[48] In Uganda, Christianity has again acted as a vital cohesive force in preserving culture and society in time of conflict.

RWANDA AND BURUNDI

The heart of Africa is one of the areas of the world where Anglicanism has managed, with some success, to transcend its anglophone roots and connections. That there are vigorous churches in Rwanda, Burundi and the Congo Democratic Republic is largely due to the evangelistic enthusiasm generated by the Ugandan church. The Ruanda Mission first established work at Gahini at a distance from centres of power, either of

[46] Margaret Ford, *Janani:The Making of a Martyr* (London: Marshall, Morgan & Scott, 1978).
[47] Yoweri Museveni, *Sowing the Mustard Seed* (London: Macmillan, 1997).
[48] Sverker Finnstrom, *Living with Bad Surroundings: War and Existential Uncertainty in Acholiland* (Uppsala: Uppsala University Press, 2003); K. Ward, '"The Armies of the Lord": Christianity, Rebels and the State in Northern Uganda, 1986–1999', *Journal of Religion in Africa* 31.2 (2001), pp. 187–221.

the Tutsi monarchy or of the Belgian administrators. The revivalist ethos of the church emphasised the equality of Tutsi pastoralists and Hutu farmers, in ways which ran counter to the increasing political polarisation between these groups. When, on the eve of independence, the first wave of killings of Tutsi began, the Anglican church centres became sites of refuge. The church gave sanctuary to the Queen Mother at Gahini Hospital and aided her escape; this was a political act. In 1963 the Tutsi pastor and Balokole leader, Yona Kanamuyezi, was butchered to death, just as the civil war was abating. Since the famines of the late 1920s Uganda had already acted as a magnet for Hutu labour. Now many Tutsi fled to Uganda. The Church of Uganda offered a welcome. In some parts of the country the Rwandan community contributed significantly to church life, in lay and ordained leadership. In Burundi, which became a separate state at independence and retained Tutsi dominance in government, there were also significant numbers of Rwandan Anglican refugees, active in Anglican church life and ministry. In Rwanda itself, Hutu tended to dominate the episcopate and other leadership roles in the church, just as they did in society at large.

In the early 1990s Tutsi refugees from Uganda invaded Rwanda. Church leadership of all denominations identified with the government in its denunciation of the invaders and the stigmatisation of the Tutsi 'enemy within', unwittingly or by design fostering the paranoia which created the genocide and the slaughter of nearly a million people. With the collapse of the old regime and the coming to power of Paul Kagame (a Tutsi born and raised in exile in Uganda), the face of the Anglican church in Rwanda changed substantially. Some of its old leaders, accused of complicity in the genocide, were forced to flee and the Archbishop to resign. Tutsi pastors returned from Uganda and Burundi to assume positions of leadership in the church. The new Archbishop was Emmanuel Mbona Kolini, trained in Uganda, who had also served as a missionary in the Congo, and had become Bishop of Lubumbashi.

The genocide inevitably poses deep moral questions on the witness of all the Christian churches. For the Anglicans, the apparent failure of the revivalist teaching of a faith which breaks down divisions was particularly acute. It starkly revealed the narrow use of Scripture, and the limits of personal piety as an answer to political responsibility. If the Revival emphasis on confession and reconciliation is to work for the healing of the new Rwanda, there is a recognition that it has to do so on a broader plane, with greater awareness of the structural as well as the individual dimensions of sin, and a wider understanding of Christian discipleship.

This also remains a challenge for the smaller Anglican church in Burundi as it exists in a society where similar tensions between Tutsi and Hutu have followed a different trajectory but remain stubbornly intractable.[49]

THE CONGO

In 1896 the first evangelists from Tooro in western Uganda travelled along the northern flanks of the Ruwenzori mountains to Mboga, in what later became the Belgian Congo. Mboga became the focus of the remarkable ministry of Apolo Kivebulaya, an evangelist and priest from Buganda, particularly among pygmy and forest peoples. This was actually a late venture, dating from the 1920s. The core of the church membership was among the Hema pastoral people, who had strong cultural links with the peoples of Bunyoro and Tooro. Kivebulaya (a nickname, literally 'that coming from Europe', perhaps a reference to his early fondness for exotic clothes) came to be regarded by the time of his death in 1933 as a saint. He was characterised by simplicity of life (he never married), a Franciscan poverty and a love of nature. He planted trees around the churches and out-stations he pioneered – inspired both by an aesthetic and a commercial interest – and planted flower gardens around his own homes. Anglicanism remained more or less confined to this remote area (remote both from the centre of political power in Kinshasha and from its Anglican roots in Kampala) until the 1970s.

Then Anglicanism, quite suddenly and unexpectedly, began to move out into other parts of independent Zaire. Part of the reason for this was the various pressures under which Christian institutions laboured during President Mobutu's long rule. He attacked the church for its foreignness, banning foreign 'Christian' names, and stressing the need for 'authenticité' in its worship and life orientation. Behind this, increasingly, there was a desire to control and tame the churches. To that end, in 1970 Mobutu ordered a rationalisation into four churches (Catholic, Protestant, Orthodox and Kimbanguist, the last a large African-instituted church founded by Simon Kimbangu in the 1920s). All Protestants had to affiliate to what became known as the Eglise du Christ au Zaire. Within this umbrella organisation, without any doctrinal or real corporate unity, a number of *communautés* pursue their own life. Government regimentation of church life and the difficulties of receiving government recognition (the

49 Meg Guillebaud, *Rwanda: The Land God Forgot? Revival, Genocide and Hope* (London: Monarch, 2002).

personalité civile legal status) led a number of smaller independent churches to seek affiliation with the Anglican church.

Other groups which had broken away from Protestant churches with more inflexible moral disciplinary codes than the Anglicans also sought shelter within the fold of the Eglise Anglicane du Zaire. This was a measure of the traditional wide boundaries of Anglican identity (seen, for example, in the Kikuyu church after the female circumcision crisis). But it could also be portrayed by other churches as a lack of seriousness. For the Anglican church it posed big problems of how best to induct these new congregations into Anglican liturgical practice. This was especially acute as Zaire became a 'failed state', with its infrastructure and educational facilities crumbling, communication problematic and printed materials of any kind – bibles, prayer books, hymnaries – difficult to attain. Nevertheless, the church continued to grow enormously, from the affiliation of independent congregations, the planting of new churches, and the presence of refugees from the West Nile district of Uganda and Zambian migrants from the Copper Belt into Lubumbashi in the South.

If in Shaba Province Anglicanism seems too foreign, back in its east Congo heartland the Anglican church has been identified as an ethnic church – moreover, one where Hema are seen as having an undue influence. In the civil wars of the 1990s, where ethnic tensions between dominant and marginalised groups have been utilised to exacerbate conflict in the interests of warlords, this ensures that the church is inextricably bound up with competing groups, however much it can justifiably point to the fact that it is a church for all. But, as in the Sudan, times of war have also produced a flowering of indigenous Christian songs deeply expressive of the response of a suffering church in times of conflict.[50]

THE INDIAN OCEAN

The francophone Province of the Indian Ocean consisted in 2000 of four dioceses in Madagascar, the diocese of Seychelles and the diocese of Mauritius. Anglican work originated with British capture from the French of the islands of Mauritius (1810) and the Seychelles (1814). Work

[50] Georges Titre Ande, 'Authority in the Anglican Church of Congo', Ph.D. dissertation, University of Birmingham, 2003; Emma Wild-Wood, 'Migration and Identity: The Development of an Anglican Church in North-East Congo', Ph.D. dissertation, University of Edinburgh, 2004; Peter Wood and Emma Wild-Wood, 'One Day we will Sing in God's Home', *Journal of Religion in Africa* 34.1–2 (2004), pp. 145–80.

in the large island of Madagascar was initiated in the 1860s, before the colonial era. Both the SPG and the CMS sent missions, but it was the SPG which continued. The London Missionary Society had established work there at the beginning of the nineteenth century, and after the end of a period of severe persecution in 1861, it had the status of a quasi-established church. The Anglican church, in contrast, developed as a free church, distanced from both local establishments and the French colonisers.

CONCLUSION

In East Africa, Anglicanism has a strong institutional presence and a strong evangelistic zeal. Organisations such as the Mothers' Union have been important training grounds for women's responsibilities, and the East African churches have, largely, been receptive to women's ministry – ordination to the priesthood occurred in Kenya and Uganda nearly a decade before it did in the Church of England. The Revival movement has stressed lay involvement and a strong internalised commitment to Christian faith and ethical standards. It has fostered autonomy and a confident local leadership, and has created strong and distinctive forms of Anglicanism which have the confidence to retain elements of the English inheritance (for example the Book of Common Prayer) and to develop a robust spirituality forged in persecution and struggle.

CHAPTER 10

The Middle East

The Anglican presence in the Middle East differs profoundly from that in other parts of the world. Scattered throughout the region there are Anglican congregations with British expatriate membership, but there are no substantial communities of British settlers. English-medium churches attract an international membership of diplomatic, business and aid-organisation personnel. It is largely transient. With the exception of the Sudan, the indigenous Anglican churches in the area are very small indeed. If Anglicanism has any importance in the Muslim heartlands, it is more in its interaction with the other Christian bodies, with Islam and with Judaism.

At the beginning of the nineteenth century, Anglican interest in the region grew out of the general missionary awakening. The French Revolution had had a profound effect on Christian relations with Judaism. It accelerated the process of Jewish emancipation within Europe. Able to participate fully in European civil society, most European Jews were nevertheless determined to retain their own religious identity. But some opted for conversion to the dominant religious culture. Many Christians, not least those most involved in the missionary movement, saw such conversions as the first fruits of a widespread conversion of the Jews. They linked both this and the preaching of the Gospel throughout the world to signs of the return of Jesus Christ and the inauguration of the millennium. In 1809 the London Society for Promoting Christianity among the Jews was founded. Like many early missionary societies, it was an inter-denominational Protestant organisation. It had powerful backing from Evangelical Anglicans such as Lord Shaftesbury, and was soon operating as a largely Anglican society, the Church Mission to the Jews. The Society particularly operated in the Prussian, Austrian and Russian areas of Poland, distributing Yiddish and Hebrew Old and New Testaments. Eventually this type of work in Eastern Europe became more restricted, as both governments and the Jewish community became suspicious of such proselytism. But it did produce a number of converts to the Anglican church, including some skilled in rabbinic teaching, people motivated to act as missionaries to their own people, including Jewish communities living in Palestine and scattered throughout the Muslim world.

Two of them became Anglican bishops – Alexander, the first Anglican bishop in Jerusalem, and Schereschewsky, the first American Episcopal bishop in Shanghai. There were also more problematic examples of Jewish Anglican missionary work. In Morocco, the Revd J. B. Ginsberg, a Polish Jewish convert employed by the CMJ, became so unpopular with the Jewish community of Mogador that in 1879 they complained to the British consul that Ginsberg was bribing people, especially the young, with bread, money and clothes. Ginsberg claimed that he was simply distributing famine relief. Eventually his position became so precarious that he sought Spanish protection and made his escape to England.[1] This brought a rather ignominious end to a mission which had previously employed a native, and more tactful, Moroccan Jewish convert, the Revd Abraham Ben Oliel.

The awakening of Protestant interest in the Jews gave the Holy Land a particular resonance. The CMJ established a base in Jerusalem in 1820 in what became Christ Church, east Jerusalem. It was only towards the end of the century that Evangelical circles began to equate their interest in the place of the Jews in the divine unfolding of history with Jewish aspirations for a Jewish homeland. But by then Anglicans were aware of other, countervailing, issues in the Middle East, and this made them cautious of endorsing Zionism.

Apart from the specialised interests of the Church Mission to the Jews, Anglican missionary activity in the Middle East focused on two areas:

relations with the ancient Christian communities; and direct evangelism among Muslims. In 1825 the CMS sent the Revd William Jowett to establish a base in Malta – it was not an ideal spot for work in the Middle East, but it was British territory and a convenient launching pad for gaining official permission to work anywhere in the Ottoman Empire. The CMS hoped to co-operate with the various Orthodox churches of the East (both Chalcedonian and non-Chalcedonian) in a mission of renewal and invigoration, to be effected by the exposure of Orthodox Christians to the Scriptures. A printing press in Malta began the task of publishing translations of the Bible and the Book of Common Prayer into contemporary Arabic, employing educated Orthodox (and Greek Catholic)

[1] Eliezer Bashan, *The Anglican Mission and the Jews of Morocco in the 19th Century* (Ramat-Gan: Bar-Ilan University, 1999), pp. 167–90.

agents for that task. The CMS did not aim to proselytise, but often found it difficult to keep to this intention. But they were never as keen as the other major Protestant mission in this area, the American Presbyterians, to form an Arab church consisting largely of converts from other Christian churches. The CMS, along with other Anglican missions in the nineteenth century, hoped for a general turning of Muslims to the Gospel. This did not happen. The expectation remained alive well into the twentieth century. But gradually Anglicans came to accept that their mission would be largely one of constructive engagement with Islam, in scholarship and action. The expectation that Islam would disintegrate in the face of the superiority of western Christian values has come to be recognised as just one aspect of western cultural arrogance.

PALESTINE

If Anglican mission cannot simply be identified with British interests,[2] some such link cannot be discounted either. This can be seen in the creation of a diocese in Jerusalem in 1841. A joint venture between the British and the Prussian governments, it was designed to provide oversight for both German and English Protestants living in Palestine. Coming at the height of the Tractarian criticism of the Erastianism of the Church, and when Newman and his friends were keen to distance themselves from continental Protestantism, the scheme was one factor in Newman's decision to leave the Anglican church.

The first two bishops came from the ranks of the CMS missionaries. The first, chosen by the British government, was Michael Solomon Alexander, a Jewish convert and former rabbi who had pioneered CMS work in Ethiopia. On his sudden death in 1845, the Prussians appointed another CMS missionary, Samuel Gobat. A French Swiss from the Reformed tradition, he had been ordained in the Anglican church (and was consecrated bishop by the Archbishop of Canterbury); but the Anglo-Catholics were suspicious of his 'Calvinist' and Evangelical opinions. Gobat, who had worked in Egypt, focused on building up an Arab church in Palestine. He professed reluctance to proselytise from among the existing Arab Christian communities. But, in reality, many if not most of the small Anglican community which emerged in Palestine came

[2] A. L. Tibawi, *British Interest in the Middle East 1800–1901*, mentioned by Cragg in Kevin Ward and Brian Stanley, *The Church Mission Society and World Christianity 1799–1999* (Richmond: Curzon and Grand Rapids: Eerdmans, 2000), p. 122.

from Christian backgrounds. The first Arab Anglican priest, ordained in 1871, Michael Kawar, had been a Greek Catholic. Gobat could also be insensitive to Muslim opinion. When the Turkish government announced a measure of religious freedom for Anglicans, Gobat offended the Nablus community by ringing the church bells and flying flags. A riot ensued.[3]

In 1882 the German government, dissatisfied with the lukewarm Anglican attitude to the joint arrangement, withdrew. The Archbishop of Canterbury persuaded both the CMJ and the CMS to contribute towards the establishment of the bishopric on a purely Anglican basis. The choice of Bishop Blyth, however, was not welcomed by the CMS. Blyth was a high churchman and was particularly keen to develop good relations with the Orthodox patriarch in Jerusalem. Blyth established the collegiate Church of St George, hoping that it would become a centre for the worldwide Anglican communion, and a welcome alternative to the previous, somewhat unsuccessful, attempts to create a Jewish or an Arab Anglican church. As one commentator puts it:

> If St George's ... was to make the English feel at home and represent the catholicity of Anglicanism, it was a success. But to those Evangelical missionaries who wanted the Anglicans to represent the 'purity of Protestantism' in a land of 'corrupt' Christianity, the new bishop and his compound seemed an unfortunate development.[4]

Anglicanism in Palestine hardly existed as a corporate body at all. There were a number of divergent forms of Anglicanism: a small and struggling Hebrew Anglican community based in Christ Church, Jerusalem, increasingly isolated; a small but viable Arab Christianity; and an English Anglicanism based at St George's, of increasing importance during the Mandate period. With the collapse of the Ottoman Empire at the end of the First World War, Palestine became a League of Nations mandate under British control. This fragmentary character was exacerbated by the fact that the Anglican church had no corporate legal standing; and Anglicans were not recognised as a *millet* (a separate religious community). The British were as reluctant as the Ottomans to accord that recognition.

A further complication was the increasing demand of Palestinian Anglicans to wrest control of their own affairs from the CMS. In this they

[3] Anthony O'Mahony (ed.), *The Christian Communities of Jerusalem and the Holy Land: Studies in History, Religion and Politics* (Cardiff: University of Wales Press, 2003), p. 154.
[4] Ibid., p. 158.

had Bishop Blyth's support. He was concerned both that the CMS should pay ordained Arab clergy properly and that the Palestinian Native Church Council should have autonomy from the mission. He supported the Revd Seraphim Boutagy in his difficulties with the CMS, and Naser Odeh, whom the CMS tried to suspend for preaching a sermon 'contrary to evangelical principles'. The Arab Evangelical Episcopal Community wanted to be Evangelical and episcopal, but it wanted to develop its own identity. Neither an Evangelical missionary society nor an English bishop whose priorities were elsewhere was sufficiently sensitive to these issues in the late nineteenth century.

The stand-off between the bishop and the CMS on the one hand and that between Palestinian clergy and the CMS on the other were ameliorated when a CMS missionary, Rennie MacInnes (1914–31), was appointed to succeed Blyth. MacInnes had served in Cairo and was much more sensitive to Arab concerns. This was particularly evidenced in the critical attitude of MacInnes to the Balfour Declaration of 1917, with its acceptance of the aspirations for a Jewish homeland, and his discomfort at what he considered to be the extremism of the Zionist movement ('generally political, very often sordid and always noisy' is how he described it privately).[5]

One of the fruits of the school system which Gobat had set up and which was continued by Blyth was the creation of a western-educated class, some Palestinian Anglican, many members of other Christian groups, many Muslim. Anglican families contributed to the reawakening of Arab nationalism. Members of St George's School and choir threatened to boycott Lord Balfour's visit in 1925 if he read a lesson.[6] The Palestinian American academic Edward Said became internationally renowned for his interpretation of the colonial encounter with non-western societies in books such as *Orientalism* and *Culture and Imperialism*: In his memoir *Out of Place*, he describes growing up in Jerusalem. His father had attended St George's School in Jerusalem in the early years of the twentieth century. He went to run the family business in Cairo (after a period in America during which he acquired American citizenship), and in 1914 he married Edward's mother. Her father was a Baptist pastor from Nazareth, and she had been educated in the American school in Beirut. Edward, born in 1935, was named after the Prince of Wales. His

[5] Rafiq A. Farah, *In Troubled Waters: A History of the Anglican Church in Jerusalem 1841–1998* (Bridport: Christians Aware, 2002), p. 92.

[6] Ibid., p. 97.

early life was divided between Jerusalem and Cairo, and he attended St George's School in Jerusalem in 1947, just before the catastrophe ('al Nakba') which overtook Palestinians – the creation of the State of Israel in 1949.[7]

The Palestinian Anglican community, though tiny, was important in the development of a Palestinian consciousness during the Mandate period. This role continued after 1949. The prosperous Anglican community, with land and businesses in what became the State of Israel, was badly affected. Some sought exile in the West Bank, Amman and Lebanon. Only two Palestinian priests remained in the State of Israel. After the 1967 war, the West Bank came under Israeli occupation. Anglicans have been closely identified with the Palestinian Liberation Front. Elia Khoury, a future bishop, was on the Executive Committee. Dr Hanan Ashrawi, a lecturer at the Bir Zayt University (the Anglican Musa Nasir's foundation in the 1940s), has become an eloquent spokesperson of the Palestinian cause.[8] Canon Naim Stifan Ateek has written passionately of justice for Palestinians, and a theology of liberation. His work emerged from the first Intifada (Uprising) against Israeli occupation in the late 1980s.[9] The experience of disruption and exile, the injustice of a Jewish 'right of return' at the expense of the dispossession of Palestinian people, the sense of a common plight uniting Palestinian Muslims and Christians, have all tended to radicalise a tiny group of Anglicans whose natural instincts would be for stability and economic conservatism. A number of Anglicans have been elected to the Knesset (parliament), one of them as a Communist delegate. But for many, the best option has been migration – particularly to the United States. This has been a phenomenon in all the lands of the Middle East, and has affected all Christian communities. It is a particularly strong option for a community which has skills and education.

The division of Jerusalem in 1949, as well as the difficulties of travel between Muslim and Jewish states, made the work of the bishop difficult. Christ Church, the centre of Anglican work among Jewish people, was left high and dry in east Jerusalem, in the Kingdom of Jordan. St George's itself was also in east Jerusalem. In 1957 the Anglican authorities decided to reconstitute Anglican work by creating an Archdiocese in Jerusalem. The Archbishop would become Primate of a province which

[7] Edward Said, *Out of Place: A Memoir* (New York: Alfred Knopf, 1999), pp. 107–12.

[8] Riah Abu El-Assal, *Caught in Between: The Story of an Arab Palestinian Christian Israeli* (London: SPCK, 1999).

[9] Naim Ateek, *Justice and only Justice* (Maryknoll, NY: Orbis, 1989).

encompassed Egypt, Sudan, Iran and the Gulf. The Palestinians pressed for a Palestinian Bishop of Jerusalem. But it was decided that the new Archbishop should be British – Campbell MacInnes, the son of the former bishop. He preached his inaugural sermon in Arabic. But this did not quite compensate for the sense that the Palestinian Anglicans had been sidelined. Najib Cubain did become the first Arab bishop when a diocese of Jordan, Syria and Lebanon was created, but it was not the outcome which the Palestinian Anglicans had campaigned for. There was the possibility that Christ Church, the first Anglican church, might become the seat of the bishop. But the CMJ was unwilling to abandon its church completely, and the Arabs felt that the Hebrew iconography and ethos of the place made it inappropriate. In the end the Arab bishop shared the St George's compound, but that too was not an ideal solution.[10]

The English culture of St George's – 'high tea at 4 o'clock Greenwich Mean Time', as Bishop Riah caustically described it[11] – continued to be an irritant to a Palestinian community in the aftermath of the Suez crisis, when there was a general Arab resentment at British policy in the Middle East. In 1976 the archbishopric was replaced by a looser grouping of Middle East Anglicans. Jerusalem at last got an Arab bishop in Faiq Haddad, the descendant of one of the first Anglican Palestinian families. His assistant was Elia Khoury, who had been active in the Palestinian resistance, and had been expelled from Israel. Events both in Israel and in the Middle East generally have not been propitious for the future of the Anglican community. Since 1968 hundreds of Arab Episcopalians have emigrated. Like Bishop Riah, many would prefer Israel to be reconstituted as a secular state in which Jew, Muslim and Christian, Arab and Israeli, can share a common citizenship. Meanwhile, some look for closer relations with the Lutheran Evangelical Church and with the Presbyterians in Syria and Lebanon as one positive attempt to survive.[12] In the mean time, St George's educational work continues primarily in an ecumenical and inter-religious context.

EGYPT

Egypt, in the aftermath of the Napoleonic Wars, was a propitious place for the CMS to attempt to assist the ancient churches 'in the recovery

[10] Daphne Tsimhoni, *Christian Communities in Jerusalem and the West Bank since 1948: An Historical, Social and Political Study* (Westport, CT: Praeger, 1993), p. 143.

[11] Riah Abu El-Assal, 'The Birth and Experience of the Christian Church: The Protestant/Anglican Perspective in the Middle East', in Michael Prior and William Taylor (eds.), *Christians in the Holy Land* (London: The World of Islam Festival Trust, 1994).

[12] Farah, *In Troubled Waters*, p. 169.

from their long sleep'.[13] The Muslim authorities, more or less independent of the Ottomans, were open to western ideas and modernity. This directly benefited the Coptic Orthodox Christian minority, freeing them for greater participation in the political life of the country. The Copts were the ancient church of Egypt, tracing their origin to St Mark. When William Jowett, from his Malta base, first approached the Coptic leaders, they were responsive. German missionaries were sent to start schools and establish a printing press in facilities offered by the Copts. In 1854 a young monk was chosen as Pope, Cyril IV. He admired the Anglican work and wanted to introduce schools, theological education and a printing press for the Coptic community itself. He died in mysterious circumstances in 1861: it was rumoured that his friendship with westerners had made him unpopular both with government and with conservative groups within his church. The long reign of Cyril V (1870–1927) was, by contrast, a time of conservative reaction. Anglicans continued to develop friendly relations with the Coptic Church, and to avoid proselytising. It was only in 1922 that the Episcopal Church in Egypt was willing openly to encourage Copts to become members.[14] By this time the American Presbyterians had developed a vigorous Arab Presbyterian church, with Coptic leadership. Aziz Atiya's comment about western churches generally, that although 'launched primarily to work among non-Christians they soon took the shorter road of proselytizing the Copts', is thus rather harsh in the case of the Anglicans, who only reluctantly modified their policy of working with the Orthodox Church after a hundred years.[15] Anglicans have continued to value relations with the Coptic Church, and have been encouraged by the biblical ministry of Pope Shenouda, the Patriarch in the latter part of the twentieth century.[16]

British political and commercial interests in Egypt were dramatically increased by the building of the Suez Canal in the 1860s. In 1881 the British bombarded the port of Alexandria in disapproval of the Urabi revolt of army officers. Thereafter British authority in Egypt was paramount, even though formal colonial rule was not acknowledged. The army and commercial presence meant the establishment of a number of expatriate English-speaking churches in the main urban centres.

[13] Eugene Stock, *The History of the Church Missionary Society*, Volume 1 (London: CMS, 1899), p. 121.

[14] Samy Shehata, 'An Evaluation of the Mission of the Episcopal Church in Egypt from 1918 to 1925 with Special Implications for the Role of the Church Today', MA dissertation, University of Birmingham, 1998.

[15] Aziz S. Atiya, *A History of Eastern Christianity* (Millwood, NY: Kraus, 1980) (1st edn 1968), p. 113.

[16] Samy Shehata, 'Ecclesiology in Contemporary Egypt: An Evaluation and a Proposal', Ph.D. dissertation, University of Birmingham, 2001.

Llewellyn Gwynne was appointed as bishop in Egypt in 1911 (he was assistant to the bishop in Jerusalem and from 1920 diocesan bishop of Egypt and Khartoum). In the 1930s Gilbert Scott designed a cathedral on the east bank of the Nile. Edward Said, who was confirmed there in 1949, describes it thus:

> The church itself was part of a grand compound facing the Nile a little to the north of the British barracks (now the site of the Nile Hilton). An impressive plaza with ceremonial driveway allowed cars entry to the cathedral's main doors, the whole of the place communicating that sense of monumental power and absolute confidence which was so much the hallmark of the British presence in Egypt.[17]

Such confidence was shattered by the Suez débâcle of 1956, after which the English bishop and the provost were required to leave the country. The cathedral itself was demolished in the 1980s to make room for a bridge over the Nile, part of a major urban redevelopment plan for the most populous city in Africa. The government financed the building of a new cathedral at Zamalek, built by a local architect, Awad Kamil Fahmi, and more in harmony with its environment.[18]

Significantly it was in 1882, just after the official inauguration of a British protectorate, that the CMS formally articulated a policy of evangelisation among the Muslim majority of the country. This was always a sensitive area, both for the Egyptian authorities and the British. The CMS established a church in the Boulac slums of Cairo. But its most important witness among Muslims was in Old Cairo at Harpur Hospital (named after its founder Dr F. J. Harpur). A Christian congregation grew based on the Egyptian workers at the hospital. The first Egyptian Anglican priest, Girgis Bishai, worked there for forty years as an evangelist, before he was ordained in 1925 – compared to the Palestinian ordinations of the 1870s this was a tardy development, partly an indication of the reluctance of Anglicans in Egypt to set up an alternative church to the Coptic. Bishai's ordination was encouraged by William Temple Gairdner, who had pastoral oversight of the Arab congregations in Old Cairo. Gairdner also looked to the establishment of a permanent deaconate, on the Coptic model, of people working in secular employment.

[17] Said, *Out of Place*, p. 143.

[18] Arthur Burrell, *Cathedral on the Nile: A History of All Saints Cathedral Cairo* (Oxford: Amate Press, 1984).

Temple Gairdner's significance in the field of Muslim–Christian relations is immense.[19] A Scot, he studied at Oxford. Influenced by the Student Volunteer Movement with its phrase 'the evangelisation of the world in this generation', he joined the CMS and followed his close friend Douglas Thornton to Cairo in 1898. Both were inspired by the heroic death of General Gordon. This was the era of high imperialism. In 1910 Rennie MacInnes, CMS Secretary in Cairo, noted that King Edward VII ruled over more Muslims than the Turkish emperor or the Shah of Persia put together, and looked forward optimistically to the opportunities this afforded for Christian evangelism. There is no reason to sense that Temple Gairdner would have dissented from this. He had just produced his *Reproach of Islam* in 1909, a book specifically designed to encourage new missionaries from the next generation of varsity students. In impassioned language he spoke of the very existence of Islam as 'reproach', a perpetual reminder of Christianity's failure 'truly to represent her Lord'.[20]

By the time of the fifth edition, aware that the title might be misconstrued, he renamed the book *The Rebuke of Islam*, which he hoped would convey more a sense of challenge to the church. But already Temple Gairdner's work in Cairo posed uncomfortable questions about the use of the language he had employed. Gairdner had established schools and reading rooms in Old Cairo, to appeal on the one hand to students (so-called 'effendi') who could afford a western-style education, and on the other hand to scholars trained in the Quran and at the al-Azhar university. Gairdner began seriously to address the questions and sceptical responses of those with whom he established relations. In 1910 he took a year of study in Germany and at Hartford, Connecticut. He came to value the writings of the Sufi mystical poet al-Ghazali, and his respect and appreciation for the spirituality of Islam deepened. He had always been impressed by the value which Islam put on universal 'brotherhood', which he saw as a challenge to Christianity. He collaborated with Thornton in producing *Orient and Occident*, a journal for serious discussion between Islam and Christianity. His production of Arabic plays on biblical themes and biblical commentaries in the style of the medieval Muslim Quranic interpreter al-Baidawi and his composition of Arabic hymns and tunes indicate Gairdner's concern to locate Anglican

[19] See Michael Thomas Shelley, 'The Life and Thought of W. H. T. Gairdner 1873–1928: A Critical Evaluation of a Scholar-Missionary', Ph.D. dissertation, University of Birmingham, 1988.

[20] William Temple Gairdner, *The Reproach of Islam* (London: Church Society, 1909), p. 335.

mission in a Muslim milieu. Gairdner, says Cragg, was 'deeply committed to Christian apologetics but served by a genuine scholarship and warmed with strong personal love'.[21]

Constance Padwick produced a biography of Gairdner in 1929, a year after his sudden death at the age of fifty-six. Padwick continued the patient journey of discovery pioneered by Gairdner. Born in 1886, she worked from 1909 to 1916 on the home staff of the CMS as the editor of the children's magazine, before going to Cairo to work for the Nile Mission Press.[22] She was involved in the editing of *Orient and Occident.* After the Second World War she worked in the Sudan, producing Arabic educational books for Nuba schools. But her great contribution to Christian–Muslim dialogue came in her retirement when, in 1961, she persuaded the SPCK to publish *Muslim Devotions.* This was a collection of Sufi prayer tracts and manuals, picked up personally by Padwick on street-stalls, in markets and outside mosques, in places as far apart as Calcutta and Tunis. She concentrated, not on the scholarly texts, but on popular literature, valued by ordinary mosque-goers. She included this rapturous prayer of Night Communion, said to be a prayer which Ali, the son-in-law of the Prophet, was overheard to recite as he looked out on the Kaaba in Mecca:

> My God and my Lord, eyes are at rest, stars are setting, hushed are the movements of birds in their nests, of monsters in the deep. And Thou art the just who knowest no change, the equity that swerves not, the everlasting that passes not away. The doors of kings are locked, watched by their bodyguards, but Thy door is open to him who calls on Thee. My lord, each lover is now alone with his beloved, and Thou art for me the Beloved.[23]

Bishop Kenneth Cragg, an inheritor of the work of Gairdner and Padwick, has creatively moved beyond the boundaries which Gairdner worked within, as a profound Christian interpreter of Islam.[24] Having worked at the American University in Beirut during the Second World

[21] Kenneth Cragg, *Muhammad and the Christian: A Question of Response* (Oxford: Oneworld, 1999), p. 3.

[22] Jocelyn Murray appears to be wrong in stating that Padwick went as a CMS missionary (entry in G. H. Anderson (ed.), *Biographical Dictionary of Christian Missions* (New York: Macmillan 1998)). It appears that she was rejected at first on health grounds, and subsequently preferred to remain a free agent as her theological position became more inclusive.

[23] Constance Padwick, *Muslim Devotions* (London: SPCK, 1961). Quoted also in Kenneth Cragg, *Troubled by Truth* (Edinburgh: Pentland Press, 1992), p. 69, part of Cragg's moving biographical sketch of Padwick.

[24] For a brief biographical sketch, see David Kerr, in Anderson's *Biographical Dictionary of Christian Missions.* For a longer appraisal, see Christopher Lamb, *The Call to Retrieval: Kenneth Cragg's Christian Vocation to Islam* (London: Grey Seal, 1997), Chapter 1.

War, Cragg taught at Hartford Seminary, where Gairdner had had such a fruitful sabbatical forty years before. In 1956 he published *The Call of the Minaret*. This was followed by *Sandals at the Mosque* in 1959 – part of Max Warren's Christian Presence series. In 1970 he was appointed by Archbishop George Appleton as assistant bishop in Jerusalem, residing mainly in Cairo. He encouraged the appointment in 1974 of the first Egyptian Anglican diocesan bishop.[25] Few Anglicans have done more than Bishop Cragg to promote the cause of Christian–Muslim dialogue in ways which respect the distinctive faith of both religions.

IRAN AND IRAQ

Henry Martyn was dying of consumption when in 1811 he arrived in Shiraz from India, bearing his Arabic and Persian manuscripts of the Bible. The Arabic text was received with satisfaction, but the scholars criticised the 'flowery and exotic Persian'. Martyn stayed for a year to work on a new translation, engaging in debates about his Christian faith with the Muslim clergy, at their request. He hoped to present his completed manuscript to the Shah in Tehran, but that did not prove possible, and Martyn journeyed into Turkey, where he died at Tokral, attended by Armenian Christians. He was thirty-one.[26]

The next Anglican engagement with this area came in the 1840s. Christian Rassam came from an aristocratic Chaldean family in Mosul. The Chaldeans were that branch of the eastern Nestorian Church which had accepted the authority of Rome some centuries previously. But there remained a section of the church which had remained distinct – the 'old church' under the hereditary patriarchate of the Shimun family, to the north of Mosul in modern Iraq. Massam was employed by the CMS in Cairo, translating *The Pilgrim's Progress* and parts of the Book of Common Prayer into Arabic. In 1835 he married Matilda Badger, sister of a CMS missionary, George Badger. Rassam and his brother-in-law began to interest high-church circles in supporting the Old Church of the Assyrians. Eventually Badger was sent by the SPG to investigate possibilities. Badger must be one of the few missionaries to have quarrelled both with the CMS and with the SPG. The project lapsed, though

[25] Brian de Saram, *Nile Harvest: The Anglican Church in Egypt and the Sudan* (Bournemouth: Abinger, 1992), pp. 203–8.

[26] For a full biography see Constance Padwick, *Henry Martyn: Confessor of the Faith* (London: SCM, 1923). The quotation is from Kenneth Cragg's reflections on Martyn in *Troubled by Truth*, Chapter 1.

Badger wrote an account of *The Nestorians and their Rituals* which kept the issue of the Nestorians before the British public.[27]

Eventually the Archbishop of Canterbury, partly through the financial support of a prominent Anglo-Catholic layman, Athelstan Riley, sponsored a mission to the Assyrians, which operated between 1885 and 1915. One of the priests who served the mission was Arthur Maclean, a Gaelic speaker, who eventually became Primus of the Scottish Episcopal Church. He and his fellow priest W. H. Browne tried to adapt their life style and costume to the local culture. They produced liturgical texts for the church. They were adamant that their work was to support the Old Church, unlike the Roman Catholics, American Presbyterians and Russian Orthodox, who seemed intent to take over the church or to proselytise. Anglicans had their own problems with the church, agonising about whether it was 'Nestorian', and had a defective Christology.

The problem for the Old Church was much more down to earth – it desperately needed financial and diplomatic support in a battle for survival. The Anglican mission was never wealthy enough to satisfy those needs. After the First World War, Anglican interest continued in a desultory way, as the Assyrian struggle to survive became an issue of the rights of ethnic minorities in the modern state of Iraq. But in 1976 the link was reaffirmed when a new Patriarch was consecrated in St Barnabas' Church in Ealing, London.

Meanwhile in Persia, an Anglican mission had been established which was to produce an Iranian Anglican Church.[28] Its founder was Robert Bruce from Dublin, who in 1869 proposed to the CMS that he start work in Persia. His first involvement was in helping the Armenian community to run a school in Isfahan. But the CMS was less reluctant to create its own church than in other places – and when Bishop French of Lahore visited in 1883, he confirmed some sixty-seven people, most with an Armenian background, and ordained as deacon Minas George. One of the first women missionaries, Isabella Read, a schoolteacher, married an Armenian CMS agent, Joseph Aidiniantz, the headmaster of the Persian boys' school in Isfahan. As Gulnar Francis-Dehqani's researches show,[29] she was somewhat shabbily treated by the CMS, which refused fully to

[27] This section is based on J. F. Coakley, *The Church of the East and the Church of England: A History of the Archbishop of Canterbury's Assyrian Mission* (Oxford: Clarendon Press, 1972).

[28] Robin Waterfield, *Christians in Persia* (London: Allen & Unwin, 1973), Chapters 13 and 14.

[29] Gulnar Eleanor Francis-Dehqani, *Religious Feminism in an Age of Empire: CMS Women Missionaries in Iran 1869–1934*, CCSRG Monograph Series 4, Department of Theology and Religious Studies, Bristol University, 2000. For a discussion of CMS women's perceptions of the position of Muslim women see G. Francis-Dehqani, 'CMS Women Missionaries in Persia:

support her when her husband's mental health broke down. Mrs Aidiniantz nevertheless remained in Isfahan, struggling to make a living and bring up her three children. Her two daughters, Nouhri and Nevath Aidin, subsequently themselves became teachers employed by the CMS. As late as 1955 Nouhri took over the running of a private elementary school when the church schools were nationalised.

Another important woman missionary in Isfahan was Mary Bird, who worked in Persia from 1891 to 1904 and again from 1911 till her death in 1914. She pioneered women's medical work, against much local opposition and hostility from male colleagues. Dr Emmeline Stuart, a qualified doctor (Mary Bird's medical skills were gained without formal training), continued this important work in Shiraz and Isfahan, focusing the work away from the Armenian community and towards the needs of Muslim women in the poorer districts of town. As in Egypt, it was often the hospital work which provided the nucleus of the local Christian community, converts from Islam.[30]

At the turn of the nineteenth and twentieth centuries, 'Mullah' Zahra (so called because she was literate and could recite the Quran) had eye trouble. She left her home in Taft and visited the CMS hospital at Yazd, taking her two daughters with her. Sekineh stayed on, trained as a nurse and became a Christian. She married a Muslim, Muhammad. Her son, Hassan, was five when his mother died. His father allowed him to go to the Christian school, and eventually to Stuart College at Isfahan. As soon as he was legally able to do so, at eighteen, Hassan Dehqani-Tafti was baptised. His family were not happy with his decision and later prohibited him from taking any part in his father's funeral. Hassan went on to study Persian literature at Tehran University during the 1940s, and then to study for ordination at Ridley Hall in Cambridge. On his return to Iran he married the daughter of the Bishop of Iran, William Thompson.

By the 1950s the church in Iran was beginning to feel the pressures of the anti-imperialist feeling generated by the western-inspired coup against President Mossadeq in favour of the Pahlavi dynasty. In 1960 Hassan Dehqani-Tafti was elected by the diocesan synod as the first Iranian Anglican bishop. During these years Muslim agitation against a Christian presence was particularly associated with the Tablighat-i-Islami

Perceptions of Muslim Women and Islam 1884–1934', in Ward and Stanley, *The Church Mission Society and World Christianity*, pp. 91–119.

30 The following material is taken largely from H. B. Dehqani-Tafti, *The Unfolding Design of my World: A Pilgrim in Exile* (Norwich: Canterbury Press, 2000).

movement. Anglicans had, in their origins, benefited from local patronage, for example from Zell-i-Sultan and the Qajar family. Now Anglicanism's associations with Britain increasingly became a liability, and with the revolution of 1978–9 it became positively dangerous to be Anglican. The hospitals and the blind school were expropriated. Arastoo Sayyah, the priest of Shiraz, was brutally murdered. Other Iranian clergy and workers, and missionaries, were imprisoned or put under house arrest. An attempt was made on the life of the bishop and his wife Margaret. Bishop Dehqani-Tafti was still able to travel abroad because of his international obligations as presiding Bishop of the Episcopal Church of Jerusalem and the Middle East. But his son, Bahram, who had returned from studies in the United States to work as a teacher, was denied a visa: it was made clear that he was being held as a hostage for his father's return. In May 1979 Bahram was assassinated.

> Love seemed at first an easy thing -
> But ah! the hard awakening.[31]

Bishop Dehqani-Tafti's lines referred to a heartbreaking poem of the great Persian Sufi poet Hafiz, whom he always treasured. The bishop and his family found refuge in England, in the diocese of Winchester, whose bishop John V. Taylor has noted:

> when their beloved son Bahram was assassinated, Hassan was able to associate it not only with the sacrifice of Christ on the cross, but also with the martyrdom of Hussain (the son of Ali), central to the devotion of Shi'ite Muslims.[32]

The bishop was not able to return to his diocese. In 1986 a group of Australian bishops and Michael Nazir-Ali of the Pakistani diocese of Raiwind did visit Tehran and consecrated Iraj Mottahedeh as assistant bishop. He was eventually elected as bishop in 1990. The future of the little Anglican church remains precarious in Iran, along with that of other Christian communities.[33]

SUDAN

The Anglican churches discussed so far in this chapter are very small indeed, and declining – their membership rarely exceeds 1,000. With the

[31] H. B. Dehqani-Tafti, *The Hard Awakening* (London: SPCK, 1981). The English version of the poem is from the translation by Arberry.
[32] J. V. Taylor's foreword to Dehqani-Tafti's *The Unfolding Design of my World.*
[33] Dehqani-Tafti, *The Unfolding Design of my World*, p. 230.

Episcopal Church in Sudan we are dealing with a very different phenomenon: a church of 5 million which has grown enormously over the last two decades. Nevertheless, the history of Anglicanism in Sudan belongs to the story of the churches in the Middle East. Historically, Sudan has been intimately connected with Egypt. Anglicanism came to the Sudan from Egypt. More importantly, the Sudanese church, in ways which are very different from almost all other parts of black Africa, is bound up with Islam. A resurgent Islam and nationalism have made Anglican church life (and Christian witness generally) increasingly problematic in much of the Muslim world. In Sudan, the pressures from a state determined to impose an Arab and an Islamic identity on the whole of Sudan have led to a remarkable growth of Christian allegiance, particularly in southern Sudan. Christian faith has become part and parcel of a struggle for identity and survival. The Episcopal Church in Sudan also has important connections with the churches further south, particularly in Uganda.

From the early nineteenth century, the Sudan was the object of political and economic domination from Egypt, which has always had a vital interest in control of the waters of the Nile. Egyptian Sudan was known as the 'Turkiyya' because Egypt was still nominally under the control of the Ottoman Empire (the Turks). The Egyptian government claimed to have a mission to end the slave trade in the area, and employed a number of British officials to act on its behalf in its suppression, the last and most famous being General Gordon. This campaign did nothing to relieve the oppressive nature of Egyptian rule as far as the people of the Sudan were concerned, and led to an Islamic revivalist uprising under the leadership of Muhammad Ahmad. In 1882 he proclaimed himself the 'Mahdi' who had come to regenerate Islam throughout the world, and to remove Egyptian misrule in the Sudan. General Gordon was killed by the Mahdi in 1886. This provoked the British to intervene. At the battle of Omdurman, Kitchener smashed what remained of the Mahdi's power. Britain already had considerable political sway in Egypt. In the Sudan they instituted what was called the 'Anglo-Egyptian condominium'.

Gordon was a supremely popular figure among British Christians – he inspired Douglas Thornton and Temple Gairdner in their decision to join the CMS as missionaries. He was also the inspiration for Llewellyn Gwynne, the Welsh missionary whom the CMS sent in 1899 to begin the Gordon Memorial Mission in Khartoum. The new British authorities were decidedly unenthusiastic about Christian missionaries working in an environment where there continued to be a strong emotional support for the Mahdi. They were intent on upholding the status of Islam as the religion of the North, but were willing to consider Christian mission in the South. The CMS was initially wedded to a mission in the North, as the fitting tribute to Gordon. They quickly began what was to be their most important institutional work in the North – education for girls.

But in 1905 they were reluctantly drawn into starting work in the South. General Wingate had imposed a system of mission spheres in southern Sudan which was particularly generous to the Anglicans, giving them a large area of the Equatoria Province to the west of the Nile and areas on both banks of the Nile in the White Nile Province among the Nilotic Dinka and Nuer peoples. The Catholics objected in principle to such arrangements and felt frustrated that they were not allowed to work in all parts of the South. The Anglicans were presented with large areas which at first they were unable adequately to exploit.

The first settlement in the South at Malek in 1906, among the Bor Dinka (the Jieng), looked very unpromising, and most of the first missionaries gave up. Archibald Shaw was the one who persevered, and he was to spend thirty-five years in the Sudan. He developed a close affinity with the Dinka people, sharing their nomadic life for long periods and respecting their cattle culture. Like nomadic cattle people elsewhere in Africa, the Dinka saw little in the missionary appeal which convinced them of the need for the fundamental change in life style which Christianity seemed to demand. But Shaw – Macuor, to give him his Dinka 'ox' name – remains a heroic figure to this day, as the patriarch and founder of Dinka Anglicanism. His adopted 'son', Daniel Deng Atong, an orphan who had been abandoned because of a congenital birth abnormality, became the first Sudanese priest (he was deaconed in 1941 and priested in 1943). He was ordained as the first Sudanese Anglican bishop in 1955, as assistant to Bishop Oliver Allison. A severe psychological illness prevented Atong from continuing in his work after 1958.

As Archdeacon, Shaw was instrumental in the consolidation and expansion of Anglican work in the other parts of the South allotted to them by the government. In Equatoria, progress was more obvious. Anglican work among the Zande people benefited from the establishment of a strong boarding-school system. Zande, a much more structured and hierarchical society which has been compared to Buganda, was able more easily than the pastoralist Dinka to adopt Christianity. It was in Zande country, at Yambio, that in 1938 the first revival movement began, promoted by a fiery British missionary, Richard Jones. It made an impact, not least on Daniel Deng Atong, who was a teacher in Loka, where revival had spread from Yambio.

Further east, on the borders with Uganda, a strong church grew up among the Bari and Lendu and Kakkwa peoples. It was here, particularly from the late 1940s, that evangelists of the East African Revival preached. The Revival made a great impact, profoundly affecting the structures of the church, allowing women to express their faith and values (especially through the introduction of the Mothers' Union, with which the Revival was closely linked) and encouraging local, informal evangelism. From these groups emerged the first substantial body of clergy, and the bishops, such as Elinana Ngalamu, who would lead the church in the post-missionary era.

The missionary era in Sudanese Anglican history was comparatively short. It came to an abrupt end soon after independence, which for the Sudanese church was traumatic indeed. In most African countries independence has been accompanied by a sense of pride and a heightened African identity. In the southern Sudan, the sudden creation of an independent Sudan in 1956 challenged its African identity in a host of ways. For most of the Anglo-Egyptian condominium, the British had had a free hand in the southern Sudan. They had deliberately limited the use of Arabic, and Islamic culture had been restricted. With independence, the future of the country became the focus of intense debate. Northern Sudanese were intent on having a unified and basically Islamic state. A vigorous policy of Arabisation was imposed in the South, especially in the schools. In 1962 the government passed the Missionary Societies Act, which severely curtailed the work, not only of missionaries, but of the local churches themselves.[34] In 1964 all foreign missionaries were expelled. The strong emphasis on a local trained ministry of catechists and priests was to be important in determining how the Episcopal Church would survive this period.

An armed struggle ensued, led by a southern rebel group known as the Anyanya. Organised church life became increasingly difficult during the first civil war. In 1965 Bishop Ngalamu was travelling from Rumbek to Juba to attend a meeting of the Episcopal Synod in Jerusalem. He spent the night at Bishop Gwynne College in Mundri. Soldiers invaded the college, seeking to arrest the bishop. The staff and students scattered into the bush, and the bishop made his escape. They eventually found shelter as refugees in Uganda. The experience of exile exposed a generation of

[34] Roland Werner, William Anderson and Andrew Wheeler, *Day of Devastation, Day of Contentment: The History of the Sudanese Church across 2000 Years* (Nairobi: Paulines Publications, 2000), p. 377. Much of this section is based on this book, and the other books in the Faith in Sudan series.

students to the educational opportunities provided by the Ugandan church. It produced a group of Sudanese Anglican clergy, such as Clement Janda and John Kanikwa, who have had important careers in African Anglican and ecumenical circles. Most importantly, it reinvigorated the strong links between Uganda and the southern Sudan.

In 1970 international Anglican leaders (Leslie Brown, formerly Archbishop of Uganda, and George Appleton in Jerusalem) – were involved in peace initiatives brokered by the World Council of Churches which resulted in the 1972 Addis Ababa Agreement. A measure of devolved government was agreed for the South, and respect for the religious identity of southerners was promised. Many exiles returned home. For ten years a measure of peace and stability was achieved, and the churches were able to consolidate and grow. In 1976 Sudan was separated from the Province of the Middle East to become the autonomous Episcopal Church of the Sudan, with four dioceses. Elinana Ngalamu was its first Archbishop. Unfortunately, in 1983 the agreement broke down. The Addis Ababa accords were abrogated, devolved government ended and Sharia law was established throughout the country. A new civil war erupted, with the Sudan People's Liberation Army, under John Garang, emerging as the foremost opposition. Large swathes of the countryside fell under SPLA control, though Khartoum kept control of the major urban centres, principally Juba. Bishop Gwynne College had to be closed down yet again. In the Yei area whole peoples had to relocate, finding shelter in the West Nile Province of Uganda. The journey into Uganda was interpreted as a new 'Exodus', with the Catholic and Anglican leaders (Fr Peter Dada and Bishop Seme Solomona) as Moses figures.

> A saga in Biblical style was established. This story told, retold and interpreted by a people steeped in the Biblical traditions of the East African Revival, has sustained the people of the Koboko camps through the intervening years, and given assurance that in the midst of the chaos and loss of a seemingly endless war, God is with his people to sustain and uphold.[35]

Throughout southern Sudan, biblical texts which speak of the Nile and Nubia are interpreted as revealing a covenantal relationship between God and the people of this area.

Perhaps even more remarkable has been the experience of the Nuer and Dinka (Jieng) people during the second civil war. This produced enormous disruption and death, as well as the wholesale destruction of

[35] Andrew Wheeler (ed.), *Land of Promise: Church Growth in a Sudan at War*, Faith in Sudan 1 (Nairobi: Paulines Publications, 1997), pp. 30–1.

the herds on which Dinka society and culture were based. Displaced young people found in the church an alternative to the families they had lost. The response was a general disillusionment with the old forms of religion which had seemed to serve so well for so long. The *jak* (traditional spirits) were now seen to be angry and punitive, and people looked to Christ as a more reliable and hopeful alternative. A prophet called Paul Kon Ajith began a campaign to remove the symbols of the old spirits. At a great gathering the symbols of the *jak* were brought and burnt and a new cruciform church built. Bishop Nathaniel Garang of Bor diocese moved in and out of the battle lines, preaching and baptising. One of the features of this movement has been the creation of a powerful symbolism in ritual and art: crosses were made from the remnants of MIG jets – turning weapons into symbols of peace. There was an outpouring of vernacular song, composed in the war zones and in the refugee camps on the borders of Sudan, such as Kakuma, in northern Kenya.

One of the problems for such a profoundly indigenous, vernacular movement is how it can be communicated outside the very specific historical circumstances which has given it birth. This remarkable movement of the spirit, born of war and dissolution, has had an equally remarkable *griot* (to use a West African term), a 'praise singer', who has given voice to this movement of the spirit. Marc Nikkel was an American Episcopalian priest, an artist and a theologian. His early death from cancer in 2000 cut short his energetic and creative ministry. His first experience of Sudan was in Bishop Gwynne College in the 1980s, when he participated in the restoration of the 'village of God' (a phrase used by David Brown, its first principal, and revived by Benaiah Pogo). Nikkel designed murals of Daniel and the young men in the fiery furnace, adapted from paintings discovered during the archaeological excavations of the ancient cathedral of the church of Nubia at Faras.[36] Nikkel was one of four expatriates who in 1987 was abducted by SPLA soldiers and eventually released after a seven-week trek to Kenya. He devoted the rest of his life to working alongside the Sudanese people, recording this Dinka Christian renaissance.[37] Nikkel's sensitivity as a liturgist enabled him to reflect on the meaning of this vernacular outpouring for an understanding of Anglicanism.[38]

[36] A photograph of this mural can be seen between pp. 528 and 529 of Werner, Anderson and Wheeler, *Day of Devastation, Day of Contentment.*

[37] The most extended account was published posthumously in 2001. Marc Nikkel, *Dinka Christianity: The Origins and Development of Christianity among the Dinka of Sudan with Special Reference to the Songs of Dinka Christians* (Nairobi: Paulines Publications, 2001).

[38] Marc Nikkel in Samuel Kayanga and Andrew Wheeler, *'But God is Not Defeated'* (Nairobi: Paulines Publications, 1999), p. 142.

In many parts of Africa dissatisfaction with the older forms of Anglicanism has resulted in a flight into new Pentecostal movements. The southern Sudanese church has shown the possibilities of Anglican liturgical renewal in desperate circumstances:

[God's] presence undergirds their astonishing spiritual vitality, their determination to survive, and rebuild and create anew, and even to celebrate – a new paradigm for survival.[39]

The Dinka have been foremost among victims of a renewed slave trade, in which young boys and girls are abducted, and brought up in the North as Muslims. Meanwhile the flight of southerners to the North, to congregate in the sprawling townships of Khartoum, has created a strong Christian presence in the North, in which churches are a focus for survival and the re-creation of a southern identity.[40]

It remains to be seen whether Sudan will survive as a single nation or whether it will be divided into a predominantly Muslim North and a predominantly Christian South. Even if division happens, the issues of the two faiths living side by side will be of great importance. The fate of the two parts has been inextricably bound together. In the North, there remains a vigorous Christian community, not only of southerners living in Khartoum, but of Nuba people in the highlands south of Khartoum: people who are thoroughly at home in the Arabic culture of the North, but who express their Nuba identity as Christians.[41] In the South, Islam remains a strong presence, especially in the towns.[42]

CONCLUSION

Concerning the Middle East, Kenneth Cragg asks the question which has troubled Christians for centuries: is there a future with Islam? His answer is that 'there is no future for Arab Christianity except with Islam'.[43] The question has become all the more critical as large numbers of Arab

[39] Kayanga and Wheeler, *'But God is Not Defeated'*, p. 148.

[40] See Oliver Duku, 'The Development and Growth of Mayo Congregations' (Mayo is a suburb of Khartoum), in Wheeler, *Land of Promise*, pp. 39–60.

[41] Justin Willis, 'The Nyamang are Hard to Touch: Mission Evangelism and Tradition in the Nuba Mountains, Sudan, 1933–1952', *Journal of Religion in Africa* 33.1 (2003), pp. 32–62, describes how the first CMS missionaries tried, unsuccessfully, to shield the Nuba from Arabic. But it was here that Constance Padwick, after the Second World War, worked at producing Arabic texts for a school system which could no longer resist the use of Arabic if the Nuba were not to be seriously disadvantaged.

[42] See Gino Barsella and Miguel Guixot, *Struggling to be Heard: The Christian Voice in Independent Sudan 1956–1996* (Nairobi: Paulines Publications, 1998).

[43] Kenneth Cragg, *The Arab Christian* (Louisville: John Knox, 1991), p. 279.

Christians of all traditions have sought security and a future by emigration to the West, and particularly to America. The long-term survival of many churches is put in question by this unparalleled exodus of the young and active. For the tiny Anglican churches in Arab lands, the question of viability remains even more acute than for the Orthodox churches. Temple Gairdner was early confronted with some of the harsh realities of work in Egypt, and wrote to his fiancée:

> I seem to have left the uncloudedness, the boyhood of life behind me for ever, and have entered into what I feel to be a sadder life . . . I see the same thing in front – this apparently hopeless effort to cope with Islam . . . these terrible disappointments . . . Indeed I grieve that I am not more sad, for this is a call to enter into a very inner chamber of the sufferings of Christ. The danger is that one should remain in the ante-room of mere disappointment and grow hard and cold in it, and settle down to a faithless, hopeless sort of existence.[44]

Anglican mission in the Middle East has had continually to come to terms with the reality of an Islamic dominant culture. Cragg in a highly sophisticated intellectual way and many Arab Christians and missionaries in practical work have attempted to enter that culture sympathetically and creatively, to mark out a place for the church. Working together with other Christian churches, both Orthodox and western (Catholic and Protestant), has also been an important aspect of continuing work. Dialogue in the Middle East is never simply a theological or pastoral exercise – it has to confront the harsh political realities. Palestinian Anglicans identify strongly with the Palestinian cry for liberation. In Sudan, the vibrant Episcopal Church engages existentially with the question of how Muslims and Christians can live together peacefully.

[44] Constance Padwick, *Temple Gairdner of Cairo* (London: SPCK, 1929), p. 95. See the comments on this letter by Cragg in Ward and Stanley, *The Church Mission Society and World Christianity*, p. 133.

CHAPTER II

South Asia

SOCIETY, RELIGION, CASTE

The India which became the focus of missionary interest from the early eighteenth century was a vast and diverse society, not least in its religious traditions. The core values of India were shaped by what became known as Hinduism. The Mogul conquest had introduced Islam to much of North India, and from there to the rest of the sub-continent. Other religious minorities were significant in specific areas, notably the Sikhs, the Jains, and the indigenous Christians of Kerala. Scattered throughout the sub-continent were 'tribal' people who were not integrated into the dominant culture of India. 'Hinduism' as a 'religion' was in many ways a construct of eighteenth-century European attempts to understand and make sense of the complex religious and social reality of India. Western intellectuals – Orientalists,[1] as they came to be called – looked to the sacred Sanskrit texts as the norm by which to understand Hinduism, applying to India understandings of religion arising from the Christian tradition. A distinction was made between 'the Great Tradition' of the classical Hindu Scriptures and 'the Little Tradition', the multiplicity of traditions of popular, village Hinduism.

Early nineteenth-century Christian missionaries tended to begin with an aggressively negative attitude to Hinduism in the abstract, though this might become tempered by the actual experience of sustained encounter. The British presence in India was mediated through the East India Company, regulated by, and responsible to, the British Parliament, but an unofficial body itself. Company rule in India had greatly extended in the eighteenth century, but applied to only a small proportion of India as

[1] See Edward Said, *Orientalism* (New York: Pantheon, 1979). Mallampalli usefully defines Orientalism as 'that body of knowledge about "the Orient" which ultimately serves the interests of colonial domination'. Chandra Mallampalli, *Christians and Public Life in Colonial South India* (London: RoutledgeCurzon, 2004), p. 10.

a whole. The first Protestant missionaries to India saw the East India Company as one of the chief obstacles to their success. They accused the Company of an easy tolerance of 'idolatry' and indifference to the radical social reform which the missionaries saw as essential. Much of the missionary critique of Indian society itself focused on the caste system, seen as the chief source of India's ills.

Basic to Indian social organisation was caste. It had ramifications both for Indian understandings of religion and for the way in which Christian missionary activity embedded itself in Indian soil. In simple terms, caste is a hierarchical ordering of groups within society. Individuals are born into a particular group, and remain there for life. They marry within that group, and perform the functions of the group for the welfare of the society as a whole. A number of these functions, especially those involving contact with bodily fluids, corpses and animal parts, are considered religiously polluting. At some time in their lives, all people are involved in activities which cause pollution, and they need to undergo elaborate and costly rituals of purification. But some people, by the nature of their occupation, are in a permanent state of pollution. They are 'outcaste' and should be avoided by other groups. They are required to avoid watering places and to live on the outskirts of the village. They must not use the public streets. According to Hindu Scriptures there are four *varna* (social groups) whose distinctive roles give them varying degrees of purity: Brahmins (Priests), Kshatriyas (Warriors), Vaishyas (Traders) and Shudras (Cultivators). In practice people belong to a particular *jati*, the endogamous local caste group. Caste is not necessarily synonymous with economic status. Some Brahmins are poor, while a group from a lower *varna* may enjoy wealth, status and power in a particular community. A group may have ambitions for higher status. In a process often called 'Sanskritisation', they may try to conform to the ideals and rituals prescribed in the Hindu Scriptures, distancing themselves from polluting practices, and thus making a bid for greater respectability. Groups outside the formal caste system are nevertheless dependent on the ideology of the caste system, both because they are poor and vulnerable and because they perform functions essential to the caste society. They are in no position overtly to challenge the dominant ideology, and implicitly accept it, competing with other, equally despised groups to distance themselves from the more polluting activities.[2] But this does not preclude strategies

[2] For a clear exposition of the caste system see Judith M. Brown, *Modern India* (Oxford: Oxford University Press, 1994), pp. 17–31.

of resistance, the creation of an alternative story, autonomous from, and counter to, the dominant ideology.[3]

It was the fact that the caste system was not as static as either defenders or opponents suggested that facilitated group conversion to Christianity. Conversion had a variety of goals and consequences for the mobility of the group as a whole, or for a section of the group. However much the Christian churches taught the abandonment of caste status within the church, caste considerations and sensibilities continued to affect the life of Christians in a number of profound ways.

THE CHURCH OF ENGLAND IN INDIA: THE 'ECCLESIASTICAL ESTABLISHMENT'

Throughout the colonial period Anglican churches had to wrestle with a problem of identity. Is the church a part of the governmental apparatus of the British Empire? Is it an extension of the parochial system of the Church of England, existing to serve English men and women abroad (whether as soldiers, administrators or settlers)? How does this essentially English body relate to the presence of a local 'native' church which has grown up as a result of the labours of Anglican missionaries? Bishop Thomas Valpy French, first Bishop of Lahore (1877–87), complained that in the Punjab there were 'two churches (native and European) . . . united under one bishop'.[4] The reference to 'two churches' was hardly consistent with Anglican ecclesial self-understanding at this period (with its emphasis on Catholicity), but it did starkly express the empirical reality. The Church of England in India was an ecclesiastical establishment from 1814 until 1930, long after disestablishment had been effected in Ireland, Wales, Canada and the Caribbean. And yet it was an establishment like no other: that of the ruling power in India, but definitely not of, or for, the indigenous population. Neither the Company nor the Raj which replaced it in 1858 desired to subvert the existing religious culture and institutions of India.

From the seventeenth century, the Company had appointed chaplains to look after the welfare of its servants, and those who identified with them (especially important were communities of Anglo-Indians through

[3] This issue is well articulated in Sathianathan Clarke's pioneering work of theological methodology, *Dalits and Christianity: Subaltern Religion and Liberation Theology in India* (Delhi: Oxford University Press, 1998).

[4] Jeffrey Cox, *Imperial Fault Lines: Christianity and Colonial Power in India 1818–1940* (Stanford: Stanford University Press, 2002), p. 45.

inter-marriage). The Company discouraged chaplains from conducting direct missionary work among Indian peoples, except in the most limited ways. The policy of non-interference in the religious sensibilities of local rulers, Hindu and Muslim, was challenged by the Evangelicals, whose egalitarian and democratic tendencies threatened the conservative and hierarchical ordering of society in both princely and Company states. Hence the remarkably hostile reaction of the authorities to the arrival of William Carey and the first Baptist missionaries in 1793.

Ironically, it was a group of Evangelical Anglican chaplains of the East India Company who were most active in urging the British Parliament to force the Company to drop its prohibition of direct mission activity. Claudius Buchanan, Daniel Corrie and Henry Martyn, while working as chaplains, actively explored the possibilities of missionary work in India. They reported back to the newly formed Church Missionary Society about fruitful lines of missionary work, and supplied information to the members of the Clapham Sect which they could use in their political campaign to reform the way in which the East India Company operated. As with their anti-slavery activity, Evangelicals aimed to free India from oppressive forces which were inimical to human freedom as well as true religion.

The former governor, Warren Hastings, had argued against allowing missionary activity because it was 'not consistent with the security of the Empire to treat the religions established in the country with contempt'. In his speech to Parliament in 1813 Wilberforce had nothing but contempt for 'the evils of Hindostan', which 'pervade the whole mass of the population'. He went on to describe caste as 'hopeless and irremediable vassalage', and to condemn polygamy, sati (the immolation of a widow on the funeral pyre of her husband) and 'obscene and bloody rites of their idolatrous ceremonies, with all their unutterable abominations'. The whole religious system was 'mean, licentious and cruel'.[5] Wilberforce had little sympathy for the 'Orientalists' of the East India Company, who, he believed, were indifferent to the urgency of radical social reform. In contrast, Wilberforce claimed to champion the millions of ordinary people trapped in the system.[6]

Wilberforce's speech swung the debate in favour of the missionaries. The new charter allowed missionary activity in so far as it was not

5 Robin Furneaux, *William Wilberforce* (London: Hamish Hamilton, 1974), pp. 326–8.

6 Said characterises Orientalists as having an overwhelming distaste for the culture and religion of those they were investigating. His book focuses largely on attitudes to the Arabic Muslim world, and would need to be qualified with reference to India.

obviously inimical to public order, and on the clear understanding that 'the principles of the British Government, on which the natives of India have hitherto relied for the free exercise of their religion, be inviolably maintained'.[7] The other important outcome was the appointment of a Bishop of Calcutta. The British were sufficiently worried about the reaction to the appointment in Bengal to take steps to ensure that Thomas Middleton's consecration in London and his enthronement in Calcutta were done with a minimum of publicity. The Evangelicals' desire for other dioceses in Madras and Bombay was not realised until 1835.

A system emerged in which these three bishops were paid by the 'Ecclesiastical establishment', which continued to appoint and deploy an expanding cohort of military and civil chaplains.[8] Both Company and British Parliament remained nervous about endorsing missionary activity as such, though individual Christian members of the Indian civil or military establishment, especially in the Punjab, were particularly friendly towards missionary activity.[9] After 1835 Parliament refused to create more dioceses by Act of Parliament. The assumption of direct British rule in India in 1858, after the Sepoy Mutiny, did not radically change this position. Queen Victoria's statement was meant to reassure Indian religious sensibilities:

> Firmly relying ourselves on the truth of Christianity and acknowledging the solace of religion, we disclaim alike the right and the desire to impose our convictions on any of our subjects.[10]

In practice, the government did accept the need for further extension of the episcopate and allowed this to happen by a number of legal expedients which did not involve parliamentary legislation, including endowment by public subscription. Dioceses of Lahore (1877), Travancore (1879), Chota Nagpur (1890) and Lucknow (1893) were thus created. By the twentieth century, the British authorities in India were not worried about the Parliament in London. Now they were anxious not to provoke Indian Nationalist criticism by overt support for the church. This was one of the reasons why, after the appointment of the first

[7] Stephen Neill, *A History of Christianity in India, 1707–1858* (Cambridge: Cambridge University Press, 1985), pp. 153–4.

[8] Bernard Palmer's *Imperial Vineyard: The Anglican Church in India under the Raj* (Lewes: The Book Guild, 1999) is largely concerned with this aspect of the Anglican presence in India.

[9] Eugene Stock was particularly appreciative of the support of people like John Lawrence. See his *History of the Church Missionary Society*, Volumes I and II (London: CMS, 1899).

[10] Cox, *Imperial Fault Lines*, p. 33.

Indian, Samuel Azariah, as Bishop of Dornakal in 1912, no other Indian diocesan bishop was appointed before the disestablishment of the church in 1930, and indeed before independence in 1947.[11]

Bishop Middleton, the first Bishop of Calcutta, had been so conscious of the limitations imposed on him in the terms of his appointment that he felt unable either to license ordained missionaries working in India or to ordain those who were not British subjects. Bishop Reginald Heber (1823–6) and Bishop Daniel Wilson (1832–58) overcame those inhibitions. By mid-century, Indian Anglicans greatly outnumbered the English, even if they remained a very small minority of Indians as a whole. But, as Bishop French indicated, the British and the Indian sections of the church operated in almost totally different worlds.

India was characterised by a great diversity of Anglican missions, and never became identified with a single Anglican church tradition in the way that many parts of Africa did. In the eighteenth century, the SPCK had financed German missionary enterprise in South India, partly because the SPG had felt precluded by its charter (which confined its work to British colonies) from engaging in any part of India. In the nineteenth century, especially after the appointment of a bishop, the SPG did finally become directly involved, some time after the CMS. In the second half of the nineteenth century, the work of the two societies was supplemented by groups of Anglican religious: the Order of St John the Evangelist (the Cowley Fathers) and 'brotherhoods' of university men from Cambridge (in Delhi), Oxford (Calcutta) and Dublin, working in co-operation with sisterhoods. Local Indian orders were also formed, such as the Brotherhood of St Andrew and the Sisters of St Mary in Bengal. The Church of England Zenana Mission had a specific role among upper-caste women.

THE BEGINNINGS OF PROTESTANT MISSIONARY WORK IN INDIA

In 1706 Bartholomaeus Ziegenbalg and Heinrich Pluetschau, Germans from the Pietist centre of Halle, had arrived under the auspices of the King of Denmark, to begin work in the area of the Danish trading fort at Tranquebar, south of Madras. Finding some hostility at first from the Danish community, they set up their centre in the area controlled by the Indian ruler of Tanjore. The connections between the Danish and the

[11] For this process see M. E. Gibbs, *The Anglican Church in India 1600–1970* (Delhi: ISPCK, 1972).

English court during the reign of Queen Anne (her husband was Danish) led to financial support from the SPCK, which from 1732 began to pay the full salaries of some of the German missionaries. The church which emerged was Lutheran in its church order, its adherence to the Augsburg Confession, and its hymnody. But as Anglican involvement grew, the German missionaries also incorporated Anglican elements, in particular translating the Book of Common Prayer into Tamil. Working on foundations already laid by previous Roman Catholic activity, the Protestant missionaries had success both among the Paraiyar (pariah) outcastes and the higher-status Velela caste (a local Sudra elite). The nascent church incorporated these caste divisions into its structures, with Velala rather than Paraiyar taking leadership positions. The seating arrangements in church reflected group distinctions and Communion was taken by Velela first, so that 'pollution' was avoided.

In the 1770s C. F. Schwartz visited a congregation which had grown up at Palayankottai, in the Tirunelveli district, under the patronage of Kohila, a Brahmin widow now living with a British soldier. Schwartz hesitated to baptise Kohila because they were not formally married, but after the soldier's death she was baptised and took the name Clarinda. With the catechist Gnanaprakasam, she promoted evangelistic work in Tirunelveli, which was to meet with a response from the Shanar (or Nadar) people. Sattianadan, a Velela catechist, was ordained by Schwartz according to Lutheran order in 1790, and worked faithfully in Tirunelveli until his death in 1815. Tirunelveli (Tinnevelly) became one of the strongest and most vibrant of the Anglican churches in India.

One remarkable Tamil Christian of this period was another Velela, Vedanayagam Pillai, the *sastri* (poet), who lived from 1774 to 1864, and who experienced the transition of the church from Lutheran to predominantly Anglican church order. Vedanayagam was a superb Tamil composer of poetry and dance-drama, utilising Tamil classical and folk traditions to create a rich body of literature in which biblical themes were expressed in a Tamil voice, such as his 'Bethlehem Kuravanci' presentation of scenes from the life of Christ.[12] His adopted daughter Jnanadipa Ammal (literally 'The Light of Wisdom') helped him in his work, learnt English, and translated a number of devotional works from English into Tamil.

[12] Indira Viswanathan Peterson, 'Bethlehem Kuravanci of Vedanayaka Sastri of Tanjore: The Cultural Discourses of an Early-Nineteenth-Century Tamil Christian Poem', in Judith M. Brown and Robert E. Frykenberg (eds.), *Christians, Cultural Interactions, and India's Religious Traditions* (Grand Rapids: Eerdmans, 2002), pp. 9–36.

Vedanayagam was critical of the new wave of missionaries who took over in the 1810s. This was a period of transition in the South Indian church. The Danes, unable to sustain the work during the disruptions of the Napoleonic Wars, invited a newly awakened British missionary movement to take over. The SPCK at first assumed some of the work but in 1825 handed over to the SPG. The CMS entered in 1815. The outstanding CMS missionary of this early period was also German, Carl Rhenius, who energetically set about transforming the church in Tirunelveli. Rhenius was undoubtedly one of the great missionaries of the age, but his abrasive style alienated many existing Christians. The new missionaries generally seemed to show disdain for their traditions and sensibilities. In particular, they felt that there was no compromise with caste: Christians should renounce caste at baptism, and eradicate caste distinctions from their fellowship, in particular at Holy Communion.[13]

Vedanayagam accused Rhenius of a brutal intolerance in his condemnation of the blending of traditional culture and Christian worship (for example through the use of flowers), his neglect of Tamil lyrics and music, his insistence on the intermingling of castes in church, and abandoning the custom of higher-caste communicants taking the elements first. A number of Velelan authors attacked the new policy in a work entitled 'The Foolishness of Amending Caste'.

The first Tamil Christian to be ordained (in 1826) according to the Anglican ordinal was Christian David, who had been working in Ceylon. He advised Bishop Heber to have a more tolerant attitude to the caste sensibilities of the Tamil church. But the strong weight of the missionary movement as a whole was against compromise. A declaration against caste became part of the baptismal liturgy of the church. All Anglican missionary societies were in agreement that caste could have no place in the Christian community.

The end of Rhenius' career was clouded by conflicts with the CMS. Rhenius wanted to ordain pastors in accordance with the old Lutheran traditions. Now that there was a bishop in India, the CMS saw no reason for such presbyteral ordinations to continue. Rhenius for a time established a schismatic church in the Tirunelveli area, but after his death the congregations were reconciled with the Anglican church. Eventually, specifically Lutheran work revived in Tranquebar itself. Nevertheless, the Tamil Anglican church cannot forget the foundations laid by the

[13] See Frykenberg's introduction to David and Sarojini Packiamuthu and Robert Frykenberg (eds.), *Tirunelveli's Evangelical Christians* (Bangalore: SAIACS Press, 2003).

Lutherans. (Equally, the strong Lutheran church of Bukoba in Tanzania takes pride in its Anglican origins from Uganda.)

ANGLICANS AND THE ORTHODOX CHRISTIANS OF KERALA

There was in neighbouring Kerala a Christian church more ancient by far than the Lutherans of Tamil Nadu. Called variously Yakoba, Syrian Orthodox and Malabar Christians, its members trace their origins back to the apostle Thomas.[14] Contacts with Roman Catholics in the sixteenth century had eventually split the church and left a legacy of mistrust of foreign intervention. Nevertheless, when Claudius Buchanan visited the Metran (Metropolitan) Dionysius I in 1806, a potentially fruitful relationship with the Anglican church was initiated.[15] Buchanan contacted the CMS, and in 1816 the first CMS missionary began working in Kerala, in what the CMS called a 'mission of help'. Bible translation into the local language of Malayalam was a priority. A seminary was established at Kottayam to train Orthodox clergy.

Very quickly, however, misunderstandings began to creep into the relationship. The early CMS missionaries tended to 'blame' those rituals and practices they disliked on Roman Catholic influences, failing to recognise that they were in fact deeply held Orthodox tenets of faith. The CMS called superstitious such practices as prayers mediated through the saints, veneration of Mary, prayers for the dead, elaborate ceremonials, and reference to the sacrament of the Eucharist as 'the sacrifice'. Such profound negativity alienated the Orthodox leadership. In turn the Orthodox frustrated the CMS missionaries, eager to do primary evangelism. Orthodox Christians blended into the caste structures of society. They had high status, and found it difficult to share the missionaries' zeal to convert Hindus from the depressed classes.

In 1836 the synod of Mavelikkara rejected the proposals of Bishop Daniel Wilson for continued co-operation with the Anglicans, and the two groups began to go their own ways. The CMS now felt free to develop its own evangelistic work, based at Travancore, which began to bear some fruit among the Ezava people (a group similar to the Tamil Nadar in occupation and status). Some Syrian Christians continued to work with the CMS, including the Revd George Mathen, originally

[14] L.W. Brown, *The Indian Christians of St Thomas* (Cambridge: Cambridge University Press, 1956). Leslie Brown, a CMS missionary in Kerala, became Bishop of Uganda.

[15] C.P. Mathew and M.M. Thomas, *The Indian Churches of St Thomas* (Delhi: ISPCK, 1967), Chapter 5.

ordained in the Orthodox Church. They began to assume leadership positions in the nascent Anglican church. This may have inhibited more lower-caste groups from joining the church. The CMS institute at Kottayam continued to provide education for Anglicans and Orthodox. Take, for example, the Poonen family: T. C. Poonen became the first person from Kerala to study for the Bar; his brother Dr E. Poonen studied medicine in Aberdeen and became head of the Travancore government medical department. Dr Poonen's daughter, Mary (1886–1976), was the first woman to study medicine at the college in Trivandrum, and eventually became the head of medical services in Travancore.[16]

The breakdown of formal relations did not end the influence of CMS Anglicans among the Orthodox. A movement for reform continued to be active, inspired particularly by the work of Abraham Malpan in revising the liturgy and translating it into Malayalam. Eventually differences between reformers and traditionalists led to the separation of the two groups and the emergence of the Mar Thoma Church as a distinct Orthodox church.[17] The Mar Thoma were deeply influenced by the biblical emphasis of the CMS: Bible reading became a vital part of individual and family worship, preaching at the Eucharist became essential, and in the 1890s revivalism (spreading over from the CMS work in Tirunelveli initiated by Thomas Walker) had an impact on Mar Thoma Christians.[18] But the liturgy continues to be called *Qurbana* (the sacrifice), and to follow the liturgical richness of Orthodoxy. The theologian M. M. Thomas has given the Mar Thoma church an international and ecumenical profile in the twentieth century. The Mar Thoma Church has always had strong fraternal relations with the Anglican church, and this has been translated into full inter-communion between it and the united Churches of South and North India.

ANGLICAN MISSION ACTIVITY IN NORTH INDIA

Anglican mission work in North India only began to take off in earnest in 1814, with the passing of the new India Act. The Baptists – William Carey, Joshua Marshman and William Ward – had already established the ground rules for Christian engagement with Bengali and Hindu culture, operating from the Danish trading station of Serampore. The

[16] Robin Jeffrey, 'Women and the "Kerala Model": Four Lives 1870s–1980s', *Journal of South Asia Studies* 12.2 (December 1989), pp. 22ff.

[17] Susan Visvanathan, *The Christians of Kerala* (Madras: Oxford University Press, 1993), p. 12.

[18] Mathew and Thomas, *The Indian Churches*, Chapter 7.

Evangelical Anglican Company chaplains were in basic sympathy with their approach, involving Bible translation and a rather polemical debate over the meaning and adequacy of the classical texts of Hinduism and Islam. Henry Martyn was prominent among the chaplains for the intensity of his missionary zeal and the quality of his biblical translation work into Arabic, Persian and Hindustani. He worked in India from 1806 to 1811, when, his health already weakened, he went to Shiraz in Persia to complete his work on a Persian New Testament. He died in Turkey at the age of 31. For the CMS he provided the benchmark of dedicated, imaginative missionary work. One of Martyn's colleagues in language work was Sheikh Salah, from a learned Delhi Muslim family, knowledgeable in Hindi, Persian and Arabic. A man with a deep, questioning spirituality, he eventually made the decision to become a Christian and in 1811 was baptised with the names Abdul Masih ('The Servant of the Messiah') in Calcutta. He was crucial in the development of CMS work in North India, and the Society asked Bishop Middleton to ordain him. But the bishop believed that he was inhibited, by the terms of his appointment, from ordaining anyone who was not a British subject. In 1820, the CMS therefore asked one of its Lutheran missionaries in Bengal to ordain Masih, as had been the established practice of the church in South India. Bishop Heber, having clarified his legal position, eventually gave Masih episcopal ordination in 1825, just two years before Masih's death.

Both the CMS and the SPG wished to influence the upper echelons of society. They hoped to create or exacerbate a discontent with the traditional religious culture (whether Hindu or Islamic) among educated and religiously knowledgeable men like Masih. One means to this end was to build up an educational system in English which would inculcate the best of western Christian learning. The most articulate exponent of this approach was Alexander Duff, of the Church of Scotland Mission, who argued that the mission priority should be to create an upper class deeply influenced by Christian values, even if only a minority formally converted. Macaulay famously argued for an education system which would produce men who were 'Indian in blood and colour. But English in taste, in opinions, in morals and in intellect'. Gauri Viswanathan has characterised this as 'a secular project to transform Indians into deracinated replicas of Englishmen even while they remained affiliated to their own religious culture'.[19] Education proved an area where missions and

[19] Gauri Viswanathan, *Outside the Fold: Conversion, Modernity and Belief* (Princeton: Princeton University Press, 1998), p. 5.

government could co-operate, though the shared ideals (of producing a socially progressive pro-British elite) masked different goals.[20]

Anglicans hastened to develop their educational institutions, but they were never easy about a wholehearted Anglicisation policy. They were always conscious that education needed also directly to serve the church, both by training clergy and catechists and by providing education for Indian Christians, who were largely from low-caste groups. They were less willing than the Scots to throw all their energies into providing education for upper-class non-Christian Indians. In Calcutta, Bishop's College was originally supported financially by both the CMS and the SPG, but the CMS gradually distanced itself from a project which did not primarily serve the needs of its church communities, and a more high-church ethos came to predominate. But where the CMS had a dominant voice, it too was keen to develop elite schools. At St John's College, Agra, in the Punjab, the CMS missionary T.V. French developed a school which he hoped would become an Indian 'Alexandria': a modern 'Catechetical School' which would train Christian apologists who could hold their own among the intellectuals of the prevailing culture (in this case primarily Muslim). When he became Bishop of Lahore, French supported the formation of the Cambridge Brotherhood, a group of young university graduates, many of them influenced by Brooke Foss Westcott, one of the foremost biblical scholars of his time. The Cambridge Mission established St Stephen's School in Delhi, the old Moghul capital, which in 1904 also became the British capital. In the old capital of Calcutta, a similar brotherhood, the Oxford Mission, was established in 1879.

INDIAN ELITE CONVERTS

The emphasis on elite conversion did result in a number of outstanding Indian apologists for Christianity. Krishna Mohan Banerjea (1813–85), a Bengali Hindu social reformer and journalist, was baptised by Alexander Duff in 1832. Eventually he became an Anglican and was ordained. He was the first Indian on the staff of Bishop's College in Calcutta. In Benares, Nilakantha Goreh (1825–95), a sceptical Brahmin intellectual, disputed the truth of Christianity at the CMS mission but eventually came under its spell. He was baptised Nehemiah. He was ordained in 1868, and his Christian pilgrimage led him to find the Anglo-Catholic

[20] J.C. Ingleby, *Missionaries, Education and India: Issues in Protestant Missionary Education in the Long Nineteenth Century* (Delhi: ISPCK, 2000).

tradition more satisfying than the Evangelicalism of his conversion. He particularly admired the Cowley Fathers (the Society of St John the Evangelist), who had established work in Poona (Pune) in the Bombay Presidency, and whose relations with the CMS were particularly fraught. Goreh was a disciplined, austere thinker, whose most famous work was *Shadarshana Darpana* (1862), translated into English as *Rational Refutation of Hindu Philosophical Systems*. 'Intellectually confident but temperamentally diffident',[21] he tried to show both the coherence of the Catholic faith and the philosophical inadequacies of Hinduism. Duncan Forrester has described Goreh's theology as 'a somewhat forbiddingly orthodox understanding of Christianity'.[22]

Religious disputation was an important element in the nineteenth-century meeting of religions. Although profoundly polemical and un-ecumenical in spirit, it did have the virtue of taking the other religion seriously. At the beginning of French's missionary career in Agra there occurred a series of formal disputations with Muslim religious leaders in which both sides set out the issues which divided them. In the 1830s, the CMS missionary Pfander had produced, in German, a refutation of Islam, which he translated into Persian as *Mizan al-Haqq* (*The Balance of Truth*). This became widely known in Islamic theological circles, and the Muslim *ulama* (teachers) in Agra were anxious to engage Pfander in debate. The Great Debate of 1854 focused on such issues as the Trinity, the prophethood of Muhammad, and questions of the corruption of sacred texts. One of the areas in which the Muslim disputants particularly discomfited the Christians was their awareness of the debates within Protestant Christianity (and particularly among Pfander's German compatriots) on the reliability of the Bible. They felt, with some justification, that the missionaries were unable adequately to answer their queries.

The Sepoy Mutiny and its aftermath meant that it became impossible for Muslim and Christian to recreate the mutual confidence to debate these issues in the academic, purely 'theological' manner which had been enjoyed in 1854. Muslims had become more wary of Christian intentions. Christians became more focused on their evangelistic work among the lower strata of society.

Some missionaries gradually came to distrust the polemical approach entirely, and to argue for a more sympathetic understanding of the role of

[21] Balwant Paradkar, *The Theology of Goreh* (Bangalore: Christian Institute for the Study of Religion and Society, 1969), p. 10.

[22] Duncan Forrester, *Caste and Christianity* (London: Curzon, 1980), p. 130.

religion. In India more positive understandings of Hinduism were associated at first with Protestant free-church missionaries such as Bernard Lucas and J. N. Farquhar (whose *The Crown of Hinduism* of 1913 argued for a 'fulfilment' view by which Hinduism is not destroyed but transformed by the Gospel). They were influenced by the wide sympathies of the English Anglican theologians F. D. Maurice and B. F. Westcott.[23] Although neither the Evangelical nor the Anglo-Catholic group in India found such theological liberalism immediately congenial, a century of encounter between Indian Hinduism and Christianity led to an increasing humility in the face of the diversity of religion.

PANDITA RAMABAI AND WOMEN CHRISTIAN CONVERTS

A major element in the missionary dispute with Hinduism was disagreement over the rights of women. Missionaries drew attention to issues of child marriage, the practice of sati and the miserable status of surviving widows, many very young. Reform movements within Hinduism equally addressed these problems. For the small number of high-caste women who converted to Christianity it was a major concern. The most notable high-caste woman convert was Ramabai (1858–1922). The daughter of a Brahmin scholar from Karnataka, she received a thorough education in Sanskrit and the Hindu Scriptures from her father. Both her parents had died by the time Ramabai was sixteen. Ramabai, accompanied by her brother, began a life of travel which made her famous as an interpreter of the Purana (Scriptures): the University of Calcutta honoured her with the titles of 'Pandita' (teacher) and 'Saraswati' when she was only twenty. She married a Bengali lawyer, from a Sudra caste and a supporter of Brahmo Samaj, the Hindu reform movement. After less than two years of marriage, her husband died, leaving Ramabai with a young daughter, Manorama. Ramabai had begun to read St Luke's Gospel, given to her husband by a Baptist missionary. Moving to Pune, Ramabai came in contact with Fr Nehemiah Goreh, who was residing with the Cowley Fathers. She also met the Sisters of St Mary the Virgin, an Anglican community whose mother house was in Wantage, England. In 1882 she left India to stay at Wantage, the beginnings of a deep but at times stormy relationship with the sisters, particularly with Sister Geraldine, who acted as her god-mother when Ramabai made the decision to be baptised.

[23] Kenneth Cracknell, *Justice, Courtesy and Love* (London: Epworth, 1995).

The Calcutta press in particular raised an outcry at this decision. It expressed concern that Ramabai, in an unfamiliar country, had been the subject of undue pressure. Ramabai was, in fact, never willing to sacrifice her autonomy, whether to the Hindu establishment in Calcutta, to Goreh, or to her English advisors, to whom she wrote sharply:

> You have never gone through the same experience of choosing another religion, for yourself, which was totally foreign to you, as I have . . . You can't interpenetrate my poor feelings.[24]

And, to Sister Geraldine:

> I am, it is true, a member of the Church of Christ, but I am not bound to accept every word that falls down from the lips of priests or bishops . . . I have just with great efforts freed myself from the rule of the Indian priestly tribe, so I am not at present willing to place myself under another similar yoke by accepting everything which comes from the priests as authorized command of the Most High.[25]

Back in Pune, Ramabai established a home for child widows. She wrote about the plight of women in a book first written in Marathi and then in English, *The High Caste Hindu Woman* (1888). But she refused simply to denounce Hinduism. To the disapproval of more conservative Christians, she continued to visit temples to expound the Purana Scriptures to women. Ceaselessly restless spiritually and intellectually, towards the end of her life she promoted a Keswick-style revival in her Pune community. It was the mystical and devotional aspects of the Keswick movement which inspired her. In this she resembles the missionary Amy Carmichael of Tinnevelly. Among her many activities were Bible translation and the composition of spiritual songs and hymns in Marathi and Hindi.

A contemporary high-caste Christian woman influenced by Ramabai was Krupabai Satthianadhan (1862–94). Like Ramabai, she was from a Brahmin family, but her father had converted and she was brought up a Christian.[26] Her home area was Nasik, north of Bombay and Pune. Nasik was famous for its CMS school, where a number of African freed slaves were educated. Krupabai trained as a doctor at the Madras Medical College, the first college to admit women. She had been prevented from

[24] Ramabai to Canon William Butler, 3 July 1885, in A. B. Shah (ed.), *The Letters and Correspondence of Pandita Ramabai* (Bombay: Maharashtra Board, 1977), p. 74, quoted in Viswanathan, *Outside the Fold*, p. 125.

[25] S. M. Adhav, *Pandita Ramabai* (Madras: Christian Literature Society, 1979), p. 131.

[26] Biographical details can be found in the new edition of her autobiographical novel: Krupabai Satthianadhan, *Saguna: A Story of Native Christian Life*, ed. Chandani Lokuge (Delhi: Oxford University Press, 1998). The novel was first serialised in the *Madras Christian College Magazine* in 1887 and 1888, and was published posthumously in 1895.

taking up a scholarship in Oxford because her American missionary mentors considered that her physical health could not withstand the British climate. In Madras she met Samuel Satthianadhan, the son of a prominent Anglican priest. Satthianadhan had just returned from Cambridge. He became a headmaster.

After their marriage in 1881, Krupabai also became involved in education, particularly girls' education. Her autobiographical novel *Saguna* has been described as the first novel in English by an Indian woman. She also began a biography of her mother-in-law, Anna Satthianadhan, herself a proponent of women's rights. But, as Krupabai's health began rapidly to deteriorate, she concentrated on completing her novel *Kamala: The Story of a Hindu Life.*[27] Strongly influenced by English Romanticism, and with an intense appreciation of nature, especially of her native Deccan, Krupabai explores the growth of two girls 'trapped in the standard mould of domesticity'[28] and their struggles for individuality and a sense of self-worth and acceptance as equals by men. *Kamala* owes much to Ramabai's campaign for justice for widows. Krupabai does not hesitate to use her novels as the vehicle for preaching her understanding of Christian faith. Her sense of longing, on the other hand, reminds me of Olive Schreiner's *Story of an African Farm*, published only a few years before. Krupabai may well have had a strong sense of her own mortality, and she was only thirty-two when she died.

THE MASS MOVEMENTS

Despite the stature of such figures as Banerjee, Goreh, Ramabai and the Satthianadhan family, it was clear by the end of the nineteenth century that the hope of a gradual acceptance of Christianity among the ruling classes was not to be realised. The missionary campaigns against social injustice had resulted in a vigorous Hindu response, both of reform and counter-attack. One area of social reform which did capture the popular imagination, however, was the missionary campaign on behalf of the Bengali *ryots* (peasant labourers), who were forced to cultivate indigo for the European planters. German CMS missionaries in Krishnagar had drawn attention to the plight of the *ryots* for a decade,[29] but in 1860 the

[27] Krupabai Satthianadhan, *Kamala: The Story of a Hindu Life*, ed. Chandani Lokuge (Delhi: Oxford University Press, 1998).

[28] Meenakshi Mukherjee, *The Perishable Empire: Essays on Indian Writing in English* (Oxford: Oxford University Press, 2000), p. 71.

[29] Geoffrey Oddie, *Social Protest in India: British Protestant Missionaries and Social Reforms 1850–1900* (Delhi: Manohar, 1979), Chapter 5.

issue took on national and international dimensions when the Irish CMS missionary James Long translated a popular satirical play *Nil Darpan* (*The Mirror of Indigo*) from Bengali into English. The enraged indigo merchants took Long to court, and he was imprisoned for libel.[30] He became a folk hero in Bengal. In post-independence India a Communist government in Bengal named a street in Calcutta after him.

Although Long was not typical in the intensity of his political commitment, increasingly missionaries turned from hoping for the conversion of the ruling classes to a concentration on evangelism among the low- or non-caste communities. In the Punjab, the second half of the century brought significant movements into the church of such groups. One of the strongest of these movements concerned the Chuhra *jati* (caste) of the Punjab. Conversions were particularly strong in areas worked by the American United Presbyterian mission, but other missions, including both the CMS and the SPG, began to reap the harvest from the 1870s. The Chuhras were 'sweepers', an indication of the menial occupation which made them ritually impure. The other group which responded to Christianity in North India, numerous in the Delhi and Agra regions, were the Charmars – 'leather workers', who also performed work regarded as causing pollution, but who had a somewhat higher status than Chuhras. In practice both groups were predominantly agricultural labourers – their position as landless labourers, ironically, was not what rendered them 'unclean'.[31] In the 1911 census Punjabi Christians included a little over 90,000 United Presbyterians, with Anglicans in second place with some 30,000. Numbers continued to grow until the 1930s, and by 1947 the total number of Christians in this area stood at nearly half a million. Further impetus for conversion occurred as Chuhras took advantage of new land allocations in the newly drained canal areas of the Punjab. Christian villages such as Clarkabad (named after a pioneering CMS missionary in the area) gave Chuhras the opportunity to break free of their traditional communal obligations, such as the disposal of carrion and cleaning of bodies.

Missionaries were not necessarily keen to deal with the depressed classes. The Cambridge Mission was taken to task for its 'authoritarian, arrogant and elitist' attitude to nascent Charmar Christian congregations around Delhi. The future Bishop of Calcutta, G. A. Lefroy, was

[30] Geoffrey Oddie, *Missionaries, Rebellion and Proto-Nationalism: James Long of Bengal 1814–1887* (London: Curzon, 1999).

[31] John C. B. Webster, *The Dalit Christians* (Delhi: ISPCK, 1994), p. 30.

apologetic about even adopting 'this work with untouchables'.[32] The fact was that much of the impetus for conversion came from the communities themselves, and had little reference to organised missionary activity, or even the work of Indian catechists. It was, to some extent, part of competition within the *jati* group for self-betterment. This had its roots in the earlier religious history of North India, in which such groups had sought to improve their lot by identifying themselves with Islam or Sikhism. Within the Christian fold, these movements had their own dynamic, and produced a strongly local spirituality:

> A pattern of religious piety based on formal and informal gatherings for the singing of hymns and Psalms, memorization of Scripture verses, festival visits by dignitaries foreign and Indian, and Christmas observance, did not conform to the pattern anticipated by Western missionaries, who envisioned stable parishes and congregations gathering weekly under regular pastoral care.[33]

It was a piety sustained by Bible women and by the use of local *bhajun* and *ghazal* tunes and local hymnody, combined with a stiff injection of Moody and Sankey's sacred songs, which became popular even in Anglican areas. Missionaries often regretted the type of piety which emerged, with its concentration on family genealogies and status, and they regretted being unable to provide proper pastoral oversight. Sometimes this resulted in apparent lapses back into Hinduism, but such families might well re-emerge as Christian later. It also produced the category of 'secret Christians', who could not be baptised without risking their livelihood in their community.

BISHOP VEDANAYAGAM SAMUEL AZARIAH OF DORNAKAL

The mass movement of depressed classes was particularly important in Andhra Pradesh in South India. Its momentum continued for longer than did other such movements, an important reason being the support given by the first Indian Anglican bishop, Vedanayagam Samuel Azariah. He became Bishop of Dornakal in 1912 at the age of thirty-eight. Azariah came from the heart of South Indian Anglicanism, in Tirunelveli, and was the son of a priest. Azariah went to the CMS school at Palamcottah and then the Madras Christian College (one of the great Christian centres founded by the Church of Scotland). He then worked with the YMCA, a Protestant ecumenical organisation which had established a strong

32 Cox, *Imperial Fault Lines*, p. 140: Lefroy's pamphlet 'The Leather-Workers of Daryaganj', 1884.
33 Cox, *Imperial Fault Lines*, p. 152.

presence in Indian colleges, encouraged Indian leadership and was sympathetic to the growing Nationalist aspirations of educated Indians. Azariah's colleague was an American Congregationalist, George Sherwood Eddy. Their partnership provided Azariah with a new vision of equality between missionaries and Indians. This seemed all too rare at the height of the British Raj. It informed his impassioned plea at the Edinburgh missionary conference in 1910, which still resonates:

> Through all the ages to come the Indian Church will rise up in gratitude to attest the heroism and self-denying labours of the missionary body. You have given your goods to feed the poor. You have given your bodies to be burned. We ask also for *love*. Give us Friends![34]

In 1908 Azariah had given up his YMCA work with its comparatively big salary, and was sent by the Indian Missionary Society of Tirunelveli to Andhra Pradesh, to work among Telugu-speaking people. His work impressed Henry Whitehead, the Bishop of Madras (and brother of the philosopher Alfred North Whitehead), who encouraged Azariah to be ordained. Whitehead was keen to promote an Indian bishop. Earlier attempts had foundered. The legal objections to an Indian appointment to the 'Church of England' in India were seen as problematic. Outside the CMS there was a growing reluctance to go along the path of 'racial' bishops, where an Indian bishop would only have oversight of Indian congregations. In any case W. S. Satthianadhan, the most obvious candidate for Bishop of Tinnevelly in the 1870s, was seen as unacceptable to the dominant Nadar Christians because he was from the higher-status Velelar group. The appointment in 1877 of two English suffragans as 'bishops in Tinnevelly' was a very unsatisfactory solution. Robert Caldwell represented the SPG tradition, and Edward Sargeant the CMS. They were good friends and worked harmoniously together. Both were keen promoters of Tamil culture and language. But the situation was anomalous. It did nothing to promote an Indian episcopate and seemed rather to reinforce the mission fragmentation of the Anglican church.

In 1896 a diocese of Tinnevelly was created, with a single English bishop. Whitehead felt that the time was ripe for an Indian bishop. His plan at first was to appoint a suffragan in the Dornakal area of his diocese, to work among Indians. The Metropolitan, Bishop Copleston of Calcutta, approved the plan, but insisted that an Indian bishop should have a diocese of his own. Azariah was consecrated bishop in Calcutta

[34] Susan Billington Harper, *In the Shadow of the Mahatma: Bishop V. S. Azariah and the Travails of Christianity in British India* (Grand Rapids: Eerdmans, 2000), p. 59.

Cathedral on 29 December 1912, just three years after his ordination as a priest.

Dornakal was a fast-growing diocese. Situated partly in the Madras Presidency of British India, partly in the territories of the Muslim Nizan of Hyderabad, it was an overwhelmingly Hindu area, with a number of depressed classes whose status had been deteriorating as a result of the severe famines of the mid nineteenth century. The Malas were a group whose economy was being undermined by cheap cotton imports from Lancashire.[35] The first Indian missionary, the Anglican Samuel Pakianathan, had actively supported the struggle to gain fair access to water resources.[36] Another *jati* influenced by Christianity were the Madiga 'leather workers', who had been helped by the Baptist missionaries to obtain work on canal construction during the famine of 1877–8. This alignment of caste group and denomination was clearly not helpful for a Christianity claiming to overcome caste divisions.[37]

As a non-Telugu bishop, Azariah worked hard to get alongside all the groups within his diocese. Churches were often on the outskirts of villages, near stagnant water or refuse dumps. Azariah emphasised the pageantry of his episcopal visits. His 'radiant robes' should signify to people something of the glory of God. All his life Azariah was enthusiastic about positive evangelism, understanding the difficulties people had in completely abandoning 'idol worship and superstition'.[38] But he had a rigorous side to him, and did not approve of 'mixed marriages', or of the use of astrology in deciding on marriage partners.[39] Azariah's Cathedral of the Epiphany was designed in the 'sarconic' style, incorporating both Hindu and Muslim elements. Educated people criticised him for a certain authoritarianism, and for not encouraging an educated clergy. But he remains one of the great figures in popular Andhra culture, remembered in praise songs to this day. He died two years before independence, and a European bishop succeeded him.

THE CHURCH AND NATIONALISM

Azariah was not directly involved in the politics of Indian Nationalism, the movement for *swaraj* (self-rule), though he shared the strong sense of

[35] Forrester, *Caste and Christianity*, p. 76. [36] Harper, *In the Shadow*, p. 179.

[37] G. Oddie, 'Religious Conversion among Non-Brahmins in Andhra Pradesh: With Special Reference to Anglican Missions and the Dornakal Diocese 1900–1936', in G. Oddie (ed.), *Religion in South Asia: Religious Conversion and Revival Movements in South Asia* (New Delhi: Manohar, 1991).

[38] Harper, *In the Shadow*, p. 190. [39] Ibid., pp. 267–9.

Indian patriotism so important for Indian Christians. His relations with Gandhi were somewhat distant. In contrast to most other parts of India, where the 'mass movements' had more or less fizzled out by the 1930s, Christian conversion under Azariah's leadership continued to be buoyant. It offered an alternative strategy to Gandhi's attack on 'Untouchability', his attempt to establish an inclusive Indian society, in which formerly despised people would be 'Harijan' (the people of God). Gandhi wanted to incorporate them into Hinduism.

The Nationalist spokesperson for the depressed classes, B. R. Ambedkar, was becoming increasingly distrustful, if not of Gandhi's sincerity, at least of his ability actually to deliver substantial benefits. He talked openly of leading a movement out of Hinduism. There was a fear in some Hindu circles that this might mean a declaration in favour of Christianity. Ambedkar eventually declared for Buddhism. He had come to argue that 'Dalits' should have a separate communal representation, similar to that given to Muslims and Sikhs.

Azariah, however, and the church generally were strongly opposed to this (as indeed was Gandhi). Christians, committed to the new India, wanted to immerse themselves wholeheartedly in the mainstream of its life.[40]

An Anglican totally committed to Gandhi's movement was Charles Freer Andrews (1871–1940) – an answer to Azariah's Edinburgh plea: 'Give us Friends!'[41] Andrews was an SPG missionary in Delhi from 1904 to 1914. He increasingly came to distrust the 'Sahib mentality'. At St Stephen's College he argued forcefully for the appointment of Susil Kumar Rubra as the first Indian Principal. Rubra came from an old Bengali Christian family and was Andrews' first close Indian friend and mentor. Andrews' desire for a more inclusive Christian witness (he wanted Baptists to be included in the college) and his growing commitment to Indian Nationalism and appreciation of Indian spirituality led to his resignation from the SPG. He decided not to exercise a priestly ministry, but 'to launch out my boat into unknown seas'.[42] His life thereafter was totally identified with Indian aspirations. He was devoted to two Indian Hindu spiritual leaders, who at times had very different

[40] For these issues, see Webster, *Dalit Christians*, pp. 212–28, and Harper, *In the Shadow*, pp. 291–351.

[41] Daniel O'Connor, *Gospel, Raj and Swaraj: The Missionary Years of C. F. Andrews* (Frankfurt: Peter Lang, 1990), p. 44.

[42] Hugh Tinker, *The Ordeal of Love: C. F. Andrews and India* (Delhi: Oxford University Press, 1979), p. 69.

aspirations and strategies: the Bengali poet and writer Rabindranath Tagore (1861–1941) and Mohandas Gandhi (1869–1948).

While in India, Andrews mainly lived at Tagore's community of Santiniketan. He was often abroad – he went to South Africa in 1914 to participate in Gandhi's *satyagraha*, 'non-violent protest' against the constitutional position of Indians in Natal. In subsequent years he travelled to Kenya to support the Indian political demands, to Fiji to secure the end to indentured labour, and to Guyana to support the Indian community. In India he advised Gandhi in his political campaigns and was active in trade union affairs. Towards the end of his life, Andrews again felt able to talk of his Christian commitment in *What I Owe to Christ*. He continued to have support from within the church, most notably from Foss Westcott, the Metropolitan of India and his life-long friend, who conducted his funeral.

Andrews admired Sundar Singh: both were associated with a short-lived Brotherhood of the Imitation of Christ. On ceasing to be a missionary, Andrews talked about becoming a *sanyasi* (a wandering holy man). Perhaps his political and social commitment was his way of fulfilling that role. Sundar Singh (1889–1929) was a convert from the Sikh religion. He was baptised on his sixteenth birthday in St Thomas' Anglican Church, Simla, and in 1909 entered St John's Divinity College in Lahore to study theology. He decided against ordination. He wanted to be an itinerant preacher, in the *sanyasi* tradition. His combination of devotion to Christ and his Indian spirituality made him attractive to European, American and Australian audiences when he conducted a world tour in the early 1920s. Some have subsequently questioned his relevance to a church predominantly of depressed classes in the Punjab.

> Sundar Singh of course preached against caste, but it was an abstract denunciation that held little practical relevance to the circumstances of labor servitude in Punjabi agriculture. His celebrity served, like mission institutions, to give the urban Indian Christian community some status, particularly as the rise of the national movement in the twentieth century left them more vulnerable to charges that they were 'denationalized' by their Christianity.[43]

Nevertheless, Sundar Singh has admirers within the Indian church. A. J. Appasamy, a Tamil Anglican and future Bishop of Coimbatore in the Church of South India, wrote his biography. He drew inspiration from Sundar Singh's life for his own attempts to infuse an Indian spiritual sensibility into the Christian Gospel, especially through an

[43] Cox, *Imperial Fault Lines*, p. 232.

emphasis on the Hindu *Bhakti* devotional tradition.[44] Appasamy was part of a wider group of Indian theologians from the Protestant churches who in 1938 produced *Rethinking Christianity in India Today*.[45]

THE CHURCH OF SOUTH INDIA

One of the major impulses motivating the search for Christian unity in India in the twentieth century was the sense that it was of very considerable importance that the church shed its 'Englishness' – a charge which Anglicans had particular reason to be sensitive about. Andrews was not alone in a passionate commitment to India and the Indianness of the church.[46] Even more, Indian Christian leaders were committed to this ideal. Bishop Azariah played a significant part in the negotiations. These were painfully slow, stretching over at least thirty years. In 1929 a 'Pledge' was agreed guaranteeing 'the consciences of all members of the uniting churches from being forced by any future administrative acts to accept ministries contrary to the long-established traditions and beliefs of those churches'. This was meant particularly to safeguard the consciences of Episcopal congregations in the new church.[47] But increasingly in England itself there was alarm from within Anglo-Catholic circles at decisions which were seen as jeopardising the Catholicity of the church: historic episcopacy and episcopal ordination. T. S. Eliot mounted a vitriolic campaign: it was, he averred, 'the greatest crisis in the Church of England since the Reformation'. Donald MacKinnon has referred to 'the venomous bitterness' of the controversy and 'the totally unchristian things which were said by men blandly indifferent to the myopic, clerical imperialism to which they were giving free rein'.[48]

Gradually Anglo-Catholics have come to accept the CSI, which since 1998 has been a full member of the Lambeth Conference (fifty years after

44 Appasamy first wrote about Sundar Singh and his significance in the early 1920s when the Sadhu was still alive. A. J. Appasamy, *Christianity as Bhakti Marga: A Study in the Mysticism of the Johannine Writings* (London: Macmillan, 1927). His other works include *The Christian Tradition in Independent India* (London: SPCK, 1951) and *Temple Bells: Readings from Hindu Religious Literature* (Calcutta: YMCA, 1930).

45 Robin Boyd, *India and the Latin Captivity of the Church: The Cultural Context of the Gospel* (Cambridge: Cambridge University Press, 1974).

46 Notably, among the episcopate: Foss Westcott (Metropolitan 1919–45), Edwin Palmer (Bishop of Bombay, 1908–29), Frederick Western (Bishop of Tinnevelly, 1929–38) and Michael Hollis (Bishop of Madras, 1942–55).

47 Bengt Sundkler, *Church of South India: The Movement towards Union, 1900–1947* (London: Lutterworth, 1954), pp. 257–63.

48 Donald MacKinnon, 'Oliver Chase Quick as a Theologian', *Theology* 96 (March/April 1993), pp. 107–8.

the union). In his reflections, Bishop Michael Hollis recognised that some felt the union had been cobbled together 'in such defiance of all sound ecclesiastical principles that it would inevitably fall to pieces', but in fact it did work: 'The aeroplane that flies is thereby better than one, however perfect in theory, which never got beyond the drawing board.'[49] Hollis talked about 'the release from the bondage of the past'. The CSI had overcome the historic divisions which have plagued English Christianity since the seventeenth century. But it did not include the Lutheran churches of South India, which was sad in view of the early Lutheran collaboration with the Anglicans.

The creation of the CSI, inaugurated a few months after political independence, enabled Indian Christianity to face the challenges and opportunities of the new era with some confidence and optimism. It produced a good deal of liturgical innovation, conservative in many ways and still bound by western traditions, but important for drawing on the resources of all the uniting churches and providing inspiration for liturgical reform in the Anglican communion in other parts of the world.[50] The CSI, in honouring the Pledge of 1929, was very concerned not to impose alien traditions on congregations, and this has meant a diversity of liturgical and organisational practice at the congregational level. Despite these sensitivities, one part of Azariah's Dornakal diocese, Nandyal, decided that it was unable to accept the union, wishing to remain an 'SPG' church. A complex set of reasons, some financial (the desire for continued SPG support, which looked likely to be withdrawn because of the SPG's initial ambivalence to the CSI), some pastoral, led to the decision. 'We see here a clash between ecumenical ideals and local realities.'[51] Nandyal remained part of the Anglican Church in India under the jurisdiction of the Metropolitan in Calcutta until 1976, when it finally became a diocese within the CSI.

In its early years the CSI was served by some outstanding missionaries, including Bishop Lesslie Newbigin, a missionary of the Church of Scotland. But missionary bishops rapidly became a small minority in an episcopate which was overwhelmingly Indian, something which had eluded the Anglican church right up to independence. If Nandyal feared

49 Michael Hollis, *The Significance of South India* (Richmond: John Knox, 1973), p. 16.

50 Leslie Brown claimed that the 'westward' position for the Eucharist was first adopted when he was Principal of Trivandrum and was then incorporated into the new liturgy of the CSI, from where it spread far and wide. See Brown, *Three Worlds, One Word: Account of a Mission* (London: Collings, 1981) pp. 67–8.

51 Adrian Hastings in his foreword to Constance Millington, *An Ecumenical Venture: The History of Nandyal Diocese in Andhra Pradesh 1947–1990* (Bangalore: Asian Trading Corporation, 1993), p. iii.

being swamped by non-Anglican traditions, other areas might with some justification fear that Anglican traditions might come to predominate. The original impetus of the CSI was for a new style of bishop, more humble and less pretentious, wearing the simple saffron robes symbolic of the renunciation of a *sanyasi*. However, the purple trappings of episcopacy began to creep back in, symptomatic of a failure adequately to work out checks and balances on episcopal power.[52] Moreover, in a system which rightly pays great attention to local feelings, episcopal elections have become the focus of unseemly political wranglings and even violence. These problems of Anglican styles of episcopacy are shared by Anglican churches in other parts of the world.

ANGLICAN UNIONS IN NORTH INDIA, PAKISTAN AND BANGLADESH

Although all the bishops of the Anglican Church in India were involved in the negotiations which brought to birth the CSI, only the dioceses of South India were directly involved. With independence in 1947 the remaining dioceses in the North now found themselves fragmented by the creation of India and Pakistan in 1947, with its momentous implications for Hindu and Muslim populations, and by the creation of a separate Bangladesh after the war of 1971. The Anglican dioceses, particularly of Lahore and Calcutta, straddled the borders of the new states, and inevitably their work was disrupted. The churches in the North were smaller and poorer.[53] The expansion of the mass movements had largely come to an end, as conversion became a political issue in the move towards independence. But converts did, on the whole, remain loyal to their Christian tradition:

> If Christianity reached a high-water mark with the 1930s, it also reached a level of stability that sustained it through the political crises and mass slaughter of the 1930s and 1940s. The majority of Christians in Indian and Pakistani Punjab remained poverty-stricken, illiterate and powerless, but they also remained Christian.[54]

A united church would strengthen the Indian character of what was a small minority faith. Negotiators were keen to avoid the problems of the CSI negotiations, and to work for a fully unified ministry from the outset.

[52] P. Victor Premasagar, 'Anglicanism and the Church of South India', in Andrew Wingate, Kevin Ward, Carrie Pemberton and Wilson Sitshebo (eds.), *Anglicanism: A Global Communion* (London: Mowbray, 1998), pp. 178–81.

[53] Gibbs, *The Anglican Church in India*, p. 390. [54] Cox, *Imperial Fault Lines*, p. 269.

The negotiations were more ambitious than those of the CSI, in that they involved Baptists, Brethren, Disciples of Christ and Lutherans, as well as the Methodists, the United Church (former Presbyterians and Congregationalists) and Anglicans who had participated in the CSI. The intention was that the united churches of North India, Pakistan and Bangladesh should be heirs to all the participating church traditions; the new churches should quickly establish a new united identity.

Nevertheless, dioceses often did, in fact, continue to represent a predominant ecclesiastical tradition. In Pakistan, the dioceses of Lahore and Karachi (from which Hyderabad was created in the new church) contained mainly Anglicans, whereas Multan was predominantly Methodist, and Sialkot was a Presbyterian area. The vast majority of Christians in Pakistan came from the Chuhra – Hindus who had been converted in the mass movements. Pakistan remained more open to missionary work than India in the decades after independence, and there continued to be opportunities for evangelism among non-Muslim people, especially tribal people outside the Hindu caste system.[55] There has, however, in more recent years, been increasing pressure on Christians and other non-Muslim minorities, with anti-blasphemy laws designed to protect Muslim sensibilities being used arbitrarily against Christian minorities.

The Church of Pakistan reckons to have some 800,000 members (out of a total Christian population of 2.5 million). In comparison the Church of Bangladesh is tiny, with an estimated membership of 12,500. The 1971 war coincided with the creation of the new united church. The United Church in Bangladesh emerged from formerly Anglican and Presbyterian communities. It had formerly been part of the diocese of Calcutta, and some of the largest parishes, originating in the CMS work in the Nadia district of Bengal, were now strung along the eastern border to the south of where the River Ganges enters the country. The other area of Anglican work was to the south and centre of the country, where the Oxford Mission to Calcutta had established work. In the years before independence in 1947, Fr Mohendra Chakrabarty of the St Andrew's Brotherhood had established work among a Tibetan-Burman aboriginal group, the Garo. The Presbyterians had also worked among the Santali tribal peoples. Traditions of Bengali hymnody were enriched in the tribal areas by the creation of a vernacular *bhajan* tradition. The united church came into being at the time of war and famine and has established ambitious

[55] Pervaiz Sultan, 'The Involvement of the Church of Pakistan in Development', Ph.D. dissertation, Open University, 1997.

programmes of relief and development, including rural fire insurance schemes, programmes directed to women's work, reforestation and micro-credit.[56] Mukti Barton's researches demonstrate the importance of women in small-scale rural development work, the impact of their Christian faith and the opportunities for working with Muslim women's organisations engaged in the same struggle for women's dignity.[57]

DALIT THEOLOGY

The attempt to contextualise the Gospel in the early part of the twentieth century, associated with the movement of Appasamy and other younger theologians, was given a great boost by the creation of the CSI in 1947. Indian Christianity could, with integrity, point to its ability effectively to transcend its western legacy, and to speak in Indian terms. But by the 1980s some of the presuppositions of that generation of Indian theologians were challenged by the rise of a Dalit self-consciousness, within the church and the wider society. In this period, those who had been variously designated as 'outcastes' or 'scheduled castes' came to designate themselves as Dalit ('oppressed'). In India as a whole, perhaps 25 per cent of the population can be classed as Dalit. One strand of the movement seeks status for Dalits as a separate community, distinct from the Hindu majority in India – in sharp contrast to Gandhi's attempts at inclusiveness. Some Dalits look for its recognition as a religion distinct from Hinduism.

Only a minority of Dalits are Christians, but a majority of Indian Christians are Dalit: 75 per cent, by some estimates. The United Churches have been involved in the Dalit movement, both in popularising the use of the term and speaking against the double discrimination of Dalit Christians, denied the affirmative action accorded to other depressed groups.[58] The United Theological College at Bangalore was important for developing a formal Dalit *theology* as a type of Christian liberation theology. One of the most sophisticated expositions is that by Sathianathan Clarke, son of a former Bishop of Madras and himself a presbyter of the CSI. His study of the Paraiyar community of Tamilnadu

[56] I am grateful to the Revd John Webber, former USPG missionary in Bangladesh, for the information he has provided on the church in Bangladesh.

[57] Mukti Barton, *Scripture as Empowerment for Liberation and Justice: The Experience of Christian and Muslim Women in Bangladesh* (Bristol: Centre for Comparative Studies in Religion and Gender, Department of Theology and Religious Studies, Bristol University, 1999).

[58] Kottapalli Wilson, *The Twice Alienated Culture of Dalit Christians* (Hyderabad: Booklinks, 1982).

emphasises the distinctive traditional religion of Paraiyar, in particular the importance of the drum as a symbol of Paraiyar resistance to domination and denial of full humanity by the dominant caste culture.[59]

The Tamilnadu Theological Seminary at Madurai has had an important role in developing more indigenous forms of worship, mission and service to the community. Its chapel was adapted from local Dravidian South Indian temple architecture, and forms of visual art and music associated by more conservative Christians with a Hindu milieu have been encouraged.[60] The college, always sensitive to its particular responsibility for poor and despised communities, has a history of engagement with social issues and its impact on how one understands the Gospel. The musician Theophilus Appavoo, from the Paraiyar community, has developed the musical traditional of the college, eschewing the Brahminical forms in which indigenous traditional worship has previously been articulated in favour of a strong folk, Dalit, musical expression. The liturgy incorporates 'metaphors, stylistic and performance devices, and cultural and religious values of rural Tamil life'.[61] The emphasis on Dalit issues highlights the rights of women as often the chief victims of discriminatory systems. On the other hand, the churches have been somewhat slow in utilising fully the ministry of women. As Andrew Wingate's investigation of former students of Tamilnadu Seminary shows, although the churches have accepted women's ordination as a theoretical possibility, in practice it remains an elusive goal for many women.[62]

As in many parts of the world, indigenisation of worship and the espousal of a politically conscious liberation theology may not be the most significant features of the church at the beginning of the twenty-first century. Pentecostalism has a strong appeal. It often seems foreign, but Pentecostalism, too, is able to tap into resources of the indigenous culture and spirituality. D. G. S. Dhinakaran comes from the Tirunelveli Anglican/CSI heartland. He has established himself as the most popular and influential preacher of healing and deliverance in South India.[63]

[59] Clarke, *Dalits and Christianity*, p. 193.

[60] Andrew Wingate, *Does Theological Education Make a Difference?* (Geneva: WCC, 1999).

[61] Zoe C. Sherinian, 'Dalit Theology in Tamil Christian Folk Music: A Transformative Liturgy by James Theophilus Appavoo', in Selva J. Raj and Corinne G. Dempsey, *Popular Christianity in India* (New York: New York State University Press, 2002), pp. 233–49.

[62] Wingate, *Does Theological Education Make a Difference?*, p. 69; T. K. Oommen and Hunter P. Mabry, *The Christian Clergy in India: Volume I: Social Structure and Social Roles* (Delhi: Sage Publications, 2000), pp. 362–8.

[63] Chris Gnanakan is engaged on doctoral studies at Leeds University concerning the ministry of Dhinakaran.

THE ANGLICAN CHURCH IN BUDDHIST LANDS OF SOUTH ASIA: SRI LANKA AND MYANMAR (BURMA)

Christianity in Sri Lanka/Ceylon has always had a somewhat different dynamic from that of India, both because of its Buddhist majority and because of the nature of its colonialism. The Sinhalese constitute about 83 per cent of the population, and the Tamils 17 per cent. Ceylon was ruled successively by the Portuguese, the Dutch and the British, who occupied the island in 1795. The Dutch Reformed Church had had a privileged status on the island. It had tried unsuccessfully to eliminate Catholicism, but had failed to attract any substantial Sri Lankan converts of its own. The Anglican church replaced the DRC as the established church of the colonisers, and for long reflected its reluctance to evangelise. Eventually both the SPG and the CMS established work among Sinhalese and Tamil communities. Tirunelveli Indian Christians established active evangelism on their own account among the migrant workers on the tea plantations. In the 1870s there was a somewhat acrimonious dispute between the CMS and Bishop Reginald Copleston (Bishop of Colombo 1875–1902), in which Copleston's strong views on the authority of the bishop and the development of ecclesiastical structures came up against CMS fears that the distinctive Evangelical characteristics of its congregations would be compromised as diocesan structures advanced. In 1880 the British government implemented a process of effective disestablishment of the Church of England, partly as a response to a growing sense of Buddhist nationalism, which intensified in the years around independence in 1948. Anglicans had established a system of elite schools (Trinity College, Kandy being the most prestigious). But, as with the Duff policy in India, these were as much concerned with educating a non-Christian elite as with catering specifically for the needs of the Christian community. The first Sri Lankan Anglican bishop was Lakdasa de Mel (1902–76). A product of Royal College, Colombo and Keble College, Oxford, he became an assistant bishop of Colombo in 1945, and in 1950 diocesan bishop of a new diocese in Kurunagala, near Kandy, the religious centre of Sri Lankan Buddhism. De Mel was the first of a number of bishops concerned with an appropriate indigenisation of the church in Sinhalese society, and with creative dialogue with Buddhism.

In 1947 the Tamil congregations of Jaffna voted to join the newly created Church of South India as a separate diocese. It was hoped that Jaffna would eventually transfer to a united Church of Sri Lanka. Serious negotiations took place to this end in the 1950s and 1960s, but legal action on the part of some disaffected Methodists prevented a union from being consummated. Thus, with the dissolution of the Anglican Church of India, Pakistan, Ceylon and Burma in 1970, the Anglican Church of Ceylon (Sri Lanka) remained as an 'intact' Anglican church, with former Tamil Anglicans part of a united church. Although this fact had little to do with the increasing tension between Sinhalese and Tamil, it was a regrettable reminder of the wider divisions in the society as a whole which were soon to produce a bitter civil war.[64]

In Myanmar (Burma), Christianity struggled to gain a foothold in the strongly Buddhist kingdom. Baptist work (pioneered by the American Adoniram Judson in 1813) was much more established than that of the Anglicans, but in the 1860s the SPG missionary John Ebenezer Marks (one of a series of remarkable Anglican missionaries of Jewish ancestry) was entrusted by the Burmese king, Mindon, with the education of the princes, in the expectation that diplomatic and commercial advantages would accrue. The king became disillusioned and withdrew his support as he came to appreciate the dangers of British power (leading to annexation in 1885). The Anglicans were able to survive royal hostility, and in 1877 a diocese of Rangoon was created. The most successful missionary work was undertaken, not among the Burmese, but among tribal Karen people in the North. Here existing work was boosted when a group of Baptist congregations joined the Anglicans, though Baptists have remained the major Christian influence in the tribal areas. Burmese independence in 1948 was accompanied both by an entrenched sense of Buddhist Nationalism, with the declaration of Buddhism as the state religion in 1960, and by political discontent from the tribal peoples, producing a long-running insurgency problem.

The first indigenous bishops were elected in 1949, and in 1966 Francis Ah Mya became the first diocesan bishop. He had a distinguished record of pastoral care during the Japanese occupation. It had not been possible, in the Burmese situation, to conduct church unity discussions parallel to those in India and Pakistan, though Anglicans were committed to good ecumenical relations among the tiny Christian minority. With the inauguration of the united churches in 1970, there was a need to establish an independent Anglican province of Myanmar. Ah Mya became the first Archbishop. Largely cut off from worldwide contacts in the last decades

[64] K. M. de Silva, 'From Elite Status to Beleaguered Minority: The Christians in Twentieth Century Sri Lanka', in *Colloques Internationaux du Centre National de la Recherche Scientifique* No. 582, *Asie du Sud: Traditions et changements* (Paris, 1979), pp. 347–52.

of the twentieth century, Myanmar Christians have deepened their local indigenous roots in both Burmese and tribal culture. In a hostile environment they have survived and developed appropriate forms of evangelism.[65]

[65] Material on Myanmar is taken from various articles in Scott W. Sunquist (ed.), *A Dictionary of Asian Christianity* (Grand Rapids: Eerdmans, 2001): 'Myanmar' by Tun Aung Chain; 'Anglican Church in Myanmar' by Paul Chen; and 'Ah Mya' by Saw Maung Doe.

CHAPTER 12

China

INTRODUCTION

In 1800, China, with a population of about 200 million, was by far the largest country in the world, about twice the size of India. There had been a Christian presence in the country since the thirteenth century, first Nestorian monks, then Roman Catholic friars. The work of the Jesuits proved particularly fruitful. Matteo Ricci's mission to the mandarin class gave the Jesuits access to the Manchu court, and some prominent officials and intellectuals converted. Later the Jesuits fell under suspicion – firstly by the Vatican for their attempts to interpret the Christian message in Chinese terms, and then by the Manchu for their foreignness. Missionaries were expelled in 1724 and Chinese Christianity was banned, though isolated Catholic communities continued a clandestine existence. Robert Morrison, a British Congregationalist missionary working for the East India Company, began Protestant activity in China in 1807, operating at first in a clandestine way. It was the start of a considerable Protestant interest, in which Americans were the major participants. By the end of the century there were some 1,300 Protestant missionaries operating in China; Catholics had also returned.

China never formally fell under colonial rule. Gradually a weak Chinese government was forced to make trading concessions to western powers which seemed to undermine its sovereignty and enfeeble its grasp of power. The humiliating end of the Opium War in 1842 (in which Britain had insisted on its right to trade in opium) opened up five treaty ports to western trade and commercial settlement. Christian missions first operated freely from these bases, gradually securing rights to evangelise in the countryside around the ports. When the Taiping rebellion broke out in 1851, missionaries often greeted the movement positively. The Taiping leader, Hong Xuiquan, was influenced by Christian values and his reading of the Bible as mediated through Chinese tracts. For a time the

'God Worshippers Society' (as Hong's movement called itself) seemed to offer the prospect of a new era in China favourable to the Gospel. Missionary enthusiasm greatly waned as Hong's teaching emerged as incompatible with Christian orthodoxy, and the enormous death rate and suffering caused by the rebellion became apparent.

Charles Gordon, a sincere but unorthodox Christian, later to be famous for his death in Khartoum, helped to put down the rebellion and to restore authority to the central government. In the aftermath the Chinese authorities made more concessions to missionary work, granting missions the right to operate inland. This led to the creation of one of the most famous missions, Hudson Taylor's China Inland Mission, an interdenominational Evangelical faith mission founded in 1867, with radical ideas of a simple and adapted approach to missionary work, adopting native dress and life styles as much as possible.

The concessions to Christian missionaries were dragged from a reluctant government. It resented what it regarded as a movement subversive of Chinese values and of obedience to authority. Christian missionaries did attack many aspects of Chinese culture – for example foot binding of women and infanticide. They tended to make gains in areas where government officials were seen as particularly oppressive or where the absence of government made communities prey to warlords and casual violence. Missionaries were accused of turning Chinese converts into western stooges. Intellectuals often saw Christianity as a way of cultural reform for China, a means of reintegrating Confucian values and ethos into modern living. Chinese Christians were totally opposed to the popular religious culture of Taoism and Buddhism, saturated by magical and supernatural phenomena. The Chinese central authorities never espoused a particular state religion. They were concerned rather to ensure that no religion was a threat to the core values of Chinese civilisation. Christianity, and particularly Protestant Christianity, remained peripheral to most Chinese. By 1900 the Protestant community was tiny – a mere 60,000. Catholics numbered some half a million.[1] But the importance of the Chinese diaspora community should not be underestimated in evaluating the importance of Christianity for the Chinese. Chinese diaspora Christians had an impact on the Chinese community throughout the Asian Pacific; these diaspora communities in turn often had an impact on their place of origin.

[1] John K. Fairbank and Merle Goldman, *China: A New History* (Cambridge, MA: Harvard University Press, 1992), pp. 221–2.

China was of deep significance for America in the way that India was for Britain. Episcopalians, a small minority in America, played a comparatively small part in American missionary activity as a whole. Their story is part of that of Protestant endeavour generally, with which they have been socially and theologically identified, however much they have wished to claim a distinctive ecclesiology and ethos. Anglicanism came to China in a particularly fragmented form, in a variety of church traditions and national identities, American, English and Canadian.

ANGLICANISM IN CHINA

American Episcopalian missionaries first arrived in China in 1835, when William Jones Boone established a permanent presence in Shanghai. He was appointed Bishop of the American (Episcopal) Church Mission in China in 1844. Huang Kuang-ts'ai, baptised in 1846, was to become the first ordained deacon in 1851, and in 1861 priest. In 1842, Hong Kong was ceded to Britain. The first chaplain there was Vincent Stanton, partly funded by the SPG. The CMS was also exploring openings on the mainland, and started work around Ningbo. In 1849 Hong Kong was established as a diocese. It was named 'Victoria', and the CMS missionary George Smith became the first bishop. The Church in Hong Kong concentrated on expatriate work until the 1860s.

On the mainland, CMS work was directed to Fujiang and Zhejiang provinces in southern China, south of Shanghai and north of Hong Kong. The first Chinese priest in this area was Huang Ch'iu-the of Fujiang, priested in 1868. In 1863 the SPG opened up its work in China by sending a missionary to Beijing. In 1872 a diocese of North China was created, and this became a predominantly SPG area. In 1886 a group of Anglican Evangelicals, the 'Cambridge Seven', started to work in Sichuan province under the auspices of the China Inland Mission. CMS also established work in this area, which eventually became an Anglican diocese of West China in 1895. In other parts of China, the CIM established its own church structures. Finally, in 1909 Canadians were given special responsibility for the Henan province of North China, to the east of the capital. The first bishop, William Charles White, had been working with the CMS in the South, and he brought a number of Chinese evangelists from that area.

This is a simplification of the complex Anglican work in China. There were many contacts between the different areas, including an active interchange of Chinese catechists and evangelists. But institutionally a unified Anglican church in China did not exist until the early twentieth century.[2] The two major players were the CMS in South China, and the American Episcopal Mission in the Shanghai area. Of the CMS work, that in Fujiang was the most successful. By the time Fujiang was separated from the diocese of Victoria in 1907, the CMS had 117 stations, largely in the countryside, with 3,556 converts, ninety-three catechists and seven Chinese ordained ministers. The mission had been noted for insisting on its rights under the treaties – it was prepared to invoke consular influence to get what it wanted. This was one reason for its growth, as it was perceived as 'powerful'. The church was seen as an important factor in enabling communities to resist the power of warlords or tax collectors, or in giving them more power with the magistrates when lawsuits threatened.

Under the strong paternalistic leadership of John Wolfe (CMS missionary from 1862 to 1915), the Anglican community developed a cohesive system of elementary education, in which women's education was considered particularly important – catechists were threatened that their meagre salaries would be docked if they did not ensure that their wives could read. Chinese Bible women also performed a significant evangelistic role. If the basic level of literacy was impressive, the CMS resisted developing complex higher-education institutions. The American mission was much more concerned about the strategic importance of higher education.[3]

SCHERESCHEWSKY AND THE AMERICAN EPISCOPAL MISSION IN CHINA

Perhaps the most remarkable of all the Anglican missionaries in nineteenth-century China was Samuel Schereschewsky, whose stature approaches that of the great Protestant missionaries Morrison and Guetzlaff. Schereschewsky was born in Lithuania, at that time part of the Russian Empire, in 1831. He received a Jewish rabbinic education; his knowledge of the Masoretic Text of the Hebrew Bible, and of midrashic literature, was to be of great importance in his later translation work. His community was beginning to look outwards, influenced by Enlightenment ideas, and receptive to Christian proselytism. In 1849 Schereschewsky

[2] G. F. S. Gray, *Anglicans in China: A History of the Zhonghua Shenggong Hui (Ching Hua Sheng Kung Huei)* (New Haven: Episcopal China Mission History Project, 1996).

[3] Ryan Dunch, *Fuzhou Protestants and the Making of a Modern China 1857–1927* (New Haven: Yale University Press, 2001).

emigrated to America. Baptised by Baptists in 1855, he studied in a Presbyterian seminary, but his application to be considered for missionary work was refused. He transferred to the Episcopalians and enrolled at General Seminary in New York. Ordained in 1859, he immediately set off for Shanghai, just as the Taiping rebellion was entering its final phase. Schereschewsky immediately devoted himself to the study of Chinese, both the local Cantonese and classical Mandarin. Between 1862 and 1874 he was based in Peking to the north, perfecting his Mandarin and acting as translator to the foreign legations there. In 1867, after a courtship of three weeks, he married Susan Waring, from Brooklyn. In 1874 Schereschewsky was recalled to Shanghai to become the third bishop. At first, he steadfastly refused, not believing that he had the required capabilities, but the authorities in America prevailed. His greatest achievement, in his relatively short time as bishop, was to establish St John's College in Shanghai. Increasingly ill and incapacitated with paralysis, he resigned in 1883. Eventually he retired to Tokyo with his wife and a number of Chinese co-workers, Lian Yingghuang, Yu Baosheng and Zhang Jierhi. He continued translation work until his death in 1906.

Schereschewsky was probably right in his reluctance to become bishop. His talents were not in that direction: he was, says his biographer, 'neither a zealous nor even an effective shepherd of souls'.[4] His major ministry was in the completion of the first version of the Chinese Bible in a form of Mandarin which was actually spoken and understood in large parts of China. Any translation had to wrestle with the perennial 'Chinese terms' question, which had plagued Christian missions since the time of the Jesuits: what term should be used to translate 'God'? There were three alternatives:

SHANGDI: 'High God'
SHEN: 'spirit', ' god' or' gods'
TIANZHU: 'Lord of Heaven', a neologism invented by the Jesuits to avoid the problems of the native Chinese terms.

Schereschewsky, unlike most of his Protestant colleagues, much preferred Tianzhu. The implicit polytheism of *shen* and the fact that Shangdi could be used for 'heaven' itself or as a title for the Jade Emperor made these terms unsuitable, in Schereschewsky's opinion. Tianzhu was the term used by Catholics and by Russian Orthodox. Schereschewsky certainly did not put an end to these debates. What his version did was to bring a more sophisticated understanding of the Hebrew of the Old

[4] Irene Eber, *The Jewish Bishop and the Chinese Bible* (Leiden: Brill, 1999), p. 1.

Testament to bear, as well as an aliveness to the contemporary use of Mandarin. It has become the basis of twentieth-century revisions in Protestant circles. Schereschewsky's other main task – that of translating the Bible into a literary Mandarin – was never as successful, if only because the revolutionary changes of the twentieth century rendered literary Mandarin itself a relic of the past Confucian bureaucratic state.

ST JOHN'S COLLEGE AND THE CHRISTIAN CONTRIBUTION TO A NEW CHINA

Schereschewsky's other great legacy was St John's College. It began as a high school whose curriculum included Chinese studies, to enable scholars to take the public exams for entry into the civil service. But it concentrated on a modern western curriculum, including, from 1900, the natural sciences, making it attractive to those seeking careers outside the official system, in commerce and industry, the army and education, and indeed in the more modern departments of government. The abolition of the classical exam system in 1905 made St John's even more attractive, and in 1906 it became a full university, the first Christian university in China. Most of the staff of St John's were American, and most of the teaching was in English, but an outstanding Chinese Christian on the staff in this early period was Yen Yun-ching.

In late-nineteenth-century China, there was a deep ambivalence about Christianity. Christianity was blamed for the chronic weakness of the late Qing dynasty – the 'Christian' western powers had, for a century, been determined to undermine Chinese independence. On the other hand, Christianity, and especially its educational institutions, was regarded as a source of regeneration for China, pointing to ways of overcoming China's chronic weakness. In the aftermath of the anti-Christian and anti-missionary Boxer rebellion of 1900, Roland Allen, an SPG missionary in North China, said:

> At present the Chinese commonly look upon the missionary as a political agent, sent out to buy the hearts of people, and so to prepare the way for a foreign dominion, and this suspicion has been greatly strengthened by the fact that western nations have ... used outrages upon missionaries as a pretext for territorial aggression.[5]

[5] Quoted in Philip Wickeri, *Seeking the Common Ground: Protestant Christianity, the Three-Self Movement and China's United Front* (Maryknoll: Orbis, 1988), p. 38.

The revolution of 1911 seemed to open a new world for Christians. Much of the dynamism of the revolution came from students who had been educated at places like St John's University. The first leader, Sun Yat Sen, was a Christian (educated in Hawaii in an Anglican school); as was Chiang Kai-Chek, an alumnus of St John's University. (Neither of these men in adulthood identified himself as an Anglican.) The Nationalist rhetoric of the first years of the republic had been profoundly influenced by a Christian agenda. Christians had supported the creation of National Assemblies before the revolution, and saw campaigns against opium as necessary for national pride and strength. 'Protestants were among the earliest to make use of symbols and methods that later became central to official Chinese nationalism.'[6] The shedding of the *queue* (pigtail) by males became a symbol of the new republic. The adoption of flag and anthem and other marks of American democratic values were in evidence. The YMCA became an important social and cultural institution for Christian and national values in the early years of the republic.

The problem was that the high profile of Christians and the obvious sense of optimism about a 'tide Christward' for China which was evident, for example, in the important meeting in Beijing of the World Student Christian Federation in 1922 served to alert other Chinese movements to the potential dangers of a Christian take-over of the new China. The Anti-Christian Campaign in schools and colleges between 1922 and 1927, particularly strong in Shanghai, showed that there remained a strong sense of resentment at the Christian presence and its perceived capture of the educational system of China. Moreover, the hoped-for democratic stability which had animated those who had worked for change in 1911 did not materialise. In the interwar years China's cohesion seemed threatened as never before, by internal war lords, by Nationalist and Communist forces, and increasingly by the Japanese.

A number of Chinese Anglican intellectuals during this period tried to relate their Christian faith to the political and social crisis of the time. One such was L. U. Wu (Wu Lei'ch'uan, 1870–1944). He had a traditional Chinese education, but converted to Christianity in 1915 and joined the Episcopal Church. He was appointed to the faculty of the Protestant Yenching University in 1922 and became the President there in 1926. He was also much involved in the YMCA. In his major work of 1936, *Chi-tu-chiao yu Chung-kuo wen-hua* (*Christianity and Chinese Culture*), Wu wrestled with the relevance of Christ for China, an issue which had

[6] Dunch, *Fuzhou Protestants*, p. 137.

affected him deeply during the Anti-Christian Campaign of the 1920s. He portrayed a Jesus who was deeply interested in social reform, and who might well have set up some kind of revolutionary regime in the Palestine of his day, if the arrest of John the Baptist had not revealed the necessity of another way. Wu interpreted the Holy Spirit as *jen*, a Confucian term referring to 'perfect virtue'. Like a number of Chinese Christian thinkers of this period he saw the attraction of Communism, which unlike so much of the warring political alternatives seemed to stand for a real commitment to social justice.

T. C. Chao was a colleague of Wu at Yenching University, who taught philosophy. He published in 1935 a *Life of Christ* (*Yeh-su Chuan*) which used Confucian concepts, and endeavoured to present a non-dogmatic Christ relevant to China. Originally a Methodist, Chao was attracted to more sacramental forms of devotion, and he became an Anglican priest in 1941. Both Wu and Chao were struggling to articulate a liberal Protestant social Gospel message in the context of a modern Confucian ethic relevant to Chinese conditions and sympathetic to the radical political critique which addressed the agony of China's political impotence and instability. Not all Chinese Christians were convinced that this was the way forward. A radically different form of Christian commitment was evidenced in the Little Flock movement of Watchman Nee, who had been educated in the early 1920s at an Anglican college in Fukien before rejecting western denominational labels to establish a more biblically based, simple community of practising Christians.[7]

THE FORMATION OF THE CHUNG HUA SHENG KUNG HUI (THE HOLY CATHOLIC CHURCH OF CHINA)

Anglicans in China at the beginning of the twentieth century were a small minority of the overall Protestant body. They were aware both of their distinctiveness from other Protestants and of the difficulties of their own fragmentation on national lines. This was felt especially among the American missionaries, who had had to grapple, more than the English, with the issues of being a minority within a strongly Protestant community in the United States. Their concern for a common ecclesial identity led in 1912 to the establishment of the Chung Hua Sheng Kung

[7] Yamamoto Sumiko, *History of Protestantism in China: The Indigenization of Christianity* (Tokyo: Toho Gakkai, 2000).

Hui (CHSKH: the Holy Catholic Church of China[8]), the corporate expression of the Anglican Church in China. The church agreed on Mandarin as its official language, and began to work towards the production of a standard Book of Common Prayer. A system of theological education was established, with the theological college at Nanjing as the general training college for the whole church. The church organised its own missionary work, independent of foreign missionaries, in Shaanxi (Shensi), in North China. There were already a substantial number of ordained Chinese in all dioceses. In the 1920s the first Chinese assistant bishops were appointed: Ch'en Yun-en (K. O. Ding) for Fujien (1927), Lindel Tsen Ho-p'u for Henan (1928), and Ku Ho-ling and Song Ch'eng-chih for West China (1929). In 1934 T. K. Shen (Shen Tzu-kao) was appointed as the first diocesan bishop of the church in China, when Shaanxi became a diocese. Later in the same year Bishop Lindel succeeded the Canadian William White as Bishop of Henan. And in 1937 Song Ch'eng-chih became the Bishop of West Sichuan. By the time of the Communist takeover in 1949 there were seven Chinese diocesan bishops for fifteen dioceses, and very quickly thereafter Chinese were appointed to fill the position in most of the others.

The CHSKH was the first church in the Anglican communion to recognise women as eligible for election to diocesan synods. It also valued the establishment of an order of deaconesses – the church had employed Bible women from early days. Dorcas Liu I'lan was one of the first to be ordained. She had an important ministry in prisons and in literacy work in Shaanxi, and died of illness and malnourishment when Xi'an (the diocesan centre) was besieged by the Communists in the increasingly vicious civil war. The attempt in the interwar years to establish a national Chinese Episcopal Church was to be important for the later thinking of the whole Protestant Christian movement as it had to face the challenges of understanding its position in a Communist China after 1949. The vision of the CHSKH has been characterised as an attempt to avoid overly dualistic categories in which church and state, religion and culture, Christian and heathen were starkly contrasted. Much of the ecclesiology of the 'Three-Self Movement' after 1949 had its basis in this kind of thinking.[9]

[8] The Pinyin form is Zhonghua Shenggong Hui. See Gray, *Anglicans in China*, p. 22.

[9] Jeffrey L. Richey, 'Catholicity and Culture in China: Anglican Ideology and the Sheng Kung Hui', *Anglican and Episcopal History* 67.2 (June 1998), p. 192.

THE COMMUNIST VICTORY IN 1949 AND THE ESTABLISHMENT OF THE THREE-SELF PATRIOTIC MOVEMENT

The coming to power of Mao Tse-tung and the Communist Party in China in 1949 was a traumatic revolution for many western Christians, and especially for the American missionaries who had invested so much energy and vision in the missionary movement there. As American foreign policy became increasingly conservative and anti-Communist with the initiation of the Cold War and the fighting in Korea, any idea that Christians might come to terms with the new regime in China seemed an unacceptable compromise. The majority of foreign missionaries had left China by 1950. There was heart searching about whether more could have been done to prevent a Communist takeover, or to prepare Christians for its triumph more effectively; about whether the enterprise had been so fatally flawed that this was a judgement of God. A lobby developed in America, fiercely supportive of Taiwan and the refugee Christians there, and critical of the Christian response within China to the new circumstances, particularly the rise of the Three-Self Patriotic Movement (TSPM). The spokesman and leader of the TSPM was Y. T. Wu (1893–1979), a Protestant theologian and leading figure in the YMCA since the 1920s. Wu expressed what many of the Christian intellectuals had felt since the revolution of 1911 – an intense patriotism and readiness to participate in the reconstruction of their country. To Wu an attitude of critical engagement should be no different because the regime was Communist. Their criticism of the foreignness of Christianity was not new. Nor was the task. In 1950, Wu was among forty Christian leaders who promised to terminate overseas financial aid as soon as possible and to respond positively to the new situation. The Anglican bishops did not sign this manifesto, opting for a more cautious statement. But a number of bishops, notably Robin Chen of Anqing diocese, did co-operate with the emerging Three-Self Movement.

The foremost Anglican participant in the TSPM was K. H. Ting.[10] Ting was born in Shanghai of Christian parents – his maternal grandfather had been an Anglican priest, and his father, a banker, was an active layman, concerned to develop financial self-support in the Chinese church. Ting got a BA from St John's University in 1937 and studied for the priesthood. He married Siu-May Kuo, also from a strong Anglican family. Ting was involved in the YMCA. During the Japanese occupation

[10] Janice and Philip Wickeri (eds.), *A Chinese Contribution to Ecumenical Theology: Selected Writings of Bishop K. H. Ting* (Geneva: WCC, 2002), pp. viii–xii.

of Shanghai in the late 1930s, when separate denominational life had not been possible, Ting was pastor of the Shanghai Community Church. After the war he studied in Canada and at Union Theological Seminary in New York. Returning to China in 1951 he became Principal of a new united theological college in Nanjing, before being appointed in 1955 as Bishop of Zhejiang, one of the last Anglican episcopal appointments made in China. By the late 1950s the government had become increasingly critical of denominational divisions. This was a very difficult time for Christian leaders. Whether conservative and defensive of government encroachment or 'leftist' and broadly supportive of the Communist regime, articulate leaders were just as likely to be accused of anti-state activities, as some leaders found to their cost when they were encouraged to voice their grievances during the brief 'Hundred Flowers' period of 1957, only to be severely reprimanded later for making such statements.

Churches were appropriated and closed, and denominational life basically ceased. The Nanjing seminary found it difficult to operate. It reopened in 1961, now as a broadly ecumenical training college for ministers, only to be closed again from 1966 to 1976, during the Cultural Revolution, when Red Guards conducted a campaign to destroy all vestiges of the 'Four Olds' (ideas, culture, customs and habits). Ironically, the church, which had for so long been deemed anti-traditional and un-Chinese, now fell foul of this campaign. The bishops were not able to operate as bishops after 1957. Ting resumed his position as Principal of the Nanjing seminary. When it was again closed, half the faculty were sent to an agricultural commune, and the buildings were used as a Red Guard headquarters. Later some teachers were allowed to return to do some translation work, and eventually the seminary began again to train ministers for the church. Ting became the chief spokesman of the TSPM after Wu's death in 1978 and also President of the China Christian Council, the body which had replaced denominational structures. Ting has become the most famous spokesman of the Three-Self Movement, someone who, while remaining immensely proud of his Anglican heritage, argues strongly that China has entered a 'post-denominational' era.[11] He has defended the Three-Self Movement in the West against those who see it as a sell-out to Communism, and against radicals who see the new church as insufficiently concerned with justice issues and liberation theology.[12]

[11] K. H. Ting, *Christian Witness in China Today* (Kyoto: Doshisha University Press, 1985), pp. 1–18.

[12] Raymond L. Whitehead (ed.), *No Longer Strangers: Selected Writings of K. H. Ting* (Maryknoll: Orbis, 1989).

Even for those Christians positive to the Communists, it was difficult to anticipate the regime's point of view. Dr T. C. Chao, whose earlier liberal theology was important in the interwar period, illustrates this well. He was imprisoned by the Japanese at the start of the Pacific war. During this time he turned away from liberalism, finding a deeper truth in (Barthian) neo-orthodoxy, and attracted to the sacramental life of Anglicanism. He became friendly with Bishop Hall of Hong Kong, who ordained him. After the war he resumed his teaching at Yenching University. He welcomed the TSPM and tended to support some of the more radical, leftist stances of the regime. This did not prevent him from being accused at various times of deviance from the party line. He was reported as having become disillusioned with religion, even as having lost his faith. But according to a former pupil, Luo Zhenfang, he continued to value the religious quest:

> Dr Chao was an explorer on the road of faith, he would seek greater light . . . On his new road of seeking, before he could reach his goal, Chao parted from this world. Because of this his search for the truth is an 'unfinished symphony'. But what does it matter? It is still a masterpiece passed on to those who would continue the work of composition.[13]

Not all Anglican Christian communities are part of the Three-Self Movement. Many churches have dissolved and no longer have any corporate existence. Some Christians have joined the house church movement; indeed, some former Anglican churches may continue to exist in a more or less clandestine form. The house church movement, living a precarious existence between legality and illegality, is not a single movement, but a pluriform expression of Christian discipleship in harsh times. The desire for more indigenous forms of Christianity which are true to the simplicity of the Gospel characterised the witness of Watchman Nee. The fact that his Little Family community had no connections with foreign religion did not protect it from persecution, and Nee spent a number of years in prison.

What has emerged as western contacts with Christians in China have resumed from the 1980s is that, despite all kinds of obstacles and the manifest difficulties of upholding institutional expressions of the faith, Christianity is surviving and growing in China. Barrett's *World Encyclopedia* figures may be optimistic, but they reckon that Christians amount to 7.1 per cent of the total Chinese population, a much higher percentage

[13] Luo Zhenfang, 'Dr T. C. Chao's Last Letter to Me', *Chinese Theological Review* (1986), pp. 71–4. The article is a translation from the Chinese by Janice Wickeri.

than in 1900 or even in 1950. The Three-Self Church is reckoned to have 10.5 million affiliated members, with almost 30 million belonging to charismatic house churches. By contrast, the figure for all types of Catholics (Clandestine, Underground and 'Patriotic') is reckoned to be 12.3 million. This would suggest that they have been disproportionately adversely affected by fifty years of attacks on the church as an institution.

HONG KONG

Hong Kong was a British colony for 150 years. In 1898 the 'New Territories', on the mainland from Hong Kong island, were leased from China for a hundred years. They became an integral part of Hong Kong, necessary for its economic viability. As the term of the lease drew near, Britain entered into negotiations with the People's Republic of China. This resulted in the retrocession of the whole of Hong Kong to China in 1997, under a system which guaranteed separate identity for fifty years. The separate identity of colonial Hong Kong had enabled Christianity to flourish under much more favourable conditions than had been possible on the mainland. By 1997 the Anglican church had a very important place in the life of the economy, particularly as a dispenser of education: its system of schools was second only to that of the Roman Catholics. Nevertheless, Anglican numbers were quite modest, with active members reckoned to be about 10,000, or less than 1 per cent of the 6 million population.[14] Although Hong Kong became a diocese in 1849, priority on the island itself was to provide for the needs of the English community, with mission work among Chinese being given less status. For much of the period there were two separate synods, operating in English and Chinese and concerned for their different constituencies. Work among the Chinese was first promoted by Lo Sam-Yuen, a Chinese catechist who had worked in the Australian gold-fields with a ministry to South Chinese migrant workers. He was ordained in 1863 and established St Stephen's, which for many years was the only Chinese-speaking church in the colony. The fact that Chinese work was largely done by the CMS meant that there was little pressure to integrate the Chinese work into the structures of the diocese – but in 1902 a Chinese church body did come into existence to give some diocesan expression to Chinese work in Hong Kong.

[14] Deborah Ann Brown, *Turmoil in Hong Kong on the Eve of Communist Rule: The Fate of the Territory and its Anglican Church* (San Francisco: Mellen Research University Press, 1993), p. xxiii.

In 1930 the Lambeth Conference formally recognised the Chung Hua Sheng Kung Hui as an autonomous province of the Anglican communion. The diocese of Victoria had an ambiguous status – it had jurisdiction in the British colony, and was thus separate from the CHSKH, but had work on the mainland in Kwangsi, Kweichow and Yunnan. The decision about who should be bishop needed to be a joint one between Canterbury and the CHSKH. The Chinese bishops suggested Ronald Hall, an English parish priest whose SCM and World Student Christian Federation work had made him known in China. Hall would not have been the natural choice in England – he was considered a maverick.[15] But the appointment went ahead, and it was an inspired choice, if often uncomfortable for more traditional Anglicans. Early on, Hall resigned from the Hong Kong club when a Chinese guest was refused entry. He soon expressed his interest in the social conditions of Chinese workers and in trade unions. He never really mastered Chinese and in 1935 appointed Mok Shau Tsang as an assistant bishop to deal with the day-to-day affairs of the Chinese church. But he was always keenly interested in the Chinese Christian intelligentsia and their attempts to explain Christianity from Chinese perspectives. Hall was keenly interested in the philosophy of Dr T. C. Chao of the Yenching University in Peking. He also encouraged James Wong, an engineer, to be ordained as a 'worker priest' – Wong was later to be bishop in Taiwan. Hall was always unconventional in his ecclesiology, combining a high-church orientation owing much to Maurice with a strongly unclerical style; at home in the creative, artistic expression of faith rather than in the dogmatic and ecclesiastical.

The Japanese invasion of China in the 1930s and the outbreak of war made connections between Hong Kong and the mainland, or with the Portuguese colony of Macao, precarious. It was in these circumstances that Hall made his most controversial decision: to ordain Florence Li Tim-Oi as a priest. Li Tim-Oi was born in Hong Kong in 1907 of parents whose origins were in South China. Her father was a teacher in the English schools in Hong Kong, and she went to English-medium schools in the colony before going to the United Theological Seminary on the mainland in Guangzhou. She began to work for the church in Kowloon, but in 1940 was sent to Macao to replace the Revd Peter Mok, who had established work among the refugees escaping the Japanese occupation of

[15] David M. Paton, *RO: The Life and Times of Bishop Ronald Hall of Hong Kong* (Hong Kong: Diocesan Association, 1985), p. 75.

the mainland. When Bishop Mok was prevented from visiting Macao on a monthly basis, Hall authorised Li Tim-Oi to celebrate Communion. He saw Florence as a 'Cornelia'. Just as the encounter with Cornelius had radically transformed St Peter's thinking, so Hall now saw that the call to priestly ministry could no longer be confined to males. He ordained Li priest on 16 December 1944. He had informed Archbishop William Temple of his intentions, explaining this unprecedented action in terms of the emergency situation. He believed that to ordain a woman as priest was less irregular than to allow lay celebration of the Eucharist. Temple, at least at first, was not unsympathetic:

> If we could find any shadow of theological ground for the non-ordination of women I should be immensely comforted, but such arguments as I have heard on that line seem quite desperately futile.[16]

Temple's death meant that his successor, Fisher, had to deal with the storm of protest which ensued, and which led to the condemnation at the Lambeth Conference of 1948. Li Tim-Oi voluntarily agreed to 'give up the title' of a priest. Much of her ministry was subsequently in China itself. At Yenching University in the early 1950s she and T. C. Chen were accused of being spies of Bishop Hall, because of their special relationship with him. Florence identified with the Three-Self Movement, taught in the seminary in Gaungzhou where she had herself trained, and did pastoral work in the Anglican cathedral. During the Cultural Revolution she was required to undergo a 're-education' programme and do hard manual work. It was only in the 1980s that she was able to travel abroad, and eventually she settled in Canada, where she died. She had been enabled to resume her ministry as a priest, and the golden jubilee of her ordination in 1994 was widely celebrated. In Hong Kong itself, Hall's successor Gilbert Baker ordained two women priests in 1971, Jane Hwang and Joyce Bennett, a CMS missionary.[17] This initiated the worldwide move to ordain women in the majority of the provinces of the Anglican communion.

Bishop Hall's relations with Communist China were almost as controversial as his ordination of a woman. Hall never shared the view that the Communist takeover was an unmitigated disaster either for China or for Christianity. It could not be a disaster that for the first time for 300 years China had a strong central government. He visited the mainland in

[16] Ibid., p. 132.

[17] *The Diocese of Hong Kong and Macao 1849–1974: A Brief History*, (Hong Kong: Diocese of Hong Kong, 1974), p. 6.

1956, a time when there seemed hope of better relations. He met Mao and Zhou Enlai and criticised the Catholic church for its implacable hostility. His successor spoke of Hall's 'quixotic desire to support the new Communist regime', which 'blinded him to the realities of its abuse of power'. But, as Li Tim-Oi's memoirs show, Hall was still regarded with suspicion by the Chinese authorities.[18] The Hong Kong Anglican Church, including Peter Kwong, the first Chinese bishop, has been criticised for being excessively concerned not to offend China in the preparation for the reintegration of Hong Kong into China.

Following the Communist Revolution, the leader Chiang Kai-Chek set up an independent Nationalist regime in Taiwan, which the People's Republic of China has never recognised. Religious freedom was granted in Taiwan under an authoritarian regime. Anglicanism thus survived 'intact' in this area. It became part of Province VIII of ECUSA, and was so fiercely anti-Communist that the election of James Pong as bishop in 1971 was put in jeopardy when it became known that he had visited Russia.[19]

CONCLUSION

It remains to be seen whether the Anglican Church in China can or should attempt to recover its organisational life. Bishop Ting and Anglicans who support the Three-Self Movement are likely to work towards consolidating the ecumenical gains of a united Protestant movement, moving from a loose 'post-denominational' Protestantism to a united church. Since 1985 there have been suggestions that such a church might consider incorporating the historic episcopate, but avoiding anything like a centralised diocesan administrative system.[20] At the moment it would seem both unrealistic and a denial of half a century of co-operation to look for a revival of a 'pure' Anglican system. As the church responds to new opportunities offered by the state, and tries to assess what is the best way of expressing a corporate life, the attitude of the church in Hong Kong may be of considerable importance. Since the retrocession of this territory to China in 1997, there has existed there a vigorous denominational Christianity, whose freedoms have been guaranteed under Chinese rule.

[18] Florence Li Tim-Oi, *Raindrops of my Life* (Toronto: Anglican Book Centre, 1996). See also Ted Harrison, *Much Beloved Daughter: The Story of Florence Li Tim-Oi* (Wilton: Morehouse-Barlow, 1985).

[19] James Pong, *Worldly Ambition versus Christian Vocation* (Taipei: Episcopal Church, n.d. [1977]).

[20] Wickeri, *Seeking the Common Ground*, p. 240.

CHAPTER 13

The Asian Pacific

JAPAN

Japan had a brief but intense encounter with Catholic Christianity in the sixteenth century which ended with the banning of Christianity in 1614, the severe persecution of Japanese Christians, and the expulsion of the Jesuits. Nagasaki remained the centre of a secret Christian community (*karure kirishitan*) which persisted for the two centuries while Japan closed its doors to all contact with the West. In the early nineteenth century, in expectation of an opening of Japan to the Gospel, Protestant missionaries working in China began to work on biblical translation into Japanese; and in 1853 US Commodore Perry forced the Japanese to begin trade and re-establish contact with the West. American missionaries soon took advantage of the concessions, and in 1859 the Revd John Liggins and C. M. Williams of the Episcopal Church arrived in Nagasaki.[1] Japan soon replicated China in the diversity of its American Protestant missions. As in China, the Anglican presence was divided between a number of nationalities and mission agencies. In addition to ECUSA, the CMS started work in 1869 and the SPG in 1873, and the Canadian Anglicans began their first overseas mission in 1888.[2]

The main appeal of the missions was to the samurai, the traditional warrior class, which also comprised intellectuals and administrators. In the aftermath of the American ultimatum, there had been a political ferment in the 'feudal' Japan of the Shogunate, which led in 1868 to the re-establishment of the rule of the Tenno (emperor). Japanese society was determined to modernise and to appropriate western science and technology, without adopting the West's alien religious traditions. However, some of those who had lost out in the 1868 reform, who were not part of the new elite surrounding the emperor, were attracted to Christianity.

1 Otis Cary, *A History of Christianity in Japan* (Tokyo: Tuttle, 1976), Volume II, p. 45 (1st edn, 1909).
2 Darren Marks, 'Canadian and Japanese Christians', *Anglican and Episcopal History* 65.4 (December 1996).

Like Confucianism before it, Christianity seemed to provide an ethical discipline, a moral compass. There is a story of Channing Moore Williams, the Episcopalian missionary. Unlike most Europeans in Japan, he chose to travel third class on the trains. When asked why, he replied that there was no fourth class. Such single-mindedness had attractions for those in the samurai tradition.[3] Williams was elected in 1866 as Episcopal bishop for China and Japan. He remained bishop in Japan until 1887, when he retired to become a parish priest in Kyoto.[4]

Those who chose Christianity, however, were always a small minority. Government was not sympathetic to conversion. Missionaries were not allowed to proselytise, and Japanese Christians, especially the *karure kirishitan*, continued to be discriminated against. Only in 1873 did the government bow to pressure to allow free mission activity and tolerate conversion. But a reinvigorated emphasis on the divine nature of the Tenno as the embodiment of Japan, and an increasing centralisation of the Shinto cult, consigned Christians to an uncomfortable and ambiguous place in Japanese society. Though the constitution of 1889 officially separated religion and the state and guaranteed freedom of religion, there was a general sense that it was not possible to be a good Japanese citizen and a Christian.[5] The Japanese tolerated religion as long as it contributed to good order, did not challenge the dominant Japanese fusion of religious and national identity, and was not under the control of foreigners. On all these counts Christianity continued to be regarded with suspicion. In response, Japanese Anglican converts stressed their desire for an autonomous Japanese church. It led to the inauguration in 1887 of the Nippon Sei Ko Kai (NSKK) – the Holy Catholic Church of Japan. This was the first autonomous province of the Anglican communion outside those in which British settlers predominated, and was thus a milestone in the development of the Anglican communion. It was achieved long before any of Venn's 'three-selves' principles could apply – there were only three Japanese deacons at the time, and a total number of adherents of only about 3,000.[6] The establishment of the NSKK was also achieved

[3] John M. Takeda, 'The Experience of Japanese Anglicans', *Anglican and Episcopal History* 65.4 (December 1996), p. 419.

[4] Ian Douglas, *Fling out the Banner! The National Church Ideal and the Foreign Mission of the Episcopal Church* (New York: Church Hymnal Corporation, 1996), p. 46.

[5] Helen Ballhatchet, 'The Modern Missionary Movement in Meiji Japan', in Mark Mullins (ed.), *Handbook of Christianity in Japan* (Leiden: Brill, 2003), pp. 35–68; Alan Suggate with Yamano Shigeko, *Japanese Christians and Society* (Berne: Lang, 1996), pp. 56–117.

[6] Barnabas Satoshi Kobayashi, 'Towards the Paradigm Change of the Anglican Church in Japan', M.A. dissertation, University of Birmingham, 1998.

despite the diverse theologies and mission priorities of the mission organisations. The CMS, in particular, was unhappy with the proposal to drop the Thirty-Nine Articles as the confessional basis in favour of the less explicit Chicago–Lambeth Quadrilateral. The NSKK embodied both a national ideal – a church for Japanese people (there was still an optimism that Japan might adopt Christianity as a national religion) – and a strong sense of catholicity. In 1923 the first Japanese bishops, Motodo and Naide, were consecrated for Tokyo and Osaka.[7]

The determination to play a role in national life was important for the nascent NSKK – for the samurai converts, religion was not a private affair but embodied duty to the state. The high quality of their educational provision in schools and universities was one way in which Christians could fulfil that responsibility. On the other hand, the promotion of Tenno devotion and Shinto (*bushido*) was always problematic for Christians, especially when the Imperial Education Rescript of 1890 demanded that the official cult be taught in all institutions of learning. Members of the NSKK, like Protestants generally, argued that this was a national rather than a religious obligation, and did not compromise adherence to the First Commandment. In this they differed from Uchimura Kanzo, the founder of the Non-Church movement, a Christian movement which eschewed connections with western denominationalism. Uchimura considered Tenno veneration to amount to idolatry and was dismissed from his post as a teacher for refusing to compromise, despite his strong patriotism.[8] The first Japanese Anglican priest, Imai Judo (1863–1919), believed that the two were compatible – the spirit of Japan (*yamato damashii*) would be perfected, rather than erased, by Christianity.[9]

With the beginnings of Japanese imperialism in the 1890s, the NSKK sent missionaries to the new Japanese territory of Taiwan. In practice their main work in Taiwan was among Japanese colonists, but it was also part of a vision for a Japanese civilising mission in East Asia in which, it was hoped, Christianity would play a vital role. Japanese Anglicans participated in missionary work to Korea in the wake of the Japanese conquest in 1910, and were keen to establish work in Manchuria after the Japanese invasion of 1935.[10] Such patriotism did not diminish the criticism of Christianity within Japan as a foreign and unpatriotic religion. As a xenophobic nationalism increased, so Christian activities fell more

[7] Daniel O'Connor, *Three Centuries of Mission: The United Society for the Propagation of the Gospel 1701–2000* (London: Continuum, 2000), p. 93.

[8] Suggate, *Japanese Christians*, p. 23.

[9] A. Hamish Ion, 'The Cross under an Imperial Sun', in Mullins, *Handbook*, p. 73.

[10] Ibid., p. 78.

under suspicion. In 1939 the Religious Corporation Law required all Protestants to merge into a single church, the Kyodan (United Church). Japanese Anglicans, especially from the more Catholic traditions, resisted this political move, which egregiously ignored essential matters of doctrine and ecclesiology. Anglicans tried to achieve a separate registration, but in September 1942 the government refused. Japan was already at war, and the government had not forgotten a speech of Archbishop Cosmo Lang in 1937 condemning the Japanese bombing of Chinese cities. In 1943 a third of the NSKK, mostly from the Evangelical dioceses, decided to join the Koydan. But Bishop Paul Shinki Sasaki of Tokyo refused. He became the inspiration for the majority of congregations which did not join but tried to maintained a precarious separate existence. Sasaki was eventually imprisoned as a 'spy and defeatist' and only emerged to reunite and direct the church after the end of hostilities.[11]

After the war, the vast majority of Anglican congregations left the Kyodan to return to a restored NSKK. Other Protestant groups withdrew too, but most remained within the Kyodan, which has remained the largest Protestant body. In the aftermath of the war, the Kyodan was outspoken in its opposition to militarism, and the first of the churches to admit its complicity in the Japanese subjugation of the peoples of East Asia and to reach out the hand of friendship to Korean and Philippine churches; but inevitably Christians were divided within themselves about how to overcome past failures.[12] Japanese Episcopalians avoided the deep divisions which these debates engendered within the Kyodan. But in 1971 a radical voice did begin to emerge. The occasion was the reunification of the diocese of Okinawa with the NSKK. The people of Okinawa, in the Ryukyu Islands, had always been regarded as ethnically different from the Japanese, and had suffered discrimination for centuries. After the war Okinawa became a US military base and came under ECUSA. The 1971 occasion provoked protest at the continuing US occupation, and drew attention to discrimination against the Okinawa people.[13]

Radical priests within the NSKK became increasingly concerned about the rights of minorities in the church and in society generally, drawing attention to the treatment of Japanese indigenous minorities such as the Ainu people of Hokkaido (the aboriginal inhabitants of all Japan) and the

[11] Takeda, 'Japanese Anglicans'.

[12] James M. Phillips, *From the Rising of the Sun: Christians and Society in Contemporary Japan* (New York: Orbis, 1981), pp. 32–47.

[13] Bishop Paul Nakamura, 'No Weapons, No War, No Fighting: An Okinawan View', *Anglican and Episcopal History* 65.4 (December 1996), pp. 459–67.

buraku people who inhabited a marginal position in many urban centres, despised as inferior and 'no people'. The presence of large groups of Korean workers, the denial of their basic rights, and the exploitation of 'illegal' immigrants were seen as an area of Christian concern and action. The NSKK was no longer able to regard the veneration of the Tenno and the Shinto cult as a harmless and beneficent expression of Japanese cultural values. There was a demand to remove the prayers for the Tenno and the royal family, and a protest at the revival of public celebrations at the Yasukuni shrine, with its strong associations with the war dead.

There was a demand for public confession by the whole church for the failures of the past. Bishop Sasaki had been alone in confessing guilt in 1946. Finally, in 1996, the whole church admitted guilt:

> Since its establishment, The Nippon Sei Ko Kai has been making compromises with the idea of a Tenno (God of Heaven) ruled nation and militarism which go against the Gospel . . .
>
> The Nippon Sei Ko Kai confesses to God and apologizes to the people in Asia and the Pacific that we did not admit our fault immediately after the end of the war, were unaware of our responsibility for the past 50 years, and have not actively called for reconciliation and compensation until today.[14]

The Nippon Sei Ko Kai remains a small Christian community – it has 60,000 members compared with the 204,000 members of Kyodan, and over half a million Catholics.[15] The NSKK is a largely middle-class community, whose educational institutions and social service provision are highly regarded in society as a whole. It has not had as high a political profile as the Kyodan, nor has it produced theologians of the calibre of such Protestants as Kagawa Toyohiko, whose witness as a Christian socialist and pacifist was outstanding, or Kazoh Kitamori, whose *Theology of the Pain of God* (1946) influenced Jürgen Moltmann. Perhaps the most distinguished academic theologian of the NSKK has been Enkichi Kan (1895–1972), who studied at Harvard and Cambridge, became an Anglican priest and worked at the Anglican-founded Rikkyo University in Tokyo. He combined a strong social concern, in the tradition of Charles Gore, with a Barthian emphasis on the transcendence of God.[16]

The NSKK expresses a high degree of formalism in its worship, resonating with the strong sense of correct performance which characterises traditional Japanese spirituality, whether Shinto or Buddhist. In

[14] *Anglican and Episcopal History* (December 1996), pp. 489–91.
[15] David Barrett, George T. Kurian and Todd M. Johnson, *World Christian Encyclopedia* (2 vols., Oxford: Oxford University Press, 2001), Volume 1, pp. 412–19.
[16] Phillips, *From the Rising*, p. 254.

1986, a new translation of the Book of Common Prayer abandoned the old literary style (*bungotai*) – another indication of the realisation that the church needed to make a break with the past.[17] As with many other traditional Christian churches, the order and formalism of Anglicanism are not the qualities which easily translate into a dynamic evangelistic sense of mission. But, despite slow numerical growth, the NSKK remains committed to participation in the public life of Japan. It has also established links with other Anglican churches in Asia (Korea, the Philippines, Bangladesh) as an expression of its international commitment.

KOREA

Korea, the 'Hermit Kingdom', was as suspicious of foreign interference as was Japan. Traditionally Korea had accepted the regional hegemony of China, and Confucian ideals suffused the Korean elite.[18] There had long been Catholic influences, emanating from China. But connections with western powers provoked severe persecution up to the 1860s. However, in the 1880s Korea was increasingly concerned about Japanese imperial ambitions, and signed a treaty with the United States, which included freedom for missionary activities. The Catholics and American Presbyterians seized the new opportunities, but not Episcopalians until British Anglo-Catholics responded. In 1889, a former Royal Navy officer, Charles Corfe, was consecrated bishop to initiate the work in Korea. He was joined in 1890 by Mark Trollope, who was to become the third bishop (1911–30). With SPG support, it was hoped that a Korean (then spelt Corean) Missionary Brotherhood, founded as a quasi-monastic missionary order by Herbert Kelly, would provide the personnel for the mission. The Sisters of the Community of St Peter in Kilburn also made Korea the focus of their mission.[19]

Respecting the 'high' culture of Korea, suffused by Confucianism, Trollope proclaimed that he wished to teach 'a new Tao', to present Christianity as a fulfilment of the religious and ethical aspirations which informed Korean spirituality, appealing to the dominant culture. This was why he decided to build a church on Kanghwa Island, the centre of the national cult in Korea. The Anglican church of SS Peter and Paul, dedicated in 1900, 'harmonized', said Bishop Corfe, 'with all the other

[17] Kumazawa Yoshinobu and David Swain (eds.), *Christianity in Japan 1971–1990* (Tokyo: Christian Literature Society of Japan, 1991).

[18] R. G. Tiedemann, 'China and its Neighbours', in Adrian Hastings (ed.), *A World History of Christianity* (London: Cassell, 1999), pp. 402–4.

[19] Mark Trollope, *The Church in Corea* (London: Mowbray, 1915).

buildings in the city, overlooking them in a quiet dignity, but without any undue or conspicuous self-assertion'. The building incorporated Buddhist, Confucian and Korean religious motifs and became the model for Anglican churches throughout Korea.

A strategy based on traditional elite Korean culture ran into immediate difficulties. Japan was rapidly replacing China as the dominant power in the area, and in 1905 began a campaign of conquest which produced a bitter guerrilla war, and in 1910 the formal cession of Korea to Japan. The churches now had to deal with new rulers, who were every bit as suspicious of Christian activity as the pre-1880 Korean authorities had been. Protestant Christianity (especially the Presbyterians) became strongly identified with a Nationalist struggle against Japanese imperialism, but the 1919 independence movement was brutally crushed.[20] Anglicans were characterised by a much more co-operative policy, accepting the reality of Japanese control, but resisting attempts to impose the Shinto cult in Korean schools. Anglicans tried to follow a two-track approach in which they directed their activities both to Koreans and to Japanese settlers. In Seoul Trollope advocated having a Korean service and a Japanese service on alternate weeks. In 1926 Trollope replaced the church which served as a cathedral in Seoul by an expansive new building on a site opposite the deserted Toksu Palace. In his interesting discussion of the architecture of Korean Anglicanism, Lee notes that Trollope had the idea of employing a 'Japanese' style for churches in the provinces (an indication, perhaps, of his willingness to regard Japanese culture as the one which would prevail in Korea), and a 'western' style for the cathedral: 'to implant the image of the Anglican Church and show the authority of the Bishop's centralizing power'. With the end of both British and Japanese aspirations to colonial grandeur, the Romanesque cathedral remains, exuding a cool, austere beauty. The diocesan website is now at pains to point out the compatibility of the cathedral (at last completed in 1996) with the restored Toksu Palace nearby:

> Bishop Mark Cho (Trollope) established this central church to show the Christian victory to the Korean people who had lost their nation and to inspire them with faith . . . The cathedral is not strange to Koreans even if it is built in romanesque style because it is so well harmonized with Korea's traditional architecture.[21]

[20] See Thompson Brown's articles 'Korea' and 'Korean Independence Movement', in S. W. Sunquist (ed.), *A Dictionary of Asian Christianity* (Grand Rapids: Eerdmans, 2001).

[21] http://www.sk.or.kr.

One of the last acts of Bishop Trollope in 1930 was to ordain as priests Paul Kim, a Korean, and John Kudo, a Japanese.[22] Kudo was to be vicar-general during the war, when all western missionaries had to evacuate Korea. Kudo resisted the forced merger of the Anglican church with the Kyodan. The end of hostilities enabled missionaries to return, but Korea was soon caught up in the war, which eventually divided Korea. The small Anglican work in the North became impossible to sustain – North Korean Christians generally returned to the secret Christian status which they had endured for so long before 1880. In South Korea, the liberation brought an end to Japanese cultural as well as political imperialism. Christianity since 1945 has progressed enormously in South Korea, so that some 40 per cent of the total population now professes Christianity. The Presbyterian Church, which was strongly identified with the Korean struggle, has become an enormous church of the people. Minjung theology, the theology of 'the people', expresses this sense of identification with the struggle and the aspirations of the common people. The Presbyterian Church in Korea has been particularly active in developing critiques of the authoritarian and corporate capitalist domination of South Korean society. Anglicans have not embodied these popular or radical concerns to anything like the same extent.

The Anglican church has grown substantially since 1945 – it now has some 110,000 adherents, a big increase from the 10,000 before 1945. But this is still a very small percentage (0.2 per cent) of the total South Korean population of 50 million, and in comparison with 9 million Protestants, 8 million members of independent churches, and 3 million Roman Catholics.[23] In 1965 the first Korean bishop, Paul Lee, was consecrated. In 1993 the three dioceses of Seoul, Pusan and Taejon which constitute the Tae-Han Song-Kong-hwei (the Holy Catholic Church of Korea) became an autonomous province within the Anglican communion.

MALAYSIA AND SINGAPORE

Stamford Raffles founded Singapore in 1819 as a free port, independent of the local Muslim rulers. In the nineteenth century it became the entrepôt of mission activity as well as of trade for the whole of South-East Asia. The Anglican church was established in the area primarily to serve the

[22] [Richard Rutt,] *The Anglican Church in Korea* (London: The Korean Mission, 1963).

[23] Barrett et al., *World Christian Encyclopedia*, Volume 1, pp. 682–7. Barrett's figures differ markedly from the 2004 *Church of England Year Book* figure of only 14,558.

British traders and planters who were residing in the region. In comparison with other Catholic and Protestant missions, Anglicanism was slow to respond to missionary opportunities outside the colonial social circle.[24] In the late eighteenth century, Dutch power in the Malay states gave way to British suzerainty. The Anglican church at Melaka had originally been a Dutch Reformed church, and was converted to Anglican use as Christ Church in 1838.

The formal ecclesiastical provision for the Anglican church in this area is as complicated as the numbers of adherents are small. At first under the jurisdiction of the Bishop of Calcutta, in 1856 a local diocese, called Labuan, was formed, with Singapore as its metropolis. Labuan, a small island off the coast of Sabah in northern Borneo, was chosen because it was a possession of the British crown, unlike Singapore, which was still under East India Company rule. The first Bishop of Labuan also became Bishop of Sarawak, a diocese created by the Rajah of Sarawak, James Brooke. An adventurer in the mould of Raffles, Brooke had helped the Sarawak Malays to shake off the authority of the Sultan of Brunei. They asked him to become Rajah in 1841. Such freelance empire-making was an embarrassment to the British government, which refused to recognise Brooke's position. Brooke promoted missionary work, which he saw as a civilising agency for the non-Muslim native Dayak people. The Borneo Church Mission Institute began work in 1846, but by 1853 responsibility was assumed by the SPG. Brooke considered it to be his responsibility and right to appoint a Bishop of Sarawak, and he chose the first missionary, Dr Francis McDougall. The British took a dim view of the exercise of such a prerogative, but agreed to appoint McDougall to Labuan also. The next bishop moved the diocesan seat to Singapore in 1868. With the demise of the East India Company, it was safely in British territory. But he continued to regard his missionary work in Sarawak as of equal importance. It was only in 1909 that Singapore became a diocese in its own right.[25]

The British authorities strongly discouraged evangelistic work among the local Muslim Malay communities. But such a prohibition did not extend to the large numbers of Chinese and Tamil workers who flocked into Malaya to work on the rubber plantations and as traders. That an

[24] Michael Northcott, 'Two Hundred Years of Anglican Mission in West Malaysia', in Robert Hunt, Kam Hing Lee and John Roxborough (eds.), *Christianity in Malaysia: A Denominational History* (Petaling Jaya: Pelanduk Publications, 1992), p. 35.

[25] Graham Saunders, *Bishops and Brookes: The Anglican Mission and the Brooke Raj in Sarawak 1848–1941* (Singapore: Oxford University Press, 1992).

Anglican Christian work did emerge in the Malayan states and Singapore among these groups was more due to the persistence and tenacity of the Chinese and Tamils themselves than to any strategic planning by the authorities. In the Penang area, Tamil labourers and tappers worked on the rubber plantations, and in 1871 Royapen Balavendrum, a Tamil catechist from South India, began work among this community. He conducted house services, since Tamils were not welcome in St George's Penang, and in 1886 built a Tamil church, in the grounds owned by St George's. He extended his work as far as Singapore and established a boys' school at Province Wellesley, where there was a large transient Tamil community. He attended Hindu festivals in order to preach the Gospel, and thus gathered converts to the church. Anglican Tamils, however, found the racial segregation of the Anglicans intolerable and preferred to have fellowship with the Methodists. Balavendrum was ordained in 1880, and a fellow Tamil catechist, Gnani Poniah, in 1887. In the early twentieth century, the Revd T. Yesudian gave notable service, establishing a Tamil Christian Association and encouraging lay readers and the use of Tamil lyrics in worship.

The Chinese experience was similar to that of the Tamils, but the racial segregation imposed by British policy meant that Chinese work developed almost completely separately. Lim Kim Soy from Amoy was active among the Chinese community of Penang. Chan Wing Tsuen, from Hong Kong, became the first Chinese priest, working primarily among the Cantonese community. Dong Bing Seng worked among those from Foochow province. Chinese Bible women were active in Malaya and Singapore, as they were in China itself.

The weakness of this pattern of development became clear during the Japanese occupation of 1942–5. Bishop Leonard Wilson and many British clergy were interned, and much of the burden rested on the Chinese and Indian clergy. For the first time, inter-racial services were held.[26] Although there were attempts to resume the previous pattern once the war had ended, and the synod continued to be dominated by British expatriates, it became clear that radical changes needed to be made. For the first time Tamil and Chinese priests were appointed as vicars and archdeacons, and in 1965 Roland Koh, a priest who originated in Hong Kong, became assistant bishop in Kuala Lumpur. He had done important work in rallying the Chinese community during the Malayan Emergency

[26] Keng Aun Loh, *Fifty Years of the Anglican Church in Singapore Island, 1909–1959* (Singapore: University of Singapore, 1963).

in the 1950s and had welcomed the influx of CMS and China Inland Mission missionaries from China after 1949. Work among Chinese people was now given some priority in diocesan thinking. In 1972 John Savirimuthu became the first Tamil bishop in Malaysia. His wife was the daughter of the great Yesudian.[27]

In contrast with Malaya, missionary work was a priority in Sarawak.[28] It had the support of Rajah James Brooke and of his successor Rajah Charles Brooke, though Charles Brooke was increasingly critical of the narrowly religious work of the Anglicans, who did not have the funds to develop the educational aspects of their work as much as Brooke would have liked. He invited Catholics and Methodists to supply what he saw as lacking in the Anglican mission. The centre of Anglican work was evangelism among the Sea Dayaks (the Iban people) and the Land Dayaks (the Bidayuh). Bible translation in both languages was undertaken, and the first ordinations occurred in the 1920s. From the early days, Charles Gomes, a Ceylonese of mixed Portuguese and Sinhalese descent, served as a missionary, and his son Edwin was ordained in 1887. Charles Koch, Joseph Daniel and Edward Gunaratnam Proctor were others of a Tamil or mixed-race Ceylonese background who worked in the mission. They found that their work was not always appreciated by the British missionaries.

An increasingly important area of mission occurred among Chinese workers in Kuching and, in the twentieth century, in the towns of the oilfields. Foo Ngyen Khoon had been the first Chinese missionary from the 1850s to the 1880s, supported by the SPG. The Hakka Chinese, working as farmers south of Kuching, had escaped persecution for their Christian faith in China. They were glad to identify with the Anglicans (though many originally had been members of the Basel Mission in China).Their leader Kong Kuin En was ordained in 1913, by which time there were already a number of other Chinese clergy. The first Chinese bishop was James Wong Chang Ling, a marine engineer – made assistant bishop in 1957. By this time the church had suffered the hardship of the Japanese invasion, in which the bishop was detained and a number of Chinese priests killed.

In Sabah, the SPG work begun in the 1880s first concentrated on Hakka Chinese communities. After the Second World War, the Australian CMS became involved in work in Sabah. In 1957, Iban missionaries from Sarawak began work among the tribal peoples of the

[27] Diocese of West Malaysia, *A Man of Vision* (Kuala Lumpur: Diocese of West Malaysia, 1985).
[28] Brian Taylor, *The Anglican Church in Borneo 1848–1962* (Bognor Regis: New Horizon, 1983).

hinterland. Some of these communities have become predominantly Christian. Elizabeth Koepping's studies of the Kadazan peoples of eastern Sabah explore the phenomenon of the rapid Christianisation of whole communities, and the issues which this raises for identity. The earlier missionary approach was often patronising in its deployment of a 'fulfilment' theology, but it was less destructive, she argues, than the demonising approaches which too often characterise the charismatic forms of Christianity which are increasingly shaping the church in many parts of the Anglican church in Sabah.[29]

With independence, Sarawak and Sabah combined with Malaya to form the federation of Malaysia. In 1965, Singapore withdrew to become a separate city state. There are now four dioceses in the Province of South-East Asia: Singapore, West Malaysia, Kuching, and Sabah. With a total membership estimated as 168,000, this province is thus considerably bigger numerically than Japan or Korea. Singapore, with its large Chinese population and its pro-western capitalist system, has been an area of strong Christian growth, though Christians constitute only about 12 per cent of Singapore. The Anglican church has been considerably influenced by the charismatic movement, not least at the cathedral, a movement with which Archbishop Moses Tay (who retired in 2001) strongly identified. It has enabled the church to renew 'what had become a moribund and elitist ex-colonial church'.[30] But it has also produced a parallel militancy to that described by Elizabeth Koepping for rural Sabah. In Singapore's highly urban setting, with its traditions of authoritarian political leadership and concern for personal as well as public morality, the Anglican church has led the way in mobilising religious opinion against homosexual practice, both in Singapore and more widely in the Anglican communion.[31] The diocese of Singapore has been active in reinvigorating the former diplomatic chaplaincy churches of the capitals of Thailand, Cambodia, Vietnam and Indonesia.

THE PHILIPPINES

In 1900, as in 2000, the Philippines was the only country in Asia with a Christian majority. Half of Asia's Christians are Filipino. The Philippines

[29] Elizabeth Koepping, paper delivered at the International Association of Mission Studies, Kuala Lumpur, September 2004.

[30] You-Leng Lim, 'Homosexuality: How the Economics and Politics of Singapore have Shaped the Anglican Diocese and its Role in the Province of South East Asia', a background paper for the 1998 Lambeth Conference. Available on http://newark.rutgers.edu/~lcrew/lenglim2.html.

[31] Ibid.

was an anomaly in another sense: it was Spanish in a Portuguese-dominated region – the mirror image of Brazil. The independence movement against Spain in the late nineteenth century was suffused with a popular Catholicism, expressive of distress and protest. But the official church staunchly supported the Spanish authorities. A Catholic priest, Fr Gregorio Aglipay, established a reformed Catholic movement which became the Philippine Independent Church (PIC), and which, in the early years of the twentieth century, looked as if it might become the major national expression of religion. In 1898, Spain was forced to concede the Philippines to the USA, a move which brought certain benefits to the Filipino people but was hardly a successful outcome of their independence struggle. One consequence of the American takeover was that Protestant missions were allowed into the country for the first time.

Bishop Charles Brent was appointed by the Episcopal Church as its bishop in the Philippines – not as a missionary, but as a part of ECUSA. Brent was a Canadian by birth. An enthusiast for the new American imperialism, he regarded himself as a chaplain to the American occupiers, and in some sense a representative of America. He was imbued with the ideal of the Episcopal Church as a 'national church', an ideal which had a new resonance as America extended its influence throughout the world. He accompanied Governor Taft to Manila in 1902, and soon established an impressive cathedral near the government quarter. He devised and executed plans for schools and hospitals. American rule brought a separation of church and state in the Philippines. Brent did not conceive his task to be to proselytise among Catholics, even though that now became possible. But he was eager to establish missionary work in those parts of the Philippines where Catholicism had not been planted. The Igorot (mountain) people of north Luzon came to be seen as suitable for such an enterprise. He was shocked when his warm feelings towards Catholics were not reciprocated and the Scheut fathers established rival work in the Episcopalian centres of Bontoc and Sagada.

The Igorot came to constitute some 80 per cent of the membership of the Philippine Episcopal Church (PEC). Sagada became the centre of Igorot work, under the leadership of Fr John Staunton. Staunton had a high-church ideal of creating a self-contained Christian society among the Igorot people of Sagada – a community which Christian civilising influence would permeate, but where the negative influences of (Roman Catholic) superstition or (Protestant) secularism would be kept at bay. This patriarchal, somewhat clerical vision later gave way to a less romantic appreciation of a dynamic traditional society when the lay missionary William Henry Scott began his work after 1945.[32]

An early convert who did not fit into the conservative pattern of Staunton was Pitapit, an Igorot from Bontoc, the old Spanish provincial capital. On conversion Pitapit took the name Hilary Clapp (the name of the priest who baptised him). He married a mestiza and trained as a doctor, working in Bontoc Hospital from 1928 to 1941, and became a representative of Mountain Province in the new Philippines legislature. He protested against the social consequences of mining in the area before the mines went bankrupt in the 1930s. He had political ambitions – but failed to be appointed governor of Mountain Province by the Americans. Eventually he was appointed to this position by the Japanese occupiers in 1942, trying to steer a hazardous course between collaboration with the Japanese and support for the resistance. He helped Americans evade arrest. But in April 1945 he was executed by the guerrillas as a Japanese sympathiser. Arun Jones calls him a 'cultural broker' – between Igorot, Spanish and American culture.[33]

Brent's successor was Gouverneur F. Mosher, who had been Bishop of Shanghai. He was an admirer of Roland Allen, and advocated much more responsibility for the local church than Staunton's rather antique version of Catholicism allowed. It was now recognised by ECUSA that the Philippines was not simply an off-shore American diocese. Mosher established St Andrew's Seminary to train Filipino priests – one of the first to be ordained was an Igorot from Sagada, Eduardo Longid, who became the first Filipino bishop in 1963. In 1946, an agreement was made with the Philippine Independent Church for joint theological training at St Andrew's. This led in 1961 to a declaration of full intercommunion, with ECUSA participating in the consecration of PIC bishops. PIC, with 5 million members and 34 dioceses, is a much bigger church than PEC, which in 2000 had a membership of about 110,000.[34] As well as the Igorot, PEC has a number of Chinese members.

[32] W. H. Scott, *The Discovery of the Igorots* (Quezon City: New Day, 1974).

[33] Arun Jones, 'Christian Missions in the American Empire: Episcopalians in Northern Luzon, 1902–46', Ph.D. dissertation, Princeton University, 2001.

[34] Barrett et al., *World Christian Encyclopedia*, Volume 1, pp. 594–601.

CHAPTER 14

Oceania

Oceania was the last part of the world to be the subject of missionary endeavour.[1] Protected by vast tracts of water from casual contact with other cultures, the societies of Oceania were peculiarly vulnerable in the face of European intrusion. Christianity aided and abetted the collapse or fragmentation of the highly specialised societies and local cultures of the aboriginal and island peoples. Settlers of European (and largely British) origin rapidly came to be the majority of the total population of the region. The Christian culture which the settlers espoused often reinforced their contempt and disdain for the aboriginal inhabitants. Missionary Christianity, on the other hand, assumed a protective role. That local culture survived at all is partly to do with the fact that Christianity enabled indigenous converts to evolve new cultural responses.

With the smallest overall population of any continent (some 30 million in 2000), Oceania has become one of the most Christian parts of the world. Over 80 per cent of the population belong to Christian churches. Anglicans are a surprisingly high proportion of the total population at 17.8 per cent. This is higher than in any other continent, including Europe (where, outside Britain, there are very few Anglicans). For long the dominant church in Australia and New Zealand, Anglicans have a strong presence in some, but not all, of the Pacific islands: an estimated 38 per cent in the Solomon Islands are Anglican, 29 per cent in Norfolk Island (a dependency of Australia), 18 per cent in Vanuatu, 6.7 per cent in Papua New Guinea, and 11 per cent in the Cocos Islands. In other islands, where the London Missionary Society, the Methodists or the Roman Catholics arrived first – Fiji, Tonga, Samoa – Anglicans are a negligible proportion of the population.[2]

[1] For a general survey see Ian Breward, *A History of the Churches in Australasia* (Oxford: Clarendon, 2001).

[2] These figures are gathered from David Barrett, George T. Kurian and Todd M. Johnston, *World Christian Encyclopedia* (2 vols., Oxford: Oxford University Press, 2001).

In 1788 Captain Phillip arrived at Botany Bay to establish the penal colony which was to dominate New South Wales for half a century. Evangelicals, already exploiting the openings afforded by chaplaincy work in India, persuaded William Pitt to include a chaplain with the military party, in the person of Richard Johnson. He was joined in 1793 by Samuel Marsden, one of the most powerful figures in the colony for over forty years until his death in 1838. Marsden, a Yorkshire man of humble origins from Farsley (near Leeds), was enabled to go to Cambridge by a scholarship from the Elland Society, a local Anglican Evangelical group. He abandoned his studies in order to answer the call to Sydney. Marsden was a man of great dynamism, on the look-out for opportunities for missionary work in the South Seas in addition to his chaplaincy work. His high repute as a Christian pioneer rests on his support for the London Missionary Society's work in Tahiti, and on his promotion of CMS work among the Maori of New Zealand. In Australia itself his reputation is more controversial.

Marsden quarrelled with a succession of governors, constantly complaining about the immorality of the soldiers and the venality of the government officials. His most spectacular dispute was with Governor Macquarie. Marsden disapproved of his schemes for the rehabilitation and settlement of convicts who had completed their sentences. Marsden was mistrustful of these 'emancipists' (freed convicts), and wanted severely to limit their role in the colony. As a magistrate at Parramatta, he became known as the 'flogging parson' for his rigid enforcement of the law and harsh treatment of offenders, the majority of whom were convicts or emancipists. Marsden strongly supported an Anglican establishment, and was distrustful of the dissenting traditions of many convicts.

He was particularly hostile to the Irish Roman Catholic convicts, whose numbers greatly increased after the repression of the 1798 Irish rebellion. Convicts were required to attend the services of the established church. Marsden was not in favour of allowing Catholic priests into the colony. Irish Catholics were 'the lowest class of the Irish Nation, who are the most wild, ignorant and savage Race that were ever favoured with the light of Civilization ... extremely superstitious, artful and treacherous!'[3] Marsden's opposition to the emancipists had a class basis – he belonged to the free settlers and became one of the great land owners in the colony like Governor MacArthur himself. At Marsden's death he owned some

[3] A. T. Yarwood, *Samuel Marsden: The Great Survivor* (Melbourne: Melbourne University Press, 1977), p. 98.

20,000 acres and thousands of sheep, and employed agents back in Yorkshire to handle the sale of his produce.

Marsden cannot take all the blame for the lack of esteem in which the Anglican church was held in the early days of the colony. But the fact was that Anglicanism was regarded by free settlers (like the 1820 settlers in South Africa more likely to be Methodist than Anglican) and convicts alike as an arm of officialdom, a repressive 'moral constabulary'. As his biographer puts it:

> For Marsden to be a clergyman and magistrate was a sufficient obstacle to parochial success . . . to be rich as well was a disaster for him professionally and for the Anglican Church in New South Wales.[4]

Marsden's attitudes to the Aboriginal inhabitants were even more negative. He had great faith in and enthusiasm about the prospects of missionary work among the Tahitians and the Maori. But he was totally negative about work among the Australian Aboriginal communities he found in the Parramatta area. Land-hungry settler sheep farmers in New South Wales soon found themselves in competition with Aboriginals for their traditional hunting grounds. The humanity of Aboriginals was traduced, their life considered cheap. When the government hanged settlers for murder, the white community felt outraged. While Marsden hardly approved of murder, his situation as a large land owner made him insensitive to Aboriginal needs.

Marsden advanced the theory that evangelism was unlikely to yield any results until natives were first shown the values of 'civilisation'. Maoris and Tahitians showed signs of responding to civilisation, and it was therefore strategically sensible to expend missionary effort on them. Australian Aborigines, conversely, refused to abandon their way of life and undertake the disciplines of labour for white people.

> Whether anything can be done with these degraded Tribes I have my doubts. It is our duty to try what we can do. The time may come when they feel more wants than they do at present. They seem to have all they wish for, Idleness and Independence.[5]

Early in their time at Parramatta, Samuel and Anna Marsden did adopt a young Aboriginal boy. His own native name jettisoned, they called him (perhaps appropriately) Tristan. Tristan accompanied the Marsdens on their first trip back to England, but jumped ship at Rio de Janeiro and spent a couple of years there before finding his way back to Sydney.

[4] Ibid., p. 227. [5] Ibid., p. 241.

Turning his back on 'civilisation' he attempted to return to his own people, but, still a young man, came back to die in a Sydney hospital.

During Marsden's final years, the Anglican church developed a more regular ecclesiastical structure. Technically within the diocese of Calcutta from 1814, Australia got an archdeacon in 1825. In 1836 William Broughton was appointed the first and only Bishop of Australia – he was, indeed, the first Anglican bishop in the southern hemisphere. Broughton, unlike the chaplains, was a high churchman. Like them he supported the idea of an Anglican establishment. He protested strongly when the Anglo-Irish governor Richard Bourke passed the Church Act of 1836, which supported the educational work of the Church of Scotland, Methodists and Roman Catholics as well as the Anglicans, along lines being developed in Ireland itself. Broughton was even more perturbed when the government allowed the establishment of a Roman Catholic hierarchy in 1842, some years before this was allowed in England.[6]

Broughton would have liked the diocese of Sydney to become the Metropolitan of Australia. Other Australian dioceses were created: Tasmania, Newcastle, Melbourne, and Adelaide in 1842, dioceses in Western Australia and Queensland somewhat later. But the creation of separate colonies, with separate governments, militated against a centralised church. From its inception, the state of South Australia was clear that the Church of England should have no special status, and the free churches were quick to criticise vestiges of Anglican superiority.[7] Tractarian visions of the church seemed particularly relevant. They provided an alternative ecclesiology to establishment, stressing the divine foundations of the church and its independence from state control. South Australia and West Australia became predominantly high church, while the willingness of the SPG to endow a large number of small dioceses outside the main urban centres led to the creation of a strongly Anglo-Catholic culture away from the eastern capitals. In Victoria, by contrast, the long Evangelical episcopate of Charles Perry (from 1847) made Melbourne an Evangelical diocese, actually before Evangelicalism had become the episcopal norm in Sydney. But by the end of the nineteenth century, the Evangelicalism of Melbourne was becoming much more inclusive, tolerant and responsive to social issues, at a time when Sydney was developing the more assertive and exclusive Evangelicalism for which it became famous.

[6] Patricia Curtboys, 'State Support for Churches 1836–1860', in Bruce Kaye (ed.), *Anglicanism in Australia: A History* (Melbourne: Melbourne University Press, 2002).

[7] David Hilliard, *Godliness and Good Order: A History of the Anglican Church in South Australia* (Netley: Wakefield Press, 1986).

To live as a voluntary religious society was not easy for Australian Anglicans, whether Evangelical or Anglo-Catholic. Evangelicals clung to the idea of establishment, not least to protect a basically Protestant form of English Christianity. Irish Anglicans exerted a strong influence towards Protestantism, as they did also in Canada. Active lay support was essential if a non-establishment form of the church was to flourish, and that was not always easy to reconcile with clerically dominated models of an Anglo-Catholic vision of the church. Anglo-Catholics relied on importing English clergy rather longer than did Evangelicals. Anglicans identified strongly with British patriotism, devotion to the royal family, and a general conservatism. They did not seem quite at home with the growing democratic aspirations of Australians, remote from an emerging radical working class with which Australian Catholicism was more in tune. Anglicans had hoped to influence Australian society through the creation of a confessional educational system. But they did not have the resources to maintain such a system. By the end of the nineteenth century they had largely given up the struggle to have a comprehensive Anglican school system, and accepted that schools should be run by the state, with a general Christian, Protestant, but not specifically Anglican character. Catholics were willing to pour much more energy and resources into their schools, a major factor in the creation of a distinctive Catholic voice in Australia. Anglicanism remained until well into the twentieth century the single most important denomination in Australia, but with a diminishing proportion of the total population. In 1881 40 per cent of Australians were Anglican; by 1966 this had been reduced to 34 per cent. By 2000 it was 21.5 per cent.[8] The decline could be explained by the increasing secularism of Australian life and the decline of the 'white Australia' policy which had confined immigration largely to groups from Britain.

ANGLICANS AND ABORIGINAL PEOPLE

When the British arrived in 1788, they found peoples whose ancestors had lived in Australia for thousands of years. There was a great variety of polities and cultures, delicately adapted to the harsh environment. Although Captain Phillip was instructed to 'live in amity and kindness' with the Aboriginal people,[9] the insatiable land demands of settler stock

[8] Barrett et al., *World Christian Encyclopedia*, Volume 1, p. 81.

[9] G. Davison et al., *The Oxford Companion to Australian History* (Melbourne: Oxford University Press, 1998), p. 14.

keepers meant that the delicate ecology was rapidly disrupted in ways which permanently damaged Aboriginal society. This was exacerbated by the disdain with which the settlers regarded Aboriginal culture. Aboriginal life was considered cheap. Men were murdered; women and children massacred. Women were raped and forced into subservient relations with settler males. Marsden, while never condoning immorality, failed to demonstrate any sympathy for Aboriginal life.[10] 'Marsden was negative about all efforts to assist Aboriginal people and doubly negative about initiatives that he did not control.'[11] Missionary efforts were feeble and under-resourced, and half-hearted attempts to create self-supporting agricultural communities were misplaced environmentally and socially corrosive. In the 1830s the CMS was approached by the governor of Tasmania to establish work there, but it did not have the resources to do so. In twenty five years almost the entire Aboriginal population had been killed.

Populations on the mainland fell dramatically as the hunting grounds were reduced by European settlement. Sexually transmitted disease, introduced by the Europeans, rose to epidemic proportions. By the second half of the nineteenth century, the viability of aboriginal societies in the south-eastern corner of Australia was severely compromised. A class of Aboriginal and mixed-race peoples was beginning to gather around the growing urban centres, unable any longer to support life in its traditional ways but prevented from participating meaningfully in the new white economy, and threatened by ill health and alcoholism.[12]

With Aboriginal society in rapid decline, it was at first individual Christian initiative rather than the co-ordinated mission of the church which addressed the challenges. For some sixty years from 1855 John Bulmer, a Methodist, and his wife Caroline, worked with the Anglican diocese of Melbourne to build a self-sustaining Aboriginal community at Lake Tyers in eastern Victoria. Towards the end of his life, in 1903, Bulmer was ordained as an Anglican priest. The Lake Tyers community attempted to be a refuge for a nomadic people. The Bulmers were limited in their appreciation of Aboriginal culture. They equated Christian mission with the civilising mission, though their views gradually mellowed, turning to a wistful nostalgia, as they recognised the dangers of the

[10] Yarwood, *Samuel Marsden*, p. 241.

[11] John Harris, *One Blood: 200 Years of Aboriginal Encounter with Christianity* (Sutherland: Albatross, 1990), p. 51.

[12] This and subsequent material in this section relies on the pioneering work of John Harris in *One Blood* and in his chapter in Kaye, *Anglicanism*.

'half-civilised' Aboriginals whom the mission was creating. The Lake Tyers settlement was eventually taken over by government. But its role as a refuge was eroded. After Bulmer's death the civil administrator expelled his widow. He could not tolerate her 'misplaced sympathies' for the people. The 1886 Aborigines Protection Act of the Victoria government had already undermined one important role of the settlement. The Act defined people of mixed blood as 'white' and excluded them from Aboriginal reserves. This had devastating consequences. A biological definition of race ignored the fact that many mixed-race people resulted from the exploitation of Aboriginal women by white men. The children grew up with their mother and identified with Aboriginal culture. Under the terms of this law they were to be forcibly 'assimilated' into white society, though never accepted as full members.[13]

In 1850 in South Australia, Archdeacon Matthew Hale established the Poonindie Institute, on the Eyre Peninsula, as a farming community for Aboriginals but set apart from Aboriginal life, a place where Christian spiritual values and a work ethic could be inculcated. Some of the initial dynamism of the community waned when Hale was appointed as Bishop of Western Australia in 1857. But it did survive, as a self-supporting settlement, a place where Aboriginal people were given space to adapt 'with dignity to the culture of the invaders' (including the adoption of cricket) and to create 'a new Aboriginality'. Unfortunately, the land became coveted by white settlers, and in 1894 it was dissolved. St Matthew's Church became the parish of the white farming community.[14]

Hale had identified gentleness and a quiet and retiring spirit as Aboriginal Christian virtues. Another important figure for Anglican mission in Australia, John Brown Gribble, demonstrated a very different set of Christian characteristics. He is in a long line of Anglican activists and campaigners, from James Long in Calcutta to Trevor Huddleston in South Africa, whose passion for justice led them to conflict and controversy. In 1879, while the Congregational minister at Jerilderie, Gribble had a legendary encounter with Ned Kelly and his gang, defending a girl whose horse had been stolen. Soon after that he became involved in Anglican Aboriginal mission work at Warangesda, and was ordained in the Church of England. Invited by the Bishop of Western Australia to work among Aboriginal people on the Gascoyne River, 1,000 km north of Perth, he was appalled by the conditions of the Aboriginals on bonded labour contracts, little different from slavery. He took up their cause in

[13] Harris, *One Blood*, pp. 205–18. [14] Ibid., pp. 334–50; Hilliard, *Godliness*, pp. 37–8.

the press and published a tract, *Dark Deeds in a Sunny Land or Blacks and Whites in North-West Australia*. His outspokenness soon became an embarrassment to the diocesan mission committee which employed him and offended vested interests in Perth society, much of it Anglican. Accused of 'lying, canting humbug' by the *Western Australian*, a Perth newspaper, Gribble sued for libel in 1887 and lost. Impoverished, he returned to the east coast to live in Sydney. But in the last year of his life he established a mission at Yarrabah in northern Queensland. He died in 1893, aged forty-five.[15]

His son, Ernest Gribble, took over this mission, now financed by the Australian Board of Mission. Ernest was as stormy a character as his father, authoritarian and driven. After a breakdown in 1908, he moved to the Forrest River Mission in Western Australia, where he witnessed police attempts to break up the Aboriginal community which resulted in a number of atrocities. The Yarrabah mission survived and produced the first Aboriginal Anglican clergyman. James Noble, born in 1876 in western Queensland, worked for a settler family as a stockman. He became a Christian and was baptised and confirmed in 1895. His wife, Angelina, had been a 'stockman's boy', a euphemism for a girl used for sexual pleasure. Intelligent and gifted in languages and deeply committed to the Christian faith they had adopted, the Nobles were employed as pioneer evangelists in the CMS Roper River mission. Gribble recognised their talent and they accompanied him to the Forrest River settlement; in 1925, Noble was ordained deacon in Perth. Noble spent his last years as a clergyman at Yarrabah. He died in 1941 and was buried next to Gribble, his friend and supporter. It had been Gribble rather than the Board of Mission who had enabled his ordination. Significantly, Noble was never priested, despite the qualities of evangelism, pastoral care and leadership which he so obviously evidenced. Angelina lived on till 1964.[16]

In the twentieth century, Anglican Aboriginal mission was seen largely as an opportunity to work among relatively 'untouched' peoples in the North. Missions were established in Roper River, Groote Eylandt, Arnhem Land and the Torres Straits Islands. In the South, Aboriginal people were often described as 'doomed to disappear'. 'Pure' Aboriginals were not classed as citizens. They were a diminishing group of people, either to be protected in inadequate reserves or to be absorbed as servants in white society. Like their counterparts in Canada, these reserves have become notorious as places in which the young were forcibly separated from their

[15] Harris, *One Blood*, pp. 497–500. [16] Ibid., pp. 499–520.

families, were deculturated, and became the objects of physical, mental and sexual abuse. The institutions bred authoritarianism and attracted people of an authoritarian disposition. Anglicans were not heavily involved in the institutionalisation of Aboriginal people. But nor did they have alternative strategies. There are relatively few Aboriginal Anglicans in south-east Australia. Aboriginal and mixed-race people hardly felt welcome in most Anglican urban, suburban or rural parishes, and have tended to form their own congregations under the auspices of the Aborigines Inland Mission or the United Aborigines Mission.

The dominant strategy for much of the twentieth century was to encourage 'assimilation' as the only realistic form of survival for Aboriginal people or those of mixed race (such as the CMS settlement at Groote Eylandt). Education and church worship were in English. Vernacular culture was ignored or despised. It was a policy which hampered the emergence of an indigenous leadership. It discouraged attempts to produce biblical or liturgical materials in local languages. Exceptions were Nell Harris and Len Harris, who utilised the Gunwinggu lingua franca of the Roper River region, and Judith Stokes, who worked on the Anindilyakwa language of Groote Eylandt. This work has produced a more favourable evaluation of local song and dance, drama and the practice of body painting, despite the concern of conservative Christians.

The church has also been active in promoting the acknowledgement of Aboriginal land rights and protection, particularly against mining concessions. In the 1960s the Groote Eylandt people found that they did not have legal protection for the mineral wealth of the islands because Aboriginal people were not recognised as citizens. The CMS took a case to court on their behalf, winning Aus. $1 million compensation, with which a Groote Eylandt Aboriginal Trust was set up. In a referendum of 1967 Australian citizens did vote to extend citizenship to Aboriginals. But in itself this did not necessarily protect Aboriginal rights. The fiction that the land was unoccupied in 1788 – *terra nullius* – effectively debarred Aboriginal people from securing their rights. On Australia Day 1972 the Oenpelli people of Queensland lost their case against a mining company and were required to pay compensation. The injustice of this roused church authorities to protest. In 1985 Dinah Garadji, an Aboriginal deaconess, made a memorable intervention in the synod of the Anglican Church in the Northern Territory, asking 'How can we obey God if they take away our land? What do bits of paper mean?'

For ten years the Torres Islanders pursued the Mabo land case, despite attempts to delay and abort the process in the Queensland courts. In 1992 this resulted in the landmark decision which abolished the *terra nullius* concept, and recognised communal ownership of land. The long struggle had politicised and empowered the Torres Island Anglican community.

From the 1970s, Aboriginal clergy began to emerge. It had been a struggle for recognition and for appropriate training. In 1970 Patrick Brisbane was ordained by the Bishop of Carpentaria, Alan Pollen, in Perth. In 1973, Michael Gumbuli of the Northern Territory was ordained. Unlike James Noble, all these people were soon ordained as priests. Gumbuli became a leader in the development of an articulate Aboriginal Anglican voice. The first Aboriginal woman, Nancy Dick, was ordained deacon in 1987. The first Aboriginal bishop was a great-nephew of James Noble, Arthur Malcolm of Yarabbah.[17]

In 1938, at the 150th anniversary of white settlement in Australia, the Aboriginal political activist William Cooper of Victoria had called for an Aboriginal National Day of Mourning. This had largely gone unheard by the churches. But at the bicentenary in 1988 a service of penitence was held for the whole Australian Anglican church, in which the Primate Sir John Grindrod issued a public apology in St Andrew's Cathedral, Sydney:

> May I express on behalf of all non-Aboriginal people of our church our profound sorrow for the suffering that your people have had to endure with its violence and hurt? We humbly ask God's forgiveness.

Bishop Malcolm responded:

> For a long time we have been hurting; our spirits have felt crushed by the wrong actions that took place between my ancestors and yours. Much suffering has been the result but it is through the message of Jesus Christ that we have learnt to forgive.[18]

Despite this new recognition of the hurt and new respect for Aboriginal sensitivities, Aboriginal people still live difficult lives, both communally and as individuals. Subject to unemployment, imprisonment and the dangers of alcoholism and despair, they remain an under-resourced and marginalised people, not least in the church.

The Australian Anglican Church 'will forever remain the colonial church while Indigenous people are not a valued and integral part of its life'.[19]

[17] John Harris, *We Wish We'd Done More: Ninety Years of CMS and Aboriginal Issues in North Australia* (Adelaide: Open Book, 1998).

[18] Harris, *One Blood*, p. 867. [19] Harris, in Kaye, *Anglicanism*, p. 245.

AUSTRALIAN ANGLICANISM AND SYDNEY DIOCESE

The penitential service for the bicentenary was held in Sydney because that was where Australian Anglicanism had its birth. Sydney remains the richest and most powerful part of the Australian Anglican communion (according to the census of 1991, 39 per cent of Australian Anglicans lived in New South Wales[20]). Because of the strong emphasis on state autonomy in the confederation of Australia, there are five independent church provinces. The Archbishop of Sydney is not automatically the Primate, though a number have been elected to that position. Despite its seniority, Sydney has stood apart from the rest of the Australian church. It has developed a unique form of Anglicanism, based on a particular understanding of its Evangelical tradition.

As Bruce Kaye has pointed out, Sydney had a mixed tradition in the nineteenth century.[21] Only later did a conservative Evangelical orthodoxy assert itself over against other, more flexible forms of Evangelicalism.[22] In the 1890s Moore College, the seminary for Anglican clergy in Sydney diocese, developed a combination of a biblical conservatism and Keswick Pietism. The church was viewed as a 'little flock' of real Christians, uncompromising in their faith and morals. This unworldly outlook was uniquely combined with an astute political savvy designed to exert the maximum influence in the church and in society at large. The Evangelical Anglican Church League became a powerful pressure group within the synod. Many Sydney Evangelicals did not entirely fit this mould. Archbishop Mowll (1934–58), who had formerly been a missionary bishop in West China, represented a more consensual form of Evangelicalism, as did the Principal of Moore College in the interwar period, T. C. Hammond.

The person most associated with developing Sydney's unique Evangelical culture was David Broughton Knox, the Principal of Moore College from 1959 to 1985. A proponent of a full-blooded Reformed (Calvinistic) theology, Knox was rigorous in his thorough-going desire to implement this theology at every level of church life: personal faith, the power structures of the diocese, the relationship with the wider Anglican world, social ethics:

> The teaching and actions of Jesus nowhere show a concern for 'social justice'. The reason is that the call for social justice springs from envy rather than from

[20] John Davis, *Australian Anglicans and their Constitution* (Canberra: Acorn Press, 1993), p. 186.
[21] Bruce Kaye, *A Church without Walls* (Melbourne: Dove, 1995), p. 46.
[22] Stephen Judd and Kenneth Cable, *Sydney Evangelicals* (Sydney: Anglican Information Office, 1987).

compassion ... Compassion, not social justice, is the motivation for Christian social action ... Poverty calls for compassion ... but a Christian is not called on to campaign for a closer equalisation of incomes either within our society, or for that matter between nation and nation. Christ's gospel is not concerned with equity, but a relationship.[23]

Sydney's stubborn determination not to compromise its Reformation heritage was the main reason for the protracted negotiations to establish an Australian Anglican Church independent of the Church of England. A draft constitution was agreed by all dioceses in 1926 – except Sydney. It was only in 1962 that a new constitution was passed. It was a compromise. Adelaide criticised it for being too rigid and designed to inhibit change. Sydney remained concerned that its provisions to safeguard biblical Reformation orthodoxy were not sufficiently watertight.[24]

We only remain united by maintaining two denominations in one organisation and allowing members of both to call themselves Anglican ... The alleged comprehensiveness of the Church ... is a chimera.[25]

It was only in 1981 that the Church of England in Australia officially changed its name to the Anglican Church of Australia.

The refusal of Sydney to conform to the supposed Anglican characteristics of tolerance, diversity and moderation has become increasingly evident as Australian society has become less clearly influenced by Christian values. Sydney has consistently opposed the ordination of women, and delayed its implementation in the rest of the church. It employs women as deaconesses, and indeed has had a good record for employing women in this capacity from as early as 1922, but it does not ordain them to the presbyteral ministry, claiming biblical teaching on the headship of the male as justification for this policy. Sydney diocese has been equally strident in opposing the decriminalisation of homosexual practice. The fact that male homosexuals had traditionally found refuge in the few Anglo-Catholic parishes in the diocese, and that there was a particularly vibrant gay culture in Sydney, reinforced the view that Sydney diocese stood for Gospel values.[26]

Sydney has always had a strong missionary interest. At a time when the high-church Bush Brotherhoods were failing to recruit celibate men for work in the outback, the Evangelical Bush Church Aid Society has

[23] Bill Lawton, 'Australian Anglican Theology', in Kaye, *Anglicanism*, p. 193.

[24] John Davis, *Australian Anglicans*, p. 186.

[25] *The Anglican Church Record 1955*, quoted in Kaye, *Church without Walls*, pp. 47f.

[26] David Hilliard, 'Sydney Anglicans and Homosexuality', *Journal of Homosexuality* 32.2 (1997), pp. 101–23.

continued to expand and prosper. Although CMS Australia was by no means solely a Sydney project (and has its headquarters in Melbourne), Sydney has contributed strongly. The character of CMS work in Tanzania has much to do with the role of the Australian CMS. One distinctively Sydney mission project has been its support for the Church of England in South Africa. Sydney first became involved in the 1930s at the instigation of the Bishop of Central Tanganyika, George Chambers. Archbishop Mowll championed Fred Morris as CESA's first bishop, and its second bishop, Stephen Bradley, an Australian, received financial support from Sydney diocese. Broughton Knox helped to found George Whitefield College in Cape Town. This policy has been followed despite the hostility of the Archbishop of Canterbury and the Anglican communion as a whole to the recognition of CESA. Sydney diocese was a sponsor of the meeting of Evangelical bishops at Kuala Lumpur in 1997 which raised the issue of homosexuality on the agenda of world Anglicanism. It is likely to be a major participant in any realignment of Anglicanism over the question of homosexuality.[27]

NEW ZEALAND AND POLYNESIA

The story of the Anglican Church in New Zealand is surprisingly different from that of Australia. In New Zealand, Samuel Marsden is honoured as the pioneer of Christianity. He is commemorated on 12 May, the day of his death in 1836. The Maori have played a decisive role in the formation of the Church. In New Zealand, the first Bishop, George Selwyn, provided the Anglican church with a constitution which gave the church a strong sense of corporate unity. The Maori are a people of Polynesian origin who first came to Aotearoa (The Land of the Long White Cloud) some 1,000 years before the arrival of the Pakeha (whites), who first came as whalers and traders in the late eighteenth century.[28]

In 1809 Marsden, returning from England, met a young Maori sailor, Ruatara, nephew of chief Te Pahi, and was impressed by his intelligence. Other contact with Maori at Parramatta convinced Marsden that they appeared 'to be a very superior people in point of mental capacity', and that although they were not 'civilized' they were prime candidates for a civilising mission.[29] Marsden accompanied Ruatara to the Bay of Islands

[27] Stuart Piggin, 'Australian Anglicanism in a World-wide Context', Chapter 9 of Kaye, *Anglicanism*.
[28] G. W. Rice (ed.), *The Oxford History of New Zealand* (Auckland: Oxford University Press, 1992).
[29] Yarwood, *Samuel Marsden*, pp. 74–5.

on the north-east tip of North Island, and, on Christmas Day 1814, preached a sermon to an assembled crowd, with Ruatara translating.[30] Marsden had persuaded the CMS to send mechanics and practical missionaries, and they were invited by Ruatara's people to settle in the area. One of them, Thomas Kendall, although he was dismissed in 1823 for gun running and adultery, did prove an important pioneer for his work on the Maori language and culture.[31]

In 1823 the Revd Henry Williams arrived. He continued Kendall's language work and put an emphasis on evangelism. By 1840 a substantial Christian community had arisen under the patronage of the chiefs: by one reckoning some 43,000 people attended Anglican churches out of an estimated total Maori population of 110,000. There was also a Methodist and Catholic presence. Ruatara died young, and Christian Rangi, baptised in 1825, became the key Maori figure in the early evangelisation of the North Island. There was a strong desire for literacy, and enthusiasm for the Bible and prayer book in Maori. On their first visit to an area, missionaries would already find a congregation conversant with Christian hymns and prayers in their own language.

By the late 1830s it was becoming clear to Maori and missionaries alike that it would be very difficult to prevent whites from settling permanently in New Zealand. The CMS petitioned the British government, opposing colonisation 'as a violation of the Rights and Liberties of Natives'. But they also advised their Maori allies that it might be in their best interests to request some kind of British rule, both to prevent other powers (such as the Catholic French) from establishing sovereignty and to control white settlement. The CMS was instrumental in securing the agreement between Maori chiefs and the British, the Treaty of Waitangi of 1840, and produced a Maori translation. Maori chiefs ceded *kawanatanga* to the crown in return for *rangatiratanga* ('full, exclusive and undisturbed possession of their Lands and Estates, Forests, Fisheries and other properties which they may collectively or individually possess' (Article 2)). William Colenso (CMS missionary, a printer, and brother of the future Bishop of Natal) later questioned whether the Maori really understood that they were ceding 'sovereignty' to Britain, noting that in the Maori NT, Pilate was described as having *kawanatanga* (governorship), the implication being that sovereignty continued to reside with the Maori

30 A. K. Davidson and P. J. Lineham, *Transplanted Christianity* (Dunmore: Palmerston Press, 1989), p. 27.

31 Judith Binney, *The Legacy of Guilt: A Life of Thomas Kendall* (Christchurch: Auckland University Press, 1968).

people. In subsequent years Maori certainly did have cause for grievance that the terms of the treaty, and particularly the assurances about land, were not honoured.[32] Yet the very fact that there was a treaty gave certain protection, and a basis for protest.

Nevertheless, the Maori suffered considerably from the influx of settlers after 1840. Their numbers began to decline, and by 1896 had reached a low of 42,000, while the Pakeha population was 700,000 and rising. Land was a focal issue of conflict, and involved Maori in protracted wars in the 1850s and 1860s. CMS missionaries, as well as Bishop Selwyn, consistently protested against infringements of the treaty. Octavius Hadfield and his brothers-in-law, Henry and William Williams, were active in defending the Ngati Raukawa tribe against what they considered unscrupulous land grabbing, provoking anger from the settler community, who asked why Roman Catholics, Presbyterians and Methodists steered clear of the politics of land, while Anglicans were at the forefront of such disputes. When Hadfield was elected Bishop of Wellington in 1870, a local newspaper commented: 'Apart from his unfortunate Maori proclivities... a most estimable man'.[33] But by then the ability of the Maori to defend their land had diminished with population decline. By the end of the century, even missionaries had reluctantly come to the conclusion that the future of the Maori people lay in assimilation with the Pakeha majority. Moreover, many missionaries themselves became settlers. Their children came to identify with settler aspirations; but their intimate knowledge of the Maori language and culture could create an enduring, if paternalist, sympathy for the Maori.

It was an indication of the importance of the Maori work that in 1840, at the very beginning of the colonial period, George Augustus Selwyn was appointed bishop.[34] Selwyn, a high churchman, would not have been the choice of the CMS, but it agreed to provide half his salary. Selwyn, in turn, established a generally cordial relationship with the missionaries. He learnt Maori and took a great interest in missionary work both in New Zealand and in the Pacific islands of Polynesia and Melanesia. Selwyn worked for a diocese inclusive of Maori and Pakeha. Though the missionaries would ideally have preferred a separate native church, they

[32] J. Simpson, 'Honouring Religious Diversity in NZ Education after the Treaty of Waitangi, 1840–77', in S. Emilsen and W. W. Emilsen (eds.), *Mapping the Landscape: Essays in Australian and New Zealand Christianity* (New York: Lang, 2000), pp. 336f.

[33] Christopher Lethbridge, *The Wounded Lion: Octavius Hadfield* (Christchurch: Caxton, 1993), pp. 245, 263.

[34] Warren Limbrick, *Bishop Selwyn in New Zealand 1841–68* (Palmerston North: Dunmore Press, 1983).

co-operated with Selwyn's vision. Selwyn's genius lay in providing, in 1857, the New Zealand church with a constitution which gave the church a legal independence from the Church of England. Selwyn was keen to ordain Maori, but was critical of the poor educational provision which the CMS had so far provided. His insistence on some knowledge of Latin and Greek, as well as English, was regarded as unrealistic by the missionaries. He ordained the first deacon, Rota Waitoa, in 1853, but kept him a deacon for seven years – it was, in fact, Bishop Williams who finally ordained him as priest in 1860.

Allan Davidson believes that this delay in promoting a Maori clergy came at a critical time for the life of the Maori church,[35] and helped to fuel the discontent which produced a series of schisms from the Anglican church: for example the King movement, which attempted to combine Christian adherence with a recognition of traditional spiritual sensibilities. The missionaries condemned the King movement as syncretistic and a revival of paganism, and their negative attitude was exacerbated by the killing in 1865 of C. S. Volker, a CMS missionary accused of being a government spy.

After a slow start, the number of Maori ordinations increased. But inexorably the importance of the Maori work declined – in the early years of Waiapu diocese, synods were conducted in Maori, but by the end of the century the diocesan centre had been moved to Napier, the white-dominated town, and English became the first language. In 1877 Hemi Matenga asked why there were Maori Members of Parliament and magistrates, but no bishop. Bishop Crowther had given Africans a black bishop. 'Let it not be said because a man is a Maori he is unfit to be a bishop.' Or had Crowther only been appointed because whites could not survive in those tropical climes?[36]

In 1902 the CMS formally withdrew from work in New Zealand at a time when the future of a distinctive Maori identity was uncertain. In the early years of the century a revival occurred within Maori parishes fostered by Wiremu Ratana, who came from a strong Anglican family from Waiapu. After the First World War he embarked on a mission of charismatic healing, preaching that God wanted to make a covenant with the Maori Remnant. Maori should forsake their reliance on *tohunga*

[35] Davidson, 'Culture and Ecclesiology', in Kevin Ward and Brian Stanley, *The Church Mission Society and World Christianity 1799–1999* (Richmond: Curzon and Grand Rapids: Eerdmans, 2000), pp. 214–15.

[36] Davidson and Lineham, *Transplanted Christianity*, pp. 149–50. Matenga was writing in a Maori-language newspaper in 1877.

(traditional religious specialists) and believe in the Trinity. Parallels could be drawn with the evangelistic work of Prophet Harris in West Africa at around the same time. At first the Anglican authorities supported the movement, but they gradually became hostile and by 1925 a separate Ratana church was formed.[37] Anglicans were again challenged about facile assumptions of assimilation. A commission, which included the Maori politician and Anglican layman Sir Apirana Ngata, recommended that a Maori diocese be created. But Maori rejected the proposal that Herbert Williams be bishop – they were not prepared to be represented by a Pakeha, even the grandson of the pioneer missionary. In 1928, F. A. Bennett, a Maori, was appointed as a suffragan to the Bishop of Waiapu with the title 'Bishop of Aotearoa'. This was not a complete success: his role 'was circumscribed by ecclesiastical restrictions and an underlying assimilationist mind-set'. By the 1980s a radical reassessment of Maori culture was taking place, which resulted in an affirmation of New Zealand as a 'bicultural' society. This led in 1992 to the radical reshaping of the church with the assertion that the one Anglican church consisted of three *tikanga* (cultural streams): Maori, Pakeha and Polynesian.[38]

POLYNESIA AND HAWAII

Bishop Selwyn had promoted missionary work among Polynesians, and spent much of his ministry visiting the islands. But he found that the LMS and Methodists were already established, and he never had the resources to make a breakthrough. The CMS also did not feel able to extend its work beyond its Maori base. Where Anglicans did begin to have an impact was among minority groups. For example, in Fiji, it had some minor success in establishing pastoral work among Solomon Islanders, descendants of plantation workers who felt marginalised. In 1902 Anglicans began work in Tonga. Methodism had become virtually the established church of Tonga, but had divided into a number of competing groups. This enabled the Anglicans to establish a niche for themselves. For the first twenty-five years the work was sustained primarily through the labours of a Chinese priest from Hawaii, Yim San Mark. The church has remained small, but has produced a steady stream of church workers and ordinands (trained at St John's College in

[37] J. M. Henderson, *Ratana: The Man, the Church, the Political Movement* (Wellington: Polynesian Society, 1972) and Lethbridge, *The Wounded Lion*, pp. 297–302.

[38] Davidson in Ward and Stanley, *The Church Mission Society and World Christianity*, pp. 223–7.

Auckland) and religious. Many have worked in other islands of Polynesia and beyond. In a strongly Protestant Christian culture, shaped by Methodism, the spirituality of the Anglican church in Polynesia, as in the Pacific islands generally, is strongly Catholic.[39]

The first Anglican bishop in Tonga had been Alfred Willis (1902–6), who came there after retiring as bishop in Hawaii. Fifty years before the arrival of Anglicanism in Methodist Tonga, Anglicans had entered Hawaii, where American Congregationalists had created a vigorous Protestant 'establishment'. The Congregationalists had been in Hawaii since the 1820s under royal patronage, especially of the Queen Mother, Kaahumanu. Some of her descendants were less than enthusiastic about the puritanism of Congregationalism. The visit of the ruler, Alexander Kamehameha, to London in 1849 led to his inviting an Anglican mission. The 'Reformed Catholic' Church which resulted was a somewhat exotic creation. It took the long episcopate of Willis, from 1870 to 1900, to enable the church to move towards a more mainstream Anglican position. In 1893 the Americans overthrew the monarchy and in 1900, when Hawaii became a dependency of the United States, the American Episcopal Church took over responsibility for its continued development.[40]

MELANESIA AND NEW GUINEA

With the Congregationalists and Methodists dominating the life of the central and eastern Pacific islands, Selwyn looked to the western Pacific, Melanesia, to establish a strong Anglican presence. Founded in 1849, the Melanesian Mission was led by John Coleridge Patteson, who in 1861 was consecrated as missionary bishop by Selwyn. The headquarters of the mission was Norfolk Island (between New Zealand and Australia), where St Barnabas College became the centre for training evangelists and catechists recruited from the islands which stretched in a chain as far as the Solomon Islands. Robert Codrington was for long head of the school. His book *The Melanesians* (1891) was a major anthropological work, which, among other things, introduced the word *mana* (supernatural power) into religious vocabulary. The approach of the missionaries was one of respect for local customs and traditions, within the framework of a benign paternalism exercised by the upper-class Oxbridge celibate

[39] A. K. Davidson (ed.), *Tongan Anglicans 1902–2002* (Auckland: College of the Diocese of Polynesia, 2002).

[40] John Garrett, *To Live among the Stars: Christian Origins in Oceania* (Geneva and Suva: WCC, 1982), pp. 262ff.

missionaries. Norfolk Island was not the ideal centre for missionary work – it was too remote from the populous Solomon Islands to the north.

The great problem facing the islands in the 1860s was 'blackbirding' – the unscrupulous and violent recruitment of islanders to work on the sugar cane and cotton plantations of Fiji or Queensland. The resentment at the activities of the recruiters led directly to the death of Bishop Patteson in 1871, on his arrival on Nakapu in the Santa Cruz cluster, one of the few Polynesian islands in this Melanesian area. Patteson was killed by an islander angry at his son's abduction by blackbirders. Patteson's martyrdom led to the first serious British attempts to clamp down on the trade. In common with much Anglo-Catholic mission strategy in the Pacific, the Melanesian Mission focused attention on village life, aiming to establish a rural Catholicism which drew its inspiration from a somewhat romantic vision of the integration of faith and life in medieval Christianity. This contrasted with the more aggressive, negative approach to 'paganism' adopted by Protestant missions, where an insensitivity to traditional culture served to produce a much more dynamic, progressive and individualistic Christian community. The drawback for the Anglicans was their slowness to take pidgin seriously as a lingua franca, and their failure to follow up Melanesians who went as migrant labourers to the plantations of Queensland or Fiji, places where workers became particularly responsive to the Christian message. The potential for such converts to return home as evangelists was enormous, and they could reach places where the mission boat, the *Southern Cross*, would never go.[41] The limitations of a mission staffed almost exclusively by single celibate priests were highlighted at the turn of the century by a succession of homosexual scandals. It was only in 1905 that women were recruited for the mission. By this time Methodist and Marist missions were providing serious competition for the Anglican work. Anglicans remained pre-eminent on the Bank Islands, and on the Nggela Islands and Santa Isabel in the Solomon range.

The traditional checks and balances of Melanesian warfare had been seriously upset by the intrusion of European traders, by fire-arms and new, deadlier forms of poison, creating what has been described as 'highly anxiety-ridden' societies in which headhunting, cannibalism and violence increased. Oblivious to the extent to which the Christian religion might contribute to this chronic insecurity, Christianity was promoted as a

[41] David Hilliard, *God's Gentlemen: A History of the Melanesian Mission 1849–1942* (St Lucia: Queensland University Press, 1978).

bringer of peace, offering new shrines and new rituals to replace the old spiritual values which had become associated with malign and fearsome forces.[42] On Santa Isabel, Mano Wadrokal, a catechist born on the island, and others like him, was crucial in the Christianisation of the whole island. One of the important changes which the new religion brought was a replacement of the older forms of religious expression, the secret societies, by strong Anglican associations and guilds: the Mothers' Union, Servers' Guilds and religious brotherhoods and sisterhoods.

One of the most remarkable of Solomon Island Christians was Ini Kopuria, from Guadalcanal. Baptised as a child, he was educated at St Barnabas College on Norfolk Island. After school he joined the colonial police force. Injured in the course of making an arrest, he found himself in hospital. Like Loyola before him, he was thus given the chance to reflect on his military life and to dedicate himself to the work of Christ. He wrote to the bishop telling him of his vision to evangelise unreached peoples beyond the coastal plains, and also among the Polynesian minority who inhabited some of the remoter islands. 'I have visited all the villages as a police sergeant and they all know me; why not go to them now as a missionary?' In 1925 Kopuria founded a brotherhood dedicated to this work.

> The purpose of the Brotherhood was evangelistic ... but as a Melanesian Kopuria evangelized in a Melanesian way. He sought not to draw the people away from their villages and communities but to take Christ to them. The coming of Christ should not go hand-in-hand with the invasion of a foreign culture and individualistic concept of personal salvation without consideration for one's own people.[43]

Kopuria himself decided to get married in 1940. The order which he founded makes the Evangelical vows of poverty, obedience and chastity. But celibacy is seen as a commitment for a particular period. Many leave the order to get married. Kopuria also created an Order of Companions in the villages evangelised by the brothers, with a commitment to prayer and financial support. The brotherhood has become an important evangelistic and social task force throughout the church in Melanesia, and beyond in Carpentaria, Papua New Guinea and Fiji. Its corporate and democratic nature contrasts strongly with the intense individualism of the Australian bush brotherhoods. Kopuria was particularly interested in

[42] Darrell L. Whiteman, 'Melanesians and Missionaries', Ph.D. dissertation, Illinois University, 1980.

[43] Richard Carter, 'Religious Orders', in Andrew Wingate, Kevin Ward, Carrie Pemberton and Wilson Sitshebo (eds.), *Anglicanism: A Global Communion* (London: Mowbray, 1998), p. 47.

conflict resolution at family, village and clan level. In recent years this has been extended to attempts at bridge building between rebels and the government in the Solomon Islands, a ministry which has led to the killing of a number of brothers. In modern church history, there are many examples of successful religious orders for women. The Melanesian Brotherhood is a rare example of a thriving and innovative order which utilises the enthusiasm and dedication of young men.

During the Second World War, some European missionaries in Melanesia were executed during the Japanese occupation. The same was true of a number of Anglican missionaries in Papua New Guinea, which was also occupied. An Anglican mission on Catholic lines (but with the participation of a Sydney Evangelical, Copland King) was established in 1891 by Fr Albert Mclaren, supported by the Australian Board of Mission and by the Archbishop of Sydney. PNG was one of the last places in the area to feel the impact of an alien culture. The missionaries, like their earlier Melanesian counterparts or the American missionaries in the Philippines, aimed to infuse the remote tribal communities of the interior with a rural civilisation based on Catholic Christian values. For a long time they neglected education in English, but were also hostile to pidgin, and although they utilised the services of Melanesian teachers from the Queensland plantations, they feared that they might corrupt a people whom they too easily described as belonging to 'a child race'.[44] The first Papuan priest, Peter Rautamara, was ordained in 1917.

CONCLUSION

Although Christianity is the dominant 'world' religion in this region, the religious situation is, in fact, surprisingly diverse. Anglicanism comes with the mark of Englishness and its establishment for the settler societies of Australia and New Zealand. But in the islands of Polynesia and Melanesia, it is small compared with Congregationalism and Methodism. Only in the western Pacific is an Anglican presence of paramount significance. Among the Aboriginal communities of Australia, there is a history of neglect and oppression. Nevertheless, especially in the North, an important Aboriginal Anglican witness has made itself felt with increasing self-confidence. Aboriginal Anglicanism remains to be fully accepted by the rest of the Anglican church in Australia. It is significant that a recent and otherwise perceptive study of Australian Anglicanism,

[44] Breward, *History of the Churches in Australasia*, p. 230.

A Church without Walls, should ignore completely the Aboriginal presence in the attempt to define the nature of Australian Anglicanism.[45] The contrast with New Zealand is profound. The 1989 prayer book, *He Karakia Mihinare o Aotearoa*, mixes English and Maori in 'a multitude of voices'. New Zealand's delight in variety has rather eluded Australian Anglicanism, still largely locked in its Catholic and Evangelical camps. New Zealand was relatively early in recognising the ministry of women: the first women priests were ordained in 1977. In Australia it took until 1992. By that time New Zealand had already elected the first Anglican woman diocesan bishop in the world, Penny Jamieson. Her consecration was, however, boycotted by Maori bishop Verco. Women's ordination remains a problem for the churches of Polynesia and Melanesia.

All societies, in their different ways, have to face the challenge of a growing secularism: Bruce Kaye speaks of a climate and life style inducing 'a laid back, even horizontal disposition'.[46] Anglicanism is losing members in many parts of Australasia at an alarming rate, not only to a non-religious approach to life, or the delights of laid-back hedonism, but also to Pentecostalism. Here Sydney Evangelicals have perhaps risen to the challenge more actively than other types of Anglicanism, by promoting charismatic worship and vigorous youth programmes. Sydney Evangelicalism is abrasively counter-cultural, but also strategic in its utilisation of the resources of urban capitalism. On the islands, Christianity has often provided ways of integrating modernity with tradition. Here too Pentecostalism is challenging the forms in which that integration has hitherto taken place, something which even Catholic forms of Anglicanism increasingly have to come to terms with.

[45] Kaye, *A Church without Walls*. To be fair to Kaye, his magnificent *Anglicanism in Australia: A History* makes up for this neglect by a long and fascinating chapter on indigenous people by John Harris.

[46] Kaye, *A Church without Walls*, p. 112.

CHAPTER 15

The Anglican communion: escaping the Anglo-Saxon captivity of the church?

> *Ecclesia Anglicana* by virtue of its provenance is English in texture and fibre . . .
> All too often the bishop has become a carbon copy of the English bishop whose office and style has been accommodated to the English culture, particularly the upper-class culture. A classic example is the African bishop being addressed as the Lord Bishop of Cape Coast or Tamale or Freetown. The title reflects an English culture and social structure which are irrelevant to the African situation . . . While African or Asian or Pacific Anglicans contribute to their own captivity to the Anglo-Saxon *ecclesia Anglicana*, the captivity is also imposed from outside.[1]

This extract from an essay by John Pobee, a Ghanaian Anglican, comes from Sykes and Booty's 1988 *Study of Anglicanism*. As if to reinforce the 'Anglo-Saxon captivity', Pobee's contribution is the only one to emanate from the South. The aim of the present book has been to demonstrate that, despite the burdens of colonialism and the 'colonisation of the consciousness' to which Pobee adverts, indigenous forms of local Anglicanism have asserted themselves. Even they, however, have been discounted and marginalised in thinking about the nature of Anglicanism. In 1965 the theologian Anthony Hanson could say of Anglicanism

> . . . this Communion is still astonishingly English in complexion. Indeed it is probably in this respect the most monochrome of all world denominations . . . the Church of England on the whole goes its way without paying much attention to the opinion and reactions of the rest of the Anglican Communion, whereas the rest of the Anglican Communion on the whole tends to look to the Church of England for approbation before any important step is taken.[2]

[1] Stephen Sykes and John Booty (ed.), *The Study of Anglicanism* (London: SPCK, 1988), pp. 395–6.
[2] A. T. Hanson, *Beyond Anglicanism* (London: Darton, Longman & Todd, 1965), pp. 20, 4.

'The Ecclesiastical Expansion of England', Bishop Barry had called it in 1894, echoing the title of a book by Sir John Seely, *The Expansion of England*, written in 1882. For him this was a triumphant development.

The creation of the institutional expression of a worldwide Anglicanism can be seen as part and parcel of that expansionism. But Archbishop Longley resisted all calls to establish a highly regimented hierarchical or centralised body, and subsequent Lambeth Conferences have emphasised their advisory and fraternal functions rather than their role as a doctrinal or legislative body. The 'captivity of the church' was to take a cultural rather than an institutional form. There were many reasons in 1867 why that should be so, not least the need to accommodate American bishops. Evangelicals had a fear of 'papalism' and any development which cast doubt on the English Protestant constitutional settlement. But the need for a 'pan-Anglican' conference was precisely that Anglicanism could no longer be accommodated within the structure of a national established church. Canada in particular, having more or less lost the bruising conflict over establishment within British North America, felt a need to overcome its isolation. There was a general desire to condemn Bishop Colenso of Natal for his unorthodoxy. The synod of the Church in Canada had already issued such a condemnation. But Longley was anxious to avert a controversy with the state and, at the first Lambeth Conference, was able to fend off an official pronouncement of condemnation. According to Stephenson, Longley's careful management of the Conference and his ability to deflect it from being primarily a meeting to condemn Colenso prevented serious acrimony and enabled the Lambeth Conference to be accepted as a 'purely advisory, deliberative, consultative body', in which the Archbishop of Canterbury does not have the status of Patriarch but is *primus inter pares*.[3]

Colenso was actually invited to attend the first Lambeth Conference, but, wisely perhaps, kept away. The only African bishop, Samuel Crowther, was invited, but did not attend. This may be connected to the indifference, if not hostility, of the CMS to the Conference. Crowther first attended the Conference of 1888, where he was appointed to a committee considering polygamy among 'heathen converts'. The Conference asserted that:

The sanctity of marriage as a Christian obligation implies the faithful union of one man with one women until the union is severed by death . . . While we have refrained from offering advice on minor points, leaving these to be settled by local

[3] Alan Stephenson, *The First Lambeth Conference* (London: SPCK, 1967), pp. 268–79, 325.

authorities of the Church, we have laid down some broad lines on which alone we consider that the missionary may safely act. Our first care has been to maintain and protect the Christian conception of marriage, believing that any immediate and rapid successes which might otherwise have been secured in the mission-field would be dearly purchased by any lowering or confusion of this idea.[4]

The Conference was anxious not to condemn those who, in the past, had followed a different practice, and was solicitous of those who might find the guidelines difficult to implement in the future. This has tended to be the style adopted by successive Lambeth Conferences on ethical questions: to establish a broad consensus, to lay down general guidelines, to be sensitive to the difficulties of practical implementation, and not to shut down debate or to preclude further development. Thus the 1920 Conference warned against 'the use of unnatural means for the avoidance of conception' (warning of physical, moral and religious dangers). But by 1930 a much more positive acceptance of birth control was enunciated.[5]

Lambeth Conferences have also been wary of defining doctrine; or, rather, defining doctrine in too precise a manner. The 1888 Lambeth Conference was particularly important in laying down, not a creedal statement of the nature of Anglicanism, but a template around which Anglican churches are structured. This is the famous Chicago–Lambeth Quadrilateral. The Quadrilateral was first mooted by William Reed Huntington (1838–1909), the rector of Grace Church in New York City. His proposal was discussed by the American bishops meeting in Chicago, and, with some modifications, these were adopted by the Lambeth Conference:

That, in the opinion of this Conference, the following Articles supply a basis on which approach may be by God's blessing made towards Home Reunion:–

(A) The Holy Scriptures of the Old and New Testaments, as 'containing all things necessary to salvation', and as being the rule and ultimate standard of faith.
(B) The Apostles' Creed, as the Baptismal Symbol; and the Nicene Creed, as the sufficient statement of the Christian faith.
(C) The two Sacraments ordained by Christ Himself – Baptism and the Supper of the Lord – ministered with unfailing use of Christ's words of Institution, and of the elements ordained by Him.
(D) The Historic Episcopate, locally adapted in the methods of its administration to the varying needs of the nations and peoples called of God into the Unity of His Church.[6]

[4] [Archbishop Davidson,] *The Six Lambeth Conferences 1867–1920* (London: SPCK, 1929), pp. 108–9, 133–5.
[5] Alan Stephenson, *Anglicanism and the Lambeth Conferences* (London: SPCK, 1978), pp. 149, 165.
[6] *The Six Lambeth Conferences*, p. 122; G. R. Evans and J. Robert Wright (eds.), *The Anglican Tradition: A Handbook of Sources* (London: SPCK, 1991), pp. 345–6, 354–5.

Huntington had originally formulated his ideas in a book written in 1870, *The Church Idea.* He saw the Episcopal Church as the 'national church' of the United States. By this he meant that the Episcopal Church had a national mission within America, to embody in some way the genius of what the United States was and stood for. But 'national' also in that Huntington hoped that his denomination could become a focus of unity for a wide spectrum of church traditions within the country, the social conscience of the nation.[7] It was in the light of this that the Lambeth Conference of 1920 made its 'Appeal to All Christian People'.[8]

Useful as the Quadrilateral has been in giving a basic definition of the essentials of what a Christian church should be, and what Anglicanism in particular claims to possess, it has not been without its critics. In 1887 it was promoted by the Americans as an alternative to the classical Anglican formularies in the definition of an Episcopal Church in Japan. Remarkable as it now seems, during these years there was some optimism that such a church could become the 'national church' of Japan – in the sense of uniting all non-Roman Christians into a common structure. Even more remarkably, there was hope that such a church, shorn of its particular western denominationalism, might be adopted by the rejuvenated Japanese state as the Japanese official religion. In the end this was rejected in favour of a revived and (re)invented Shintoism in the Constitution of 1891. But the Nippon Sei Ko Kai is testimony to the strength of the American national ideal.

But if, in Japan (and later in early-twentieth-century China), the idea of a 'national' church translated into an assertion of a common interest between diverse nationalities and episcopal churchmanship, it could also be transposed into another key. The idea of a national church could fire American ideas of manifest destiny and British ideas of imperial grandeur. In 1899, Bishop Montgomery, soon to become General Secretary of the SPG, looked forward to the church becoming 'more completely an imperial Church'. In 1909, he expanded on this vision:

> Our wide experience in temperaments, even to extremes, within the church of our race, [is] one of our greatest assets in helping to create race Churches in all Continents . . . to us it is an axiom, born of temperament, that while the church must be Catholic it must also be racially and nationally expressed and the government must be national . . .[9]

[7] Ian T. Douglas, '"A Light to the Nations": Episcopal Foreign Missions in Historical Perspective', *Anglican and Episcopal History* 61. 4 (December 1992), p. 457.

[8] Evans and Wright, *The Anglican Tradition*, p. 378.

[9] Quoted by Jeffrey L. Richey in 'Catholicity and Culture in China', *Anglican and Episcopal History* 67.2 (June 1998), p. 198.

Yates' comment on Montgomery seems apposite:

It is a sad fact that Henry Venn, who never left his office desk in London, showed a far greater grasp of what Anglican mission should become than the widely travelled Montgomery. Here, rather than the self-governing, self-extending 'native' churches, was a vision of imperial Anglicanism, which bound the colonial churches to Britain in perpetuity, a corollary of which was white leadership by Europeans.[10]

However, this cannot be taken as a contrast between the two main Anglican mission societies, the CMS and the SPG. It is more symptomatic of the difference between the mid- and late-Victorian understandings of empire. The growing sense of a worldwide Anglican identity coincided with the age of high imperialism. This set the tone for the development of 'diocesanisation' and the creation of local autonomous provinces within the Anglican communion. The strong sense of catholicity entailed in this progress was somewhat subverted, for the first half of the twentieth century, by the strong idea of imperial tutelage.[11]

'Diocesanisation' described the process by which churches which had been under missionary supervision achieved autonomy. However, in the period of high imperialism, it was overwhelmingly under the tutelage of a bishop who was British. Even in those colonies which achieved dominion status, with substantial settler populations, clergy from England were chosen, sometimes with no overseas experience at all. In South Africa and Australia this remained the norm until well into the twentieth century. As a result, the representation of Anglicanism worldwide at an international level remained overwhelmingly white and British well beyond the demise of empire.

Geoffrey Fisher, Archbishop of Canterbury from 1945 to 1961, presided over two Lambeth Conferences. The post-war meeting of 1948 included a number of Chinese and Japanese bishops, but not those from the newly formed Church of South India, though Bishop de Mel, assistant bishop in Colombo (Ceylon), did attend.[12] The main controversy at this meeting was the status of the CSI, and full recognition was denied. Chinese bishops were absent from the 1958 Conference, though by then there were bishops from North India, and a number of African bishops. Fisher was

[10] Review by T. E. Yates, *Theology* 108 (January/February 2005, p. 65, of Andrew Porter (ed.), *The Imperial Horizons of British Protestant Missions 1880–1914* (Grand Rapids: Eerdmans, 2003).

[11] Ken Farrimond, 'The Policy of the Church Missionary Society concerning the Development of Self-Governing Indigenous Churches 1900–1942', Ph.D. dissertation, University of Leeds , 2003.

[12] Edward Carpenter, *Archbishop Fisher – His Life and Times* (Norwich: Canterbury Press, 1991), p. 459.

the first Archbishop to travel widely. The visits to West and East Africa were to inaugurate new autonomous provinces and to consecrate the first African diocesan bishops. In many ways, under Fisher, Canterbury achieved its greatest influence in the communion worldwide. Fisher was involved in more episcopal appointments than ever. The continuing pull of empire can be seen in his farewell to the bishops at the Lambeth Conference of 1958:

> He was particularly moved to see standing in front of him R. H. Owen, Archbishop of New Zealand, whom he had known at Oxford and who had been headmaster of Uppingham while he was at Repton. As they departed he said: 'We have in the last five weeks been living close to the kingdom of heaven' and then his voice faltered. He ended hurriedly and turned to go out. He had burst into tears.[13]

But if Owen represented the belated importance of English public-school establishment figures within the global communion, there were also the African bishops whose consecration Fisher had been involved in, who represented the first signs of a future communion: 'an international and inter-racial Christian fellowship, rather than an almost accidental imperial and missionary prolongation of the Established Church of the English nation'.[14]

Fisher relied heavily for his understanding of the general movements within Africa and Asia on Max Warren, the General Secretary of the CMS from 1942 to 1963. In his pioneering Memorandum of 1944, Warren discerned that the most important issues with which the 'sending' churches would need to deal in a post-war world were nationalism and the growth of autonomous indigenous churches. Warren combined considerable abilities as a diplomat (able to communicate with government as well as in ecclesiastical circles) with an ability to articulate a theology of mission which was responsive to the aspirations of Asians and Africans. He stressed 'Christian presence' as a missionary theme, one of careful, prayerful listening, 'a theology of attention'. If Warren prepared the English church for the revocation of power, and the transition from mission to church, his successor as CMS General Secretary, John V. Taylor, explored the continuing importance of mission in a world where missionaries did not, and should not, exercise power.[15]

[13] Ibid., p. 476.

[14] Adrian Hastings, *A History of English Christianity 1920–1985* (London: Collins, 1986), p. 449.

[15] Kevin Ward, ' "A Theology of Attention": The CMS Tradition at the End of the Colonial Era in Africa', in Frieder Ludwig and Afe Adogame (eds.), *European Traditions in the Study of Religion in Africa* (Wiesbaden: Harrassowitz Verlag, 2004), pp. 227–36.

The financial strength of the US Episcopal Church was, in the post-war years, vital for creating and sustaining the institutional life of the Anglican fellowship. In 1959 Fisher appointed Stephen Bayne (Bishop of Olympia, Washington State) as the first Anglican Executive Officer. Bayne expressed his sense of the changing nature of the communion at the Toronto Anglican Congress in 1963:

> The Anglican Communion is not an organisation by which older and stronger Churches can extend their influence over younger and weaker Churches. We are not interested in branch offices around the world. We care rather for a household within which many Churches, representing many cultures and peoples, take their self-reliant and buoyant place in full brotherhood, each giving and receiving, each receiving and learning. Therefore our organisation must both reflect this and nourish it.[16]

At the Toronto Congress, Bayne issued a challenge for the communion to engage in 'Mutual Responsibility and Interdependence in the Body of Christ'. The idea became a watchword: 'MRI'. It was intended to promote a redistribution of resources of money and expertise from richer parts of the communion to the poorer in a more concerted way, one in which the whole communion actively shared; but in the end the MRI process failed in its goal to overcome the division between 'giving' and 'receiving' churches, the process sometimes becoming a shopping list of requirements rather than real engagement.[17]

The successors to MRI, the Partners in Mission programmes, have tried, with varying success, to overcome these limitations. Another attempt to develop robust forms of association came with the establishment, in 1969, of the Anglican Consultative Council, with clerical and lay as well as episcopal membership. The first meeting was held in 1971 in Limuru, Kenya, and there have been regular meetings outside the north Atlantic. In 1971 John Howe, formerly bishop of St Andrew's, Dunkeld and Dunblane, in Scotland, became the first Secretary General of the ACC. In his reflections on his eleven years with the ACC, he notes two 'watersheds'. One had been reached and crossed by the 1970s – the internationalisation of the Anglican communion and its development as a 'world-wide family'. The other watershed had yet to be negotiated:

> The indigenous sharing of a faith requires an adequate universal agreement on the acceptable limits of faith and practice in the Anglican Communion. The

[16] John Howe, *Highways and Hedges: Anglicanism and the Universal Church* (Toronto: Anglican Book Centre, 1985), p. 79.

[17] John Clarke, in Kevin Ward and Brian Stanley, *The Church Mission Society and World Christianity 1799–1999* (Richmond: Curzon and Grand Rapids: Eerdmans, 2000), p. 328.

> need is not for acceptance of a universal, total, and therefore imposed, canon law. In people and situations so different, there will always be diversity, and a measure of diversity is welcome. The norm does not require the same details everywhere ... The emphasis here is on the need to agree the limits of interpretation, and consequently of practice.[18]

By and large, liturgical revision has been accomplished in many of the provinces of the church without becoming a major issue for the unity of the communion as such, though it has often been accompanied by very heated debates within provinces. This is especially so in the United States. Though once the Book of Common Prayer was seen as a touchstone of what it meant to be Anglican, from the 1970s the idea of variety and flexibility in liturgy seems to have been accepted as part of appropriate contextualisation and indigenisation of the church. The debate on women priests and bishops has not been so unproblematic. It has been an issue which has seriously divided provinces, especially in North America and in Britain, and, for substantial minorities, has thrown in doubt the bonds of unity. Although the first ordinations of women to the priesthood occurred in Hong Kong, theological controversy about the propriety of women's ordination was largely an issue for the churches of the 'North'. Women's ordination was seen by some in the Anglo-Catholic tradition particularly as threatening the fourth article of the Chicago–Lambeth Quadrilateral with its distinctive view of Christian ministry. It was this article which was always a major stumbling block in ecumenical relations. The 1968 Conference had decided that the arguments for women's ordination were inconclusive, and advised caution. The 1978 Conference was faced with the fact that not only Hong Kong, but Canada, ECUSA and New Zealand had ordained women. In a carefully worded statement, and by a large majority, the bishops urged all member churches to respect provincial autonomy and to acknowledge 'the legal right of each Church to make its own decision about the appropriateness of admitting women to Holy Orders'. While recognising that such acceptance of 'variety of doctrine and practice' would be disappointing to Catholic and Orthodox churches, the resolution stressed that 'the holding together of diversity within a unity of faith and worship is part of the Anglican heritage'. It affirmed that those who did ordain women intended to ordain them into 'the historic ministry of the Church'.[19]

[18] John Howe, *Highways and Hedges*, p. 17.

[19] http://www.anglicancommunion.org. 1978 Lambeth Conference: Resolution 21.

Significantly, although there had been no strong call for women's ordination in much of Africa, and the issue was widely regarded as part of the secular liberal agenda of western societies, women's ordination has proceeded in many of the African Anglican provinces without a great deal of anguish or indeed much heated theological debate. Uganda and Kenya began to ordain women in the 1980s without waiting for the Church of England to act. By and large, clerical conservatism has not proved too much of an obstacle in East Africa. Although the avenue to ordination has been opened up for women, their position as priests remains a rather marginalised one in the church as a whole in Kenya and Uganda: women priests are few, and they have yet to achieve positions of real authority within male-dominated structures. The Church of the Province of Southern Africa has ordained women as priests. But the Church of Nigeria, which has always demonstrated extreme conservatism in its adherence to its traditional Evangelical heritage, has not done so. But, when the Episcopal Church of Sudan agreed to ordain women, it explicitly included ordination to the episcopate.

Not long after the 1988 Lambeth Conference, women were ordained to the episcopate: in 1989 Barbara Harris, an African American priest from Philadelphia, was made assistant bishop in the Massachusetts diocese. Later that year Penny Jamieson was elected as Diocesan Bishop of Dunedin in New Zealand, and consecrated in 1990. Potentially this created even greater problems for those opposed to women's ordination, since it was seen as having ramifications for the validity of all Anglican orders. Recognising the 'impaired communion' which the ordination of women to the episcopate might have caused, the 1998 Conference simply urged member churches to recognise that both groups were 'loyal Anglicans'.[20] Eleven women bishops were at the 1998 Conference. As one website puts it: 'There was some sullen non-cooperation, but little overt hostility from the male bishops.'[21]

One might ask why this issue, enormously contentious and divisive as it has been, has yet been handled with much less strain on the fundamental structures of the Anglican communion than the issue of homosexuality, which began to dominate discussions about the nature of the Anglican communion from 1998. In searching for some answers one can point to the slow incremental growth of the women's movement, which

[20] http://www.anglicancommunion.org. 1998 Lambeth Conference: Resolution III.2, 'The Unity of the Anglican Communion'.

[21] http://www.anglicancommunion.org. Katie Sherrod, 'First Female Bishops Find Warm Welcome at Lambeth Conference', 30 July 1998.

made the ordination issue the culmination of a long process beginning in the nineteenth century, and indeed was expressed first of all within the missionary movement. The issue has divided the churches in the North, uncovering deep theological division. But it has not sparked the same amount of animosity in the churches of the South. Social conservatism, rather than strongly held doctrinal or biblical considerations, has inhibited the movement for women's ordination in most churches of the South. Furthermore, no province has declared that this is an issue by which the communion stands or falls. Most have been content with the recommendation of the Eames Report, that the ordination of women generally, and of women bishops in particular, should be subject to the principle of 'reception' by which the validity of the changes can be assessed over time.

The issue of homosexuality, by contrast, erupted suddenly. It arouses the passions of the churches of the South in ways which women's ordination did not. Like women's ordination, it is considered by opponents to challenge the authority of Scripture and tradition. But in the case of homosexuality, a number of provinces have demonstrated that they are willing to see the communion fragment on this issue – it is a 'first-order' issue, that is, one of fundamental doctrinal importance. This is at first somewhat puzzling in that, whereas there were no women priests in the Anglican communion until the twentieth century, there have almost certainly been male clerics with a homosexual orientation for centuries, including Archbishops. The question becomes not primarily about the presence of homosexuals in the church, but about the condemnation of same-sex practice, and specifically whether such activity can be tolerated among the clergy.

At Lambeth 1978 the issue of homosexuality was raised in the context of general issues of relationships, marriage and sexuality:

> While we reaffirm heterosexuality as the scriptural norm, we recognise the need for deep and dispassionate study of the question of homosexuality, which would take seriously both the teaching of Scripture and the results of scientific and medical research. The Church, recognising the need for pastoral concern for those who are homosexual, encourages dialogue with them. (We note with satisfaction that such studies are now proceeding in some member Churches of the Anglican Communion.)[22]

The very fact that the issue was openly discussed was used by President Idi Amin of Uganda as a way of discrediting the Church of Uganda. He

[22] http://www.anglicancommunion.org. 1978 Lambeth Conference: Resolution 10.

had allowed the bishops to attend Lambeth, but they were accompanied by a body of security men posing as reporters or embassy officials. This was a year after the assassination of Archbishop Luwum, and Amin was deeply suspicious of the church. He also liked to mock the Anglican church as being the creation of the lust of Henry VIII for more wives.[23]

Lambeth 1988 reaffirmed the previous declaration, but put the issue within a context of human rights and of pastoral care for persons of homosexual orientation. The Conference also revisited the decision of the Lambeth Conference of 1888, and recommended that under certain strictly defined conditions, a polygamist 'who responds to the Gospel and wishes to join the Anglican Church may be baptized and confirmed with his believing wives and children'. But he had to promise not to enter into any new polygamous union.[24] The tenor of the resolutions on homosexuality and on polygamy suggests an openness to new insights, rather like the changes in attitudes to contraception between 1920 and 1958. But any such progression was negated by the experience of the Lambeth Conference of 1998.

No previous Lambeth Conference had generated such polarisation as Resolution 1:10 of the 1998 Conference, eventually agreed, after an emotional debate:

This Conference

a. commends to the Church the subsection report on human sexuality
b. in view of the teaching of Scripture, upholds faithfulness in marriage between a man and a woman in lifelong union, and believes that abstinence is right for those who are not called to marriage;
c. recognises that there are among us persons who experience themselves as having a homosexual orientation. Many of these are members of the Church and are seeking the pastoral care, moral direction of the Church, and God's transforming power for the living of their lives and the ordering of relationship. We commit ourselves to listen to the experience of homosexual persons and we wish to assure them that they are loved by God and that all baptised, believing and faithful persons, regardless of sexual orientation, are full members of the Body of Christ;
d. while rejecting homosexual practice as incompatible with Scripture, calls on all our people to minister pastorally and sensitively to all irrespective of sexual orientation and to condemn irrational fear of homosexuals, violence within marriage and any trivialisation and commercialisation of sex;

[23] K. Ward, 'The Church of Uganda amidst Conflict' in H. B. Hansen and M. Twaddle (eds.), *Religion and Politics in East Africa* (London: James Currey, 1995).

[24] http://www.anglicancommunion.org. 1988 Lambeth Conference: Resolutions 64 and 26.

e. cannot advise the legitimising or blessing of same sex unions nor ordaining those involved in same gender unions
f. [asks for a monitoring process of work done on these issues]
g. [notes the significance of the Kuala Lumpur Statement on Human Sexuality . . .][25]

The Resolution was affirmed by 526 bishops and opposed by 70, with 45 abstaining.[26] Despite the large majority, this was not a compromise motion reconciling differing views. In fact, the motion was revised during the debate to give it a harder edge. In this regard Resolution 1:10 is a departure from previous practice, aimed at achieving consensus. Resolutions on women's ministry, for example, had been primarily concerned with maintaining unity despite those differences. At the very first Lambeth Conference in 1867, a resolution condemning Bishop Colenso might well have so divided the Conference that no further meetings would have been possible. Archbishop Longley skilfully avoided putting the issue to a formal resolution. The previously most divisive issue was that concerning the status of the united Church of South India in 1948. The failure to reach any satisfactory conclusion had resulted in the isolation of the CSI from Anglican gatherings for some forty years.

Another sign that the 1998 resolution on human sexuality appears to depart from the usual Lambeth practice is that it has come to be regarded as a touchstone of orthodoxy, a way of defining the limits of change and of curbing provincial autonomy. The authorisation of a service of blessing for same-sex partners in the Canadian diocese of New Westminster in 2003, the agreement of the General Convention of the Episcopal Church of the USA to consecrate Gene Robinson (an open homosexual living with a partner) as Bishop of New Hampshire, and his consecration on 2 November 2003, caused a huge outcry. As well as encountering objections on biblical and theological grounds, these acts were condemned as an ostentatious flouting of the clear will of the 1998 Lambeth Conference as expressed in Resolution 1:10.

One of the novel features of this crisis, which has been noted again and again, is the importance of the churches of the South. The polarised positions have become more entrenched since 1998. To put the issues simply and simplistically: in the view of the South, a liberal majority in the churches of the North has dominated the affairs of Anglicanism, at least since the 1960s, giving in again and again to a secular liberalising

[25] http://www.anglicancommunion.org. 1998 Lambeth Conference: Resolution 1:10.
[26] The figures are given in Stephen Bates, *A Church at War: Anglicans and Homosexuality* (London: I. B. Tauris, 2004), p. 139.

agenda, and fatally compromising biblical orthodoxy and Catholic tradition. Although designed to halt the decline of the church, this policy has in fact simply colluded in the erosion of Christian values in society, has contributed to the growing irrelevance of the church and has assisted the disastrous numerical decline in church adherence. Meanwhile, in the South the church stands for an uncompromising Gospel. Biblical faith and traditional Christian morality are taken seriously. The church grows at a phenomenal rate. For long the Anglican churches of the South were marginalised and felt excluded from the affairs of communion. Their numerical growth was not matched by the weight of their contribution. They deferred to the experts from the older parts of the Anglican communion. Finally, in 1998, they were able to find their voice, to take an active part in shaping what kind of communion Anglicanism should be. In this determination, they have found allies from within sections of the older provinces, disaffected and silenced minorities within Evangelical and traditionalist Anglo-Catholic circles, who now at last find their understandings of Christian orthodoxy confirmed and supported after being on the defensive for so long. This feeling is clearly expressed by the campaigning group Anglican Mainstream, founded in the midst of the row in England over the appointment of a gay assistant bishop in the Oxford diocese in 1993: 'we may be marginalised in England, but we represent the vast majority of Anglicans of the two-thirds world'. The phrase 'two-thirds world' is often used by the Oxford Centre for Mission Studies (some of whose members were important in the establishment of Anglican Mainstream) and is meant to express the importance of the churches of the South, where Christianity is growing and vibrant. The older 'third-world' designation, by contrast, has come to signify the marginalisation of the South, its third-class status.

These ideas, somewhat crudely stated in the previous paragraph, are part of a more sophisticated reassessment of world Christianity associated with the missiological work of Andrew Walls and Lamin Sanneh, and expressed by Philip Jenkins in *The Next Christendom*: 'the center of gravity in the Christian world has shifted inexorably southwards, to Africa, Asia and Latin America'.[27] On the issue of homosexuality, Jenkins writes:

In the issues of homosexuality too, a chasm divided the world's religious communities, nowhere more visibly than in contemporary Africa . . . Viewed

[27] Philip Jenkins, *The Next Christendom: The Coming of Global Christianity* (Oxford: Oxford University Press, 2002), p. 2.

> over the span of history, African cultures are no more homogeneous in these matters than those of Europe ... In recent years, though, the revolutionary change in social attitudes toward homosexuality in Europe and North America has created a social gulf with many Third World societies ...
> The main difference is that these communities have not yet experienced the kind of secularizing and modernizing trends towards liberalization in these matters, to 'join the modern world'. They are doubly unlikely to do so, since these same trends are associated with Western cultural imperialism, and are blamed for the decline of religion in Europe and North America. Why should southerners wish to join this world if they have any chance of remaining separate?[28]

This neatly articulates the arguments also used by conservative Anglicans in the present crisis; and, as an objective argument in its own right, it makes sense. But it does not quite explain why the issue of homosexuality should have become the presenting issue which threatens the unity of the communion.

The issue began seriously to exercise Anglican bishops in the South in the preparation for the 1998 Lambeth Conference. In 1997 Anglican Christian leaders from the South met in Kuala Lumpur, Malaysia, for the second 'Anglican Encounter in the South' under the chair of the Archbishop of Nigeria, Joseph Adetiloye. The first Encounter meeting had been organised by the Council of the Anglican Provinces of Africa (CAPA) and had met in Limuru in 1994. A 'Statement on Human Sexuality' was issued by the 1997 meeting, which subsequently became a core document in the crisis over homosexuality. It acknowledged 'the complexity of our sexual nature' and human vulnerability to sexual sin. It stressed that human sexuality is to be expressed solely in the life-long union of marriage between a man and a woman; and that therefore all homosexual practice is sinful. Biblical teaching is unambiguous. But there is no conflict between 'clear biblical teaching and sensitive pastoral care'. The statement ends:

> 10. We are deeply concerned that the setting aside of biblical teaching in such actions as the ordination of practising homosexuals and the blessing of same-sex unions calls into question the authority of the Holy Scriptures. This is totally unacceptable to us.
> 11. This leads us to express concern about mutual accountability and interdependence within our Anglican Communion. As provinces and dioceses, we need to learn how to seek each other's counsel and wisdom in a spirit of true unity, and to reach a common mind before embarking on radical changes to Christian discipline and moral teaching.

[28] Ibid., pp. 200–1.

12. We live in a global village and must be more aware that the way we act in one part of the world can radically affect the mission and witness of the Church in another.[29]

The statement is eloquent in its expression of disturbance about changing understandings of sexuality in Britain and North America. In the absence of critical historical and theological assessments of the background to the Kuala Lumpur statement, it remains unclear why this issue, rather than others, should have been singled out for attention. It is intended as a warning to the churches of the 'North' and invokes the motto of the 1963 Toronto conference on mutual interdependence to stress the need to involve the South in the debate about changing sexual mores. As a statement of biblical principle it could be considered timely by those who sympathise with this reading of the Bible. But, it is questionable whether this is an issue about which it is possible or advisable to issue quasi-confessional statements, meant to close down debate rather than to continue to explore. Although, as Jenkins stated in the earlier quotation, many of the countries of the South have not yet confronted the issue of homosexuality, this ignores both the presence of indigenous forms of homosexual practice within traditional societies and the impact of 'modern' understandings even in the South. Christianity in Africa and Asia has in fact been one of the prime conveyers of the 'modern'. Modern Christian understandings of sexual relations – as being primarily between individuals and based on mutual attraction and affection, rather than on more social or economic considerations – are precisely the conditions which erode more traditional attitudes to sex and marriage in non-western societies. They also often undermine the traditional benign attitude to same-sex affective relationships (which are not seen as competing with obligations to marry). One of the deeply unfortunate consequences of the polarised positions on homosexuality has been the increase in homophobia within the countries of the South. Homophobia is as much a western intrusion as is modern homosexual identity. The inflammatory statements of Archbishop Akinola of Nigeria about homosexuals, in the short run at least, has made life for Nigerian gays more difficult. A similar situation has arisen in Uganda.

Southern Anglicans have also felt aggrieved at the statements of those whom they regard as arrogant 'liberals', campaigners such as Bishop Spong of New Jersey. Integrity, an American Episcopalian gay advocacy

[29] Statement on Human Sexuality, Kuala Lumpur Second Anglican Encounter in the South, 10–15 February 1997.

organisation, has developed a high-profile, in-your-face rhetoric, strategically understandable in an American context. But applied to Uganda, it profoundly alienated and irritated the bishops and was seen as demonstrating a neo-colonialist spirit. The consecration of Gene Robinson as Bishop of New Hampshire has been regarded as an intolerable attack on Christian values and has caused a number of provinces to declare that they are no longer in communion with ECUSA.

The crisis has been seen by African and Asian Christian leaders as a coming of age, the 'emergence from man's self-incurred immaturity', immaturity being 'the inability to use one's own understanding without the guidance of another'. Kant's definition of enlightenment seems rather ironic in this context. But the anti-liberal stance on homosexuality can also appeal to 'enlightenment' values. The Ugandan bishops have declared homosexuality to be 'unbiblical and inhuman'. Archbishop Akinola has compared homosexuality to an 'enslavement' from which the Gospel brings liberation – thus invoking the anti-slavery humanitarian movement which brought the Gospel to Nigeria in the first place. Archbishop Josiah Idowu-Fearon, of Kaduna, has been somewhat more restrained in his denunciations. He sees the problem as originating in American 'cultural arrogance'. Like Archbishop Orombi of Uganda he has defended the policy of refusing grants from ECUSA – distinguishing between 'sweet' and 'bitter' money. He has turned the metaphor of mature and young churches on its head – accusing the American church of being an unruly child whom the rest of the family must discipline. But if it will not come into line, then it may have to leave home.[30]

The Church in South Africa has had a very different stance on the issues from the East or West African bishops. The history of the struggle against apartheid has made the church sensitive to any form of discrimination which seems to exclude one group. Both Archbishop Tutu and his successor as Archbishop of Cape Town, Njongonkulu Ndungane, have been passionate in their appeal for the inclusion of homosexual people in the life of the church. But a group of Anglicans in the CPSA have questioned this stance, wondering whether the Church in South Africa really wants to ally itself with the declining churches of the North rather than the vibrant churches of the rest of Africa.

[30] For further discussion on these issues, see K. Ward, 'Marching or Stumbling towards a Christian Ethic? Homosexuality and African Anglicanism', in Terry Brown (ed.), *Other Voices, Other Worlds* (London: Darton, Longman & Todd, 2006), pp. 129–41.

Africa has its own intractable struggles with regard to sexual morality. Christians in Africa generally have failed to convince the majority of their membership that the strict marriage discipline taught by the churches is either practical or easily adaptable to African conditions. The African church has consistently refused to lower its standards in the face of laxity, and it feels that this strictness should equally apply to issues of homosexuality. But few pastors or leaders have been satisfied with a situation in which a large proportion of the congregation are denied Holy Communion because their marriage or partnerships are not approved by the church. And, within Anglicanism at least, marriage in the church is not the condition for baptism or membership of the church. The rules are, however, enforced rigorously for the clergy, and that is what makes the particular question of ordaining active homosexuals so hard to swallow for the African church.[31]

Yet there is a long tradition in African Anglicanism of debate about sexual ethics and discipline, which strict formal regulations have not inhibited. Unfortunately, outside South Africa, the strength of episcopal condemnation of homosexuality has stifled any debate on these issues among clergy and laity alike; and has helped to exacerbate or create a homophobic climate which contrasts with earlier, more relaxed attitudes.

In Africa, Christian preoccupation with homosexuality as an alternative life style is of fairly recent origin, precipitated by the debates at Lambeth in 1998 rather than expressing chronic anxieties. In Singapore, a burgeoning westernising, multi-ethnic society has prospered under a morally prescriptive and authoritarian rule. The success of the charismatic movement within the Singapore Anglican church since the 1960s has both given it a strong evangelistic, expansive impetus and heightened its tendency towards a hard-line moralism. According to the analysis of You-Leng Lim, this has reflected the anxieties of Singaporean society generally, embracing many 'western' values and yet suspicious of those which are deemed too permissive or subversive:

> The confidence of Singapore and other South East Asian countries in matters of politics, economics and church is accompanied by its shadow: the fear of subversion, deflection and heresy... The mistake is for any community to completely externalize this into an international 'clash of civilization', or project it into a Manichaean struggle of heretics and orthodox. Walking the Anglican

[31] K. Ward, 'Same-Sex Relations in Africa and the Debate on Homosexuality in East African Anglicanism', *Anglican Theological Review* 84.1 (2002), pp. 81–111.

middle path with a measure of consciousness for the complex and symbolic might well provide a welcomed sobriety for all.[32]

It is difficult to accept that the moral absolutism evinced in the homosexuality debate is primarily concerned with the divergence between a largely doctrinally and ethically conservative South and a liberal and permissive North. In many ways, indeed, it is a spill-over of the mounting civil war within American society between liberal and conservative religion. It is highly possible that the conflict within ECUSA will produce a fragmentation and an institutional split. This would be ironic in that the Episcopal Church was one of the few Protestant churches which avoided division over slavery in the nineteenth century or over fundamentalism in the early twentieth century. But now, it appears to be heading for a major and profound disruption over sexuality.

Conservative groups within ECUSA have been particularly successful in convincing the Asian, African and Latin American Anglican leadership of the righteousness of their cause, and thus exporting the sexuality debate in its western forms to the rest of the communion. The Windsor Report urges expressions of regret by ECUSA and the Church of Canada, and a moratorium on further moves which would signal acceptance of homosexual activity. It also asks that those churches in Africa and Asia which have regarded it as their moral duty to give help to disaffected congregations within the American church will exercise restraint. The Windsor Report suggests the adoption of a Covenant which would commit provinces to working in partnership and to avoid taking actions which are offensive to other parts of the communion. The Report condemns actions which clearly appear to infringe Resolution 1.10 of the 1998 Lambeth Conference; but also condemns those provinces outside ECUSA which have intervened to provide alternative episcopal support for conservative parishes which feel alienated from their own diocesan bishop. Conservatives were angered by this even-handed rebuke, and the somewhat mild recommendation that ECUSA 'be invited to express its regret that the proper cords of affection were breached'. They demand 'repentance' for the action itself rather than simply regret that the action caused offence. The stakes have been raised, with conservatives seeing themselves as 'orthodox' in contrast to the 'revisionists' who are dismantling the faith.

[32] You-Leng Lim, 'Homosexuality: How the Economics and Politics of Singapore have Shaped the Anglican Diocese and its Role in the Province of South East Asia'. A paper prepared as background material for the 1998 Lambeth Conference, http://newark.rutgers.edu/~lcrew/lenglim2.html.

ECUSA's apparent obsession with canonical form is seen as hollow when substantial issues of the Gospel are at stake.

It remains difficult to predict whether the Archbishop of Canterbury, and the Church of England (itself internally divided on these issues), can sustain dialogue with both ECUSA and its dissidents, and keep the churches of Africa, Asia and Latin America satisfied. The Windsor suggestion of a binding covenant which would help to enforce a common discipline is attractive to some Evangelicals. Maurice Sinclair, when he was Archbishop of the Southern Cone, advocated some enhancement of the office of the Archbishop of Canterbury to effect just this. But this has always seemed a strange proposal from Evangelicals, who traditionally have been most suspicious of ecclesiastical (and episcopal) authoritarianism. In this regard the diocese of Sydney more clearly articulates traditional Evangelical fears in its wholesale rejection of a Covenant:

> *The [Windsor] Report* is wrong in suggesting a tightening up of the Anglican communion and an increase in the powers of its various 'Instruments'. On the contrary, it is important that freer structural relations are promoted within the Communion.[33]

In the view of Sydney the time has come to avoid prevarication:

> Deliberately misleading rhetoric, and the ambiguous language that occurs in Church politics, should be jettisoned once and for all. If Anglicans are so proud of their 'diversity', then it is time to be truly honest about it. Those who do not hold to the Apostolic Faith and who are prepared to say so, are being honest. At least then it becomes clear who is aligned with whom, and congregations can be clear about the true situation to which they must respond. Pretending to be united is of no help to anyone.[34]

But Sydney is probably unique in the Anglican communion in the dogmatic clarity with which it holds its clear and narrowly defined version of Reformed Anglicanism. It would be unlikely that an Anglican Communion (as opposed to a looser association of Evangelical Protestantism) could be sustained on this basis. Sydney's theological certainties are not likely to be congenial to the 'orthodox' in ECUSA, whether they are from Catholic or Evangelical traditions. Nor would a Sydney theological dictatorship be long acceptable to the diverse Anglicanism of much of the global South.

[33] Peter Bolt et al. (eds.), *The Faith Once for All Delivered* (Sydney: Australian Church Record, 2005), p. 139.

[34] Ibid., p. 140.

Nor, in the South, would plans to set up more powerful central structures (whether based on the personal esteem of the Archbishop of Canterbury or on more conciliar mechanisms) accord with the autonomy of non-western Christianity. The Anglican communion has evolved as a 'family' with a well-defined external structure which allowed rather considerable flexibility and individuality. Previously such individuality was constrained by the presumption of the priority of 'English' norms. The mystique of Englishness and an acceptance of the superiority of western values have been shattered. But not completely. The fact that the conflict has focused so fiercely on homosexuality is itself an indication of the way in which what is essentially a conflict within modern western secular society has spilled over to the rest of the world, itself coming to terms with modernity and the increasing dominance of secularity and its discontents.

The old forms of Anglicanism are shattered. Anglicanism as a worldwide communion can no longer exist in the old ways. There will be a period, perhaps a generation, of confusion about whether Anglicanism exists at all. Possibly from that chaos there will arise a new sense of fellowship. The Anglican church worldwide can no more contrive permanently to marginalise homosexual people or remove them from its fellowship than it could continue to accept slavery, the inferiority of women, or the natural superiority of European civilisation.

CONCLUSION

Colonial power, by definition, does not seek the consent of the people who come under its dominion. The peoples of the global South had limited control over the type of missionary Christianity they encountered. In certain circumstances they were able to play off rival versions against each other to their own advantage, or to opt for what appeared to be a more congenial form of Christianity. But in their response, the 'recipients' of missionary activity were circumscribed – by formal colonial power, by the norms and expectations, the cultural horizons and preconceptions, of the foreign missionaries. Those who became Anglican usually did so in the context of British colonial power. They were introduced to liturgical forms and declarations of faith which were not truly 'indigenous', even when translated into local languages. Spirituality and moral conduct reflected the values of the sending culture, but were presented as universal and normative.

Despite all these constraints, it has been the thesis of this book that the agency of the indigenous church was always operative. The message could, in most cases, be refused as well as accepted. Where it was heard and received, it could be appropriated and utilised in complex ways and to different effect. For the majority of receiving peoples, the first missionaries were, in any case, not people from the North, but evangelists from neighbouring regions and culturally similar ethnic groups, who had already decisively shaped the message in accordance with their understandings and their own sense of what was demanded.

Indigenous forms of Anglican Christianity thus emerge from the very beginning of the encounter. They did not originate in the late twentieth century, with the end of formal colonialism. That it should appear so is primarily the perception of the former colonisers. To put it somewhat simplistically, they imagined that they could create a Christianity in their own image. But then colonialism collapsed. Ashamed of the colonial past, members of the once dominant group deem the Christianity of the South to be a regrettable colonial hangover. Alternatively, those in the North who lament the decline of Christianity as central to their culture somewhat sentimentally regard the South as the preserver of its lost values, and long for the South to re-evangelise a pagan North. The first perspective fails to recognise the autonomy of Christianity in the South. The second perspective caricatures the Christian faith in the South as unrealistically pure and simple and underestimates the challenge of evangelisation.

Christianity, of course, never simply fits into local culture. There is always a creative tension between conformity and opposition. What may be a right balance in one era may become unbalanced in another. The church always comes under the judgement and mercy of God, and can never congratulate itself on its own success. Scripture, tradition and reason, an evangelical message and a Catholic ecclesiology – all these marks of Anglicanism exist in diverse local forms and traditions. A too precise or authoritarian attempt to foster a common faith may create a sense of unity and communion for like-minded sections of the communion, whether geographically or theologically defined. The danger is that such a highly regimented communion will cease to be communion at all and become an oppressive uniformity, likely to fragment into several opposing factions, some more authoritarian, others more tolerant.

One possible scenario in the early-twenty-first-century crisis of Anglicanism is of a dominant 'southern Anglicanism', in alliance with northern allies, imposing its rigorous version of Christian orthodoxy on the North. This is premised on the assumption that there is a common southern 'orthodoxy' and that it is uniformly unsympathetic to northern secularity and 'revisionism'. That there should be such a reversal in the traditional role of North and South may have its attractions in terms of retributive justice, but it would belie the complexity of Christian mission. Rarely have missionaries worked for long in a new culture before they have been converted to a deeper and more appreciative understanding of the richness of that culture as well as a greater awareness of its hidden resistance to the Gospel. Such an understanding, in turn, transforms the missionaries' understanding of their own inherited faith and heightens an awareness of the richness and recalcitrance of their own cultures. It could be said that a definition of successful mission is the extent to which that conversion, that transformation, is made. Indigenisation is a process for the North as well as the global South.

Northern Christians may need to listen with humility, no longer able to dictate terms. But it would be unfortunate if this reversal failed actually to address the modern and post-modern, the secular and post-secular cultures, of the North in their own terms, in their own richness and recalcitrance. Moreover, a Christianity which ignores the fact that modernity and secularity, post-modernity and post-secularity, are actually transforming the face of southern cultures deeply and rapidly is not likely to have sustaining power.

Anglicanism avoided major splits over questions of biblical modernism at the beginning of the twentieth century. At the beginning of the twenty-first century it is convulsed by forces of acrimony and fragmentation. Divisions over homosexuality are presented as symptomatic of fundamental divisions over biblical interpretation and doctrine. Many Anglicans resist attempts to define membership of the communion by inflexible or narrow criteria, on the grounds that this is alien to what it means to be Anglican, as well as a betrayal of Christian values. A wide variety of theological debate and practice has always been encouraged within Anglicanism, based on a general consensus of faith and order. To insist on strict definitions of orthodoxy may lead to a great schism in which the communion splits into two, with the majority of 'northern' Anglican churches and the majority of 'southern' churches ranged in two rival, uncomprehending, versions of Anglicanism. But, more likely, perhaps, is the rise of networks of mutual recrimination, and an erosion of the geographical basis of Anglican provinces. Competing versions of Anglicanism will co-exist in the same space, the 'Anglican communion' existing as a single, ideal, unattainable 'invisible communion', to be set against the lamentable fragmentary nature of actual Anglicanism. But there is also the possibility that the communion will weather this storm. There are strong forces within the Anglicanism of the South which value Anglican qualities of tolerance and hospitality, generosity of spirit and open debate, a hesitancy about defining the faith too rigidly or too narrowly. Moreover, the ethical dimensions of the specific issue of homosexuality are themselves likely to change radically in the South itself. Other areas of sexual morality and family life styles will be opened to examination, alongside other equally important areas of Christian ethical engagement, conducted in a more profound, less sterile, atmosphere of biblical and theological enquiry and reflection. It is my hope that issues of sexual orientation will cease to be the defining issues of Christian identity, and that new forms of co-operation and mission, on a global scale, will emerge within the Anglican communion.

Maps

MAP 1

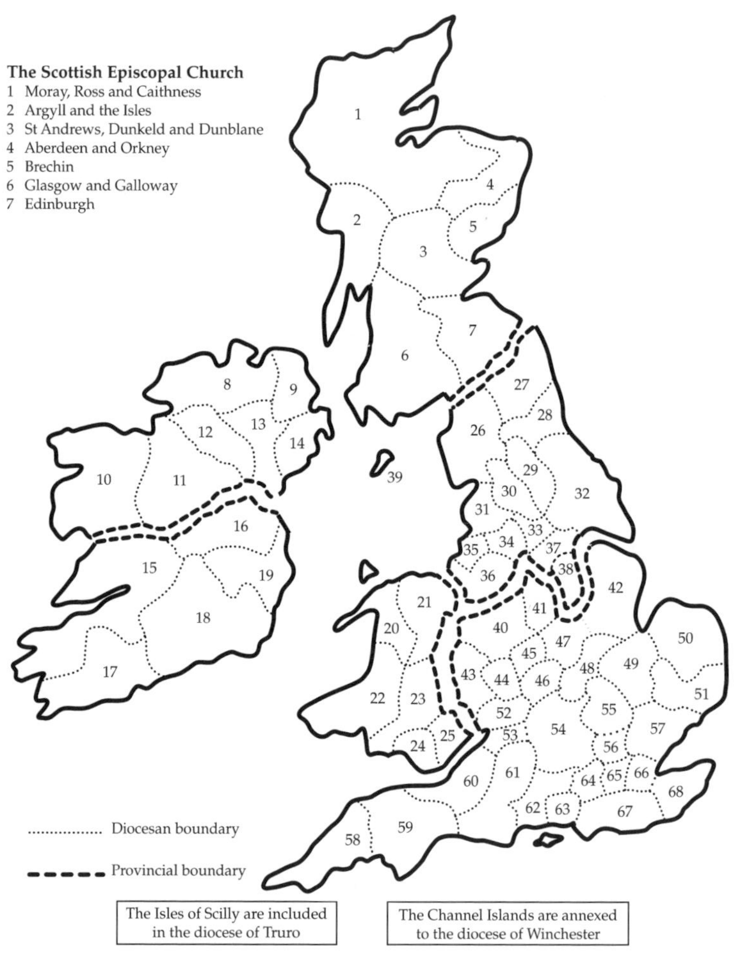

Map 1 The Church of England; the Church of Ireland; the Scottish Episcopal Church; the Church in Wales

The Church of Ireland
Province of Armagh
8 Derry and Raphoe
9 Connor
10 Tuam, Killala and Achonry
11 Kilmore, Elphin and Ardagh
12 Clogher
13 Armagh
14 Down and Dromore

Province of Dublin
15 Limerick and Killaloe
16 Meath and Kildare
17 Cork, Cloyne and Ross
18 Cashel and Ossory
19 Dublin and Glendalough

The Church in Wales
20 Bangor
21 St Asaph
22 St Davids
23 Swansea and Brecon
24 Llandaff
25 Monmouth

The Church of England
Province of York
26 Carlisle
27 Newcastle
28 Durham
29 Ripon and Leeds
30 Bradford
31 Blackburn
32 York
33 Wakefield
34 Manchester
35 Liverpool
36 Chester
37 Sheffield
38 Southwell
39 Sodor and Man

Province of Canterbury
40 Lichfield
41 Derby
42 Lincoln
43 Hereford
44 Worcester
45 Birmingham
46 Coventry
47 Leicester
48 Peterborough
49 Ely
50 Norwich
51 St Edmundsbury and Ipswich
52 Gloucester
53 Bristol
54 Oxford
55 St Albans
56 London
57 Chelmsford
58 Truro
59 Exeter
60 Bath and Wells
61 Salisbury
62 Winchester
63 Portsmouth
64 Guildford
65 Southwark
66 Rochester
67 Chichester
68 Canterbury
Diocese in Europe

Extra-provincial dioceses
Bermuda
Lusitanian Church
Spanish Episcopal Reformed Church
The Church of Ceylon
Falkland Islands

The Anglican Church of Australia

Province of Western Australia
1 North-West Australia
2 Perth
3 Bunbury

Province of South Australia
4 Willochra
5 Adelaide
6 The Murray

Province of Queensland
7 The Northern Territory
8 North Queensland
9 Rockhampton
10 Brisbane

Province of New South Wales
11 Riverina
12 Bathurst
13 Armidale
14 Grafton
15 Newcastle
16 Sydney
17 Canberra and Goulburn

Province of Victoria
18 Ballarat
19 Bendigo
20 Wangaratta
21 Melbourne
22 Gippsland

23 Tasmania (extra-provincial)

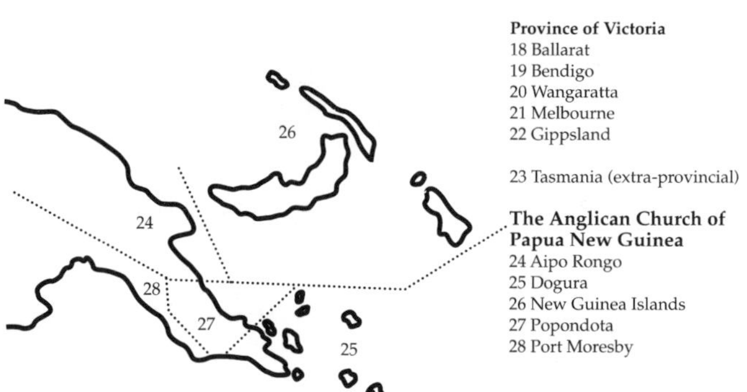

The Anglican Church of Papua New Guinea
24 Aipo Rongo
25 Dogura
26 New Guinea Islands
27 Popondota
28 Port Moresby

Map 2 The Anglican Church of Australia; the Anglican Church of Papua New Guinea

MAP 3

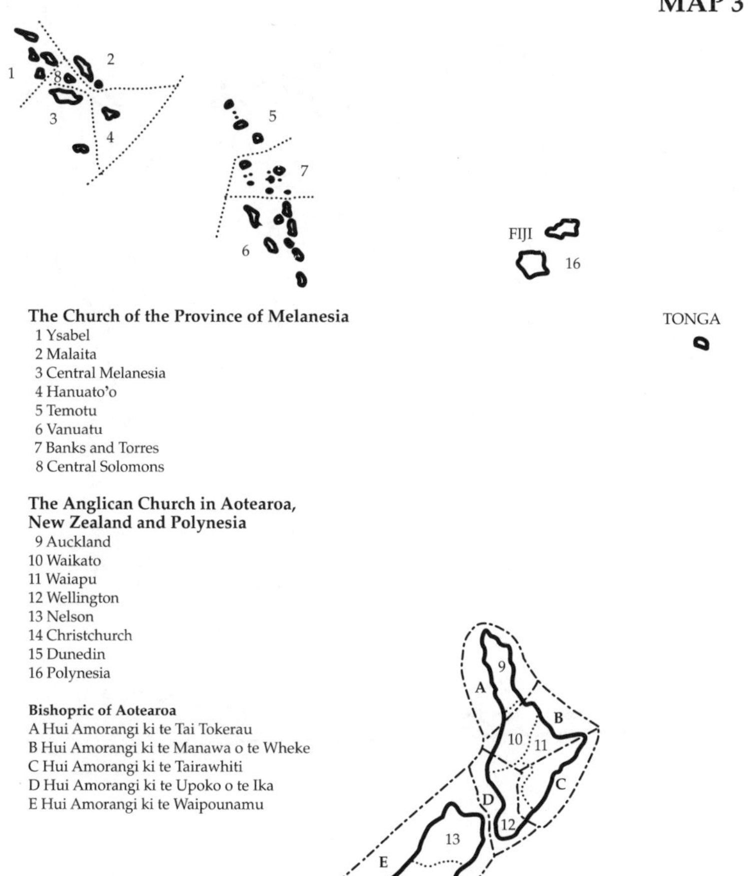

Map 3 The Anglican Church in Aotearoa, New Zealand and Polynesia; the Church of the Province of Melanesia

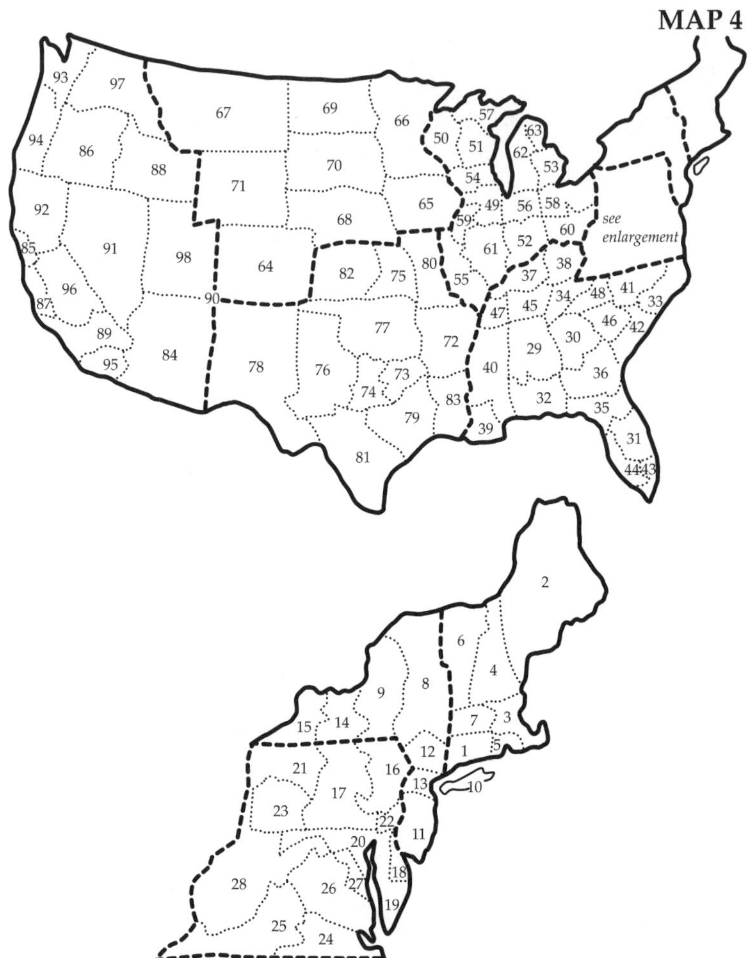

Map 4 The Episcopal Church in the United States of America

The Episcopal Church in the United States of America

Province I
1 Connecticut
2 Maine
3 Massachusetts
4 New Hampshire
5 Rhode Island
6 Vermont
7 Western Massachusetts

Province II
8 Albany
9 Central New York
10 Long Island
11 New Jersey
12 New York
13 Newark
14 Rochester
15 Western New York
Haiti (*see Map* 5)
Virgin Islands (*see Map* 5)
Convocation of American Churches in Europe

Province III
16 Bethlehem
17 Central Pennsylvania
18 Delaware
19 Easton
20 Maryland
21 North-Western Pennsylvania
22 Pennsylvania
23 Pittsburgh
24 Southern Virginia
25 South-Western Virginia
26 Virginia
27 Washington
28 West Virginia

Province IV
29 Alabama
30 Atlanta
31 Central Florida
32 Central Gulf Coast
33 East Carolina
34 East Tennessee
35 Florida
36 Georgia
37 Kentucky
38 Lexington
39 Louisiana
40 Mississippi
41 North Carolina
42 South Carolina
43 South-East Florida
44 South-West Florida
45 Tennessee
46 Upper South Carolina
47 West Tennessee
48 Western North Carolina

Province V
49 Chicago
50 Eau Claire
51 Fond du Lac
52 Indianapolis
53 Michigan
54 Milwaukee
55 Missouri
56 Northern Indiana
57 Northern Michigan
58 Ohio
59 Quincy
60 Southern Ohio
61 Springfield
62 Western Michigan
63 Eastern Michigan

Province VI
64 Colorado
65 Iowa
66 Minnesota
67 Montana
68 Nebraska
69 North Dakota
70 South Dakota
71 Wyoming

Province VII
72 Arkansas
73 Dallas
74 Fort Worth
75 Kansas
76 North-West Texas
77 Oklahoma
78 Rio Grande
79 Texas
80 West Missouri
81 West Texas
82 Western Kansas
83 Western Louisiana

Province VIII
84 Arizona
85 California
86 Eastern Oregon
87 El Camino Real
88 Idaho
89 Los Angeles
90 Navajoland
91 Nevada
92 Northern California
93 Olympia
94 Oregon
95 San Diego
96 San Joaquin
97 Spokane
98 Utah
Hawaii
Alaska (*see Map* 6)
Taiwan (*see Map* 14)
Micronesia

The Anglican Church of the Southern Cone of America

25 Argentina
26 Chile
27 Northern Argentina
28 Paraguay
29 Peru
30 Uruguay
31 Bolivia

41 Bermuda (extra-provincial to Canterbury)
42 Haiti (province II of ECUSA – *see Map* 4)
43 Virgin Islands (province II of ECUSA – *see Map* 4)

Map 5 The Anglican Church of the Central American Region; the Episcopal Anglican Church of Brazil; the Episcopal Church of Cuba; the Church in the Province of the West Indies; the Anglican Church of Mexico; the Anglican Church of the Southern Cone of America

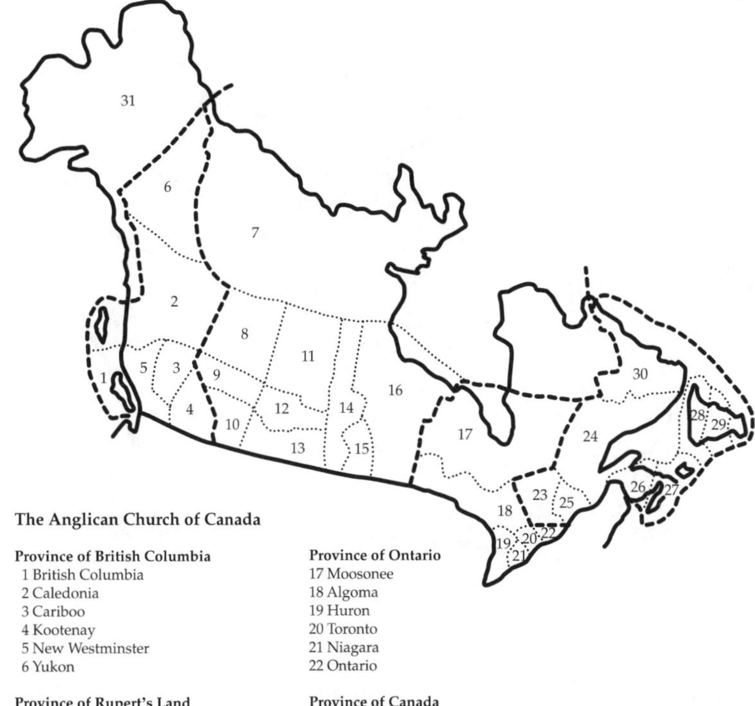

The Anglican Church of Canada

Province of British Columbia
1 British Columbia
2 Caledonia
3 Cariboo
4 Kootenay
5 New Westminster
6 Yukon

Province of Rupert's Land
7 Arctic
8 Athabasca
9 Edmonton
10 Calgary
11 Saskatchewan
12 Saskatoon
13 Qu'Appelle
14 Brandon
15 Rupert's Land
16 Keewatin

Province of Ontario
17 Moosonee
18 Algoma
19 Huron
20 Toronto
21 Niagara
22 Ontario

Province of Canada
23 Ottawa
24 Quebec
25 Montreal
26 Fredericton
27 Nova Scotia and Prince Edward Island
28 Western Newfoundland
29 Central Newfoundland
30 Eastern Newfoundland and Labrador

31 Alaska (in province VIII of ECUSA)

Map 6 The Anglican Church of Canada

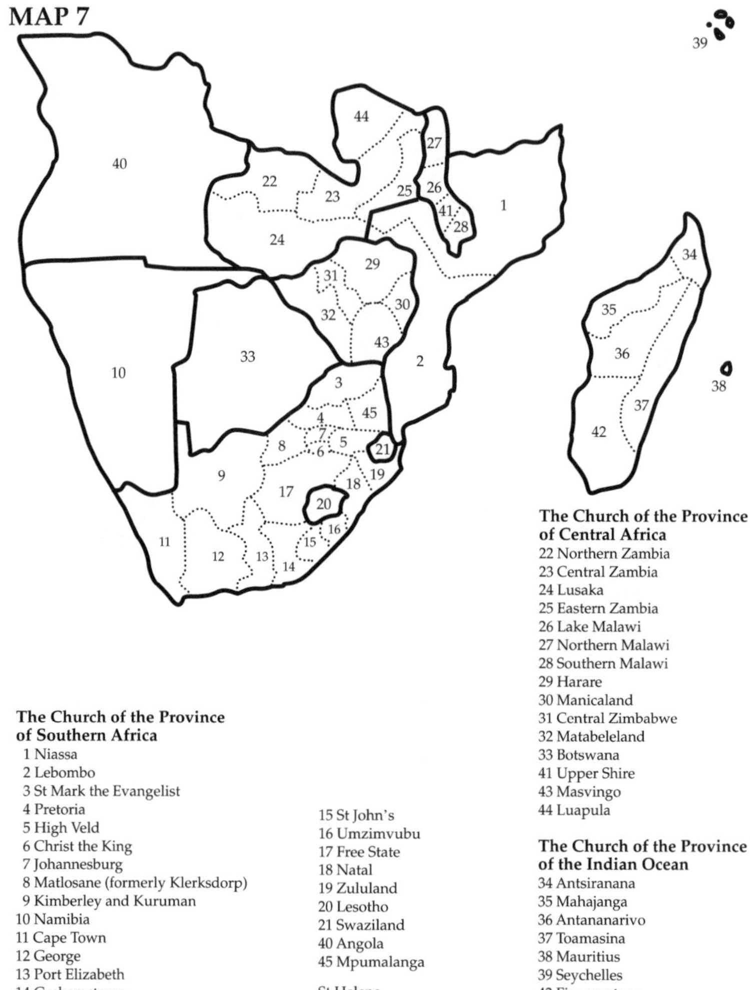

Map 7 The Church of the Province of Central Africa; the Church of the Province of the Indian Ocean; the Church of the Province of Southern Africa

MAP 8
see enlargement
10 and 48
The Anglican Church of Kenya
1 Nambale
2 Bungoma
3 Katakwa
4 Maseno North
5 Maseno West
6 Maseno South
7 Southern Nyanza
8 Butere
9 Mumias
10 Nairobi
11 Mount Kenya South
12 Mount Kenya West
13 Nakuru
14 Nyahururu
15 Embu
16 Mbeere
17 Mount Kenya Central
18 Eldoret
19 Kitale
20 Kirinyaga
21 Meru
22 Machakos
23 Kajiado
24 Mombasa
25 Taita Taveta
26 Kitui
44 Thika
45 Bondo
48 All SS Cathedral
The Anglican Church of Tanzania
27 Morogoro
28 Zanzibar
29 Dar-es-Salaam
30 Ruaha
31 Rift Valley
32 Tabora
33 Western Tanganyika
34 South-West Tanganyika
35 Ruvuma
36 Masasi
37 Kagera
38 Victoria Nyanza
39 Mara
40 Mount Kilimanjaro
41 Central Tanganyika
42 Mpwapwa
43 Southern Highlands
46 Kondoa
47 Tanga
49 Kiteto

Map 8 The Anglican Church of Kenya; the Anglican Church of Tanzania

MAP 9

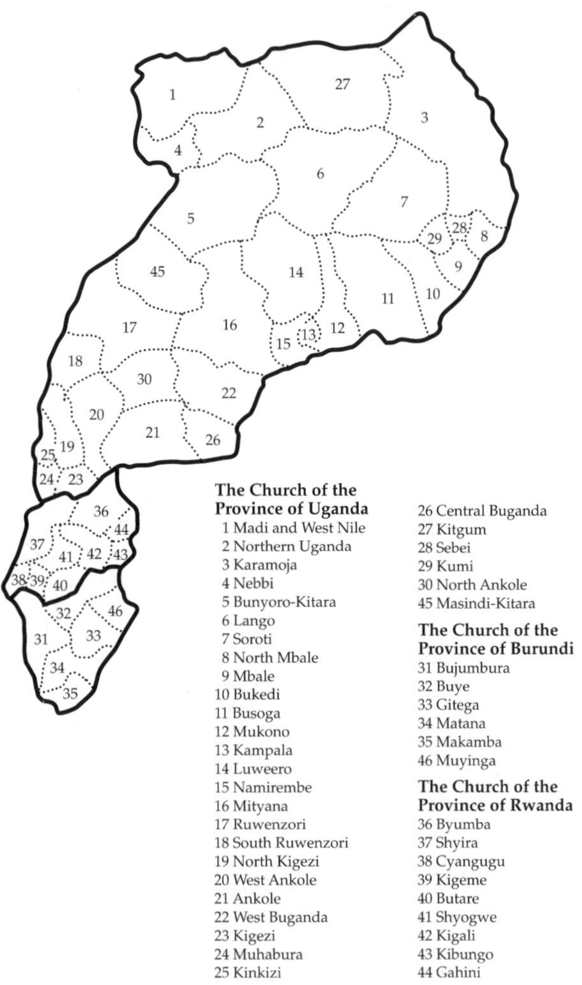

Map 9 The Anglican Church of Burundi; the Episcopal Church of Rwanda; the Church of the Province of Uganda

MAP 10

Map 10 The Episcopal Church of the Sudan; the Church Province of the Congo

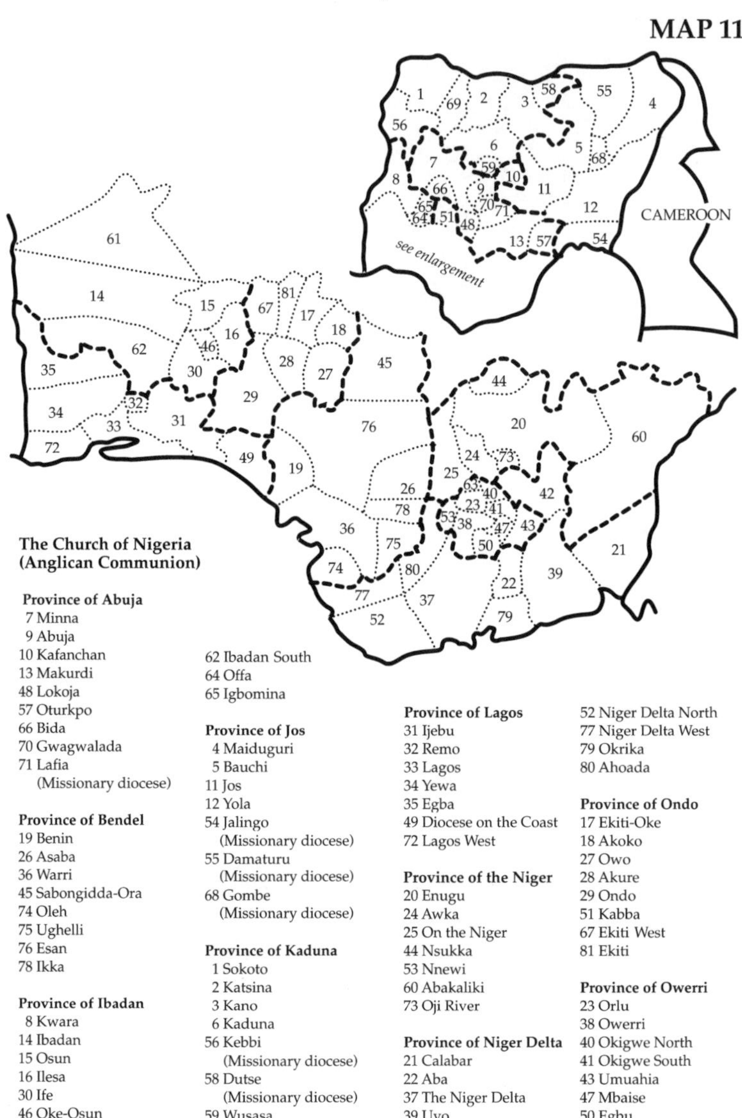
MAP 11
CAMEROON
see enlargement
The Church of Nigeria (Anglican Communion)
Province of Abuja
7 Minna
9 Abuja
10 Kafanchan
13 Makurdi
48 Lokoja
57 Oturkpo
66 Bida
70 Gwagwalada
71 Lafia (Missionary diocese)
Province of Bendel
19 Benin
26 Asaba
36 Warri
45 Sabongidda-Ora
74 Oleh
75 Ughelli
76 Esan
78 Ikka
Province of Ibadan
8 Kwara
14 Ibadan
15 Osun
16 Ilesa
30 Ife
46 Oke-Osun
61 Ibadan North
62 Ibadan South
64 Offa
65 Igbomina
Province of Jos
4 Maiduguri
5 Bauchi
11 Jos
12 Yola
54 Jalingo (Missionary diocese)
55 Damaturu (Missionary diocese)
68 Gombe (Missionary diocese)
Province of Kaduna
1 Sokoto
2 Katsina
3 Kano
6 Kaduna
56 Kebbi (Missionary diocese)
58 Dutse (Missionary diocese)
59 Wusasa
69 Gusau
Province of Lagos
31 Ijebu
32 Remo
33 Lagos
34 Yewa
35 Egba
49 Diocese on the Coast
72 Lagos West
Province of the Niger
20 Enugu
24 Awka
25 On the Niger
44 Nsukka
53 Nnewi
60 Abakaliki
73 Oji River
Province of Niger Delta
21 Calabar
22 Aba
37 The Niger Delta
39 Uyo
42 Ukwa
52 Niger Delta North
77 Niger Delta West
79 Okrika
80 Ahoada
Province of Ondo
17 Ekiti-Oke
18 Akoko
27 Owo
28 Akure
29 Ondo
51 Kabba
67 Ekiti West
81 Ekiti
Province of Owerri
23 Orlu
38 Owerri
40 Okigwe North
41 Okigwe South
43 Umuahia
47 Mbaise
50 Egbu
63 Ideato

Map 11 The Church of Nigeria (Anglican Communion)

Map 12 The Anglican Communion in Japan; the Episcopal Church in Jerusalem and the Middle East; the Church of the Province of West Africa

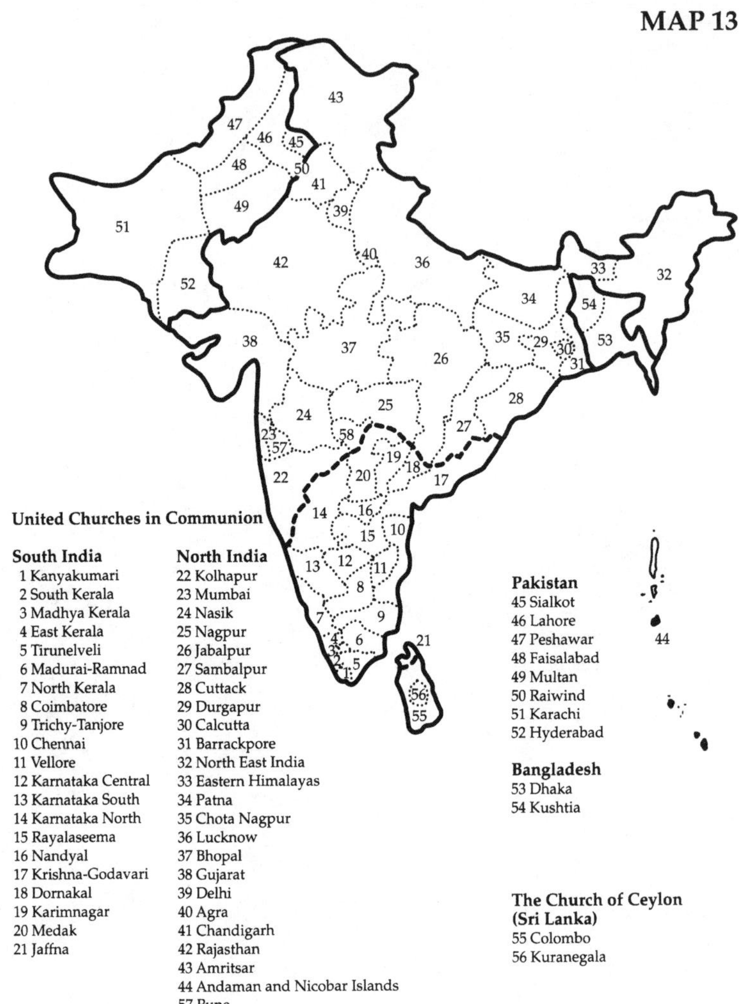

Map 13 The Church of North India (united); the Church of South India (united); the Church of Pakistan (united); the Church of Ceylon; the Church of Bangladesh

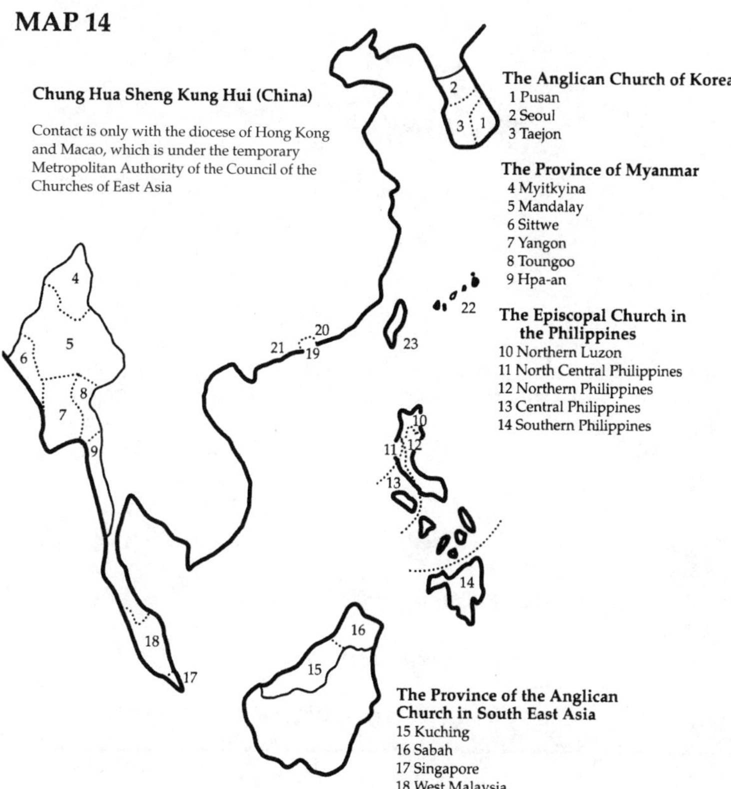

22 Okinawa
(diocese in the Anglican Communion in Japan)

23 Taiwan
(diocese in Province VIII of ECUSA)

The Holy Catholic Church in Hong Kong
19 Hong Kong Island
20 Eastern Kowloon
21 Western Kowloon

Map 14 The Anglican Church of Korea; The Church of the Province of Myanmar (Burma); The Episcopal Church in the Philippines; the Church of the Province of South-East Asia; Hong Kong Sheng Kung Hui

Bibliography

Abdallah, Yohanna B., *The Yaos/Chiikala cha Wayao,* arranged, edited and translated by Meredith Sanderson (London: Frank Cass, 1973).

Achebe, Chinua, *Things Fall Apart* (London and Lagos: Heinemann, 1959).

Acheson, Alan, *A History of the Church of Ireland, 1691–2001* (Dublin: Columba Press, 2002).

Ackermann, Denise, *Claiming our Footprints: South African Women Reflect on Context, Identity and Spirituality* (Matieland: Institute for Theological and Interdisciplinary Research, 2000).

Ackermann, Denise, et al. (eds.), *Women Hold up Half the Sky* (Pietermaritzburg: Cluster, 1991).

Adebiyi, T. B., *The Beloved Bishop. The Life of Bishop A. B. Akinyele* (Ibadan: Daystar Press, 1969).

Adhav, S. M., *Pandita Ramabai* (Madras: Christian Literature Society, 1979).

Ajayi, J. F. Ade, *A Patriot to the Core* (Ibadan: Anglican Diocese, 1992).

Akenson, Donald H., *Small Differences: Irish Catholics and Irish Protestants 1815–1922* (Kingston: Queen's University Press, 1988).

Akiri, Raphael Mwita, 'The Growth of Christianity in Ugogo and Ukaguru', Ph.D. dissertation, University of Edinburgh, 1999.

Alexander, Peter, *Alan Paton* (Oxford: Oxford University Press, 1994).

Ande, Georges Titre, 'Authority in the Anglican Church of Congo', Ph.D. dissertation, University of Birmingham, 2003.

Anderson, Gerald H. (ed.), *Biographical Dictionary of Christian Missions* (New York: Macmillan, 1998).

Anderson, Owanah, *400 Years: Anglican/Episcopal Mission among American Indians* (Cincinnati: Forward Movement, 1997).

Anderson, W. B., *The Church in East Africa 1840–1974* (Dodoma: CT Press, 1977).

Appasamy, A. J., *Christianity as Bhakti Marga: A Study in the Mysticism of the Johannine Writings* (London: Macmillan, 1927).

Temple Bells: Readings from Hindu Religious Literature (Calcutta: YMCA, 1930).

Appiah, Kwame Anthony, *In My Father's House* (Oxford: Oxford University Press, 1992).

Armitage, David, *The Ideological Origins of the British Empire* (Cambridge: Cambridge University Press, 2000).

Ateek, Naim, *Justice and Only Justice* (Maryknoll, NY: Orbis, 1989).

Atiya, Aziz S., *A History of Eastern Christianity* (Millwood, NY: Kraus, 1980).

Avis, Paul, *Anglicanism and the Christian Church* (Edinburgh: T. & T. Clark, 2002) (1st edn 1989).

Ayandele, E. A., *Holy Johnson: Pioneer of African Nationalism 1836–1917* (New York: Humanities Press, 1970).

Ballhatchet, Helen, 'The Modern Missionary Movement in Meiji Japan', in Mark Mullins (ed.), *Handbook of Christianity in Japan* (Leiden: Brill, 2003).

Barnard, Toby, *Irish Protestant Ascents and Descents 1641–1770* (Dublin: Four Courts Press, 2004).

Barrett, David, Kurian, George T., and Johnson, Todd M., *World Christian Encyclopedia* (2 vols., Oxford: Oxford University Press, 2001).

Barry, Gerald J., *Trinity Church: 300 Years of Philanthropy* (New York: The Hundred Year Association, 1997).

Barsella, Gino, and Guixot, Miguel, *Struggling to be Heard: The Christian Voice in Independent Sudan 1956–1996* (Nairobi: Paulines, 1998).

Barton, Mukti, *Scripture as Empowerment for Liberation and Justice: The Experience of Christian and Muslim Women in Bangladesh* (Bristol: Centre for Comparative Studies in Religion and Gender, Department of Theology and Religious Studies, Bristol University, 1999).

Bashan, Eliezer, *The Anglican Mission and the Jews of Morocco in the 19th Century* (Ramat-Gan: Bar-Ilan University, 1999).

Bates, Stephen, *A Church at War: Anglicans and Homosexuality* (London: I. B. Tauris, 2004).

Beidelman, Thomas O., *Colonial Evangelism* (Bloomington: Indiana University Press, 1982).

Benson, G. P., 'Kenya's Protestant Churches and the *Nyayo* State', in H. B. Hanson and M. Twaddle (eds.), *Religion and Politics in East Africa* (London: James Currey, 1995), pp. 177–99.

Berkley, Claude, 'Partnership is a Leaky Ship: An Evaluation of the Relationship between the Church in the Province of the West Indies (CPWI) and the United Society for the Propagation of the Gospel since the Time of Independence', unpublished M.Phil. dissertation, University of Birmingham, 2000.

Biko, Steve, *I Write What I Like* (London: Penguin, 1988).

Binney, Judith, *The Legacy of Guilt: A Life of Thomas Kendall* (Christchurch: Auckland University Press, 1968).

Bolt, Peter, et al. (eds.), *The Faith Once for All Delivered* (Sydney: Australian Church Record, 2005).

Boobbyer, Philip, 'Moral Re-Armament in Africa in the Era of Decolonization', in Brian Stanley (ed.), *Missions, Nationalism, and the End of Empire* (Grand Rapids: Eerdmans, 2003), pp. 221–36

Borer, Tristan Anne, *Challenging the State* (Notre Dame: Notre Dame University Press, 1998).

Boyd, Robin, *India and the Latin Captivity of the Church: The Cultural Context of the Gospel* (Cambridge: Cambridge University Press, 1974).

Breward, Ian, *A History of the Churches in Australasia* (Oxford: Clarendon, 2001).

Brooks, Leroy Errol, 'The Church and the Abolition Movement in the British Caribbean', unpublished M.Th. dissertation, Columbia Theological Seminary, 1986.

Brown, Deborah Ann, *Turmoil in Hong Kong on the Eve of Communist Rule: The Fate of the Territory and its Anglican Church* (San Francisco: Mellen Research University Press, 1993).

Brown, Judith M., *Modern India* (Oxford: Oxford University Press, 1994).

Brown, Judith M., and Frykenberg, Robert E. (eds.), *Christians, Cultural Interactions, and India's Religious Traditions* (Grand Rapids: Eerdmans, 2002).

Brown, Leslie W., *The Indian Christians of St Thomas* (Cambridge: Cambridge University Press, 1956).

Three Worlds, One Word: Account of a Mission (London: Collings, 1981).

Brown, Terry (ed.), *Other Voices, Other Worlds* (London: Darton, Longman & Todd, 2006).

Browne, George D., *The Episcopal Church of Liberia under Indigenous Leadership* (Lithonia: Third World Literature Publishing House, 1994).

Bryan, Dominic, *The Politics of Ritual, Tradition and Control* (London: Pluto Press, 2000).

Burkett, Randall K., *Garveyism as a Religious Movement* (Metuchen, NJ: Scarecrow, 1979).

Burrell, Arthur, *Cathedral on the Nile: A History of All Saints Cathedral Cairo* (Oxford: Amate Press, 1984).

Butler, Patrick, 'The Growth of the Evangelical Church in South America and the Place of the Anglican Church within that Movement'. Unpublished dissertation, All Nations College, 1994. In the SAMS Library Collection, Crowther Hall, Selly Oak, Birmingham.

Campbell, James, *Songs of Zion* (Oxford: Oxford University Press, 1995).

Campbell, P. F., *The Church in Barbados in the Seventeenth Century* (Bridgetown: Barbados Museum and Historical Society, 1984).

Canny, Nicholas, *The Origins of Empire: British Overseas Enterprise to the Close of the Seventeenth Century* (Oxford: Oxford University Press, 1998).

The Oxford History of the British Empire, Volume I (Oxford: Oxford University Press, 1988).

Carpenter, Edward, *Archbishop Fisher – His Life and Times* (Norwich: Canterbury Press, 1991).

Carrington, Philip, *The Anglican Church in Canada: A History* (London: Collins, 1963).

Cary, Otis, *A History of Christianity in Japan* (Tokyo: Tuttle, 1976) (1st edn, 1909).

Chadwick, Owen, *Mackenzie's Grave* (London: Hodder & Stoughton, 1959).

Chidester, David, *Savage Systems* (Charlotteville: Virginia University Press, 1996).

Christie, Kenneth, *The South African Truth Commission* (Basingstoke: Macmillan, 2000).

Christophers, Brett, *Positioning the Missionary: John Booth Good and the Confluence of Cultures in Nineteenth-Century British Columbia* (Vancouver: University of British Columbia Press, 1998).

Church of England Year Book 2000 (London: Church House Publishing, 2000).

Church of England Year Book 2004 (London: Church House Publishing, 2004).

Clark, J. C. D., *English Society 1660–1832* (Cambridge: Cambridge University Press, 2000).

Clarke, Knolly, 'Liturgy and Culture in the Caribbean: What is to be Done?', in Idris Hamid (ed.), *Troubling the Waters* (San Fernando, Trinidad: St Andrew's Theological College, 1973).

Clarke, Sathianathan, *Dalits and Christianity: Subaltern Religion and Liberation Theology in India* (Delhi: Oxford University Press, 1998).

Coakley, J. F., *The Church of the East and the Church of England: A History of the Archbishop of Canterbury's Assyrian Mission* (Oxford: Clarendon Press, 1972).

Cochrane, James, *Servants of Power: The Role of English-Speaking Churches in South Africa 1903–1930* (Johannesburg: Ravan, 1987).

Colgrave, Bertram, and Mynors, R. A. B., *Bede's Ecclesiastical History of the English People* (Oxford: Clarendon, 1969).

Committee on Black Anglican Concerns, *Seeds of Hope: Report of a Survey on Combating Racism in the Dioceses of the Church of England* (London: General Synod of the Church of England, 1991).

Committee for Minority Ethnic Anglican Concerns, *The Passing Winter: A Sequel to Seeds of Hope* (London: Church House Publishing, 1996).

Cox, Jeffrey, *Imperial Fault Lines: Christianity and Colonial Power in India 1818–1940* (Stanford: Stanford University Press, 2002).

[CPK Provincial Unit of Research,] *Rabai to Mumias: A Short History of the Church of the Province of Kenya 1844–1994* (Nairobi: Uzima, 1994).

Cracknell, Kenneth, *Justice, Courtesy and Love* (London: Epworth, 1995).

Cragg, Kenneth, *Muhammad and the Christian: A Question of Response* (Oxford: Oneworld, 1999).

The Arab Christian (Louisville: John Knox, 1991).

Troubled by Truth (Edinburgh: Pentland Press, 1992).

Crampton, E. P. T., *Christianity in Northern Nigeria* (London: Cassell, 1975).

Cross, F. L., and Livingstone, E. A., *The Oxford Dictionary of the Christian Church*, 3rd edn (Oxford: Oxford University Press, 1997).

Crummey, Donald, *Priests and Politicians: Protestant and Catholic Missions in Orthodox Ethiopia 1830–1868* (Oxford: Clarendon Press, 1972).

Cundall, Frank, *The Life of Enos Nuttall, Archbishop of the West Indies* (London: SPCK, 1922).

[Davidson, Archbishop], *The Six Lambeth Conferences 1867–1920* (London: SPCK, 1929).

Davidson, A. K. (ed), *Tongan Anglicans 1902–2002* (Auckland, 2002).

Davidson, A. K., and Lineham, P. J., *Transplanted Christianity* (Dunmore: Palmerston Press, 1989).

Davis, John, *Australian Anglicans and their Constitution* (Canberra: Acorn Press, 1993).

Davis, Kortright, *Cross and Crown in Barbados: Caribbean Political Religion in the Late 19th Century* (Frankfurt: Verlag Peter Lang, 1983).

Emancipation Still Comin': Explorations in Caribbean Emancipatory Theology (Maryknoll: Orbis, 1990).

Davison, G., et. al., *The Oxford Companion to Australian History* (Melbourne: Oxford University Press, 1998).

Dayfoot, A. C., *The Shaping of the West Indian Church 1492–1962* (Kingston: University of the West Indies, 1999).

de Gruchy, John, *The Church Struggle in South Africa* (Cape Town: David Philip, 1979).

de Saram, Brian, *Nile Harvest: The Anglican Church in Egypt and the Sudan* (Bournemouth: Abinger, 1992).

de Silva, K. M., 'From Elite Status to Beleaguered Minority: The Christians in Twentieth Century Sri Lanka', in *Colloques Internationaux du Centre National de la Recherche Scientifique* No. 582, *Asie du Sud: Traditions et changements* (Paris, 1979).

Dean, David M., *Defender of the Race: James Theodore Holly, Black Nationalist Bishop* (Boston: Lambeth Press, 1979).

Dehqani-Tafti, H. B., *The Hard Awakening* (London: SPCK, 1981).

The Unfolding Design of my World: A Pilgrim in Exile (Norwich: Canterbury Press, 2000).

Denniston, Robin, *Trevor Huddleston: A Life* (New York: St Martin's Press, 1999).

Devine, Thomas, *Scotland's Empire* (London: Penguin, 2003).

Diocese of West Malaysia, *A Man of Vision* (A festschrift for Bishop Savarimuthu) (Kuala Lumpur: Diocese of West Malaysia 1985).

Doe, Norman, *Canon Law in the Anglican Communion* (Oxford: Clarendon, 1998).

Donovan, Mary S., *A Different Call: Women's Ministries in the Episcopal Church 1850–1920* (Wilton: Morehouse-Barlow, 1986).

Douglas, Ian T., '"A Light to the Nations": Episcopal Foreign Missions in Historical Perspective', *Anglican and Episcopal History* 61.4 (December 1992), pp. 447–82.

'Anglicans Gathering for God's Mission: A Missiological Ecclesiology for the Anglican Communion', *Journal of Anglican Studies* 2 (2004), pp. 9–40.

Fling out the Banner! The National Church Ideal and the Foreign Mission of the Episcopal Church (New York: Church Hymnal Corporation, 1996).

du Boulay, Shirley, *Tutu: Voice of the Voiceless* (London: Hodder & Stoughton, 1988).

Duffy, Eamon, *The Stripping of the Altars* (New Haven: Yale University Press, 1992).

The Voices of Morebath (New Haven: Yale University Press, 2001).

Dunch, Ryan, *Fuzhou Protestants and the Making of a Modern China 1857–1927* (New Haven: Yale University Press, 2001).

Dunn, D. Elwood, *A History of the Episcopal Church in Liberia 1821–1980* (Metuchen: Scarecrow Press, 1992).

Eber, Irene, *The Jewish Bishop and the Chinese Bible* (Leiden: Brill, 1999).

El-Assal, Riah Abu, *Caught in Between: The Story of an Arab Palestinian Christian Israeli* (London: SPCK, 1999).

'The Birth and Experience of the Christian Church: The Protestant/Anglican Perspective in the Middle East', in Michael Prior and William Taylor (eds.), *Christians in the Holy Land* (London: The World of Islam Festival Trust, 1994).

Ellis, Stephen, *The Mask of Anarchy: The Destruction of Liberia and the Religious Dimension of an African Civil War* (London: Hurst, 1999).

Elphick, Richard, and Davenport, Rodney (eds.), *Christianity in South Africa* (Cape Town: David Philip, 1997).

Emilsen, S., and Emilsen, W. W. (eds.), *Mapping the Landscape: Essays in Australian and New Zealand Christianity* (New York: Lang, 2000).

England, Frank, and Paterson, Torquil (eds.), *Bounty in Bondage: The Anglican Church in Southern Africa* (Johannesburg: Ravan Press, 1989).

Enwerem, Iheanyi M., *A Dangerous Awakening: The Politicization of Religion in Nigeria* (Ibadan: Institut Français de Recherche en Afrique, 1995).

Equiano Olaudah, *Equiano's Travels*, edited and abridged by Paul Edwards (Oxford: Heinemann, 1996).

Evans, G. R., and Wright, J. Robert (eds.), *The Anglican Tradition: A Handbook of Sources* (London: SPCK, 1991).

Fairbank, John K., and Goldman, Merle, *China: A New History* (Cambridge, MA: Harvard University Press, 1992).

Falola, Toyin, *Violence in Nigeria: The Crisis of Religious Politics and Secular Ideologies* (Rochester: Rochester University Press, 1995).

Farah, Rafiq A., *In Troubled Waters: A History of the Anglican Church in Jerusalem 1841–1998* (Bridport: Christians Aware, 2002).

Farrant, Jean, *Mashonaland Martyr: Bernard Mizeki and the Pioneer Church* (Cape Town: Oxford University Press, 1966).

Farrimond, Ken, 'The Policy of the Church Missionary Society concerning the Development of Self-Governing Indigenous Churches 1900–1942', Ph.D. dissertation, University of Leeds, 2003.

Faupel, J. F., *African Holocaust* (London: Geoffrey Chapman, 1962).

Fingard, Judith, *The Anglican Design in Loyalist Nova Scotia 1783–1816* (London: SPCK, 1972).

Finnstrom, Sverker, *Living with Bad Surroundings: War and Existential Uncertainty in Acholiland* (Uppsala: Uppsala University Press, 2003).

Fleming, Archibald, *Archibald the Arctic* (New York: Appleton-Century-Crofts, 1956).

Ford, Margaret, *Janani: The Making of a Martyr* (London: Marshall, Morgan & Scott, 1978).

Forrester, Duncan, *Caste and Christianity* (London: Curzon, 1980).

Francis-Dehqani, Gulnar Eleanor, *Religious Feminism in an Age of Empire: CMS Women Missionaries in Iran 1869–1934*, CCSRG Monograph Series 4, Department of Theology and Religious Studies, Bristol University, 2000.

Freeman-Grenville, G. S. P., *The Mombasa Rising against the Portuguese, 1631* (Oxford: Oxford University Press, 1980).

Frey, Sylvia, and Wood, Betty, *Come Shouting to Zion: African American Protestantism in the American South and British Caribbean to 1830* (Chapel Hill and London: University of North Carolina Press, 1998).

Fryer, Peter, *Staying Power: The History of Black People in Britain* (London: Pluto Press), 1984.

Furneaux, Robin, *William Wilberforce* (London: Hamish Hamilton, 1974).

Gairdner, William Temple, *The Reproach of Islam* (London: Church Society, 1909), revised as *The Rebuke of Islam* (London: United Council for Missionary Education, 1920).

Garrett, John, *To Live among the Stars: Christian Origins in Oceania* (Geneva and Suva: WCC, 1982).

Germond, Paul, and de Gruchy, Steve, *Aliens in the Household of God: Homosexuality and Christian Faith in South Africa* (Cape Town: David Philip, 1997).

Gerstner, J. N., *The Thousand Generation Covenant* (Leiden: Brill, 1991).

Gibbon, Geoffrey, *Paget of Rhodesia* (Cape Town: Africana Book Society, 1973).

Gibbs, M. E., *The Anglican Church in India 1600–1970* (Delhi: ISPCK, 1972).

Gifford, Paul, *African Christianity: Its Public Role* (London: Hurst, 1998).

Christianity and Politics in Doe's Liberia (Cambridge: Cambridge University Press, 1993).

Gilroy, Paul, *The Black Atlantic: Modernity and Double Consciousness* (London: Verso, 1993).

Githiga, Gideon, *The Church as Bulwark against Authoritarianism: The Development of Church–State Relations in Kenya 1963–1992* (Oxford: Regnum, 2001).

Goedhals, Mandy, 'The Order of Ethiopia', in Daniel O'Connor, *Three Centuries of Mission: The United Society for the Propagation of the Gospel 1701–2000* (London: Continuum, 2000), pp. 382–94.

'Ungumpriste: A Study of the Life of Peter Masiza, First Black Priest in the CPSA', *Journal of Theology for Southern Africa* 68 (September 1989), pp. 17–28.

Goodridge, Sehon S., *Facing the Challenge of Emancipation: A Study of the Ministry of William Hart Coleridge, First Bishop of Barbados 1824–42* (Bridgetown: Cedar Press, 1981).

Gordon, Shirley C., *God Almighty Make Me Free: Christianity in Preemancipation Jamaica* (Bloomington: Indiana University Press, 1996).

Gordon-Carter, Glynne, *An Amazing Journey: The Church of England's Response to Institutional Racism* (London: Church Publishing House, 2003).

Grant, John Webster, *A Profusion of Spires: Religion in 19th Century Ontario* (Toronto: Toronto University Press, 1988).

Moon of Wintertime: Missionaries and the Indians of Canada in Encounter since 1534 (Toronto: Toronto University Press, 1984).

Gray, Charles, *The Life of Robert Gray* (2 vols., London: Rivington, 1876).

Gray, G. F. S., *Anglicans in China: A History of the Zhonghua Shenggong Hui (Chung Hua Sheng Kung Huei)* (New Haven: Episcopal China Mission History Project, 1996).

Grotpeter, John J., *Historical Dictionary of Namibia* (Metuchen: Scarecrow Press, 1994).

Guelzo, Allen C., *For the Union of Evangelical Christendom: The Irony of the Reformed Episcopalians* (Pennsylvania: Pennsylvania State University Press, 1994).

Guillebaud, Meg, *Rwanda: The Land God Forgot? Revival, Genocide and Hope* (London: Monarch, 2002).

Guy, Jeff, *The Heretic* (Pietermaritzberg: Natal University Press, 1984).

The View across the River: Harriette Colenso and the Zulu Struggle against Imperialism (Cape Town: David Philip, 2001).

Haliburton, G. M., *The Prophet Harris* (London: Longman, 1971).

Hallencreutz, Carl, and Moyo, Ambrose, *Church and State in Zimbabwe* (Gweru: Mambo Press, 1988).

Hamid, Idris (ed.), *Troubling of the Waters* (San Fernando, Trinidad: St Andrew's Theological College, 1973).

Hansen, H. B., *Mission, Church and State in a Colonial Setting: Uganda 1890–1925* (London: Heinemann, 1984).

Hansen, H. B., and Twaddle, M. (eds.), *Religion and Politics in East Africa* (London: James Currey, 1995).

Hanson, A. T., *Beyond Anglicanism* (London: Darton, Longman & Todd, 1965).

Harper, Susan Billington, *In the Shadow of the Mahatma: Bishop V. S. Azariah and the Travails of Christianity in British India* (Grand Rapids: Eerdmans, 2000).

Harris, C. C., and Startup, R., *The Church in Wales: The Sociology of a Traditional Institution* (Cardiff: University of Wales Press, 1999).

Harris, John, *One Blood: 200 Years of Aboriginal Encounter with Christianity* (Sutherland: Albatross, 1990).

We Wish We'd Done More: Ninety Years of CMS and Aboriginal Issues in North Australia (Adelaide: Open Book, 1998).

Harrison, Ted, *Much Beloved Daughter: The Story of Florence Li Tim-Oi* (Wilton: Morehouse-Barlow, 1985).

Hastings, Adrian, *A History of English Christianity 1920–35* (London: Collins, 1986).

The Church in Africa 1450–1950 (Oxford: Clarendon, 1994).

Hastings, Adrian (ed.), *A World History of Christianity* (London: Cassell, 1999).

Hayes, Alan L. (ed.), *By Grace Co-workers: Building the Anglican Diocese of Toronto 1780–1989* (Toronto: Anglican Book Centre, 1989).

Hayes, Stephen, *Black Charismatic Anglicans* (Pretoria: UNISA, 1990).

Henderson, J. L. H., *John Strachan 1778–1867* (Toronto: Toronto University Press, 1969).

Henderson, J. M., *Ratana: The Man, the Church, the Political Movement* (Wellington: Polynesian Society, 1972).

Henkel, Reinhard, *Christian Missions in Africa: A Social Geographical Study of the Impact of their Activities in Zambia* (Berlin: Dietrich Reimer Verlag, 1989).

Hilliard, David, *Godliness and Good Order: A History of the Anglican Church in South Australia* (Netley: Wakefield Press, 1986).

God's Gentlemen: A History of the Melanesian Mission 1849–1942 (St Lucia: Queensland University Press, 1978).

'Sydney Anglicans and Homosexuality', *Journal of Homosexuality* 33.2 (1997), pp. 101–23.

Hinchliff, Peter, *John William Colenso* (London: Nelson, 1964).

The Anglican Church in South Africa (London: DLT, 1963).

Hodgins, Jack, *Sister Island: A History of CMS in Ireland* (Dunmurray: CMS Ireland, 1994).

Hodgson, Janet, 'Mission and Empire: A Case Study of Convergent Ideologies in 19th Century Southern Africa', *Journal of Theology for Southern Africa* 38 (March 1982), pp. 34–48.

Hodgson, Janet, and Kothare, Jay, *Vision Quest: Native Spirituality and the Church in Canada* (Toronto: Anglican Book Centre, 1990).

Hofmeyr, Isabel, *The Portable Bunyan* (Princeton: Princeton University Press, 2004).

Hollis, Michael, *The Significance of South India* (Richmond: John Knox, 1973).

Holmes, David, *A Brief History of the Episcopal Church* (Harrisburg: Trinity Press, 1993).

Honoré, Deborah Duncan (ed.), *Trevor Huddleston: Essays on his Life and Work* (Oxford: Oxford University Press, 1988).

Howe, John, *Highways and Hedges: Anglicanism and the Universal Church* (Toronto: Anglican Book Centre, 1985).

Howe, Stephen, *Ireland and Empire* (Oxford: Oxford University Press, 2000).

Huddleston, Trevor, *Naught for your Comfort* (London, 1956).

Hunt, Robert, Lee, Kam Hing, and Roxborough, John (eds.), *Christianity in Malaysia: A Denominational History* (Petaling Jaya: Pelanduk Publications, 1992).

Ingleby, J. C., *Missionaries, Education and India: Issues in Protestant Missionary Education in the Long Nineteenth Century* (Delhi: ISPCK, 2000).

Isichei, Elizabeth (ed.), *Varieties of Christian Experience in Nigeria* (London: Macmillan, 1982).

Israel, Jonathan, *The Dutch Republic* (Oxford: Clarendon, 1995).

Jacob, W. M., *The Making of the Anglican Church Worldwide* (London: SPCK, 1997).

Japin, Arthur, *The Two Hearts of Kwasi Boachi*, translated from the Dutch by Ina Rilke (New York: Knopf, 2000).

Jeffrey, Robin, 'Women and the "Kerala Model": Four Lives 1870s–1980s', *Journal of South Asia Studies* 12.2 (December 1989), pp. 12–32.

Jenkins, Philip, *The Next Christendom: The Coming of Global Christianity* (Oxford: Oxford University Press, 2002).

Johnson, Samuel, *The History of the Yorubas* (London: Routledge & Kegan Paul, 1921). Reprinted in 1966.

Johnson, T. S., *The Story of a Mission* (London: SPCK, 1953).

Johnson, Wallace R., *A History of Christianity in Belize, 1776–1838* (Washington: University Press of America, 1985).

Johnson-Odim, Cheryl, and Mba, Nina Emma, *For Women and the Nation: Funmilayo Ransome-Kuti of Nigeria* (Chicago: Illinois University Press, 1997).

Jones, Arun, 'Christian Missions in the American Empire: Episcopalians in Northern Luzon, 1902–46', Ph.D. dissertation, Princeton University, 2001.

Judd, Stephen and Cable, Kenneth, *Sydney Evangelicals* (Sydney: Anglican Information Office, 1987).

Kalu, Ogbu, *Divided People of God* (Lagos: NOK Publishers, 1978).

Kalu, Ogbu (ed.), *History of Christianity in West Africa* (London: Longman, 1980).

Karanja, John, *Founding an African Faith: Kikuyu Anglican Christianity 1900–1945* (Nairobi: Uzima, 1999).

Kater, John, Jr, 'At Home in Latin America: Anglicanism in a New Context', *Anglican and Episcopal History* 57 (1988), pp. 4–37.

'The Beginnings of the Episcopal Church in Panama, 1852–1904', *Anglican and Episcopal History* 57 (1988), pp. 147–58.

Katjavivi, Peter, et al. (eds.), *Church and Liberation in Namibia* (London: Pluto, 1989).

Kayanga, Samuel, and Wheeler, Andrew, '*But God is Not Defeated*' (Nairobi: Paulines Publications, 1999).

Kaye, Bruce, *A Church without Walls* (Melbourne: Dove, 1995).

Kaye, Bruce (ed.), *Anglicanism in Australia: A History* (Melbourne: Melbourne University Press, 2002).

Kibira, Josiah, *Church, Clan and the World* (Uppsala: Gleerup, 1974).

Kiwanuka, M. S. M., *A History of Buganda: From the Foundation of the Kingdom to 1900* (London: Longmans, 1971).

Kobayashi, Barnabas Satoshi, 'Towards the Paradigm Change of the Anglican Church in Japan', M.A. dissertation, University of Birmingham, 1998.

Koepping, Elizabeth, 'Spiritual Representation, Priests and the Borneo Villager', *Studies in World Christianity* (2002), pp. 141–66.

Krapf, Johann Ludwig, *Travels, Researches and Missionary Labours* (London: Frank Cass, 1968) (1st edn 1860).

Lamb, Christopher, *The Call to Retrieval: Kenneth Cragg's Christian Vocation to Islam* (London: Grey Seal, 1997).

Lamming, George, *In the Castle of my Skin* (Ann Arbor, MI: University of Michigan Press, 1991) (first published 1953).

Langley, Nina, *Sir Christopher Codrington and his College* (London: SPCK, 1962).

Lawson, Winston Arthur, *Religion and Race: African and European Roots in Conflict – A Jamaican Testament* (New York: Peter Lang, 1996).

Lethbridge, Christopher, *The Wounded Lion: Octavius Hadfield* (Christchurch: Caxton, 1993).

Lewis, Harold T., *Yet with a Steady Beat: The African American Struggle for Recognition in the Episcopal Church* (Valley Forge: Trinity Press, 1996).

Lim, You-Leng, 'Homosexuality: How the Economics and Politics of Singapore have Shaped the Anglican Diocese and its Role in the Province of South East Asia'. A background paper for the 1998 Lambeth Conference. Available on http://newark.rutgers.edu/~lcrew/lenglim2.html.

Limbrick, Warren, *Bishop Selwyn in New Zealand 1841–68* (Palmerston North: Dunmore Press, 1983).

Linden, Ian, with Linden, Jane, *Catholics, Peasants, and Chewa Resistance in Nyasaland 1889–1939* (London: Heinemann, 1974).

Loh, Keng Aun, *Fifty Years of the Anglican Church in Singapore Island, 1909–1959*, (Singapore: University of Singapore, 1963).

Ludwig, Frieder, *Church and State in Tanzania: Aspects of a Changing Relationship 1961–1994* (Leiden: Brill, 1999).

Ludwig, Frieder, and Adogame, Afe (eds.), *European Traditions in the Study of Religion in Africa* (Wiesbaden: Harrassowitz Verlag, 2004).

Lynch, Hollis, 'The Native Pastorate Controversy and Cultural Ethnocentrism in Sierra Leone 1871–4', in Ogbu Kalu (ed.), *History of Christianity in West Africa* (London: Longman, 1980), pp. 270–92.

McCracken, John, *Politics and Christianity in Malawi 1875–1940*, 2nd edn (Blantyre: Kashere, 2000).

MacCulloch, Diarmaid, *Reformation* (London: Allen Lane, 2003).

Thomas Cranmer (New Haven: Yale University Press, 1996).

MacKinnon, Donald, 'Oliver Chase Quick as a Theologian', *Theology* 96 (March/April 1993), pp. 107–16.

Mallampalli, Chandra, *Christians and Public Life in Colonial South India* (London: RoutledgeCurzon, 2004).

Mann, Kristin, *Marrying Well: Marriage, Status and Social Change among the Educated Elite in Colonial Lagos* (Cambridge: Cambridge University Press, 1985).

Mann, Wendy, *An Unquenched Flame: A Short History of the South American Missionary Society* (London: SAMS, 1968).

Maracle, Brian, *Crazywater: Native Voices on Addiction and Recovery* (Toronto: Viking Press, 1993).

Marks, Darren, 'Canadian and Japanese Christians', *Anglican and Episcopal History* 65.4 (December 1996), pp. 442–58.

Markwell, Bernard Kent, *The Anglican Left: Radical Social Reformers in the Church of England and the Protestant Episcopal Church 1846–1954* (Brooklyn: Carlson, 1991).

Marshall, Joan, *A Solitary Pillar: Montreal's Anglican Church and the Quiet Revolution* (Montreal: McGill University Press, 1995).

Mathew, C. P., and Thomas, M. M., *The Indian Churches of St Thomas* (Delhi: ISPCK, 1967).

Mauney, Mardi, *Episcopal Windows on Brazil* (New York: Episcopal Church Centre, 1998).

Maxwell, David (ed.), with Lawrie, Ingrid, *Christianity and the African Imagination* (Leiden: Brill, 2002).

Mbali, Zolile, *The Churches and Racism: A Black South African Perspective* (London: SCM, 1987).

Millam, Peter J., 'A Brief History of the Diocese of the Falkland Islands', 1996. In the SAMS Library Collection, Crowther Hall, Selly Oak, Birmingham.

Miller, Calvin, and Wallace, Ian, 'A Review of Iniciativa Cristiana of the Diocese of Northern Argentina and Tear Fund' [n.d., early 1990s]. In the SAMS Library Collection, Crowther Hall, Selly Oak, Birmingham.

Miller, J. R., *Shingwauk's Vision: A History of Native Residential Schools* (Toronto: Toronto University Press, 1996).

Skyscrapers Hide the Heavens: A History of Indian–White Relations in Canada (Toronto: Toronto University Press, 1991).

Miller, Walter, *An Autobiography* (privately printed in Zaria, Nigeria, nd.) (Miller died in 1952; published posthumously).

Millington, Constance, *An Ecumenical Venture: The History of Nandyal Diocese in Andhra Pradesh 1947–1990* (Bangalore: Asian Trading Corporation, 1993).

Mills, Frederick V., Sr, *Bishops by Ballot* (New York: Oxford University Press, 1978).

Milmine, Douglas, *The History of Anglicanism in Latin America* (London: South American Missionary Society) 1994; a translation of Bishop Milmine's original Spanish work, *La Comunión Anglican en America Latina* (Santiago, Chile: La Verdad os Hará Libres, 1993).

Minter, R. A., *Episcopacy without Episcopate: The Church of England in Jamaica before 1824* (Upton-upon-Severn, Worcs.: Self-Publishing Association Ltd, 1990).

Morgan, Derec Llwyd, *The Great Awakening in Wales* (London: Epworth, 1988).

Morgan, E. R., and Lloyd, Roger (eds.), *The Mission of the Anglican Communion* (London: SPCK and SPG, 1948).

Moses, Wilson J., *Alexander Crummell: A Study of Civilization and Discontent* (New York: Oxford University Press, 1989).

Mukherjee, Meenakshi, *The Perishable Empire: Essays on Indian Writing in English* (Oxford: Oxford University Press, 2000).

Mullin, Robert Bruce, *Episcopal Vision/American Reality: High Church Theology and Social Thought in Evangelical America* (New Haven: Yale University Press, 1986).

Murray, Jocelyn, 'A Bibliography of the East African Revival Movement', *Journal of Religion in Africa* 8 (1976), pp. 144–7.

'The Kikuyu Female Circumcision Controversy', Ph.D. dissertation, University of California, 1974.

Museveni, Yoweri, *Sowing the Mustard Seed* (London: Macmillan, 1997).

Nakamura, Paul, 'No Weapons, No War, No Fighting: An Okinawan View', *Anglican and Episcopal History* 65.4 (1996), pp. 459–67.

Namata, Joseph, *Edmund John, a Man of God: A Healing Ministry* (Canberra: Acorn Press, 1986).

Neill, Stephen C., *Anglicanism* (Harmondsworth: Penguin, 1958).

A History of Christianity in India, 1707–1858 (Cambridge: Cambridge University Press, 1985).

A History of Christian Missions, revised edn (London: Penguin, 1986).

The Unfinished Task (London: Edinburgh House Press, 1957).

Niekerk, Marlene van, *Triomf* (London: Little, Brown, 1999).

Nikkel, Marc, *Dinka Christianity: The Origins and Development of Christianity among the Dinka of Sudan with Special Reference to the Songs of Dinka Christians* (Nairobi: Paulines Publications, 2001).

Northcott, Michael, 'Two Hundred Years of Anglican Mission in West Malaysia', in Robert Hunt, Kam Hing Lee and John Roxborough (eds.), *Christianity in Malaysia: A Denominational History* (Petaling Jaya: Pelanduk Publications, 1992).

Nthamburi, Zablon (ed.), *From Mission to Church* (Nairobi: Uzima, 1991).

O'Brien, Conor Cruise, *The Great Melody* (London: Sinclair-Stevenson, 1992).

O'Connor, Daniel, *Gospel, Raj and Swaraj: The Missionary Years of C. F. Andrews* (Frankfurt: Peter Lang, 1990).

Three Centuries of Mission: The United Society for the Propagation of the Gospel 1701–2000 (London: Continuum, 2000).

Oddie, Geoffrey, *Missionaries, Rebellion and Proto-Nationalism: James Long of Bengal 1814–1887* (London: Curzon, 1999).

Social Protest in India: British Protestant Missionaries and Social Reforms 1850–1900 (Delhi: Manohar, 1979).

Oddie, Geoffrey (ed.), *Religion in South Asia: Religious Conversion and Revival Movements in South Asia* (New Delhi: Manohar, 1991).

Okullu, Henry, *Quest for Justice: An Autobiography* (Kisumu: Shalom, 1997).

Olson, Gilbert W., *Church Growth in Sierra Leone* (Grand Rapids: Eerdmans, 1969).

O'Mahony, Anthony (ed.), *The Christian Communities of Jerusalem and the Holy Land: Studies in History, Religion and Politics* (Cardiff: University of Wales Press, 2003).

Oommen, T. K., and Mabry, Hunter P., *The Christian Clergy in India: Volume I: Social Structure and Social Roles* (Delhi: Sage Publications, 2000).

Orland-Mensah, H. F., 'The Ministry of the Laity as Agents for the Growth of the Anglican Church of Ghana', D.Min. dissertation, Episcopal Divinity School, Cambridge, MA, 1993.

Packiamuthu, David and Sarojini, and Frykenberg, Robert (eds.), *Tirunelveli's Evangelical Christians* (Bangalore: SAIACS, 2003).

Padwick, Constance, *Henry Martyn: Confessor of the Faith* (London: SCM, 1923).

Muslim Devotions (London: SPCK, 1961).

Temple Gairdner of Cairo (London: SPCK, 1929).

Page, Jesse, *The Black Bishop* (London: Hodder & Stoughton, 1909).

Palmer, Bernard, *Imperial Vineyard: The Anglican Church in India under the Raj* (Lewes: The Book Guild, 1999).

Paradkar, Balwant, *The Theology of Goreh* (Bangalore: Christian Institute for the Study of Religion and Society, 1969).

Paton, Alan, *Apartheid and the Archbishop: The Life and Times of Geoffrey Clayton* (New York: Scribner, 1973).

Cry, the Beloved Country: A Story of Comfort in Desolation (New York: Scribner, 1948).

Paton, David M., *RO: The Life and Times of Bishop Ronald Hall of Hong Kong* (Hong Kong: Diocesan Association, 1985).

Peart-Binns, John, *Ambrose Reeves* (London: Gollancz, 1973).

Archbishop Joost de Blank: Scourge of Apartheid (London: Muller, Blond & White, 1987).

Peel, J. D. Y., *Religious Encounter and the Making of the Yoruba* (Bloomington: Indiana University Press, 2000).

Peterson, John, *Province of Freedom: A History of Sierra Leone 1787–1870* (Evanston: Northwestern University Press, 1969).

Phillips, James M., *From the Rising of the Sun: Christians and Society in Contemporary Japan* (New York: Orbis, 1981).

Pieterse, Hendrick (ed.), *Desmond Tutu's Message* (Leiden: Brill, 2001).

Pirouet, Louise, *Black Evangelists* (London: Rex Collings, 1978).

'Religion in Uganda under Amin', *Journal of Religion in Africa* 11.1 (1980), pp. 13–29.

Strong in the Faith (Kampala: Church Press, 1969).

Pong, James, *Worldly Ambition versus Christian Vocation* (Taipei: Episcopal Church, n.d. [1977]).

Porter, Andrew, *Religion versus Empire? British Protestant Missionaries and Overseas Expansion, 1700–1914* (Manchester: Manchester University Press, 2004).

Porter, Andrew (ed.), *The Imperial Horizons of British Protestant Missions 1880–1914* (Grand Rapids: Eerdmans, 2003).

Presler, Titus, *Transfigured Night: Mission and Culture in Zimbabwe's Vigil Movement* (Pretoria: UNISA, 1999).

Prior, Michael, and Taylor, William (eds.), *Christians in the Holy Land* (London: The World of Islam Festival Trust, 1994).

Raboteau, Albert J., *Slave Religion: The 'Invisible Institution' in the Antebellum South* (New York: Oxford University Press, 1978).

Railton, N., *No North Sea: The Anglo-German Evangelical Network in the Middle of the Nineteenth Century* (Leiden: Brill, 2000).

Raj, Selva J., and Dempsey, Corinne G., *Popular Christianity in India* (New York: New York State University Press, 2002).

Ranger, Terence O., and Kimambo, Isaiah N., *The Historical Study of African Religion* (London: Heinemann, 1972).

Rasmussen, Lissi, *Christian–Muslim Relations in Africa* (London: British Academic Press, 1993).

Reed, Colin, *Pastors, Partners and Paternalists: African Church Leaders and Western Missionaries in the Anglican Church in Kenya, 1850–1900* (Leiden: Brill, 1997).

Reeves, Ambrose, *Shooting at Sharpeville* (London, 1960).

Reisner, M. E., *Strangers and Pilgrims: A History of the Anglican Diocese of Quebec 1793–1993* (Toronto: Anglican Book Centre, 1995).

Renouf, Robert, 'Anglicanism in Nicaragua, 1745–1985', *Anglican and Episcopal History* 57 (1988), pp. 382–96.

Rice, G. W. (ed.), *The Oxford History of New Zealand* (Auckland: Oxford University Press, 1992).

Richey, Jeffrey L., 'Catholicity and Culture in China: Anglican Ideology and the Sheng Kung Hui', *Anglican and Episcopal History* 67.2 (June 1998), pp. 191–211.

Robbins, Catherine, 'Tukutendereza: A Study of Social Change and Sectarian Withdrawal in the Balokole Revival', Ph.D. dissertation, Columbia University, 1975.

Rogozinski, Jan, *A Brief History of the Caribbean: From the Arawak and Carib to the Present* (New York: Facts on File Inc., 1999).

Ross, Robert, *Status and Respectability in the Cape Colony 1750–1870* (Cambridge: Cambridge University Press, 1999).

Rowell, Geoffrey, Stevenson, Kenneth, and Williams, Rowan, *Love's Redeeming Work: The Anglican Quest for Holiness* (Oxford: Oxford University Press, 2001).

Rutt, Richard, *The Anglican Church in Korea* (London: The Korean Mission, 1963).

Rutto, Christopher, 'Nandi Identity and Christian Denominationalism', Ph.D. dissertation, University of Birmingham, 2003.

Sachs, William L., *The Transformation of Anglicanism* (Cambridge: Cambridge University Press, 1993).

Said, Edward, *Orientalism* (New York: Pantheon, 1979).

Out of Place: A Memoir (New York: Alfred Knopf, 1999).

St John, Patricia, *Breath of Life* (London: Norfolk Press, 1971).

Sands, Kirkley, 'The Anglican Church and Bahamian Cultural Identity: The Role of Church-Sponsored Education, Prayer Book Liturgy and Anglo-Catholic Rituals in the Development of Bahamian Culture 1784–1900', unpublished Ph.D. dissertation, University of Edinburgh, 1998.

Sanneh, Lamin, *Abolitionists Abroad: American Blacks and the Making of Modern West Africa* (Cambridge, MA: Harvard University Press, 1999).

'World Christianity and the New Historiography: History and Global Interconnections', in Wilbert R. Shenk (ed.), *Enlarging the Story: Perspectives on Writing World Christian History* (Maryknoll: Orbis, 2002), pp. 94–114.

Satthianadhan, Krupabai, *Kamala: The Story of a Hindu Life*, ed. Chandari Lokuge (Delhi: Oxford University Press, 1998).

Saguna: A Story of Native Christian Life, ed. Chandari Lokuge (Delhi: Oxford University Press, 1998).

Saunders, Graham, *Bishops and Brookes: The Anglican Mission and the Brooke Raj in Sarawak 1848–1941* (Singapore: Oxford University Press, 1992).

Schneider, Herbert and Carol (eds.), *Samuel Johnson, President of King's College: His Career and Writings: Volume I* (New York: Columbia University Press, 1929).

Schoffeleers, Matthew, *In Search of Truth and Justice: Confrontations between Church and State in Malawi 1960–1994* (Blantyre: Kachere, 1999).

Scott, Michael, *A Time to Speak* (New York: Doubleday, 1958).

Scott, W. H., *The Discovery of the Igorots* (Quezon City: New Day, 1974).

Seekings, Jeremy, *UDF: A History of the United Democratic Front* (Cape Town: David Philip, 2000).

Shah, A. B. (ed.), *The Letters and Correspondence of Pandita Ramabai* (Bombay: Maharashtra Board, 1977).

Shank, David, *Prophet Harris, The 'Black Elijah' of West Africa* (Leiden: Brill, 1994).

Shattuck, Gardiner H., Jr, 'A Whole Priesthood: The Philadelphia Ordinations (1974) and the Continuing Dilemmas of Race in the Episcopal Church', EDS Occasional Papers, No. 6 (Cambridge, April 2001).

Episcopalians and Race: Civil War to Civil Rights (Lexington: Kentucky University Press, 2000).

Shehata, Samy, 'An Evaluation of the Mission of the Episcopal Church in Egypt from 1918 to 1925 with Special Implications for the Role of the Church Today', MA dissertation, University of Birmingham, 1998.

'Ecclesiology in Contemporary Egypt: An Evaluation and a Proposal', Ph.D. dissertation, University of Birmingham, 2001.

Shell, Robert C.-H, *Children of Bondage: A Social History of the Slave Society at the Cape of Good Hope 1652–1838* (Hanover: Wesleyan University Press, 1994).

Shelley, Michael Thomas, 'The Life and Thought of W. H. T. Gairdner 1873–1928: A Critical Evaluation of a Scholar-Missionary', Ph.D. dissertation, University of Birmingham, 1988.

Shenk, Wilbert R., *Henry Venn: Missionary Statesman* (Maryknoll: Orbis, 1983).

Shenk, Wilbert R. (ed.), *Enlarging the Story: Perspectives on Writing World Christian History* (Maryknoll: Orbis, 2002).

Shorten, Richard, *The Legion of Christ's Witnesses* (Cape Town: Centre for African Studies, University of Cape Town, 1987).

Shyllon, Folarin, *James Ramsay: The Unknown Abolitionist* (Edinburgh: Canongate Press, 1977).

Sigmund, Paul E. (ed.), *Religious Freedom and Evangelization in Latin America: The Challenge of Religious Pluralism* (Maryknoll: Orbis, 1999).

Simmons, G. C., 'The History of Codrington College, Barbados 1710–1875', Doctor of Education dissertation, Graduate School of Education, Harvard University, 1962.

Sitshebo, Wilson, 'Towards a Theological Synthesis of Christian and Shona Views of Death and the Dead', Ph.D. dissertation, University of Birmingham, 2001.

Smith, H. Maynard, *Frank, Bishop of Zanzibar* (London: SPCK, 1926).

Soyinka, Wole, *Ake: The Years of Childhood* (New York: Random House, 1981).

Stanley, Brian (ed.), *Missions, Nationalism, and the End of Empire* (Grand Rapids: Eerdmans, 2003).
Stanton, Hannah, *Go Well, Stay Well* (London: Hodder & Stoughton, 1961).
Steere, Douglas, *God's Irregular, Arthur Shearly Cripp* (London: SPCK, 1973).
Stephenson, A. M. G., *Anglicanism and the Lambeth Conferences* (London: SPCK, 1978).
The First Lambeth Conferences (London: SPCK, 1967).
Stewart, Robert, *Religion and Society in Post-Emancipation Jamaica* (Knoxville: Tennessee University Press, 1992).
Stock, Eugene, *The History of the Church Missionary Society* (4 vols., London: CMS, Volumes I–III, 1899; Volume IV, 1916).
Strayer, Robert, *The Making of Mission Communities in East Africa: Anglicans and Africans in Colonial Kenya, 1875–1935* (London: Heinemann, 1978).
Strong, Rowan, *Episcopalianism in Nineteenth-Century Scotland* (Oxford: Oxford University Press, 2002).
Suberg, O. M., *The Anglican Tradition in South Africa* (Pretoria: UNISA, 1999).
Suggate, Alan, with Shigeko, Yamano, *Japanese Christians and Society* (Berne: Lang, 1996).
Suggit, J., and Goedhals, Mandy, *Change and Challenge* (Cape Town: CPSA, 1998).
Sultan, Pervaiz, 'The Involvement of the Church of Pakistan in Development', Ph.D. dissertation, Open University, 1997.
Sumiko, Yamamoto, *History of Protestantism in China: The Indigenization of Christianity* (Tokyo: Toho Gakkai, 2000).
Sundkler, Bengt, *Bantu Prophets in South Africa* (London: Lutterworth, 1948).
Church of South India: The Movement towards Union, 1900–1947 (London: Lutterworth, 1954).
Sunquist, Scott W. (ed.), *A Dictionary of Asian Christianity* (Grand Rapids: Eerdmans, 2001).
Sykes, Stephen, and Booty, John (eds.), *The Study of Anglicanism* (London: SPCK, 1988).
Takeda, John M., 'The Experience of Japanese Anglicans', *Anglican and Episcopal History* 65.4 (December 1996), pp. 412–30.
Tasie, G. O. M., *Christian Missionary Enterprise in the Niger Delta 1864–1918* (Leiden: Brill, 1978).
Taylor, Brian, *The Anglican Church in Borneo 1848–1962* (Bognor Regis: New Horizon, 1983).
Taylor, John V., *Christianity and Politics in Africa* (London: Penguin, 1957).
The Diocese of Hong Kong and Macao 1849–1974: A Brief History (Hong Kong: Diocese of Hong Kong, 1974).
The Growth of the Church in Buganda (London: SCM, 1958).
The Kairos Document: A Theological Comment on the Political Crisis in South Africa, 2nd edn (London: CIIR/BCC, 1986).
Thompson, Phyllis, *An Unquenchable Flame: The Story of Captain Allen Gardiner, Founder of the South American Missionary Society* (London: Hodder & Stoughton, 1983).

Throup, David, 'The Politics of Church–State Conflict in Kenya 1978–1990', in H. B. Hansen and M. Twaddle (eds.), *Religion and Politics in East Africa* (London: James Currey, 1995), pp. 143–76.

Tim-Oi, Florence Li, *Raindrops of my Life* (Toronto: Anglican Book Centre, 1996).

Ting, K. H., *Christian Witness in China Today* (Kyoto: Doshisha University Press, 1985).

Tinker, Hugh, *The Ordeal of Love: C. F. Andrews and India* (Delhi: Oxford University Press, 1979).

Trollope, Mark, *The Church in Corea* (London: Mowbray, 1915).

Tsimhoni, Daphne, *Christian Communities in Jerusalem and the West Bank since 1948: An Historical, Social and Political Study* (Westport, CT: Praeger, 1993).

Verryn, T. D., *A History of the Order of Ethiopia* (Cleveland, Transvaal: Central Mission Press, 1972).

Visvanathan, Susan, *The Christians of Kerala* (Madras: Oxford University Press, 1993).

Viswanathan, Gauri, *Outside the Fold: Conversion, Modernity and Belief* (Princeton: Princeton University Press, 1998).

Walshe, Peter, *Church versus State in South Africa: The Case of the Christian Institute* (London: Hurst, 1983).

Ward, Kevin, '"A Theology of Attention": The CMS Tradition at the End of the Colonial Era in Africa', in Frieder Ludwig and Afe Adogame (eds.), *European Traditions in the Study of Religion in Africa* (Wiesbaden: Harrassowitz Verlag, 2004), pp. 227–36.

'Archbishop Janani Luwum: The Dilemmas of Loyalty, Opposition and Witness in Amin's Uganda', in David Maxwell (ed.), with Ingrid Lawrie, *Christianity and the African Imagination* (Leiden: Brill, 2002), pp. 199–224.

'"Eating and Sharing": Church and State in Uganda', *Journal of Anglican Studies* 3 (June 2005), pp. 99–120.

'Marching or Stumbling towards a Christian Ethic? Homosexuality and African Anglicanism', in a collection edited by Bishop Terry Brown, forthcoming.

'Obedient Rebels: The Mukono Crisis of 1941', *Journal of Religion in Africa* 19.3 (1989), pp. 194–227.

'Same-Sex Relations in Africa and the Debate on Homosexuality in East African Anglicanism', *Anglican Theological Review* 84.1 (2002), pp. 81–111.

'"The Armies of the Lord": Christianity, Rebels and the State in Northern Uganda, 1986–1999', *Journal of Religion in Africa* 31.2 (2001), pp. 187–221.

'The Church of Uganda amidst Conflict', in H. B. Hansen and M. Twaddle (eds.), *Religion and Politics in East Africa* (London: James Currey, 1995), pp. 72–105.

'The Church of Uganda and the Exile of Kabaka Muteesa', *Journal of Religion in Africa* 28.4 (1998), pp. 411–49.

'The Development of Protestant Christianity in Kenya 1910–1940', Ph.D. dissertation, University of Cambridge, 1976.

'Tukutendereza Yesu', in N. Nthamburi (ed.), *From Mission to Church* (Nairobi: Uzima, 1991), Chapter 3.

Ward, Kevin, and Stanley, Brian (eds.), *The Church Mission Society and World Christianity 1799–1999* (Richmond: Curzon and Grand Rapids: Eerdmans, 2000).

Waterfield, Robin, *Christians in Persia* (London: Allen & Unwin, 1973).

Webster, John C. B., *The Dalit Christians* (Delhi: ISPCK, 1994).

Welbourn, F. B., *East African Rebels* (London: SCM, 1961).

Welbourn, F. B., and Ogot, B. A., *A Place to Feel at Home* (Nairobi: Oxford University Press, 1966).

Weller, John, *Mainstream Christianity to 1980 in Malawi, Zambia and Zimbabwe* (Gweru: Mambo Press, 1984).

Werner, Roland, Anderson, William, and Wheeler, Andrew, *Day of Devastation, Day of Contentment: The History of the Sudanese Church across 2000 Years* (Nairobi: Paulines Publications, 2000).

West, Gerald O., *The Academy of the Poor: Towards a Dialogical Reading of the Bible* (Sheffield: Sheffield Academic Press, 1999).

Westfall, William, *Two Worlds: The Protestant Culture of Nineteenth Century Ontario* (Kingston: Queen's University Press, 1989).

Wheeler, Andrew (ed.), *Land of Promise: Church Growth in a Sudan at War*, Faith in Sudan (Nairobi: Paulines Publications, 1997).

White, Gavin, 'Kikuyu 1913: An Ecumenical Controversy', Ph.D. dissertation, London University, 1970.

The Scottish Episcopal Church: A New History (Edinburgh: General Synod of the Scottish Episcopal Church, 1998).

Whitehead, Raymond L. (ed.), *No Longer Strangers: Selected Writings of K. H. Ting* (Maryknoll: Orbis, 1989).

Whiteman, Darrell, 'Melanesians and Missionaries', Ph.D. dissertation, Illinois University, 1980.

Wickeri, Philip, *Seeking the Common Ground: Protestant Christianity, the Three-Self Movement and China's United Front* (Maryknoll: Orbis, 1988).

Wickeri, Janice and Philip (eds.), *A Chinese Contribution to Ecumenical Theology: Selected Writings of Bishop K. H. Ting* (Geneva: WCC, 2002).

Wigger, John, *Taking Heaven by Storm: Methodism and the Rise of Popular Christianity in America* (New York: Oxford University Press, 1998).

Wild-Wood, Emma, 'Migration and Identity: The Development of an Anglican Church in North-East Congo', Ph.D. dissertation, University of Edinburgh, 2004.

Wilkinson, John L., *Church in Black and White* (Edinburgh: St Andrew's Press, 1993).

Williams, Glanmor, *The Welsh and their Religion* (Cardiff: University of Wales Press, 1991).

Williams, Peter, *The Ideal of the Self-Governing Church: A Study in Victorian Missionary Strategy* (Leiden: Brill, 1990).

Willis, Justin, 'The Nyamang are Hard to Touch: Mission Evangelism and Tradition in the Nuba Mountains, Sudan, 1933–1952', *Journal of Religion in Africa* 33.1 (2003), pp. 32–62.

Wilson, Kottapalli, *The Twice Alienated Culture of Dalit Christians* (Hyderabad: Booklinks, 1982).

Wingate, Andrew, *Does Theological Education Make a Difference?* (Geneva: WCC, 1999).

Wingate, Andrew, Ward, Kevin, Pemberton, Carrie, and Sitshebo, Wilson (eds.), *Anglicanism: A Global Communion* (London: Mowbray, 1998).

Winter, Colin, *Namibia* (Grand Rapids: Eerdmans, 1977).

Wiseman, E. M., *Kikuyu Martyrs* (London: Highway Press, 1958).

Wood, Peter, and Wild-Wood, Emma, 'One Day we will Sing in God's Home', *Journal of Religion in Africa* 34.1-2 (2004), pp. 145–80.

Worsnip, Michael, *Between the Two Fires: The Anglican Church and Apartheid* (Pietermaritzburg: Natal University Press, 1991).

Yarwood, A. T., *Samuel Marsden: The Great Survivor* (Melbourne: Melbourne University Press, 1977).

Yates, T. E., *Venn and Victorian Bishops Abroad* (London: SPCK, 1978).

Yoshinobu, Kumazawa, and Swain, David (eds.), *Christianity in Japan 1971–1990* (Tokyo: Christian Literature Society of Japan, 1991).

Zhenfang, Luo, 'Dr T. C. Chao's Last Letter to Me', *Chinese Theological Review* (1986), pp. 71–4.

Index